# PROJECT PAIN RELIEVER

## A JUST-IN-TIME HANDBOOK FOR ANYONE MANAGING PROJECTS

Dave Garrett

J.ROSS
PUBLISHING

Copyright © 2012 by Dave Garrett

ISBN-13: 978-1-60427-039-6

Printed and bound in the U.S.A. Printed on acid-free paper.

10 9 8 7 6 5 4 3 2 1

**Library of Congress Cataloging-in-Publication Data**

Project pain reliever: a just-in-time handbook for anyone managing projects/ edited by Dave Garrett.
    p. cm.
Includes bibliographical references and index.
ISBN 978-1-60427-039-6 (hardcover: alk. paper)
1. Project management—Handbooks, manuals, etc. I. Garrett, Dave, 1965-
HD69.P75P7624 2011
658.4'04—dc23

2011037065

Phone: (954) 727-9333
Fax: (561) 892-0700
Web: www.jrosspub.com

# CONTENTS

# DEDICATION

*This book is dedicated to my amazing family—my wife Julie, Spencer, Olivia, Zachary, and Max. Their happiness and success is the most important project of my life. Seeing them help others is my greatest joy.*

# PREFACE

Project management can be a lonely and even painful job. Part of that pain comes from driving organizational change, which is what project managers do. However, most of the difficulty people have is simply due to their new role as a project manager. The majority of those responsible for leading projects are doing it as one role that they play, but not as their profession. These *accidental* project managers run into the same issues and problems frequently faced by professional project managers, but often lack the relevant knowledge and experience to properly address them. This handbook, developed by more than 30 leading project management experts, was designed to help accidental project managers, or any manager responsible for project results, to quickly find specific solutions to the problems they are desperate to fix, right now!

As CEO of gantthead.com, I have spent more than a decade observing project managers asking project-critical questions of one another. The questions are never: "Could you list and describe the process areas covered by the *PMBOK® Guide*?" or "What is a good process for managing issues?" The questions always describe more of a *feeling* than anything matching up with a best practice solution. Project managers bring up problems such as:

- My sponsor wants more than I can deliver.
- The schedule is totally unrealistic.
- We do not have the resources we need.
- The team is frustrated with *rework* based on changing requirements.
- My team will not listen to me.
- My team does not understand what we are doing.

With those and other questions in mind, *Project Pain Reliever* is a compilation of common questions and problems, coupled with solid solutions described by an expert. This reference was built to address a large number of problems directly without making you read through significant amounts of text to find solutions. These are certainly not the only solutions to each problem. Rather, they represent the most common and effective approach to the problem, based on deep practitioner experience. My goal was to make this book as *plug and play* as possible.

## Real Problems and Experienced Problem Solvers

The solutions within this book were written by practitioners who have used them in the past with great success, not by academics passing along what they've read recently. So there is none of the vicarious problem solving that has become an issue in business and academia today. This book is a collaborative effort on a number of levels:

- First, the *list of problems* in this book was selected based on a decade of discussions that I have observed on gantthead.com. *Crowdsourcing* was a buzzword a few years back, essentially meaning that numerous people could collaborate virtually to build things that were traditionally built by companies with employees. In this sense, the structure of the book itself is defined based on the wisdom of the crowd: thousands of online voices over many years. It has been my experience that a similar set of problems crop up year after year. There is variation in the way the issues and questions were expressed, but people universally stumble over the same things covered in this book.

- On a second level, gantthead has always been a delivery vehicle for *practitioner-generated content*. I like that phrase better than the commonly used "user generated content" because it makes a distinction between *anyone* and people who have experience (either positive or negative) in the field. This book took it one step further and asked practitioners who are active online to provide real-world solutions to specific crowd-defined project management problems, then review the solutions that their peers have created, and tell a story about each problem that would make it easy for the reader to relate to. The stories are nearly always a reflection of the practitioner's experience in dealing with the same problem. In a way, these are essentially *lessons learned*, told by the project manager who learned them.

- Third, discussions around each of these problems can continue online. This will occur on gantthead.com, projectsatwork.com, and the blogs of each contributing author. In this way, we will provide more solutions to problems as we identify and resolve them through online discussion.

## How the Book Is Organized

The book is divided into two parts. Part A: Leadership—The Art of Project Management covers problems related to critical soft skills. Part B: Management—The Science of Project covers problems related to technical skills. Each part is divided into chapters, which are designed to help users quickly narrow their search by type of problem, such as *effectively communicating, planning, or dealing with constraints, assumptions, and scope.* Each chapter is further divided into subchapters. Each subchapter, expressed as an intuition, emotion, or question, addresses a very specific and common project management problem, and takes you through:

- A clear definition of the problem in a straightforward way
- A list of warning signs to help understand if you have this particular problem
- A brief description of what may happen if you do nothing
- A coherent solution to the problem
- Step-by-step guidance on how to respond to the problem

To help users retain their new knowledge, summaries of *What you have learned* for addressing each problem are available from the Web Added Value™ Download Resource Center at www.jrosspub.com. Additional problems with solutions and other useful resources may be found here as well.

## How To Use This Book

The table of contents is organized by problem, so users can look there, find the problem, read through the solution, and apply it. While looking for the problem you need to solve now, you might see other problems that apply to your project. Hopefully, as you browse through the contents, guided by your specific needs, you will see that this is a book filled with solutions.

## Benefits of This Book

Accidental project managers should find this book eye-opening, as it provides an easy way to connect their problems with the time-proven methods typically used to resolve them. Although much of project management is IT-focused, these are problems that are universal across all business functions and industries where people lead projects.

Project managers can effectively use this book to improve personal performance, and, by extension, the performance of their projects and organization. Every project manager has daily struggles relating project management-dogma to everyday work. They often lose sight of common solutions and end up feeling like they are between a rock and a hard place. Hopefully, these quick solutions will help projects get *unstuck*.

Project sponsors, portfolio managers, and executives may also find this handbook very useful. Each chapter can be viewed as a quick and easy mentoring tool to fix problems that project managers bring to you every day. Using this handbook could help to improve project results within the organization.

This reference may also be useful as a supplemental resource for professional training of new project managers or for academic courses in project management.

If you still have trouble with a problem for which a solution is not forthcoming, please drop us an email at contactus@gantthead.com and we will do our best to help. I hope this book returns many times its cover price in saved time and decreased frustration. If that is the case, then this handbook is a success.

Dave Garrett, Editor

# ACKNOWLEDGEMENTS

Gratitude for contributors to this book is all about *the crowd*. Thousands of project managers contributed on some level by repeatedly asking questions that are addressed in this book. However, the authors of each subchapter deserve credit for providing practical solutions that come from real-world experience. Each of the 35 authors in this book made a substantial contribution. I am grateful to each author for his or her efforts.

There were a few authors, however, that I would like to acknowledge here. Andy Jordan not only contributed 14 subchapters to the book, but also reviewed and assisted in editing nearly all of the manuscript. His advice helped to guide me through the manuscript process and in the end, pushed it to completion. It always surprises me when people like Andy take time away from their personal lives and consulting practices to help other people be more successful.

Also deserving of special recognition is Michael Wood's ten sections that focus on requirements, covering some of the toughest challenges that project managers face every day. He is always willing to help a fellow traveler. We are all lucky to have him as a contributor.

In addition, J. Chris White's ten to-the-point solutions are some of the most easily applied. His tireless work was exceedingly helpful.

I would also like to thank Arjun Malhotra for giving me a word of encouragement when this project seemed to slow down. Sometimes motivation makes all of the difference.

I also deeply thank my wife Julie for dragging me over to the computer on a regular basis, then formatting content in a way that I never could. I am in her debt.

Dave Garrett

# CONTRIBUTORS

## Gina Abudi

As Partner and SVP of Strategic Solutions at Peak Performance Group, Gina Abudi, MBA, oversees projects with global clients in a variety of strategic areas, including organizational analysis and design, project and process management, corporate education, talent optimization, leadership development, executive coaching and team development. She has written numerous articles and white papers, and presented at various forums on project management and leadership. Abudi provides guidance to a variety of clients in developing a strategic approach to project management. Abudi has a blog at www.GinaAbudi.com. In this book: Subchapters 3.7, 4.7.

## Panagiotis Agrapidis

Panagiotis Agrapidis, MS in Civil Engineering, is a project management consultant to private and public companies and institutions. Between 1996 and 2004, under the auspices of Greek Prime Minister, Agrapidis established a Strategic PMO, involving ministries, regional governments, and public companies: collecting data from 7,500 offices; coordinating 53,916 projects with a budget of €47.8 billion; improving the efficiency in the utilization of public funds; and supporting the organization of the Olympic Games. He also participated in major construction projects such as the 2nd Bosporus Bridge and Arak Petrochemical Complex. He often speaks at PMI and IPMA World Congresses and at many events in Greece. He can be contacted at fiap@ath.forthnet.gr. In this book: Subchapter 1.9.

## Imad Alsadeq

As consultation director of THIQAH, a management and engineering solutions company, Imad Alsadeq, PMP, PMOC, PMI-RMP, MCP, is contributing to his region's development by providing and facilitating consultation, training and technical solutions. He was one of Organizational Project Management Maturity Model OPM3® second edition volunteers. In addition to leading the author team to develop the first Arabic Project Management templates book, Alsadeq has delivered various papers for several international conferences about portfolio management and other topics. He was recently recognized by PMI for his service on the PMI Global Congress 2010—EMEA Project Action Team. In this book: Subchapter 7.14.

## David Arias

David Arias, PMP, is President of PMR, Inc., based in San Juan, Puerto Rico. His focus is on the effective management of projects within the full range of business functions, including strategy, marketing, finance, IT systems, and development. Reflective of his practical approach to these areas, his company's tag line is, "Converting challenges into real solutions." In this book: Subchapter 7.13.

## Harlan Bridges

Harlan Bridges, PMP, has extensive experience in Web, IT, and technical communication. He has managed multiple complex, multimillion dollar projects with global teams of up to 40 developers. He has a reputation for improving process efficiency and quality standards by devising and implementing innovative development procedures. He has demonstrated an ability to interpret client business requirements and develop effective technical solutions. Bridges' expert project management skills include risk assessment, requirements gathering and analysis, usability testing, business model and strategy development, budget and project plan creation, and resource allocation. In this book: Subchapter 4.6.

## Alex S. Brown

Alex Brown, PMP IPMA-C, has been a project leader for the past 15 years. Brown is currently President and CEO at Real-Life Projects, Inc. He is fascinated with project management, strategic planning, and blending these topics into *strategic project management*. He writes and speaks frequently to audiences of project managers and senior executives. His professional goal is to help business people improve their understanding of projects, and to help project people improve their understanding of business. In this book: Subchapters 1.10, 9.9.

## Peter Carothers

Peter Carothers, PMP, has extensive experience in leading information technology programs and projects in the government and private sectors, combining *PMBOK® Guide* expertise with pragmatic real-world experience to get results. As program manager, he has planned and implemented PMOs, and managed ongoing PMO operations, including operational process improvement, PM standards, project execution, and staff development. His analytical, strategic, process-focused, and communication-centric problem-solving skills have helped him build high-performance teams. In this book: Subchapter 9.2.

## Luis Antonio Crespo

As PMO Senior Project Manager with experience in the financial and insurance verticals, Luis Crespo, PMP, CSM, is passionate about project management and the development of project management organizations. Luis is taking project management to the masses by teaching project management frameworks to businesses after successfully making these classes available to an IT group of more than 200 users. Luis has been involved in the development and improvement of project management organizations across several different enterprises. Luis measures his success the same way he measures the success of a PMO: Project Success! In this book: Subchapters 3.11, 9.5.

## Craig Curran-Morton

Craig Curran-Morton works as the Manager of Business Process for Ledcor. He has developed a passion for assisting clients in identifying their challenges and working with them to find solutions that are both implementable and sustainable. His real passions are project management, BPM, the *PMBOK® Guide*, and environmental issues. He views much of his work through a *green lens*. He wants individuals and organizations to have a greater awareness of the needs of people and the planet in their drive for profit. Craig has been an active contributor to gantthead.com and he enjoys speaking on project management topics at PMI dinners and conferences. In this book: Subchapter 3.2.

## Mike Donoghue

Mike Donoghue is a member of a multinational information technology corporation where he collaborates on the communications guidelines and customer relationship strategies affecting the interactions with internal and external clients. He has analyzed, defined, designed, and overseen processes for various engagements, including product usability and customer satisfaction, best practice enterprise standardization, relationship/branding structures, and distribution effectiveness and direction. He also established corporate library solutions to provide frameworks for sales, marketing, training, and support divisions. In this book: Subchapter 7.11.

## Ed Evarts

Ed Evarts is a leadership development and team success coach based in Boston and the practice leader at www.evartscoaching.com. He partners with mid- to senior-level professionals and their teams in corporate environments to achieve clarity, gain insight, and take action. With over 25 years of leadership and management experience, Ed is known for business acumen, ability to resolve complex human relations issues, and an enthusiastic, genuine, accessible, and responsive style. Armed with a certificate in Project Management from Boston University, Ed is passionate about helping busy individuals assess ways to influence, impact, and evolve the thinking and behaviors of others in positive and fulfilling ways. Ed is a frequent speaker on networking, leadership development, and personality preferences. In this book: Subchapter 3.12.

## Cicero Ferreira

Cicero Ferreira led many complex management consulting projects while a Principal for PricewaterhouseCoopers and IBM Global Business Services. As founder and CEO of Omega Consultoria in Sao Paulo, Brazil, Ferreira currently dedicates himself to creating high value services for clients through the application of best practices in project management, business process management, and shared services operations. As a university professor, Ferreira taught MBA courses in PM, BPM, and SSO at leading universities in Brazil. He is also an experienced lecturer, researcher, and author of articles in those areas of expertise. In this book: Subchapters 5.7, 8.4.

## Andrew Filev

Founder and CEO of Wrike, Andrew Filev focuses on improving project management tools and practices with the help of new technologies. His innovative ideas are applied in an online project management solution used by thousands of companies from 55 countries. Filev's views on changes in contemporary project management are reflected in his Project Management 2.0 blog. Filev has written more than 30 articles on new trends in project management and the deployment of next-generation Web-based applications. He has given speeches at the UTD PMI Symposium, Office 2.0 Conference, Enterprise 2.0 Conference, and other events. In this book: Subchapters 7.6, 7.8, 8.7.

## Cornelius Fitchner

Cornelius Fitchner, PMP, is owner and host of The Project Management Podcast and The Project Management Prepcast. Fitchner has been working as a project manager in his native Switzerland, in Germany, and in the U.S. for 16 years. Fitchner has led projects for a management consulting company, a national retailer, and an internet startup company. Currently, Fitchner works as a project manager for a financial service provider. His passions are project management methodologies and PMOs. Cornelius served as the 2007 Chair of the Project Management Institute, Orange County Chapter. In this book: Subchapters 7.4, 7.7.

## Michael B. Flint

As a business consultant specializing in project management, Michael B. Flint, PMP, has a track record for delivering results and benefits with an approach that marries practical real-world challenges with academic theory. Flint is a business-focused consultant and project management expert. He serves as president of MBF Consulting Services, Inc., with clients across North America in all sectors of the marketplace, providing services to enable organizations to realize value through the effective use of project management. As Director and former President of the Project Management Institute, Southern Ontario (Toronto) Chapter, he has been an active volunteer and was winner of the PMI Volunteer of the Year Award in 2008. He is an international speaker on project management processes and approaches. In this book: Subchapter: 1.3.

## Elizabeth Harrin

As CEO of The Otobos Group, and publisher of *A Girl's Guide to Project Management*, Elizabeth Harrin aims to demystify project management by bringing clarity to the subject. Harrin's goal is to show how project management permeates everyday life, and that project managers can use what they learn at work and outside of work to improve their projects. Harrin is the author of *Project Management in the Real World* and *Social Media for Project Managers*, and writes regularly for project management and business publications. A founding member of PMI's new media council, Elizabeth often speaks on project management topics, and has a blog at www.pm4girls.co.uk. In this book: Subchapters 2.6, 5.9.

## Andy Jordan

As President of Roffensian Consulting Inc., Andy Jordan focuses on strengthening project management environments through the development of teams and individuals. Jordan is a prolific writer with over 100 published articles on a number of project management topics, and is an accomplished presenter and instructor on project management and leadership. Jordan is driven to improve the quality of project management by providing project managers with the skills they need to become accomplished people and task leaders, as well as encouraging them to challenge accepted project management norms. In this book: Subchapters 1.11, 3.8, 3.9, 4.1, 4.8, 5.4, 5.5, 7.3, 7.5, 7.12, 8.2, 9.1, 9.6, 9.7.

## Ty Kiisel

As an *accidental* project manager and marketing veteran with over 25 years of experience, Ty Kiisel makes project management concepts and best practices for project management tools accessible to both the expert and novice project professional by weaving personal experiences, historical references, and other anecdotes into daily discussions around effective leadership approaches that maximize the effectiveness of project teams. Ty is also the host of the popular podcast *TalkingWork.com*. In this book: Subchapters 1.8, 2.4, 3.5, 3.6.

## Paul S. Lukas

As Manager of Complex Infrastructure Projects for a leading technology company, Paul S. Lukas, PMP, CPA, manages multi-million dollar, multi-national infrastructure updates, and reengineering projects. Lukas is known as the *Conductor* for his skills in managing people and technology by getting individuals to perform from the same score. He has held leadership positions in financial management, operations management, outsourcing contract negotiation and administration, customer service strategy, technology planning, IT development, and IT finance. Lucas is an active speaker and former Co-Chair of the PMO Special Interest Group of the Association of IT Professionals. Paul is a survivor of the September 11, 2001 attacks and his sub-chapter contribution is based on lessons learned during that experience. In this book: Subchapter 9.10.

## Jerry Manas

Jerry Manas is President of the Marengo Group, and author of *Managing the Gray Areas* (RMC Publications, 2008) and *Napoleon on Project Management* (Nelson Business, 2006). A sought-after author, speaker, and consultant, he is cofounder of the popular blog site *PMThink*, and a founding member of The Creating We Institute, a leadership think-tank dedicated to fostering *we*-centric organizations and teams. In this book: Subchapters 2.2, 3.3, 4.10.

## Alexander Matthey

Alexander Matthey is an expert project manager, PM consultant, coach, and trainer with 26 years of experience in managing projects of varied size and complexity on several continents. Matthey set up and led PMOs in the telecommunications industry in Switzerland, trained hundreds of project managers on several continents (the trainer of 33% of all Swiss PMPs), and is an active expert of 3PM Experts, delivering services in the Geneva/Lausanne area as well as in the United Arab Emirates and GCC. Matthey is particularly interested in complex project management and program management services with an emphasis on behavioral change management, and works fluently in English, French, Hungarian, and Bulgarian. In this book: Subchapter 5.1.

## Stephen Maye

Stephen Maye loves to tell a story. Presently, the story is about how we can better strategize, plan, and execute projects that will achieve full realization and not stop at installation. Maye's success in the project space is achieved through a commitment to keeping an eye on the ball, a gift for connecting the parts, and a passion for communicating what matters. As an independent consultant, Stephen has over 15 years of management experience with a focus on effectively driving cultural change. He is a frequent contributor to gantthead. In this book: Subchapter 7.9.

## Josh Nankivel

Josh Nankivel, BSc in Project Management, PMP, coaches new and aspiring project managers to achieve their career goals through various publications and training courses. He founded pmStudent in 2006 to help himself and others learn more about project management as a discipline and career. He has managed IT and non-IT projects in computing, financial services, telecommunications, and aerospace industries. In this book: Subchapters 1.6, 7.2, 8.3.

## Mark Price Perry

As Vice President of BOT International, and Director of PMO Services for gantthead .com, Mark is dedicated to helping organizations with PMO setup. Perry is the author of *Business Driven PMO Setup—Practical Insights, Techniques and Case Examples for Ensuring Success* and host of The PMO Podcast with over 200 episodes. He has written and presented on several topics from business-driven PMO setup to PMO strategies for complex adaptive systems. Having worked with and learned from hundreds of PMOs of all shapes and sizes around the world, Mark's mission is to serve the PMO domain and provide practical guidance to organizations seeking to set up, manage, and improve upon their PMOs. In this book: Subchapter 4.4.

## Aaron Porter, MBA, PMP

Aaron Porter, MBA, PMP, is a project manager for the Utah Health Information Network (UHIN), the state-recognized Health Information Exchange, and a non-profit organization that operates an electronic value-added network providing EDI services to the health care community in Utah. Prior to working for UHIN, Porter worked for almost seven years in the combined role of business analyst and project manager in IT Operations at Delta Dental of California. He has two primary objectives as project manager: to help others gain a better understanding of the profession and to help project managers achieve their professional objectives. Toward these ends, Porter maintains a blog about preparing for the PMP exam and maintaining the PMP credential. He also serves as Vice President of Education and Certification for PMI, Northern Utah Chapter. In this role, he hopes to be able to provide his peers with the resources they need to identify and achieve their own professional development goals. In this book: Subchapters 1.7, 9.3, 9.8.

## Dave Prior

Dave Prior is the President of ProjectWizards, Inc., and responsible for North American sales, service, training, and support for Merlin, a project management application. He has done volunteer work aimed at establishing a strong bridge between the Agile and PM communities, and also focuses on helping project managers add Sun Tzu's *The Art of War* into their PM tool set. His blog, *DrunkenPM*, appears on gantthead.com and he has a podcast called *ProjectPotion* with Bas de Baar, the Project Shrink. Dave has spoken at numerous project management, IT, and Agile conferences around the world. In this book: Subchapters 2.1, 3.1, 4.9, 8.1, 8.8.

## Jennifer Russell

As President of Mastodon Consulting, Jennifer Russell drives good governance practices, from developing corporate social responsibility programs to driving regulatory compliance and strategic execution. She uses project management as her *secret sauce* to take on intractable problems for multinational corporations, and develop and implement practical solutions. Profiled by Ziff-Davis Media as a *Great Mind in Development*, Jennifer has taught project managers all over the world about governance, risk, and strategy. She serves as an advisory board member for the San Francisco Chapter of PMI, and is active on several other boards. She would like to remind you that volunteering is a great way to learn new skills and make new contacts. In this book: Subchapters 4.3, 8.11.

## Fran Samaras

Fran Samaras has provided vision in the field of project management and much experience in implementing a strategic mix of process, change, and technology initiatives. As Vice President of Enterprise PMO, Life and Specialty Ventures, Samaras manages a team that is responsible for the execution of enterprise projects. She is responsible for developing a culture of project management discipline, setting the strategy for portfolio prioritization and high performance in project management and implementation. Her experience includes past roles as Vice President, PMO and Enterprise Project Manager at Zurich NA, Manager at Accenture, and Project Team Lead at AMA

Insurance Agency, Inc. She believes that effective project management can bring calm to chaos, deliver results, and achieve goals. In this book: Subchapters 2.5, 4.5, 5.3, 5.8.

## Alec Satin

Alec Satin sets up organizational processes for an international services firm. He cares deeply about the health of work environments, and consults for leaders who want to change their companies for the better. As a mentor and coach, Satin helps new project managers reach their stride. He also writes for blog.alecsatin.com. In this book: Subchapter 2.3.

## Aaron Smith

Aaron Smith has 20 years of experience in publishing as an editor and writer, including his role as Editorial Director of ProjectsatWork.com, an online magazine for project management professionals. Prior to this role, Smith led and worked on award-winning editorial teams covering a diverse spectrum of fields and industries, including university academics, healthcare, wine, music, and construction. In this book: Subchapter 3.4.

## Ian Stewart

As a Vice President and Team Lead in SunTrust Bank's Corporate Program Management Office, Ian Stewart is committed to building consistent, repeatable project results through reasonable, yet sound, project governance and compliance practices. Stewart has contributed to two PMI project management standards—Project Estimation and the Organizational Project Management Model (OPM3®). He also co-developed a set of Project Management Professional Exam test preparatory materials and authored articles on a variety of project management topics. Stewart's mission is to help organizations to effectively leverage investments in projects and programs. In this book: Subchapter 7.10.

## Peter Taylor

As "The Lazy Project Manager", Peter Taylor is a successful author, public speaker, and trainer. In his day job, he leads a PMO for Siemens Industry Software; on which he has based the book *Leading Successful PMOs*. Peter wants project managers to work a little less hard and be more effective—to be *productively lazy*. He shares his thoughts through several Web sites as well as free podcasts for download on iTunes. In this book: Subchapter 4.2.

## J. Chris White

J. Chris White has a passion for helping companies move their plans *from paper to performance*. White is the President of ViaSim Solutions, the makers of pmBLOX, a simulation-based project planning tool that goes beyond the traditional Critical Path Method and uses the Dynamic Progress Method as its foundation. He co-authored *Strategic Quality Management*, and has written and presented papers on the topics of leadership, management, and simulation. White is also a Six Sigma Lean Master Black Belt. In this book: Subchapters 1.4, 1.5, 2.7, 3.10, 5.2, 5.6, 7.1, 8.6, 8.9, 9.4.

## Jennifer Whitt

Jennifer Whitt, PMP, is a speaker, trainer, certified performance coach, author, and President of Optimo, Inc., a consulting firm specializing in project management and leadership development. She is the Editor in Chief of *The Optimo Exchange Newsletter*. Most recently, Whitt launched *PDUs 2Go* for *Project Managers on the Go*. From experience, she knows how difficult it can be to make time for classroom or online learning, so she developed a new way for project managers to Earn n' Learn while on the go. Customers have branded this site *iTunes for Project Managers*. In this book: Subchapters 8.10.

## Michael Wood

As a nationally recognized thought leader in enterprise value delivery improvement, Michael Wood helps organizations pursue and deploy stakeholder value-driven projects and initiatives. His *Helix Factor* books enjoy international distribution, and represent the first *Lean How-To* books in the business process improvement field. Wood has written more than 100 articles ranging from IT strategy to governance, and portfolio to project management. His time-tested methods and approaches grew out of real-world practice. He is a sought after speaker and workshop leader. Wood's mission is to help organizations, through their people, to become stewards of stakeholder value through exemplary execution and stellar delivery. In this book: Subchapters 6.1-6.9, 8.5.

# ABOUT THE EDITOR

**Dave Garrett**

Dave Garrett earned a B.A. from the University of Maryland and M.S. in Information Systems from The American University. As President and CEO of gantthead.com, Dave is dedicated to creating value for the project management community and the continued growth of its media network (gantthead.com, projectsatwork.com, and others), which now reaches over 600,000 project managers worldwide. His strategic, management and technical expertise has enabled him to guide the gantthead team in the development and refinement of resources that are unmatched in the project management industry.

Gantthead is a subsidiary of Headstrong, Inc., a global IT consulting firm. Prior to cofounding and building gantthead into a profitable web-based business from the ground up, Dave was Director, Advanced Technology Group for Headstrong, Inc. In this role, he managed multiple projects and was responsible for all aspects of intranet management and development, including global knowledge management, ongoing systems development, and administration. Dave also authored and managed the development of webWAVE intranet methodology.

Gantthead.com is the world's largest online community of IT project managers. Developed by project managers for project managers, gantthead serves as a destination where project managers go to get support for their projects. Members of gantthead have access to:

- How-to articles covering project management from every angle
- Free templates, checklists, project plans, and other documents to solve immediate problems
- Entertaining and insightful blogs from the brightest minds in project management
- Videos and webinars to earn free PDUs
- Participation in member groups to connect with peers
- A social network that can help with specific issues
- Online learning opportunities to build a resume and sharpen skills

Dave's strategic, management, and technical expertise has enabled him to guide the gantthead team in the development and refinement of resources.

Web
Added
Value™

*Free value-added materials available from*
*the Download Resource Center at www.jrosspub.com*

At J. Ross Publishing we are committed to providing today's professional with practical, hands-on tools that enhance the learning experience and give readers an opportunity to apply what they have learned. That is why we offer free ancillary materials available for download on this book and all participating Web Added Value™ publications. These online resources may include interactive versions of material that appears in the book or supplemental templates, worksheets, models, plans, case studies, proposals, spreadsheets and assessment tools, among other things. Whenever you see the WAV™ symbol in any of our publications, it means bonus materials accompany the book and are available from the Web Added Value Download Resource Center at www.jrosspub.com.

Downloads for *Project Pain Reliever: A Just-in-Time Handbook for Anyone Managing Projects* include "What you have learned" summaries for addressing problems contained within the book, additional problems with solutions, and other useful resources.

# PART A

## Leadership—The Art of Project Management

# 1

# FOCUSING YOUR EFFORTS

## 1.1 Whom do I have to please?

By Dave Garrett

### 1. Problem

Every problem can make you feel like you have to please a thousand different people who all want different things. However, the problem isn't only, "whom do I please?" It is also, "which needs are truly important?"

### 2. Warning Signs

- You are wasting a lot of time going back and forth between people, and trying to figure out what your project should accomplish.
- No one seems to be confident in your ability to deliver.

### 3. What will happen if I do nothing?

Trying to please everyone means that you will end up pleasing no one. This is how a lot of folks lose their jobs or get moved to a position that doesn't require managing people.

### 4. Solution

You need a clear set of goals and a real understanding of how everyone's

---

**Are You Like Susie "the Pleaser"?**

Snap! Those stylish tortoise shell polycarbonates sure make a sharp sound when they finally give way. Susie, the project manager for an app project, stared at the two pieces of an "unbreakable" whole, like she hadn't been twisting them back and forth in frustration for 20 minutes. Sunglasses clearly could be broken, but was her career just as fragile?

She thought she had the new web app project set up for success after the launch meeting. The meeting participants had all of the requirements for "Build your own specs" defined, and everyone seemed to know exactly what needed to be done. Then came the visitors.

First, Sharon, the Marketing VP, dropped by to talk about how happy she was that the online product catalog was being replaced by this new app. The catalog replacement was never mentioned in the meeting, but to Sharon it was a logical part of the project. Susie let her go without committing to anything, but she also didn't say that it wouldn't be done.

Next, Bob, the Product Manager, presented Susie with a list of reports that he wanted the application to produce for him. Again, none of this was covered in the meeting, but Bob was a really important person in the company, so Susie said, "I'll do what I can."

After lunch, with a nagging feeling of dread, Susie found a new email from Steve, the Technical Lead on the project, letting her know about three core systems that needed modifications to work with

*Continues*

3

needs affect what you're doing (shown in Figure 1.1). In short, you need:

1. A high-level executive, a sponsor, whose work is closely tied to the outcome of your project, to make the tough calls.
2. A scope document to make sure that you understand exactly what needs to be done.
3. A defined way to work with the sponsor to address everyone else's needs.

the new application. Tons of effort would need to be spent beyond the application itself, but the efforts needed to be done to make everything work together.

It was clear to Susie that none of the additional needs could be addressed without causing massive delays and increased costs to the project. Rather than send the email she had composed in her head, telling everyone to forget their needs and wants, Susie took a deep breath and tried to figure out what to do next.

## 5. What should I do?

When you don't know who to please, you need to identify a sponsor as the one person you need to please most. Then, you need to develop a scope document, which essentially outlines how you will please that person and accomplish something valuable to the organization.

There are two sets of people you need to be concerned with when managing a project: sponsors and stakeholders. The sponsor is the one you ultimately answer to. He or she should work with you to define *success* in a way that also pleases stakeholders. You

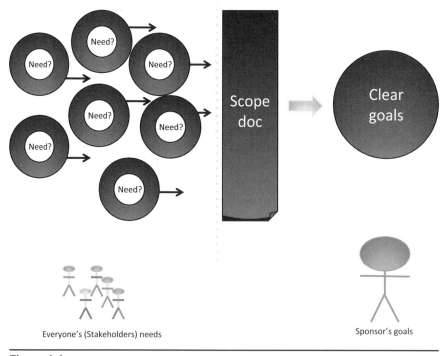

Everyone's (Stakeholders) needs

Sponsor's goals

**Figure 1.1**

define *success* in a scope document, then stick to doing what is in the scope document and accomplish what you set out to do.

### 5(a) Sponsor

Gather what you have in terms of goals and support materials, and make sure you have the best description of what the project aims to do before looking for a sponsor. Then identify your sponsor *candidates*. In this context, the best sponsor will most likely be someone you know or at least know of. It may or may not be the person to whom you've been reporting status. Think about:

- Executives you report to
- Executives tied to the function
- Which executive has the most to lose if your project fails

To identify a sponsor, think about these questions:

- Who has the financial power to be a sponsor for this project?
- Who has the political influence in the organization to be a sponsor?
- Who has a history of backing successful projects?
- Will this sponsor defend the project as it runs into challenges or starts to lose organizational support?
- Would you have a good working relationship?
- Who will provide the project direction and focus, and at the same time, ask the right questions to help you be successful?
- Is the sponsor positioned to take ownership in the resulting product of the project?

The sponsor is a *buck stops here* person. He or she is a business leader within the organization who:

- Is tied to the success of your project in a meaningful way
- Helps define the scope and objectives of the project
- Sets priorities and resolves conflicts
- Has the power to make changes to the project in order to achieve the goal(s)
- Can approve assignment of people and resources
- Has enough influence to communicate effectively to every group involved in the project
- Communicates with the executive team to ensure continued support

Think about the first three bullet points for a moment. Someone in the business, above you, has likely committed to executive management that your project will be a success. His or her reputation probably depends on it. You just need to make the sponsorship role clear and official, so that there is a single person (or small group) who can define success and resolve conflicts.

Once the right person has agreed to be your sponsor, work with them to identify stakeholders and plan to address their needs. Also, work with them to set and document the project scope.

### 5(b) Stakeholders

The project's stakeholders are probably all of the people who have been asking you for things. They have a vested interest in the project, and would like to make their priorities yours. This isn't a bad thing, but you can't please everyone. Identify and group stakeholders with the help of your sponsor. Understand whose needs you can and cannot serve, which needs are incompatible with each other, and any conflicts those needs may present.

To understand what you are dealing with, you want to first separate stakeholders into groups. Ask yourself, are stakeholders:

- End-users of what the project is creating?
- People whose jobs will be affected by what you are doing?
- People who will be better or worse off in a specific way, based on the outcome of the project?
- People who are on competing projects?
- Sharing other reasons to care about your project?

Grouping stakeholders will give you a better idea of what you are dealing with. You can't give people everything that they want, but hopefully you can give them what they need by working with the sponsor to create an effective scope document.

### 5(c) Scope document

Then you will work with your sponsor to create a scope document. The scope document defines what you are doing and *not* doing. At a minimum, it defines:

- The goals and objectives of the project.
- How the project aligns with your organization's goals and strategies.
- Assumptions that you've made about the project (things you assume are already taken care of).
- Constraints that you are placing on the project (objectives you are *not* trying to achieve or items that you will *not* do).

The scope document can include other items and take various forms. Often, it is a business case or project charter, but the important part is that your participation in the project is documented, agreed upon, and reflective of the sponsor's definition of success.

# 1.2 How do I define *success* on this project?

By Dave Garrett

## 1. Problem

When you started the project, it felt like you understood the goals. Lately, it has become clear that what you thought were your goals are not well-defined or meaningful anymore.

It is a common mistake to take someone's word about the importance of the project without completely understanding the goals. It happens to many project managers. The project is just something to be done, and you've been chosen to do it. Or, perhaps, you knew what you were doing early on and now everything changed. Either way, the fact that goal changes happen often does not offer a lot of comfort when you're left holding the bag.

## 2. Warning Signs

- People seem to misunderstand the project in general.
- You have little pressure to get things done—and that makes you nervous.
- Your sponsor went away or changed.
- You can't explain the value of your project to others in a clear and unstanderable way.

### Is Your Project Managing You?

Don just didn't have the heart to tell him. Simon couldn't wait for Don's project to produce a new headrest design that would fit well with his hot new 2-seater. His eager anticipation started to sound like "are we there yet?"—hard to take from someone who was so adamantly anti-back seat.

It started innocently. Don asked Simon to participate in a focus group, and then came the follow-up questions from Simon. In a matter of weeks, Simon had become a central figure on the project. He gave Don great guidance on designing super-safe headrests. When Don asked for his input, Simon dove right in, spending countless hours not only answering questions, but sacrificing his personal time to make sure Don's project was going well. It seemed like every report Don gave to management was riddled with "Simon says..."

By the time Don realized that Simon thought he was producing actual designs, it was too late. Maybe he could squeeze in designs and change the scope of the project. Don thought, "Nobody seems to care right now and it does seem like a useful thing to do." Don's sponsor left early in the project, which was about "Designing Safety into Production Processes"—whatever that meant. The sponsor left before the goal of the project was really clear.

Now, Don had a choice, either figure out what the project was supposed to accomplish without looking like a fool, or change the scope of the project to accomplish something he knows will be useful. The problem is that Don doesn't know where to start.

## 3. What will happen if I do nothing?

If you do nothing, the work might be easy, but you'll regret it later when the project is cancelled or completed with little to show for it.

Your project's success depends on a unique set of needs. Your career in business depends on making measurable, meaningful contributions to the organization—otherwise, you are wasting time. The project needs to be important to your organization *and* important to someone who has a loud, influential voice within the organization. You'll find that:

- Everyone around you has needs, and a lot of them could be important to your organization. However, you can't be all things to all people.
- It is easier to get things done if the people you ask things of believe your project's goals are aligned with their needs. Of course, you shouldn't mislead people as to your project's goals.

Picture yourself describing what you accomplished on this project when you're competing for your next position. How does that look if you've done nothing to ensure this effort is meaningful?

Also picture yourself explaining to senior management why you satisfied another person's needs without officially changing the scope of your project. That might work for Robin Hood, but is unlikely to work for you.

## 4. Solution

There are always more than one set of possible goals, and people will always make assumptions about what you're doing, according to their interests. If what you are doing has no impact on them, they likely won't care about the outcome of your project. So, to get things on track, you need to reset the goals in alignment with your sponsor's needs and the overall organizational direction. As shown in Figure 1.2, you need three things to define success on a project.

1. A high-level executive (preferably one), a sponsor, whose work is closely tied to the outcome of your project, to make the tough calls.
2. A clear understanding of why the outcome of this project is important to both the organization and to your sponsor.
3. A business case to make sure you understand exactly what needs to be done.

## 5. What should I do?

When you are unclear about your project's goals, it is important to define your sponsor, goals, and business case, in that order. Otherwise, you will waste a lot of time.

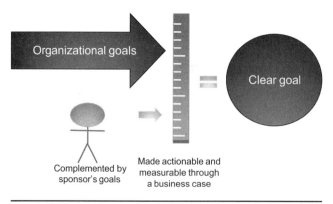

**Figure 1.2**

### 5(a) *Find a sponsor*

Your sponsor is often the person who actually defines what success will look like. They may not define it clearly up front, but that is why you need to refine goals and create an actual business case for yourself. You will likely have some goals and support materials defined at this point. Use what you have to create the best description of what the project aims to do before looking for a sponsor. Then, identify sponsor *candidates*. The best sponsor will likely be someone you know or at least know of. It may or may not be the person to whom you've been reporting status, so conduct your sponsor search with an open mind. Think about:

- Executives to whom you report
- Executives tied to the function or functions the project will touch
- The executive who has the most to lose if your project fails

To identify a sponsor, think about these questions:

- Who has the spending authority to be a sponsor for this project?
- Who has the political influence in the organization to be a sponsor?
- Who has a history of backing successful projects?
- Will this candidate defend the project as it runs into challenges or starts to lose organizational support?
- With whom will you have a good working relationship?
- Who will provide project direction and focus? Will they ask the right questions to help you be successful?
- Is the candidate positioned to take ownership in the resulting product of the project?

The sponsor is a person with final say over nearly all project decisions. He or she is a business leader within your organization who:

- Is committed to the success of your project in a meaningful way
- Helps define the scope and objectives of the project
- Sets priorities and resolves issues and conflicts
- Has the power to make changes to the project plan, budget, and timing in order to achieve the goal(s)
- Can approve assignment of people and resources
- Has enough influence to communicate effectively to every constituent group involved in the project
- Effectively communicates with the executive team to ensure continued support

Think about those first three bullet points for a moment. Someone in the business, above you, has likely committed to executive management that your project will be a success. Their reputation probably depends on it. You just need to make the sponsorship role clear and official, so that there is a single person (or small group) who can define success and resolve conflicts. Making it official also focuses the sponsor's attention on the importance of the project, verifying their responsibility for the project's success.

Once the right person agrees to be your sponsor, work with them to refine your goals.

### 5(b) Goals tied to the organization's goals or strategies

If you've chosen the right sponsor, that person's interests are closely tied to some part of the organization's strategy. Reach as high as you can into your organization's strategy, goals, or objectives. Understand how your project supports those goals and your sponsor's goals in a complementary way.
First, have a talk with your sponsor. Ask him or her to:

- Describe the goals of the project as they understand them
- Descrobe how those goals tie to the strategy
- State how s/he would measure success in a way that ties to the strategy
- Point out why those measures are important to him or her personally

Then, do a little research. The organization's strategic initiatives are sometimes published as a stand-alone document, a business plan, a mission statement, within existing information systems plans, or in C-level announcements describing business problems that the organization is intent on solving. Understand the organization's short- and long-term business goals, and see if your project can help achieve those goals. The trick is to:

- Figure out how your sponsor's input ties in with the documents that define what's important to the organization
- Identify ties between project goals and specific strategic goals of the company
- Identify specific success metrics that clearly tie to the organization's strategic objectives

If you can't quantify the business goals and objectives (make them measurable), work through it with your sponsor.

### 5(c) Define the business case

The business case makes everything achievable by making goals and measures clear. It defines what you are doing, and why it's important, in a way that everyone can understand. Usually, you would build a case to get initial funding for the project, but you need it now as a reference point for decisions you are making every day on the project. You want to be sure that everything you do helps you to realize a business objective that you've laid out in this document—otherwise, you are wasting resources. At a minimum, the business case defines:

- The goals and objectives of your project
- How the project aligns with the organization's goals and strategy
- How you will measure the results in a very tangible and objective way
- Risks (what could cause you to fail) and how you plan to deal with them
- Assumptions that you've made (things you assume are already taken care of or are out of this project's scope)

- Constraints you are placing on the project (objectives you are *not* trying to achieve or things that you will *not* do)
- Estimated cost
- Estimated return on investment

The business case is usually done at the beginning of the project to justify its existence, so it can be very detailed. Yours can be as short as a page, but can be longer if what you're writing helps to clarify the value you are creating. The exercise of writing it will clarify the goals in your mind, as well as on paper. You want to be able to tell anyone who asks exactly what you are doing and why it's important. You also want goals and measures that guide you when deciding what will and will not make the project succeed.

# 1.3 Different people want different things at different times.

## By Michael Flint

### 1. Problem

Despite following the methodology, the standard approach, and delivering what was asked of you, your project did not meet expectations and it might be considered a failure.

You know how to start a project, gather requirements, identify objectives—what is in scope and out of scope, etc. You plan, schedule, and get commitments for deliverables. You document everything and get all of the necessary approvals. The methodology helps to guide you through the process, deal with issues as you go, and manage change requests, mitigate risk, and deliver the final product—with all of this happening on time and within budget. You did what you said. The project should be a complete success. So how could it be considered a failure?

Stakeholders, and, in particular, the sponsors may have expectations of what the project will deliver and when. These expectations may be very different than the

> **Are We Developing a Product or a Brand?**
>
> Time was slipping by as Jerry bounced between co-sponsor opinions. Erin and Brett would not stop pulling him in different directions. Suddenly, Erin wanted the product masthead and product logo that the team had thrown together to become a central feature of the overall corporate brand. She felt like it would be easy to quickly make refinements, but those refinements had already cost the project 5 person-weeks of effort. Erin wanted to make the logo fresh and new, but still fit the overall company standards. However, she can't put what she wants into words. Brett just wants to be done with the logo and for the team to get moving on the rest of the project. Executives feel like they both have a point, and want a collaborative resolution to the differences of opinion.
>
> Future users of the system are starting to provide random input. Owners of related systems want to integrate development efforts to accomplish their own goals. Brett is in so deep that he barely has time to talk to anyone.
>
> At the end of the day, it's Jerry's call and his responsibility. He just doesn't know who to listen to. It's a classic no win situation for him.

answers received during the requirements gathering process. Not all stakeholders are known or declared at the initiation, so their needs, requirements, and expectations can not all be quantified early in the project. Often, you will have to deal with cosponsorship of projects, which might provide additional guidance and support. However, it dramatically increases the chances that you are dealing with different expectations for the same project.

The bottom line is that upon completion of the project, even offer delivering what was asked and meeting requirements, some projects are still deemed to have failed. They met requirements, but did not deliver what was *expected*.

## 2. Warning Signs

- There is more than one person providing direction or requirements for the project
- There are frequent *side* meetings to ensure that parts of the project are looked after
- You don't understand how this project fits into the organization's strategic direction
- You feel like you aren't getting the full story from anyone about what is really wanted
- Your inability to meet expectations seems like a timing issue

## 3. What will happen if I do nothing?

You seem to have a relatively simple job: determine what is required and deliver it. However, if you ignore warning signs and just push through using this simple approach, there is a good possibility that, at the end of the project, you will have failed. You will have delivered to the specified requirements, but failed to meet the spoken or unspoken expectations of the stakeholders.

This is a clear case of delivering what was asked of you not being good enough.

## 4. Solution

More than anything else, you need to get all of the decision makers in a room and agree on scope and a set of goals. During this meeting, you need to do more than just accept requirements as written or spoken. You need to hear more than just the words and statements. You need to tune into the unspoken processes, observe the relationships, and follow through on how things work in the organization. You need to use all of your senses and not just record the words given in answer to the question asked. You need to probe deeper and ask *stupid* questions. Don't stop until you have a complete understanding of every expectation that matters.

## 5. What should I do?

Do not assume that all the people are *at the table* when defining the project charter and planning the schedule. Bring them to the table and ensure that decisions are made.

### 5(a) Make sure all stakeholders are identified

Some stakeholders are known, obviously connected to the project, and easily identified. Others are not. Some stakeholders will have clear expectations, having defined them for the project team through vision statements or structured reviews and documents. Others will not know what they want and appear to support the status quo. Barring a conclusive meeting, this group may only have a concrete opinion after the project ends.

### 5(b) Start with a skeptical view of the organization

Assume that information has not been fully communicated. This is easier for the consultant who comes into an organization with little or no prior knowledge of the culture and limited preconceived ideas. Resident project managers must adopt a consultant's persona.

### 5(c) Treat each person as an individual and prioritize whose goals are more important

Understand that the sponsor's stated needs are likely to be most important, but that others can help or undermine you along the way, based on their personal interests. Be aware of the organizational culture and become effective in *reading* the individuals who may impact the project. You need to tune into each individual's interests to pick up early warning signals on the project, the project team, and anything else that you may not have thought about. The bottom line is that projects are made up of different people who will want different things at different times.

### 5(d) Translate and document nonspecific expectations into project plans and goals

You must be able to not only hear, but translate expressed needs into quantifiable, prioritized requirements that express the overall *intent* of the project. This is traditionally done by:

- Reviewing the stated goals and success measures of the project
- Capturing each stakeholder's perception of what the project should achieve and how it varies from the official goals
- Documenting the intersections and divergences at a detailed level; consider drawing out cases as needed
- Achieving and documenting concurrence among the group

Traditionally, we drive for statements to describe requirements to identify the order of things and bring clarity to the concept that was enunciated to bring us on board. This is almost always step 1. It is also where new project managers tend to stop thinking about goals and objectives. More seasoned managers identify all key stakeholders and their expectations for the project, as well. The project charter, while providing the official direction, scope, and critical success factors, does not identify the project for all people. For example, reviews with regional managers, individual local managers, and the users of a software product will reveal requirements and expectations that have not been captured when initiating the project at the head office.

# 1.4 I'm technically on track, but not accomplishing what people wanted.

By J. Chris White

## 1. Problem

By all relevant project metrics (e.g., earned value, milestones), your project is right on target, if not exceeding goals. However, no one seems to be looking at those metrics, and instead, feel that progress is not as far along as expected.

## 2. Warning Signs

- The project sponsor, executive, or end customer feels the constant need to clarify their requirements.
- Even though the project is on budget and on schedule, the end customer is not happy.
- Team members are getting frustrated with minor changes.
- You strongly feel that the project will fall short of its objectives or that it is not accomplishing what it is supposed to accomplish.

## 3. What will happen if I do nothing?

Regardless of how good the project looks from a metrics perspective, in the eyes of the project executive and end customer, the project may not meet its objectives. As the project manager, this may be a black mark on your record that you cannot escape, which means it could have a drastic impact on the subsequent projects you are assigned (if any), as well as your long-term career.

## 4. Solution

There are some cases in which things change drastically during the middle of a project and the original objectives change so much that some of the work done to date is no

---

### You Can't Please Everybody!

At every weekly project status meeting, Steve, the project manager, got updates on how the project was progressing. Every week the status of the project was right on track with the original plan. This was quite an accomplishment. His team was engaged and enthusiastic, team members helped each other and shared information, and weekly status meetings were actually fun, not the typical "beating" that everyone was used to. "Who could ask for more?" thought Steve.

Apparently, his project sponsor and the end customer *could* ask for more, and they often did. The periodic meetings with these two stakeholders were not nearly as fun as the weekly status meetings with the team. Instead, they questioned the content of the project deliverables, changed scope on several key tasks, and added other requirements that were not in the original plan.

This caused several problems for Steve and his project team. They often had to rework some of the deliverables that they thought they had successfully completed on budget and on schedule. Or, they had to add new tasks and activities that weren't in the original baseline plan, which resulted in a scheduling nightmare as tasks and resources needed to be shifted and reallocated to keep the entire project on schedule with the hard due date.

Over a period of a few weeks, Steve and the project team would get things back in order and be back on track. But, once again, the next meeting with the project sponsor and end customer resulted in more changes. "Why does this keep happening?" wondered Steve. "I'm managing the project as best I can, but they're still not happy with the results."

longer helpful or applicable. We will not deal with this situation in this chapter. For advice on that type of situation, please see:

- Chapter 1.5: I feel like I need to start over.
- Chapter 5.2: Everything has changed. I need to reset goals and expectations.

Here, we will focus on the most probable other cause for this situation—a lack of full understanding of the requirements and expectations for the project. In this case, the solution is to get a full understanding of the requirements and expectations for the project. This means talking a lot with the project sponsor, executive and the end customer.

## 5. What should I do?

The fundamental problem in this situation is a lack of understanding of the requirements and expectations for the project. On any project, we have a natural tendency to want to get going, start working immediately, dive in, and accomplish something quickly. For example, on a software development project, developers may begin writing software code for the parts of the application that they already know how to code, yet they may not know exactly what the entire application is supposed to do. Of course, when you begin without having a full vision of the end result, it makes the correct end result difficult to achieve.

Here is a basic equation to remember:

$$UNCERTAINTY = RISK$$

Anytime the project manager and the project team do not completely understand, without a doubt, what the project is supposed to accomplish, they are accepting some level of risk. The more that is unknown to the project manager and team, the higher the risk. The more that is known, the lower the risk. Uncertainty and risk are proportional. Because you, the project manager, are leading this project and are in charge of organizing all resources and deliverables, the bulk of the responsibility for understanding the full range of end customer (or project sponsor) requirements falls squarely on your shoulders. You will be held accountable.

Every project starts in some *abstract* form and gains *detail* as it progresses. The key is to capture as much detail up front, as quickly as possible, so that the project moves from abstract to details without loss from waste or unproductive effort (that is, money and resources). It does not matter that a task is on budget and on schedule if it is the wrong task or an incomplete task.

Several things can cause a person to not fully understand the details of the requirements for a project. Typically, a different set of people (separate from the project team) could be the ones setting the requirements. Because they are not part of the team, additional knowledge or insight could have been *lost in translation* as the requirements were passed on. This is common when a sales team has the interface with the end customer and the implementation of the project is handled by a separate project team. Another reason is that the end customer (or the project executive within the company) is pushing for an accelerated schedule. With pressure to move along quickly, details are skipped in favor of *getting something done*, so that it looks like progress is being made on the shortened deadline.

Whatever the reason, it is time to do something about it. To let it continue will only cause more problems (and possibly larger, catastrophic problems) later. So, what do you need to do now? There are several key actions that you need to take:

### 5(a) Review the original requirements

The first thing you need to do is to immediately sit down with your end customer (and/or project sponsor, depending on who has defined the objectives of the project) and walk back through the original requirements. Wherever there is doubt, ask questions. There is no room for error. If you don't understand all the technical details about the project or its requirements, bring in team members who do have the technical expertise. Also, ask about any expectations that the end customer and/or project sponsor may have that are not *technical* requirements, such as the desire to participate in weekly status meetings or the desire to talk directly with some of the key team members. Make sure all of these requirements, objectives, and expectations are documented and recorded. Read them back to the end customer and/or project sponsor to ensure they were captured correctly.

### 5(b) Review current work and tasks

While still working with the end customer and/or project sponsor, review current work and tasks to see if anything was missed and why. You may need to get several other key team members involved in this step. Get a full understanding of any gaps that currently exist. Take these gaps to your full project team to see if cost, schedule, and resource estimates need to change. If estimates need to change dramatically, that's an entirely different situation because major renegotiations will be necessary. The two chapters referenced earlier in this section are good chapters to read if this is the situation. For now, we will assume that major changes in cost, schedule, and resource estimates are not required.

### 5(c) Define corrective actions and get sponsor approval

After understanding gaps and any changes in estimates, define corrective actions that are needed and get the project sponsor and end customer to sign-off on the changes. This is extremely important because this change document now becomes a paper trail that can be referenced if other scope changes or new requirements are introduced downstream on the project.

### 5(d) Manage performance against the plan

As suggested in other chapters when changes arise, the next thing to do is to aggressively manage project performance against the revised plan. As project manager, you are accountable for this project, so you will definitely want to stay on top of things and address any deviations as soon as possible to prevent problems from propagating.

After getting this project back on course, make sure to implement these types of up-front clarification discussions and documentation efforts on future projects (if it is not already part of your company's normal project process).

# 1.5 I feel like I need to start over.
## By J. Chris White

### 1. Problem

The project is going downhill, and fast. You're not sure how the project got to this point, but it's getting extremely difficult (if not impossible) to get resources, budget, and schedule back on track.

### 2. Warning Signs

- Information shared at meetings is growing vague.
- People are beginning to "distance" themselves from the project.
- Plan updates need to be published more frequently.
- The project does not seem to be accomplishing anything useful.
- You find yourself going back and forth on key decisions.
- You point to the original plan and everyone laughs.

### 3. What will happen if I do nothing?

Simply put, your project runs a very high risk of crashing and burning. If this project is not important to the company, perhaps crashing and burning is not a big deal and can be absorbed as a loss. Most likely, though, the project is important enough that a complete failure is not an option. You cannot continue making *minor fixes* to the project with the hope that things will get back on track by themselves. Hope is not a strategy.

---

**Should I "Throw in the Towel"?**

Jim used to really enjoy going to work. With this latest project, however, he was beginning to dread walking through the front door of the office. "How did it get this bad?" he often wondered to himself. "Should I just cut my losses and tell my project sponsor that this is a no-go?" Weekly status meetings were brutal.

Jim felt like he was pulling teeth trying to get useful, relevant information out of other team members. He found himself constantly making adjustments to the project plan because information would change frequently. As much as he tried to stay on top of things, people just weren't enthusiastic anymore, and they seemed reluctant to want to do anything about it. "Could they see the dead end, too?" he wondered.

Jim wasn't sure what to do. He had been to plenty of project planning training classes, but this subject was never covered. When you find yourself making *corrections* on top of previous *corrections*, something is not right. When you find yourself going back and forth on decisions because the *real* information keeps changing, something is not right. When you find it hard to get a straight answer from other team members because it's always bad news, something is not right. When attempts to get the project back on track only push it later and make it more costly, something is definitely not right.

Jim knew he had to do something or his career might come to a grinding halt. This was a very important project to the company and to his project sponsor, so canceling the project was out of the question. But, knee-jerk reacting to each problem only created additional problems. "How did we get so far from the original plan?" he asked himself. "More importantly, how do we get back to the original plan? Or, does the original plan even matter anymore?"

## 4. Solution

In the human body, when a bone breaks severely enough, it needs to be reset. Projects are often the same. If they get off-track too badly from the initial baseline, they need to be re-baselined. This means gauging the current status of all activities and starting over with new estimates for how the remaining work will be accomplished. Don't be surprised if the new baseline looks nothing like the initial baseline.

## 5. What should I do?

This is probably one of the biggest nightmares that a project manager can face. The beautiful plan that got you out of the gate is now one of the ugliest things that you've ever seen; communication among team members is poor or non-existent; additional requirements (and, thus, new tasks) got added after the project started; new stakeholders appeared and need to be involved; scope is creeping, and so on. You need to do several things:

### 5(a) First, take a long, hard look in the mirror

You are partially (and perhaps mostly) to blame for the current situation. The project outlook is this bleak because you were not making sufficient course corrections along the way to keep communication vibrant, to minimize scope creep and additions to the requirements, and such. There are many possible reasons for this situation:

- You may have started with a completely unrealistic baseline plan. If you knew this going into it, shame on you. If you did not know this, then you may have relied too heavily on the estimates provided by others or trusted their estimates without reviewing or challenging some of their assumptions. You are just as responsible and accountable as they are for that estimate. If your name is on the project, make sure you pay attention.
- When you saw things beginning to go wrong, you did not step in. Perhaps you did not want to offend other team members or make it look like you were micro-managing them. Or, perhaps you hoped that things would improve somehow. Keep in mind, errors propagate. If there is a small mistake in the beginning of a project, it will only grow and ripple throughout the project. It is easy to be too relaxed about the project status early in the project because there is a lot of time left. That time burns up quickly. Nip the problems in the bud. Be quick and thorough. You don't have to be rude, but a lot of times you do have to be assertive.
- You received bad status information and never knew the real project status until it was too late. You are still responsible for *managing* the team members, not just the work. This means gaining trust and respect, and setting the right expectations for behavior and performance. Similar to errors propagating, bad habits and behaviors of team members only get worse. Put in the time and effort at the beginning of the project with managing resources, and you can avoid a lot of problems. Furthermore, when there are problems, you'll have a base of respect and understanding to build from.

Whatever the reason(s), face up to them and accept them. Learn from them. Remember this pain so that the lesson sinks in. Even though this is a nightmare situation, many good project managers have experienced it. At least you can have solace that it's a common nightmare. Welcome to the School of Hard Knocks.

That being said, the other team members are also partially to blame. They need to hear this and be aware of how their decisions and/or behaviors have impacted the project. As a project manager, you have to be firm at this point. Your job is to manage the project to achieve intended objectives. If major change is involved, then so be it. But, if team members are not aware of their contribution to the poor status of the project, they will likely continue their current course of action, which is detrimental. This type of discussion is often handled best in a group setting, so that no one is singled out. In addition, if the project is in this bad of shape, many resources are to blame, not just one.

### 5(b) Second, establish a new plan immediately (i.e., re-baseline)

Approach team members individually and get their buy-in on the new plan and estimates. People often find strength in numbers and may challenge big changes when presented in a group setting. If approached individually, the team members will feel like their concerns are being heard and that they are being given a fair deal. You are not trying to *trick* someone into accepting a new plan that meets your needs as a project manager, but which is completely unrealistic for the other team members.

Your goal is to get a new plan, get consensus from everyone participating, and then make sure the new plan is followed diligently. Some micromanagement will definitely be involved to show people that you are serious about the new plan and any new behavior or performance expectations. If, or when, complaints roll in, remind them of the necessity of the new baseline and that they participated in developing the new estimates. You don't want a project failure on your resume, and they don't want one either.

### 5(c) Third, talk to the project sponsor or executive and explain the situation

A major re-baselining effort will most likely require project sponsor or executive approval. You must be able to tell them what happened, why the project is in its current state, and what you (and your team) plan to do to remedy the situation. Always make sure those who are looking out for you and those who are held organizationally accountable for your project are in the loop.

Typically, a new estimate will be longer or more costly than the original plan. The project sponsor needs to be aware of additional cost as soon as possible so that he or she can take appropriate action. This may involve fighting for additional resources, negotiating with the customer of the project, or passing the unfortunate news up the chain of command. In any case, forthrightness and transparency are keys. *Ostrich managers* don't get very far.

# 1.6 I feel all alone. Where can I turn for advice?

By Josh Nankivel

## 1. Problem

You want to make the processes for managing projects better, but sometimes feel as if you are the only person working on a project. Others are so busy with other activities and priorities that you find little support.

## 2. Warning Signs

- When you start talking about how to improve project management, you immediately see eyes glazing over.
- People in your organization do not know what structured project management is or why it is important.
- You can't seem to find anyone who might serve as a mentor within your organization.

### Is Anybody Out There?

Stan had been managing projects for years, mainly as one of those *other duties as assigned*. He started to enjoy managing these projects though, and wanted to learn more about the various methodologies for project management that he was hearing about.

He found himself trying to bounce ideas about how to better run projects with the other people who were running projects against their will. Most of them started drifting off immediately when Stan approached them on this topic, and a few nodded their heads politely. No one was offering their own ideas, though, and the answer to most of Stan's questions was, "I don't know. This is how we've always done it."

Seeking a mentor, Stan identified a few individuals who had been with the company for decades and running projects during that time. Unfortunately, they either did not care to talk about how projects get managed, or didn't seem to want to spend time talking to Stan about project management. Dejected, Stan murmured to himself, "I feel all alone. Where can I turn for advice?"

## 3. What will happen if I do nothing?

Eventually, your motivation to make projects more successful through continuous improvement and a common set of processes will fade. You will slip into status-quo land with the other *zombies*, and your passion for effective project management will be replaced with the phrases, "good enough," and, "at least it's not my fault."

## 4. Solution

What is missing are other people who care enough about the discipline of project management to have lively debates and discussion about it. You need someone to bounce ideas off of, someone to learn from who has faced the same types of challenges you are wrangling with.

## 5. What should I do?

Don't worry, there are plenty of options for you to explore. You can find other zealots of project management all over the place.

### 5(a) Within your own organization

Within your own organization, it is likely there are others who have the same mindset toward project management, but you have not found each other yet. Start by setting up a meeting over the lunch hour and invite everyone in the company for your new "Project Management Lunch Club." Send an agenda in advance to discuss a specific topic or line up a presentation on a particular topic. (It may even be you doing most of the presentations at first.)

### 5(b) Local PM organizations and groups

If you live in or near a fairly large city, chances are there is an established project management group waiting for you. Go to *Google.com* and type in: project management events [your city name], project management group [your city name], or project management organization [your city name].

   You will find Web sites of individual groups and potentially other sites like *Meetup* or *LinkedIn*, which store information about project management events and groups.

   When you find a group, give them a call or send them an email to find out more. Usually you can attend a regular meeting as a guest the first time, so you can get a feel for the group before you join. Membership fees are usually reasonable and worth it; if you are in school, there is usually a discount, student rate.

### 5(c) Online links to PM groups

The Internet has opened up many doors for interacting with like-minded people. Social networking and media sites are a few places to find a project management group. Examples of sites include:

- *LinkedIn.com*—Many great discussion groups available.
- *Twitter.com*—Go to *search.twitter.com* and look for #PMOT (Project Managers On Twitter) or #FTPM (First Time Project Managers), and you will find lots of information and people to follow.
- *Gantthead.com*—Browse the many departments and discussion groups available; connect with other project managers, and have fun!
- Blogs—Articles and editorials. Use *blogsearch.google.com* to find them for specific topics you are interested in.
- Podcasts—Audio or video shows. Search for *project management* in iTunes or other podcast directories.

# 1.7 Management just changed the goals. How do I reset the direction?

By Aaron Porter

## 1. Problem

You thought the project was making good progress, but you found out that management had changed the goals for your project. How do you get more information about the changes and then share that information with your team, so that you can make the appropriate changes to the project direction?

## 2. Warning Signs

Goals of a project can change at any time. The earlier they change the easier and less expensive it will be to make the appropriate adjustments to the project. But there aren't always a lot of warning signs that management is going to change direction on a project.

Once goals change, they remain changed. There will be no more warning signs. Two indicators that goals are at risk of changing are when objectives are not (1) clearly defined or (2) widely accepted. If you are trying to make progress on the project, but the goals are not clearly defined or accepted, at some point someone is going to either question them or define them for you. Even if that someone is you, it could result in the need to reset project direction. So, how can you tell when goals are not clearly defined, understood or widely accepted?

> ### Remember Last Week When Things Were on Track?
>
> John was worried. This was his first day back from vacation and he was catching up on e-mails. He had to create a new folder for a string of e-mails discussing technology that had not been considered during planning for the Thin Client project; he'd never make it through his other e-mails, otherwise. The new technology would require completely different hardware and software, cost more, take longer to implement, and be more complex to maintain and support.
>
> The last email really got his attention. It said:
>
> > John,
> >
> > Come see me!
> >
> > Mark
>
> "John, have a seat," said Mark. "Thanks for meeting with me. I know you are busy catching up, but we need to talk about the Thin Client project."
>
> "I just got off the phone with Tim. He went to a conference last week and met with some vendors. I forwarded you several emails about a new technology he found. He wants us to drop everything else and go with the new technology."
>
> Back at his desk, John wondered if the decision to change was made on the golf course or at the bar. He could keep the same resources, but didn't know if they would need training on the new system. He didn't look forward to getting the new budget approved, or explaining why it was going to cost more or take longer. John quickly got on the phone and placed the order for the new server racks on hold, in case they were incompatible with the new system.
>
> "Time to gather the troops," John said to nobody, as he sighed and set up a new meeting on the calendar.

- Stakeholders and/or team members express confusion about the project goals.
- Stakeholders and/or team members ask about work that you think is out of scope.
- The project team has difficulty coming up with a design for the solution.

- Project deliverables are not accepted even though they were created according to design and meet quality requirements.

## 3. What will happen if I do nothing?

It is possible to finish a project even if you do nothing about the expected changes. You may finish the project on time. You may even finish the project within budget. But you risk branding the project, and yourself, as a failure if you don't deliver the desired product or service. Management will, most likely, make the changes for you if you don't demonstrate your support and act in your capacity as project manager.

## 4. Solution

There is an option for resetting direction after management changes project goals—use change management. The outcome of change management will vary according to the project and the changes that management makes, but you shouldn't let the change management process slide just because the changes came from higher-level management.

Whether you need to stop the project and start over, or make a few minor changes to the project's scope, it is critical that you understand the gap between where you are and where management wants you to be, the requirements to get there, and any risks associated with the changes to make an educated decision regarding how to proceed. Then the burden falls on you to get acceptance of the required changes from your project team and stakeholders.

## 5. What should I do?

The assumption is that you are going to implement management's changes. How the changes are implemented depends upon what you find as you gain greater understanding of the changes. It is possible that a detailed assessment of the changes may lead to the conclusion that the project should be canceled. In that case, your job is to make recommendations and act upon the decisions of management. In this case, however, your job is to get the work done.

### 5(a) The sponsor

Your starting point is your gateway to management—the project sponsor. As soon as possible, sit down with your sponsor and discuss the changes. You need a good understanding of what is being requested, and if the changes allow for additional funds or time, to be able to explain the changes to your project team.

Before you are done meeting with your sponsor, outline a plan for how you are going to proceed, so that your sponsor knows what you intend to do and can provide input into the plan (most sponsors love providing input, even if they won't admit it, and they even have good suggestions on occasion). This planning step will help build your sponsor's confidence in you and give him or her a plan to take back to management. The outline could look something like this:

- Perform a quick assessment of the changes
- Communicate the changes and assessment results to project team and stakeholders

- Notify the Change Control Board (CCB) of the changes
- Make a detailed assessment
- Plan

You may also be asked for a schedule for how long these activities will take. The first three can be done as quickly as you can assess the changes and get everyone together for a briefing. The rest will depend upon how much work is involved with the detailed assessment and planning. You may have to estimate and then get back to the sponsor with a real schedule after you get started. Whatever the results, maintain regular communication with your sponsor throughout the process.

### 5(b) A quick assessment

Perform a quick assessment of the changes so that you understand how they affect project scope. Your sponsor may want to do this with you, or you may do it on your own. You should ask yourself:

(1) What work needs to continue?
(2) What work needs to stop?
(3) What work needs further review to make a decision on whether or not it can continue?

Due the nature of the changes, it may be difficult to separate the first two types of work from the third by yourself. That's okay; the purpose of this assessment is to identify critical work so that the project does not lose momentum while the impact of the changes is evaluated, and to help you explain the changes to your team and stakeholders. Management may not want critical work to slip while you figure out the rest of the changes, and you want your team to have the best understanding of what is expected of them.

### 5(c) The project team and stakeholders

After your quick assessment, share the information you have with your team and stakeholders. Explain the impact to the project—what needs to stop, what needs to continue, what may or may not change—and let them know that the changes will be going through a detailed assessment; some of the team may even be involved in the process. This is important because very few people enjoy change, and you want your team and stakeholders on board with where you are at and where you are going. Do not assume that because management made the change everyone will agree with the new direction. You may have to perform some conflict management to keep the work on track.

### 5(d) Change management

Change management has a slightly different implementation from company to company. In some companies, it is simply an approval process. In other companies, it is a hands-on process that involves fully understanding the impact of the changes. You can find a spectrum of activities between both points at other companies. You want all of it, even if it all doesn't come from the CCB.

Where do you start? Get the changes on the change request log, first. You should document the changes and where they came from. This information will also help you as you close out the project, when reviewing what was successful or unsuccessful. Was it because the original objectives weren't defined correctly? Was a key stakeholder left out during initiation who had additional insight into the project? Or was it due to changes in technology or the marketplace?

If you can gain insight into why management made the changes, you may be able to avoid or respond more quickly to similar situations in the future. Because the changes came from management, CCB approval may just be a formality, but verify this before proceeding. Whether you or the CCB are responsible for a detailed assessment of the change, the following questions should be considered:

- How have the deliverables and requirements changed? (current state versus desired state)
- How will the budget and schedule change?
- What risks to the budget, schedule, and success of the project do the changes create?
- How are you going to get from *here* to *there*?

The results of the assessment need to be documented, and the document needs to be shared with the project team, stakeholders, and sponsor. But you're not done, yet.

### 5(e) Planning for change

Now that you know the deliverables, the scope of the changes, and the requirements, it's time to plan. How does planning help you reset the direction? It solidifies the direction the proposed changes are going to take, and provides tangible efforts that can be observed and evaluated. The only difference between this planning and the planning you did at the beginning of the project is that you may be incorporating new work into an existing plan instead of starting from scratch. It is still work, has risks, and needs to be prioritized, and you still need resources and budget.

So, what do you do? Work with your team to identify the resources, work, risks, schedule, and budget. Update your project schedule. Update your project management plan. Create a one-page summary that highlights the changes to the project, including costs and schedule, and review the information with your sponsor. The decision to continue may be simple, may need to go before the CCB, or may need to go to top management. Having a one-page summary of the changes will aid in acceptance of the new work to be done. You may find managers willing to read a 20-page project plan, but you are more likely to have a decision made quickly, and in your favor, if you can boil the information down to its core details for management's consumption.

### 5(f) Move forward

Once the decision to move forward is made, share the decision with your team and stakeholders. If the change was drastic, consider a new project kick-off in order to build excitement about the changes. It is important to make sure that you have the support of all involved parties in making this work. You should have involved your team and stakeholders during the detailed assessment and planning, and should have their support in completing the work, but you also want to make sure they understand that they have management's support in completing the new work as currently planned.

As mentioned, very few people enjoy change. Even fewer people enjoy working on projects that constantly change direction. Some team members may harbor this fear, and fear can be debilitating to a project. Even if your team's concern is valid, it is important that you reinforce the dedication of management to the new project direction with the team, so that your team will continue to function effectively.

When all is said and done, and the project is over, take the time to recognize your team for all of their efforts in making the project a success. Celebrate the team's adaptation to change. Work with your sponsor to get someone from management to speak to the team and express gratitude for a job well done; this is a chance to build trust between management and the team, which will help make adapting to changes on future projects easier.

### 5(g) Additional thoughts

Years ago, when I was doing some freelance Web development, a mutual friend put me in touch with a growing cookie sales company that worked with schools for fundraisers. The owner gave me the requirements for the Web site and indicated that he wanted to run it on a desktop PC in his office. His reasoning was that he sent a lot of e-mail through tools provided by his ISP, and they regularly blocked his site because they thought he was sending out bulk spam e-mails; he wanted control.

After looking at the Web site traffic thresholds and the requirements for his e-mail software, I let him know that his Web server would not be able to handle the traffic while running on a PC, due to hardware and software limitations; he needed a physical server or the Web site would be down more than it was up. His response was that this was not only a great opportunity for me to build my resume, but also for ongoing income. I chose to pass on the opportunity because he wanted a solution that was not viable and was unwilling to listen to alternatives. I could not envision a good working relationship, and felt that I was right and he was wrong. This also meant a little more time taken out of other work for me.

I bring this story up because it is possible that the results of the detailed assessment could lead to the conclusion that the project should be canceled. As project manager, it is not your decision to cancel a project, but you are responsible for presenting your findings (and alternatives in some cases) to your sponsor, who in turn is responsible for presenting the information to management, so that they can make the decision. Management may choose to continue with the project in spite of your recommendation; there may be more details behind their decision than they have shared with you. If you are asked to continue the project, you need to choose how to proceed. Whatever you choose, don't limit yourself solely because you think your way is right. If nothing illegal or unethical is going on, ask yourself if your way really is the only way or best way, or if you are just being stubborn. Whatever you decide, do your best.

# 1.8 I'm having trouble making decisions.

### By Ty Kiisel

## 1. Problem

You feel somewhat lost concerning a project. Some of the options you have don't seem to make sense. You might even feel like some of the decisions shouldn't be yours to make.

Project manager *is* a decision-making position. Unfortunately, many organizations don't foster good decision-making practices—making it difficult for project managers to answer these questions:

1. Who is responsible for making decisions?
2. Are there decisions I can make alone?
3. How do I ensure that I am making smart decisions?
4. How do I avoid making bad decisions?

Sound familiar? You're not alone. One of the biggest challenges faced by project managers is effectively defining the decision-making process.

## 2. Warning Signs

Organizations and project teams that struggle with making decisions tend to

**Trust the Marines**

The "fog of war" is what military leaders call battle-field uncertainty during the fighting. The term is attributed to the Prussian military analyst Carl von Clausewitz, who wrote in his book *On War* (Book II, Chapter II), "The great uncertainty of all data in war is a peculiar difficulty, because all action must, to a certain extent, be planned in a mere twilight, which in addition not infrequently—like the effect of fog or moonshine—gives to things exaggerated dimensions and unnatural appearance."

Although von Clausewitz wasn't describing the decision-making challenges of managing projects, he could have been. Regardless of your work management approach, everyone doing project-based work will at times face the need to make decisions without all the needed information.

The U.S. Marines are trained to make decisions in the fog of war. They call it "the 70% solution":

1. If you have 70% of the information you'd like to have,
2. If you've done 70% of the analysis that you think is required,
3. And feel 70% confident that you are right—get on with it.

The Marine Corps teaches young officers that a well-reasoned decision, that's well executed, has a fair chance of success, but taking no action has no chance of success.

The next time that you need to make a tough decision in the heat of battle, give some thought to the 70% solution. If it's good enough for the U.S. Marines, it might work for you.

languish under the *paralysis of analysis*. They spend a lot of time researching possible scenarios, creating presentations and sophisticated spreadsheets—causing projects to struggle and ultimately fail. Poor decision making can often result in lost opportunities as decisions take too long to make, enthusiasm for a particular decision is lost as the process languishes, or even poor decisions are made resulting from analyzing too many variables or nonessential information. In this situation, you might feel like:

- There are more challenges than solutions.
- Every decision you make is critical; there is no room for error.
- You need to back up every decision with *proof* that it was the right one to make.
- You need to involve many people in each decision.

## 3. What happens if I do nothing?

If you make no decision, you could wreck your career as a project manager. The refusal to make decisions is akin to voting yourself *off the island*. Although it's possible for a willing project leader to learn how to make *good* decisions, if you just can't make decisions at all, it might be time to rethink your career as a project manager—*before* your boss does it for you.

## 4. Solution

Because decision making is such a critical part of project management, here are some things you can do to make project decisions a little easier and more successful:

- Plan for procrastination.
- Don't forget Occam's razor, which suggests the simplest solution, is often the best.
- Sometimes any decision is better than no decision (see Sidebar).
- Don't forget the project objectives.
- You can't always trust your gut.
- Build consensus for quick implementation.

## 5. What should I do?

### 5(a) Project management is decision making

Many organizations do not foster good decision-making practices, which handicaps project mangers, project teams, and organizations. The answers to the following three questions will help your organization foster a workable decision-making process:

1. *Who?* Prior to the beginning of any project, determining who has decision-making power is step 1. Of course, on most projects there are likely to be several decision-makers.
2. *What?* Different members of the team probably have different decision-making responsibilities based on their role. Identifying the scope of everyone's responsibility, regarding the type of decisions they can and can't make, avoids confusion and makes it possible to streamline the process. Nobody wants to "Mother, may I?" for every move they want to make, nor should a project manager or stakeholder be expected to make every decision.
3. *How?* Identifying how decisions are made and how they are shared with project team members is almost as important as the decision itself. Making decisions in a vacuum is not the answer (more about this later).

### 5(b) Decisions, decisions!

The Swiss philosopher Henri Frederic Amiel said, "The man who insists upon seeing with perfect clearness before he decides, never decides."

This can be said of most project-based work. Fear of making a bad decision has contributed to the downfall of many projects. It has also been said that *good decisions come from experience*, and *experience comes from bad decisions*. Making what some people would call a *bad decision* isn't always bad, as long as you learn from it. In this regard, I agree with the U.S. Marine Corps (see the Sidebar), that a well-reasoned decision that is well executed has a reasonable expectation of success. Making no decision *guarantees* failure.

However, sometimes in the heat of battle, as circumstances change, some project leaders can procrastinate in making decisions. With that in mind, planning for procrastination in the same way that planning for allocation of resources, project return, and risk are done might be a valuable decision-making tool.

Planning for procrastination means making as many decisions up front as possible—reducing the need for spontaneous decision making when it's crunch time. That doesn't mean there is no room for making decisions as situations change, but it does eliminate the need to make decisions about the things that could easily be made in advance. Here are some examples:

1. *When to end a failing project?* Determining in advance the criteria for a failed project eliminates the need for a project manager or stakeholder fully invested in the project to attempt to make an unbiased decision regarding a project that has little or no chance of success.
2. *Who is the firing squad?* Along with predetermined criteria for labeling a project *Dead on Arrival*, determining who will decide that the failure is complete is also important. This is usually a function of the PMO or designated stakeholders. Nevertheless, pre-project decision making ensures that organizations won't be throwing good money after bad.

Establishing criteria for decisions relating to given circumstances ahead of time also makes sense for many projects that are regularly repeated. Although you can't anticipate everything, you can plan for many of common challenges and situations that might occur.

### 5(c) Keep it simple

Simplicity is sometimes called *Occam's razor:* "Entities must not be multiplied beyond necessity." In other words, the simplest solution is often the best solution.

The principle, attributed to the English theologian and Franciscan friar, William of Occam, is considered a rule of thumb today as scientists develop theoretical models. In the scientific method, Occam's razor might not be considered an irrefutable principle of logic, but is a valuable tool for keeping scientists from overcomplicating simple solutions.

It's easy to make project decisions more complicated than they need to be. I once worked with a colleague who was so reticent to make a decision that he would spend days building PowerPoint presentations and collecting data for superiors, hoping they would make the decision for him. This proved to be an insurmountable bottleneck to the rest of the team, and ultimately demonstrated his lack of decision-making ability. Don't overcomplicate what should otherwise be a simple solution or a simple decision-making process.

### 5(d) What were we talking about?

When making project decisions, keep the business goals and objectives of the project front and center. Staying focused on the stated objectives of the project will give context to project decisions. Sometimes you might need to step back and look at the big picture. Resist the urge to keep your head down, wrapped up in minutia—allow yourself to step back and *see the forest for the trees*.

For example, I have sometimes watched colleagues strain over the most insignificant details, putting entire projects at risk. I once worked with a graphic designer who was so meticulous and attentive to the most insignificant detail that this designer would spend excessive amounts of time on many of the simplest projects—making those projects unwieldy and often over budget. Keeping business objectives front and center when making decisions helps project managers and teams avoid spending too much time on tasks that do not contribute to the project goals.

### 5(e) You can't always trust your gut

Lev Virine and Michael Trumper, in the book *Project Decisions: The Art and Science* (2008, p. 21), believe that project managers should steer clear of making decisions based on gut feelings because it can often lead to costly mistakes. This is true for a variety of reasons, but just at a very basic level, the authors state, "It is hard to eliminate the personal interests of team members or managers from the project without removing the individuals themselves."

It doesn't matter who you are—trusting your gut can be dangerous. Anecdotally, it might seem like you can make quick and successful decisions based upon your superior gut, but statistically, it is about the same as tossing a coin.

According to Virine and Trumper (2008, p. 249), human thoughts are often influenced by certain behaviors, perceptions, and the ability to recall details. We're predisposed to rely on certain variables when making decisions, such as, the manner in which the information is presented to us, and we also lean toward the belief that scenarios with greater detail are more probable. They suggest that *it is important to make small sequential choices* to improve the success of overall decision making.

In other words, as the consequences of decisions become more complicated, your gut becomes more unreliable. This doesn't sound good for managers, executives, or even project managers who believe their gut instincts are what set them apart as great decision-makers, does it? Of course, it is possible that your gut could be a statistical anomaly—but it probably isn't.

A structured, data-driven approach to decision-making provides a better model for making good decisions. That being said, some people make a lot of really good decisions—but not when they involve big and complex projects. Because many of the project decisions you will be required to make are driven by how the project performs against measureable milestones or projections, data-driven decision-making will generally lead to predictable results and successful projects. My advice would be to leave your gut to making decisions about what to eat for lunch.

### *5(f) Because I said so!*

It didn't really matter what it was about, if the only reason my father could give me was, "Because I said so," I automatically didn't like his decision. However, as a father, I admit there were times when I pulled the *because I said so* card.

Despite what some business leaders who still believe in a command-and-control leadership model think, "Because I said so" wasn't a very good way to explain decisions with my children, nor is it an effective way to explain decisions with project team members. Today's workforce doesn't respond well to that type of authoritarian decision-making process (and I have doubts as to whether is *ever* really worked in most businesses).

Although politicians take a lot of heat for consensus building when making decisions, in the workplace, it's actually a very good approach for making and sharing decisions. Making decisions alone, in a vacuum, often causes implementation challenges associated with the surprise announcement of any single decision. Particularly with decisions that initiate change, involving others in the decision-making process enables better buy-in by those who will be impacted by the change. Although there are some leaders who believe that involving others as decisions are being made slows down the process and costs time, whatever time is lost during the decision-making process is more than compensated for during implementation by employees who feel engaged and accept a level of ownership in the decision.

I once worked with a man who really embraced this type of decision making. He used to say, "It's easy for me to make a mistake, but it's unlikely that we will collectively make big mistakes." He fostered an environment where ideas were freely exchanged, differences of opinion were discussed, and consensus was reached. His was a very successful organization where everyone on the team felt empowered to positively impact the enterprise. Unfortunately, some entrepreneurs look down their nose at the word "consensus."

## References

Virine, L., and Trumper, M. *Project Decisions: The Art and Science*. Tysons Corner: Management Concepts, 2008.

von Clausewitz, C. *On War*. FQ Books, 1832.

# 1.9 Sponsors won't decide what they want.

By Panos Agrapidis

## 1. Problem

You have been asked to manage your project in the best possible way in order to satisfy the organization's strategic goals. However, although sponsors should give the necessary directives and support to your effort, they seem to be distant and reluctant. You are starting to question your way of conducting the project and the importance of your project to the organization. Maybe it is better to evaluate the possibility that the sponsors don't have clear ideas about the real impact of your project on the organization's strategy!

## 2. Warning Signs

- Project delays arise because you are waiting to receive sponsors' answers to questions that you have formulated, both officially and unofficially.
- You get contradictory answers from sponsors to your requests.
- Sponsors are trying to avoid project meetings or are reluctant to set up an appointment with you.
- You get continuous sponsors' requests for clarifications.

## 3. What will happen if I do nothing?

If you do nothing, the following may happen:

- The targets fixed during the starting phase will become *moving targets*, which are difficult to hit. Many projects experience scope creep when sponsors start asking questions about project objectives.

### The Most Exciting Project

Andrea was excited. She was ordered to start a new project, the most exciting project she could hope for. Her organization announced the creation of a PMO and appointed her as the project manager. Until now, only major projects were running, following project management rules and procedures. Now the big chance for Andrea was here, a once in a lifetime opportunity!

It was also a great moment for the organization. The new CEO wanted to show that she was ready to make all necessary changes. The project plan was approved, and Andrea was immersed in the project with both heart and mind. Not all appointed team members were adequate to cover the foreseen positions, but the enthusiasm for PMO creation was enough to overcome any possible obstacle.

Initially, the warning signs were unperceived: an appointment fixed in delay; a small cut in the project's procurement budget; the substitution of a qualified team member with one less qualified.

As the project advanced, bigger problems were created due to the sponsor's indecision. No reply was received regarding an increase in the budget in order to finance personnel seminars in project management. At the same time, the necessary consultancy for project management software implementation was still pending.

Were the sponsors unwilling to decide, or was the organization evaluating to withdraw or resize the project?

Andrea didn't hesitate. She prepared and submitted to the sponsors a detailed road map providing, in a one month period, a solution to two major problems in data collection and elaboration. It was not foreseen in the original project scope, but it was a top management request to the sponsors who could not satisfy the CEO's needs successfully.

The attitude of the sponsors towards PMO creation had changed radically and all pending issues were solved immediately. It was a project to save at any cost, and stakeholders were obligated to succeed.

- Project teams can only move forward in a committed way if each individual understands the goals and is playing their role in achieving it. If one person stops moving in the right direction, it impacts everyone's ability to move forward (see Figure 1.3).
- External support from other organization sectors will become *loose*.
- You will be the scapegoat to which they can attach the blame of project failure!

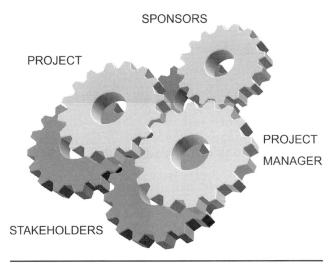

**Figure 1.3**

## 4. Solution

You are the project manager, but you do not own the project. You are acting on behalf of the organization. You are executing perfectly the originally approved project plan, but probably now this doesn't represent the best solution for the needs of the sponsors, stakeholders, or the organization. You have to focus on the following parameters continuously:

1. The changing environment around you—changes in strategy or strategy execution, macro and micro economic changes, interpersonal relationships inside the organization and between the organization and the external customers, subcontractors, and stakeholders
2. Communication, communication, communication with all stakeholders and at every occasion
3. The need to propose solutions and necessary changes before the sponsors stop making decisions, or decide without having the necessary information at their disposal

## 5. What should I do?

As a general rule, everything around us is in continuous evolution and changes are increasing both in magnitude and velocity over the last few decades.

- A strategic target, or a market, can become obsolete in a few months' time. A good customer can become a serious threat because of economic position (i.e., debt exposure, market position, geographical expansion).
- A *golden* sponsor can be seen as a serious threat if his or her positions are found in contrast with the changes imposed by the organization.

If you don't pay attention to the changes that can influence the execution of your project, you may find yourself in the middle of a hurricane. To avoid such dangerous situations, you must monitor the *weather* continuously. If the *captain* is capable to capture the signs well in advance, then s/he has several choices if any weather event threatens the ship. But whatever decision the captain may reach, the uppermost priority is always the safety of the vessel and the passengers. The captain can change the route and even the itinerary, but the real target is to reach a desired port successfully, even if that port is not the one originally planned.

### 5(a) Deal with the continuously changing environment

*Change* will be the word that all management manuals will try to "translate" more frequently in the next few years. Project managers must find ways to manage change in a complex environment. Project management methodologies can become the most powerful tools to manage change. We must always be ready to capture changes and support the sponsors and project accordingly, acting proactively and proposing the necessary corrective actions.

*Changes in strategy*

Changes in the organization's goals and strategy are going to take place with increasing frequency. The project regarding the development of a new product or a software will be necessary to change its original specifications or targets even at the end of its execution because of the changing external (i.e., economical, technological) or internal (i.e., management changes, property changes, new alliances) environment. You can't always wait to receive instructions from your sponsors. You must capture the profiled changes and be ready to propose ways to direct the organization's efforts regarding your project. The sponsors will appreciate your intention to support them, and they will support you in order to execute your project correctly, according to the organization's revised strategy.

*Economic changes*

The local as well as the world economy are found in a turbulent environment, which will produce instability for a long period. Two common cases can be used as examples:

- A new market opportunity occurs suddenly, while a *safe* one vanishes.
- The client who ordered your project can increase profits or be found in economic difficulty.

You must be open and discuss such matters with sponsors, trying to correctly position your project within the relative organizational context.

## 5(b) Deal with interpersonal relationships

From experience, you know that it is risky to deal with your team members' interpersonal relationships. Try now to evaluate how difficult and hazardous it is to deal with the interpersonal relationships between the sponsors, sponsors and top management, top management and the client, and so on. Consider that stakeholders not only have different characters, but also different behaviors, cultures, targets, and even language. We have to unify different worlds toward a common scope, transmitting the project goals and proposing necessary changes, when required, to all stakeholders.

### Internal relationships

A new CEO or General Director wants to implement positive changes in an organization. He or she will re-evaluate all projects, as well as the sponsors' work. If we, as project managers, support the sponsors adequately, we will gain precious allies ready to take the necessary decisions for the common good.

### External relationships

Client representatives (i.e., project manager, division managers) are not the client. They are members of the client organization. As could happen to your organization, the client's organization is also subject to changes. If you support client representatives in their work adequately, they will be ready to smooth differences between the two organizations regarding your project.

Local or central state authorities, institutions, subcontractors, press, or communities could influence or be actively involved in your project. Act accordingly.

If you manage the interpersonal relationships between the key players correctly, the sponsors will appreciate the *peaceful* running of your project. Less trouble equals more support received from sponsors. Don't forget also to share relative information with them. It will be useful for their relationships, and they will support a precious ally in a moment of difficulty.

## 5(c) Communication, communication, communication

Communication is an art, but also a gift. In any case, communication is obligatory. You *must* follow your project's communication plan and keep in mind that it is more important to communicate the project progress rather than achieve the project progress itself!

Project managers with a specific background (i.e., engineers, architects, and economists) are often more focused on obtaining the project's technical/economic progress or producing the necessary technical/economic changes, rather than communicating them in the sponsors' *language*. Sponsors must always be aware of what is happening within your project and you must communicate with them in the proper way.

## 5(d) Propose solutions and necessary changes

There are specific rules to follow:

- You have to always act proactively.
- You are the key player for your project, so you have to propose solutions and all necessary changes to the sponsors well in advance.

- You must keep the sponsors informed about all important issues concerning your project. At the same time you must submit to them a few alternative proposals on how to deal with project challenges (a contingency plan).
- You must take into consideration that in parallel to your own project the sponsors are involved in other projects as well. Try to cooperate and exchange information with other project managers in order to mitigate possible conflicts.

# 1.10 What my sponsor wants doesn't make sense.

## By Alex Brown

## 1. Problem

You think your sponsor might be pushing you to do the wrong things.

Yes, we all know that the sponsor is the authority for the project. He or she is in charge and is the final decision-maker. But what if you are asked to do something that doesn't make sense? Do you have to do it?

## 2. Warning Signs

- Your team jokes that the next change request will be to fill in the hole that they just dug.
- You have trouble explaining the project to your team.
- You have trouble keeping a straight face when you describe the sponsor's latest request.
- After you tell people about your project, their first question is always, "Are you serious?"

> **You Want What?**
>
> Bob could not believe his ears. He had to make sure he had heard John, the Chief Operating Officer, correctly.
>
> Bob had asked, "I just told you that the system is broken, and you want to roll it out to MORE people?".
>
> "Yes," said John.
>
> "But people will not be able to do their jobs. We will both get fired."
>
> "Exactly, except for the getting fired part. Because once everyone has the new system, we will be able to fix it. Listen, I cannot argue with you all day about this. I need it done," John picked up his papers and got ready to leave.
>
> "Fine," sighed Bob. "You are the customer and the customer is always right. I will go tell the team."
>
> The more Bob thought about this conversation, the worse he felt. But what could he do? John was his manager's boss. He signed the paychecks for everyone in the department.

## 3. What will happen if I do nothing?

Doing nothing is not an option. If you do nothing, you get fired for ignoring the sponsor. The problem is, you might get fired even if you do what the sponsor asks!

## 4. Solution

There are a few possibilities here:

1. You are wrong, and the sponsor is right. You just do not understand the whole picture.

2.  You are right and the sponsor is wrong. You understand, and your sponsor does not.
3.  You are both wrong. Bad—very bad.
4.  You are both right. The sponsor has a great project plan, and so do you. Unfortunately you are not talking about the same project.

Your first step is figuring out which situation you are in, then finding a way out or a way to improve the situation.

## 5. What should I do?

First, take a deep breath. Take a step back from the situation. *Right* and *wrong* are black-and-white, judgmental words. As soon as you find yourself saying, "The sponsor does not make sense," you have become part of the problem.

Somehow, in some way, what the sponsor says *does* make sense. At least to him or her. Your challenge is to understand *why* he or she is saying these things to you. Here are some possibilities:

*   Your sponsor may have been given a message from their boss or sponsor, and they might just be passing it along.
*   You might not understand what your sponsor is asking you to do.
*   Your sponsor might not understand your team's situation.
*   You might be smarter than your sponsor, and might see things more clearly.
*   Your sponsor might be smarter than you, and might see things more clearly.

No matter the root cause of the disagreement, there is one thing for sure—you have a communication problem. Somehow you and the sponsor are not looking at the project the same way. Your point of view is so different that the sponsor does not make sense to you. Chances are excellent that your concerns and objections do not make any sense to your sponsor either.

Treat the situation the same way you would if you saw poor communication on your team:

*   Slow down
*   Add more communication channels
*   Improve existing communication channels

### 5(a) Slow down

Probably the one, best course of action—no matter who is wrong or who is right—is to slow down. Putting the project team into overdrive to try to do something that seems impossible is a recipe for disaster.

Look at your project plan and figure out what is the cheapest, fastest thing that you can do in order to make progress and keep options open. If certain work *must* be done to make a delivery date, you might need to start that work right away. If possible, though, consider delaying the start of expensive tasks.

Invest the time in a prototype, document, or review meeting—anything to confirm that you and the sponsor are actually in agreement on what to do next.

### 5(b) Add communication channels

If you and your sponsor usually discuss the project on the phone, try having an in-person meeting. If you usually meet in person and write little down, start taking more notes and sharing them with your sponsor.

Communication is a funny thing. We all think we understand, and that we are easy to understand. Unfortunately, people often misunderstand each other. Look for ways to reinforce the same message or repeat it in different ways. Whether you or your sponsor has trouble talking, listening, writing, or reading, repeating the message gives you more chances to get it right.

### 5(c) Improve existing communication channels

You might already be communicating clearly in writing, in person, on the phone, in email, and through every other channel you have available to you. What do you do next?

Take a look at how you are communicating and look for obstacles to remove. Do you write long detailed reports? Maybe your sponsor is not reading them because they are too long. Consider shortening them. Conversely, do you try to give just an *executive overview*? Maybe it is time to spend some time explaining the details.

Watch people who work well with your sponsor. Try to get copies of their status reports and other project communications. See if they are doing something different from what you are doing.

### 5(d) What if nothing works?

There is a serious side to this problem. Sometimes, no matter what you try, you and your sponsor cannot agree on what to do next. What do you do then? The *right* answer depends a lot on the situation.

Some project managers face real ethical and safety problems. If your sponsor is asking you to do something unethical or unsafe, you should probably say, "No." Even if you get fired, you will feel better about what you have done. Sometimes other people will see the problem, and your sponsor will be fired instead of you. Do not count on this, though; life is not always fair.

You might be able to quit. There are ways to quit your project and still keep your job. Say to your sponsor, "Look, I am not the best person to lead this effort. I do not believe in your vision." If you can find someone else who would be happy to lead the effort, you can quit the project without hurting your reputation. In some organizations, you may even be rewarded for dealing with the problem quickly and honestly.

In extreme situations, you may need to actually quit your job. If a situation is intolerable, there is just one thing to do—stop tolerating it! Get out! There are lots of jokes about these situations. There is a good reason why many of those jokes involve someone writing a letter to the *next* project manager.

# 1.11 What makes my project important?

## By Andy Jordan

## 1. Problem

You have a project that has been approved, but you aren't really sure why. You understand the features that the project is supposed to deliver, but you aren't clear on why those things are important. Your team is looking for you to explain things to them because they don't understand why they are being asked to do the work either, and there seems to be a sense that the whole project is a waste of time. This is leading to a team that is lacking motivation and feels left out of the important work.

This is a common problem for project managers who understand the specific deliverables of the project, but lack an understanding of the "big picture" that led to the project in the first place. As a result, they feel like they are operating within a vacuum, with no context for the project.

## 2. Warning Signs

- The sponsor seems to be talking about a different project to you, and you can't relate your deliverables to his or her questions and concerns.
- The stakeholders are concerned about things that don't seem important to you, and don't seem worried about what you consider important.
- Your decisions on project issues are being challenged, when they seem sound to you.
- You can't answer the question "What is this project going to do for the business?"

### Why Are We Here Again?

Aaron looked at the requirements document for what must have been the tenth time that morning and slowly shook his head, sighing deeply. He couldn't figure it out—the requirements made perfect sense. It was clear what was supposed to be done, and all the right people had signed off, but he just didn't get it.

No matter how hard he thought about it, there seemed no point in doing this project—sure, the team would build the requirements, but they seemed so pointless. Aaron felt like the whole thing was just a big *make work* project, a pointless exercise in work for the sake of it. He felt a lack of motivation and knew that his team felt the same way. With so many important projects going on, it seemed like his team was being pushed to one side on something trivial, and that seemed hugely unfair after everyone had said what a great job they had done on the last project.

Meanwhile, Trish had her own problems in the executive suite. She was seriously second guessing herself on the decision to appoint Aaron to the critical project that would shape the entire future of the company. Everyone had said that he was the man for the job, and the last few projects that he had led his team on had been great successes. But now, with this radical departure into something totally different, Aaron didn't seem to be stepping up to the plate.

He seemed uninterested, bored almost, at the prospect of leading the project, and it seemed to be rubbing off on the rest of the team. Everything had been approved; they had the clear requirements and the resources that they needed to start making progress. Yet there was no spark, no excitement, no leadership from Aaron. It seemed like the time was fast approaching to replace him with someone who could do the job.

## 3. What will happen if I do nothing?

If you remain focused on the deliverables, the *what* of the project, then you will be unable to make the right decisions when problems occur, and that may prevent the project from achieving its ultimate goals. In addition, there is a chance that the sponsor will lose faith in you, feel that they have to take a closer supervisory role, or potentially replace you. Your project team may start second guessing you, putting your authority at risk because you don't seem to have a grasp on what is really going on.

Stakeholders see the deliverables of the project as simply the means to achieve their business goals, if you don't focus on those goals in addition to the tangible deliverables, then you aren't giving the stakeholders what they need.

Further, both the project team and you are likely to be disillusioned with the initiative. You will get a sense that the project is pointless, and that you have been given something to manage that the organization thinks is unimportant.

## 4. Solution

Projects don't exist in a vacuum, and they aren't created just for the sake of it. There is a business need that has to be addressed, and the specific deliverables are simply the way that the need is going to be met. If you don't understand this need, then you won't be able to explain it to your team, make the right management decisions, or provide stakeholders with the information that they are looking for. Therefore, you need to:

- Understand the purpose of the project, the *why* behind the initiative from the sponsor's and stakeholders' perspectives
- Consider the business need and be aware of the impact when making project decisions, recommending solutions and discussing issues with stakeholders
- Ensure that you are aware of any changes in priorities as the project moves forward

## 5. What should I do?

You should start by reviewing all of the project documents for any information on why the project is being undertaken. In particular, the business case and charter should have sections on why the project was approved, why now, and what the expected business benefits are.

When you have reviewed those, or if those aren't available to you, then you should contact your sponsor and arrange to sit down with him or her to discuss the reasons behind the project.

### 5(a) Meeting with your sponsor

The sponsor is the person who ultimately drives your project forward. He or she is responsible for ensuring that the expected benefits from the project are realized, so there is no one better to explain to you the business need that the project is seeking to address. When meeting with the sponsor, you should be looking to understand the following:

- What is the project expected to deliver to the business? It might be a cost saving, an increase in revenue, a reduction in risk, compliance with a regulatory requirement or any number of other goals. It isn't simply the *thing* that the project will deliver, but rather the advantage that the organization will receive from that *thing*.

- What would happen if the project were not undertaken? In some cases, things may get worse rather than stay the same (i.e., the organization may be in breach of regulations; a competitor may steal market share).
- What else is dependent on this project? Your project may be a stand-alone initiative, but it may also be part of a much larger initiative that cannot move forward until your project has been completed.

Your conversation with the project sponsor should be very specific. Projects shouldn't have progressed to the point where project managers are appointed without first going through a cost benefit process that establishes the benefit of doing the project in financial and time terms. The project sponsor should be able to share that information with you in order to assist you in understanding its importance. A conversation with the sponsor should also help you answer the related question of "why is my project important now?" You should have a better understanding of the implications of a schedule delay and a budget overrun on your project, which, in turn, will help you with your decision making.

The sponsor's reasons for championing the project are important to you, but their perspective is not the only one that you need to be aware of. You also have to consider why the project is important to other stakeholders.

### 5(b) Meeting with stakeholders

Stakeholders will have a slightly different view of the project than the sponsor. The sponsor is focused on the benefit of the entire project on all impacted areas; individual stakeholders are more concerned with the specific impact on them and their areas of responsibility. This can be different from the sponsor—a new system to automate work that is currently manual may deliver millions in savings, but to the department being automated it may mean job losses and, as a result, the stakeholder representing that department may not be in favor of the initiative.

Stakeholders may not be as open about what is important to them as the sponsor; their goals may differ from the stated goals of the project and that is not something that they are going to be likely to admit. Stakeholders may recognize it as internal politics and will try to *play the game* to their advantage. As the project manager, you need to understand each of their positions so that you can put their comments, recommendations, and requests into the larger context of why the project is important. Recognize that, at the extreme, they may wish to see the project fail.

If you are unable to understand the different perspectives of the different stakeholders, then you will find that the answer to the question of why the project is important will change depending upon who you speak to, and that will make it impossible for you to be successful.

### 5(c) Managing the project

The first advantage that you get from understanding the project's purpose is that you can communicate it to your project team, and you should do so as soon as possible.

Like you, they want to understand why they are being asked to do the work, and it's a lot easier to motivate them if they appreciate the importance of their work and the role that they are playing in the big picture.

The question of why the project is important should also be a major guide to you as you manage the project. Plans never go exactly as expected and you will be faced with many occasions when you have to make decisions in order to keep the project on track. An understanding of why the project is important can guide you through these times and help you make the right decision against the larger picture of the business need. Effectively, by understanding the larger picture of why the project is being completed, you can make the best decisions in that bigger picture.

As a simple example, if you know that your project is designed to launch a product before your competitors, you will be looking to make decisions that preserve the timelines of the project so that the need to beat the rival is maintained.

There will also be times when you are faced with a number of different options on the project: how to react to a change request, how to overcome an issue, etc. When making recommendations to the sponsor and stakeholders, an understanding of why the project is important will not only allow you to make better recommendations, it will allow you to position those recommendations in a way that the stakeholders can relate to.

Finally, an understanding of why your project is important to different stakeholders will help you to communicate with them. If you know that one stakeholder is concerned with the budget of the project more than anything else, you can tailor communications to that stakeholder around the current financials.

### 5(d) Priorities change

Projects often take months or even years to complete, and as a result, the business need may change. In addition to driving changes to the project, those evolving business needs may change why your project is important. You need to maintain a good relationship with your sponsor and stakeholders in order to understand when these changes occur and what the likely impact is on you. Only then can you be sure that you are making decisions with the most up to date understanding of the project drivers.

# 2

# MOTIVATING PEOPLE

## 2.1 I feel like I'm the only one who cares.

By Dave Prior

## 1. Problem

Your current project is mission-critical to the organization you are working for. For weeks, you've been burning the midnight oil and pushing yourself, your team, and the organization to do what is necessary to reach delivery. For awhile, things were good and everyone rallied around the idea of a big push to meet the deadline, but lately you've noticed that you are the one leading the charge, and you seem to be the only one still trying. What happened to the team spirit? Doesn't the team see how important this project is? Why do you seem to be the only one who cares? Most importantly, what are you going to do about it?

## 2. Warning Signs

1. Team members have gone from being enthusiastic to disinterested in regard to the team's recent performance.
2. Your attempts at encouraging the team to rally behind the demands of the project are met with sarcasm or outright hostility.

### The Forgotten Project

When Brian's boss asked him if he would mind helping out on Gina's project, he jumped at the chance. He was excited to be part of the team and had heard that Gina was the best PM in the company. Brian didn't know exactly how much of his time had been promised, but he felt pretty sure that his boss would keep it in mind when he assigned him other work. Of course, that was about three weeks before the new, hot project arrived. This new project was vital to the business and Brian's boss had been told to put him on the project at 100%.

Unfortunately, Brian's boss "forgot" to tell Gina the news. Gina kept assigning work to Brian, but it wasn't getting done and her project was falling further and further behind because of his missed deadlines.

Gina could not understand what was going on with Brian. All of the sudden, he was not showing up for meetings, not completing his assignments, and she had no idea why. She decided it was time to set Brian straight and make sure he was aware of her expectations and his responsibility. After all, her project was really important to the company, and he seriously needed to get on board. She had picked up on some frustration from Brian, but still couldn't understand why he didn't see how important this project was and how unacceptable it was to keep putting it at risk. He didn't seem to care.

Is this the best way for Gina to solve her problem, or are there other things she needs to consider and address?

3. Team members are showing up late, leaving early, and missing meetings.
4. The team's work output is showing a drop in quality, and the team doesn't seem to care.
5. The project's stakeholders are unresponsive.
6. If you, as the PM, are starting to feel a little burnt-out, you can bet your team is too.

## 3. What will happen if I do nothing?

If you do not take steps to deal with the declining morale and lack of interest from your team, it is likely that their output will continue to drop in quality, and they'll begin missing deadlines (if they aren't already). The more they lose faith and interest, the more it will wear you down, since you are the primary cheerleader behind the work.

If you have unresponsive management and you do not take steps to turn things around, it may become increasingly difficult for you to get the project across the finish line due to a lack of interest and support from the people responsible for acting as your product owners, who sign off on work, etc.

## 4. Solution

Finding yourself in the midst of a project in which you seem to be the only one who cares is unfortunately all too common. In the example given above, there are three levels on which you should address the situation: personal, team, and stakeholder. This chapter provides you with some tools and techniques to help you respond. It will not be easy and it is not always possible to accomplish this without a degree of fallout. However, as the PM, you are responsible to the project and when you face situations in which you are the only one who cares, you have to respond. Whether your interpretation is accurate or not, no one else is going to be able to fix this for you. So, to join the long list of leaders who have paraphrased Hillel the Elder, ask yourself, "If not you, who? If not now, when?"

## 5. What should I do?

If you have reached a point where you feel like you are the only one who cares about the project, then approach your project with a fresh perspective. Evaluate the mindsets of yourself, your team, and the stakeholders.

### 5(a) Evaluate your thinking

The first thing you need to address is the simple fact that on a personal level, this is how you are seeing the project. The reason this is an important first step is because in thinking "I am the only one who cares," you may be allowing yourself to be the victim of something you (as a leader on the project) are actually responsible for doing something about. What is worse, it implies that those who have lost interest are to blame for having done so. Both of these create divisions between you and the other participants and you will need to remove these before you can move into the next two steps.

While you may be looking at the project as though the other participants have abandoned you, in most cases, what has actually taken place is that aspects of the project (scope changes, length of time, over-allocation, technical challenges, other priorities, etc.) are in the way of the team maintaining the level of enthusiasm that you are trying to foster. Even when you are facing a complete breakdown in interest or support for your project, it is always going to have come about as the result of some other thing. Either the participants have been given reasons not to care, or they have not been given a reason to care.

The good part is that correcting this mindset may be the easiest challenge you face in this scenario. It can be as basic as shifting how you think of the issue at hand. Rather than asking, "Why am I the only one who cares?" try to think "What are the impediments preventing the others from sharing my level of enthusiasm?" This will help you to reengage as someone who has the ability to change what isn't working and get things back on track.

### 5(b) Determine causes and work out a plan

A simple shift in mindset prepares you for the second step, which is determining the cause(s) of the drop in interest, and then working out a plan to enable the team to become fully engaged in a collective response to the challenges of this project. This is not going to be easy, and it could involve anything from a simple team activity to show them how appreciated they are, to having a frank discussion with them about the state of things. In extreme cases, you may even need to switch out some team members.

If the team has gone from caring to not caring, spend some time with them listening to what caused the change. If the team still trusts that you will have enough influence to create change, then they may be forthcoming. If not, you may need to find simpler, more subtle ways to obtain the information. It is important to remember though, that if your end goal is a motivated team, you can't just tell them to be motivated and expect it to happen. You need to give them a reason, or, at least, remove the things keeping them from being motivated.

There may be many layers of blockers that need to be removed. There will likely be some that cannot be cleared away (like issues team members may have with ineffectual senior leadership or the company itself.) When this is the case, if you have been able to establish enough of a rapport with the team, by proving that you will support them, you may be able to ask them to lay aside their concerns for a time to work with you.

If you cannot resolve the issues blocking certain team members, or if they are just set on not supporting the project, you may need to have them removed from the project. This should always be a last resort because at best, you may scare the other team members into temporary motivation based on fear of getting removed from the project. This will not last, and will more than likely result in resentment, which makes you one of the blockers.

### 5(c) Reengage stakeholders

The third level on which you need to respond to this situation is the stakeholder level. Regaining the interest and attention of stakeholders or management who have been distracted by higher prioritized projects (in their view), or lost focus, is not always possible. However, you are the PM and it is your responsibility to make every effort to do so.

It is simple for project managers to fall back into the *I'm the only one* trap when it comes to disengaged management. The problem here is that as PMs, we focus on our projects and watch over them with great care. Stakeholders and management often have a number of other things competing for their time and attention, and there are times when the efforts we are managing simply may not be at the top of their list. While we can't ensure that our project will always be his or her top priority, what we can do is make an effort to gain a better understanding of what their priorities and interests are, and what motivates them.

Once we understand what the goals/objectives and interests of management and stakeholders are, we can begin to develop a plan to raise the issue of their engagement in a way that speaks to their specific areas of interest. This may take some trial and error, but there will be times when the effort alone will pay off. There will also be times when sitting down with the senior manager and/or stakeholder and having a frank discussion about how important their role is, and how much the team needs them, will be enough. Unfortunately, there will also be times when it will not be possible to reengage senior management. This too, however, can be used to an advantage, as adversity might be able to help draw the team tighter together.

# 2.2 Team members are not excited about their work.

By Jerry Manas

## 1. Problem

Your team seems as if they're reluctantly serving on the project, barely involved and doing just the minimum to get by. Indeed, you feel like you're the only one who cares about the project's outcome.

## 2. Warning Signs

When people start to lose their excitement for the project, the problem can quickly spread. You need to spot and act on these warning signs quickly:

- People don't seem happy or engaged when working on your project.
- You get very few comments, if any, during team meetings.
- Quantity and quality of work output is lacking in general, and people seem more interested in other work.
- There is an increase in absenteeism and/or a decrease in people's availability in general.

### What Makes a Leader a Good Motivator?

When people hear the word *motivator*, they often picture a larger-than-life character giving a rousing speech that rallies everyone toward a big goal. In reality, the most effective form of motivation is when people feel instinctively compelled to *want* to contribute. Few people are motivated by speeches or slogans. However, there are other ways to create an environment that can foster a sense of excitement and commitment. For instance, if people feel that they can make a significant contribution toward a goal they care about, they will be substantially motivated. So the key is to create interest and make sure people are working in their area of strength. Napoleon once said that there are two levers for moving people—interest and fear. We are always better off motivating with interest.

We can conclude that a good motivator understands people and creates an environment in which they can shine. Each person is different, but most everyone is motivated by making a difference. They can only do that if they are working within their areas of strength toward a purpose they believe in. Many people are also motivated by their relationships at work. There are also demotivators, such as an overly rigid environment, excessive multitasking, finger-pointing, or lack of goal clarity. Your job as a leader and motivator is to be aware of all this, and to create an environment where people can excel without demotivators slowing them down.

## 3. What will happen if I do nothing?

If nothing is done, you run the risk of your team growing more apathetic, possibly leading to project deliverables coming in late or inaccurate. Worse, they could potentially become resentful of the project and even look to undermine the project. Additionally, if you don't respond to team members who lack motivation, you are sending a message that the behavior is acceptable and it will likely become more prevalent. Ultimately, you may gain a reputation as a nonmotivator.

## 4. Solution

First, you need to find out what is causing the seeming lack of interest and find a way to appeal to people's natural tendency to want to help. To assist with this, you need to be sure that your project is tied to a clear need, and that everyone on the team understands their role in achieving the project's objectives. It's also important to rule out other factors that could be contributing to their lack of engagement, and address the barriers accordingly.

## 5. What should I do?

There are a number of actions that can be taken that can demystify the cause of the apathy and begin to generate some excitement on your project.

### 5(a) Rule out overload

To start with, find out what else is on your team's plate. What you perceive as a lack of excitement could in fact be fatigue if they are overburdened with too many concurrent tasks or initiatives. An organization is a complex system, with many interrelating variables. A lack of any type of demand filtering and/or resource capacity assessment methodology could lead to an intake of too many concurrent projects, leading to excessive multitasking, which in turn leads to errors and fatigue. On the flip side, if people are allowed to focus, apathy can turn into excitement.

### 5(b) Engage people in decisions

Another reason people are often disengaged from project activities is if they are not included in decisions—not only related to the project outcomes, but related to the project management methodology as well. People tend to embrace that which they helped create. A flexible organization will understand this, and allow people to participate in shaping the project methodology when possible, even making project-specific decisions about approach. You might also try sharing a list of milestones, and enlisting the team in exploring ways to overcome barriers to meeting them. Often without a high level milestones list, people can't see the forest through the trees, so they're less likely to recognize the impacts of delays. If the team is working together to solve problems, they'll be more engaged.

### 5(c) Tell a story

In order to embrace a project, people also need to understand and buy into its purpose. If a clear tie to organizational value is communicated effectively, it can go a long way toward increasing interest. This does not mean merely stating or declaring the objectives, it means *selling* the objectives.

There are proven ways to get a message across, and none are more effective than storytelling. If there is a story or example you can share that can help make a strong case, people will be more likely to remember and embrace it. The emotional angle is a strong motivator. While bland declarations are often ignored, emotional stories remain with people. Instead of saying "Our objectives are to deliver x, y, and z," try to share an example of how the customer is struggling without it, or how another organization benefited from achieving it. Share what life will be like for the customer once the objectives are achieved. Better yet, schedule a *field trip* so your team can see firsthand what the customer is facing and how the project will make a difference.

### 5(d) Create a community

A little camaraderie can go a long way. Try having a team lunch, allowing people to get to know each other. Some people are motivated more by relationships than by *causes*. They get motivated when they feel comfortable around the people with whom they are working. Not everyone is motivated by the same thing, and very few people, if any, are motivated by speeches or declarations. Don't expect to make a rousing speech and suddenly find everyone excited. That only works in the movies. If it has a good story angle, some people will embrace it. Others need to like who they're working with (and for), and that can't happen unless there's some social time. Be careful not to infringe on people's personal time, though. Otherwise it could serve to cause more stress.

### 5(e) Make sure people are in the right roles

Sometimes a team has all the right people in all the wrong roles. For instance, if someone isn't good at following up, pair him or her with someone who is. If one person is more analytical than customer-focused, put refrain from that person in a customer-facing role. Likewise, make sure people have some level of challenge in the work they are given. According to psychologist and author Mihaly Csikszentmihalyi, people work their best when they are put in a role where two elements exist: a high level of challenge and where their strengths are a good fit. Without adequate challenge, people get bored. Without adequate skills, they get frustrated. When both challenge and strengths are in full gear, people are at peak focus, what Csikszentmihalyi calls a state of *flow*.

### 5(f) Ask the team

When in doubt, simply ask. There's nothing wrong with meeting with people, either individually or in a group, to ask why they don't seem all that interested in the project. You may be surprised at the answer. Be aware that some people may be more apt to share individually than in a group.

You could also probe for ideas on how to make the project more appealing, or the environment more engaging. People naturally love to help. Most importantly, you could ask what barriers may be in their way, either inside or outside the realm of the project.

### 5(g) Ask yourself some questions

There are a number of questions you can ask yourself that may shed light on a team's lack of interest. For example, "Would I be excited to work on this project? What would make me excited to work on this project? If I am not excited to be working on this project, why would that be? Is there something in my project management style that is affecting the team's morale? Is the team's excitement level a reflection of my own? Is the team excitement level perhaps a reflection of corporate culture? Maybe a recent round of layoffs, or rumor of layoffs, is the culprit?"

You could also ask, "Is the perceived lack of excitement of the team stemming from a lack of interest by the project sponsors? If the project sponsors don't care, why should the team? Why should you? Is this the right project for the company and for the business? Should the project continue?" Perhaps the project was someone's pet idea and the person is no longer in the company. If the project is in trouble and the team is reluctant to work on a project, is it time to end the project?

# 2.3 Team members question whether the project is worth doing.

## By Alec Satin

Years ago, one of my favorite stickers read, "Question Authority!" While antiauthority rhetoric is less prevalent (or accepted) than it used to be, there is a place for it in all well-functioning teams. The best project managers go out of their way to encourage their team to constantly question assumptions, risks, and anything else that could impact the project's success.

At its core, project management is about judgment. As a project manager you are constantly making decisions as to which items to focus upon and when, what to communicate to the project team and other stakeholders, and how often to remind people of upcoming deliverables. In project management, as in life, leaving things to chance is itself a choice. It is up to you to think, plan, and then, do!

> ### He Should Do *Stand-up*
>
> "So what—do you think a solution will just magically appear before our eyes? Come on, we have to deal with reality here!" Butch got such a good laugh from the team, they completely failed to realize that he was seriously undermining their best efforts. He had a way of describing situations that seemed so logical and insightful. It also didn't hurt that he was consistently funny. At the end of the day, he set the tone in a way that Kerry, the project manager, could never hope to do.
>
> Kerry looked on hopelessly. Unable to turn the tide, she ended the meeting. She spent the rest of the day roaming among people she knew didn't believe in the project—or in her as a leader. She fielded countless questions that were paraphrased segments of Butch's complaint list, spending more time playing his game than running the project. People came in late, left early, and constantly talked about how much they wanted the project to be over.
>
> The whole situation felt hopeless.

Whatever your particular style as a project leader, it is imperative that you trust what you are doing and how you are doing it. Your team will respond to your true level of trust in yourself and, just as importantly, your trust in them. Their willingness to trust and follow your lead will be enhanced—or compromised—by your actions and attitude.

## 1. Problem

You are on a project with team members who question whether the project is worth their time or the company's resources.

## 2. Warning Signs

- You don't really care if the team questions whether the project's worth doing. They just need to get to work.
- You agree with the team. The project really isn't worth doing.
- One or more team members are standout troublemakers. They are making trouble on your project, just as they may have done on many others.
- The team is demoralized due to uncertainty in the organization.

## 3. What will happen if I do nothing?

Productivity on the project will be low, and team members will not address the real *intent* of the project because they do not understand its significance.

## 4. Solution

The solution depends on your view of the root cause of the problem. Take a look at the options below.

## 5. What should I do?

What happens when you are on a project with team members who question whether the project is worth doing? As you'll see, it depends on your perspective and the approach you have taken to the problem so far. By the time you finish this chapter, you'll be well on your way to handling all of the typical problems and solutions to the problem of people asking "Is this project really worth it?"

Here are some common situations that project managers find themselves in when their teams are questioning the value of the project itself.

### 5(a) Determine which statement most accurately describes how you think

*You don't really care if the team questions whether the project is worth doing. The team just needs to get to work.*

This is the *You're in the Army now* style of project management. Much of the real U.S. military moved on from this 1950's model, but many project managers still adopt this attitude. The problem here is not the team—it's you. Technical authority is granted by your organization, but real authority is something you earn through your interactions with the team. If *just do it* is the approach you take, it won't be long before the team's productivity drops off significantly. By the time that happens, it's often difficult to fix your relationships and move on.

You can, however, change your approach any time you like. The trick is to create an atmosphere of openness and ownership throughout your project team. Each person must feel like they helped define their part of the solution and therefore *owns* the result. Given that you believe in their approach, your job is then to merely guide things at a high level and check in to be sure things are on track. Encouraging collaboration, openness, and most of all ownership will likely lead to better performance and quicker response to project risk.

One important thing to note is that changing your *persona* is probably the hardest part. However, the difficulty is all in your head. Tell yourself, "just do it," (change your management style) rather than focusing on the deficiencies of the team. Look at it this way—it might be uncomfortable to change your style mid-project, but it's better than failing.

*You agree with the team. The project really isn't worth doing.*

The good news is that you and your team are in agreement. The bad news is that you are in a difficult situation, which will require a broad range of fairly advanced leadership skills. You're right to feel a little nervous. A large part of leadership is the willingness to say what needs to be said when it needs to be said no matter the response. If you do the prep work, you will know what needs to be said. You will also be prepared to communicate effectively.

First, be sure that you are right. What is the real intent of your project? How is everyone measuring the value it is delivering? Maybe the scope was defined poorly or the business reality has changed. If so, documenting the scope and goals of the project is the first step here. Once you have documented clear goals and scope, take a step back and see if it looks like the project is worth doing at this point. It could be that the project champion is no longer present or committed. Is there another sponsor to take his or her place? If you have presented the goals and value of the project to all of the right members of management and no one wants to sponsor it, the project is not worth doing because the goals don't matter to anyone. It's possible that there are political issues casting a dark cloud over the project. Take a piece of paper, write down or mind map all the reasons that your project may be devalued politically. In other words, the project may be worth doing, but perhaps not worth the personal political cost to each of your team members.

Once you have gathered all the reasons you can come up with, it will be time to approach your team. See *Opening Pandora's Box* later in this chapter for the best way to do this.

*There is a troublemaker on my team, affecting everyone's attitude on the project just like in the past.*

Every organization has its complainers, troublemakers, and mischief-makers. If you've never had one on any of your project teams, you likely will at some point, so it's good to be prepared. These types of team members often come to a team through transfer or you encounter them when you inherit a project. It is important to clearly distinguish intelligent questioning intended to improve the project from destructive mischief, which is almost always intended to tear down you or other team members. If you have a destructive person on your project, you must act consistently and decisively. Even if you have no time to spend on what you perceive to be a personality issue, you cannot safely neglect this situation. Ignoring it can put your project at risk.

At best, troublemakers are frustrated innovators or leaders. Thinking of them in this way may help you to see their potential and be less likely to feel irritated or enraged by their behaviors. To address this potential, you need to make extra time to listen to and work with the person one on one. Seek out their ideas privately. It may be advisable to be wary of giving them full rein in meetings unless you are certain you can bring back control as needed. Nothing can tear down a team's morale faster than a naysayer holding court for 25 minutes of a 30 minute status meeting. So don't let that happen.

Often, troublemakers merely want to make an important contribution. The easiest way to do that is to block progress in areas where the goals are questionable. The trick here is to spend enough one on one time with each *project detractor* that you can develop a shared understanding of the challenges and goals—then jointly define solutions that you can both own and work toward. Incorporate your detractor's ideas whenever possible as long as they don't threaten the quality of the end result.

This will help reduce negativity and create increasingly higher levels of ownership as you move forward. Most project managers assume that troublemakers must be dismissed as soon as possible. The fact is that they are often needed in some capacity (or they wouldn't be on the project in the first place) and harder to dismiss than you think. You should assume that the project detractor will be on your team for the duration of the project. Making them a partner in your project's success should be your number one goal.

*Your team is demoralized due to uncertainty in the organization.*

Layoffs, rumors, and ill-conceived organizational transformation are common components of project management reality. The cure is to show your team that they can count on you no matter what happens in the organization as a whole. People long to be part of something greater than themselves. Create a calm, predictable atmosphere on your project. This will help your team in a real way.

Communicate clearly and repeatedly that you will inform the team whenever you know anything that will positively or negatively impact them or the project. Let them know that you take what they say seriously. Make it *safe* to speak with you. This means, in part, that you will never betray their confidence or use anything that they say against them. Doing these things tells your team, in a practical way, that you care about their well-being.

Don't forget to follow through by doing what you promise. If you *say* and don't *do*, you are worse off than if you had never said anything. People are smart. They will know if you are sincere.

Once you have built a solid trust relationship, your team will be far more open to hearing about the value of your project. At that point, it's just a matter of communicating that value in a meaningful way.

### 5(b) Opening Pandora's Box

If the project is worth doing, but the team fails to see its value, sometimes you need to hash things out in a more direct way. In other words, *open Pandora's Box*. (In Greek mythology, Pandora opened a box that released evil into the world.) Everything that your team is saying behind the scenes needs to be brought out in the open. An in-person meeting is preferable for this type of exercise, because reading body language and other visual cues are important during confrontational discussions. However, if a conference call is the best that can be arranged, that will have to be good enough. The invitees should include only your core project team. Exclude anyone who is not actually doing the work.

You'll start the meeting by letting the whole group know that you believe there are serious questions about the project. Explicitly give people permission to speak their minds freely and without consequences. Next, briefly (25 words or less) provide the official explanation of why the project is worth doing. You can take this from the project charter, business case, or scope, but more importantly, ensure that you believe in what you are saying. Just make sure it's no longer than a few sentences and stated in clear, understandable language.

Next, transition to a discussion about the problem by explaining that changes in the business or the environment often make projects more or less valuable as they are executed. It is perfectly valid for people to talk about how the value of this project may have changed over time. Acknowledge that the project team is often closer to what is happening than stakeholders and even the project manager. You can then open up the meeting to a brainstorm, or other means that you are comfortable with, to identify the reasons the team questions whether the project is worth doing.

Your effectiveness in facilitating this meeting will depend on factors such as:

- How well the team knows and trusts you
- The organizational culture's attitude towards open communication
- Your experience and skill in facilitating meetings

A little trepidation is normal. You can take comfort in the fact that having the meeting shows courage and foresight. If you are sincere in your care and concern for the well-being of both the project and the team members, it will be recognized.

Don't be surprised if no one speaks up. You may need to *prime the pump* by using a whiteboard to write a few possible reasons why they may be questioning the project. Start with what you believe to be a lesser reason. Name it. Then ask others to speak out with how this might be a true issue or risk.

Close the meeting by thanking the team members for their participation. Tell them that you will consider what to do with the information gained from the meeting, and will let them know when you make a decision.

### 5(c) How to decide what to do next

Separate all the concerns from the meeting into categories of *major* and *minor*. Start with the assumption that all concerns are valid. For the minor concerns, make plans to resolve any that you can clear easily. Set these aside.

For each major concern, identify the real issue or risk. It may not be exactly the same as it was stated by the team. Once you've clarified it, analyze. Can you fix it? If not, who can? If it were addressed, determine what would be the positive or negative impact on:

- Project scope
- Delivery time
- Budget
- Quality

If not addressed, do any items show a potential 10 percent or greater impact to the project's cost or schedule? If so, you should immediately write up a brief, one page assessment and discuss it with your line manager. Get in the habit of communicating potential issues well in advance. *No surprises* is good practice in project management.

Whatever happens, make sure to communicate the actions you took on your team's behalf and the results. You may or may not be successful with every issue— but most people will give you a lot of credit for listening, hearing, and then acting.

# 2.4 People feel like they don't get credit for the work they do.

By Ty Kiisel

## 1. Problem

Traditional, top-down project management approaches are designed to make you good at calling out team members when projects fall behind, but seldom offer much attention on giving positive feedback when all progress indicators are green. Without appropriate praise, individual project team members become discouraged and disengage from the process.

Command and control approaches simply do not help you foster an atmosphere where team members are recognized for their accomplishments. If the only time a team member hears from the project manager is when there is something wrong or something more needs to be done, the result will be team turnover or project failure.

**Recognizing Accomplishment Is Different Than Insincere Praise**

Ralph gave a lot of lip service to recognizing team accomplishments. He made a point everyday of visiting his team to tell them they were doing a great job: "Keep it up, you're the best, can't do it without you," etc.

Unaware of exactly what they were working on or how successfully they were doing, Ralph's insincere platitudes fell to the floor like lead balloons. Mary, a popular and important member of the team, did a great Ralph impression, quoting his *praise lines* as she moved through the room. She didn't do it behind his back, but rather as he would enter the room on his morning rounds. Even after weeks of heckling, he still failed to get the hint, even taking the teasing as evidence of his bond with the team. The loud muttering after every one of his visits did not even clue him in to the problems that his *happy talk* was causing.

## 2. Warning Signs

People let you know they are not getting enough credit by:

- Directly saying they don't feel appreciated
- Expressing frustration about the value they are adding
- Expressing a dislike or distrust of management
- Complaining to their peers

## 3. What happens if I do nothing?

Although most organizations claim that their workforce is one of their most valued assets, the actions of their managers often indicate otherwise. Team members feel ignored or unappreciated, and the process suffers. Projects and tasks can fall behind or fail, the quality of work can diminish, and project teams experience high turnover. Ultimately, this can be expensive for organizations as project costs increase and dissatisfied customers look for other solutions.

## 4. Solution

With most challenges faced by project leaders, there is rarely a magic solution. It would be an oversimplification and condescending to suggest that giving team members more *atta-boys* would consistently solve recognition problems. That being said, people take pride in their work and care about what their managers and peers think of them and their accomplishments. Therefore, managers who recognize individual team member accomplishments and contributions foster an environment where team members are more inclined to participate in the project management process—and ultimately contribute to project success.

## 5. What should I do?

### 5(a) Recognizing accomplishment is only a part of successful team communication

As most business leaders loudly proclaim, an organization's workforce is their most valuable asset. This is why business leaders need to give the same attention to people as they do to other assets.

A friend told me of a conversation he once had with his oldest child. Unhappy at the result of the conversation, the child smacked her younger brother, who kicked the dog that then snapped at the cat. After witnessing the aftermath of the *conversation*, he was unable to contain himself—he had to step outside for a few minutes to laugh before he went back inside to address the situation. Although this amusing anecdote about how children react to scolding is not the same as work-related discussions that take place within project teams, I have watched coworkers *kick the dog* from time to time. (By the way, responsibility for morale rests at the top of the org chart.)

Regardless of whether or not your project teams are serving internal or external customers, a discouraged and disengaged workforce *kicking the dog* does not serve your customers or your project teams. Maintaining a positive work environment, where communication is cordial and considerate, is the first step to creating conditions where team members feel their accomplishments are appreciated and recognized.

### 5(b) A spoonful of sugar *helps the medicine (bad news) go down*

Mary Poppins, the magical nanny from London, of children's movie fame, was right. Like neglectful parents in the movies, if the only time project managers ever talk to members of the project team is when there is a problem, they will be avoided, ignored, and disregarded. However, that doesn't mean that you need to add Mary Poppins' *spoonful of sugar* to every *medicinal* conversation about how to remedy a situation. There is a better way:

- *Clearly define your expectations up front:* Most people want to do a good job. However, as project leader, you can't assume that they will automatically know what a good job is. It is up to the project manager to make sure team members understand what is expected.
- *Hold team members accountable to do a good job:* When team members understand expectations, and are regularly held accountable to meet them, they tend to meet (or exceed) the expectations.
- *Acknowledge the good, the bad, and the ugly:* When team members know what is expected of them and are relied upon to perform to expectations, it is important that project leaders recognize performance. Project mangers

need to acknowledge and recognize positive accomplishments as they occur, as well as the negative outcomes that need to be addressed, to create an atmosphere where teams feel their contributions are recognized and appreciated.

### 5(c) Is a team member worth an occasional kudo for a job well done?

On most project teams, everyone contributes to the success of projects with different talents and skills. Although there may be team members who share the same job description, their contribution and skill sets are not always the same. So it is important to understand each person's contribution. Can you specifically identify the value each individual brings to the team? Is it something you can live without? If it's not, then whenever *special value* is delivered, it is certainly cause for praise.

It makes sense to recognize team member accomplishments when appropriate. If that's not something you do with your project teams, you run the risk of losing high-quality people as situations change. People don't tend to leave a job for financial reasons. It is usually unfavorable working conditions or a negative relationship with the boss. They may not quit abruptly, but they will be on the lookout for their next opportunity, which eventually presents itself.

### 5(d) Recognizing accomplishments without creating prima donnas

Of course, like everything else, it is possible to overdo praise. It's natural for people who receive nothing but continual praise to acquire an exaggerated opinion of themselves. Creative people or people with specialized skills tend to be very confident and naturally self-assured. How you praise is as important as the praise itself. There has been much written about the best ways to discipline employees, but we seldom talk about the proper way to praise and recognize accomplishments. When offering praise, the following approaches are important:

- *Make it meaningful:* Make the praise commensurate with the accomplishment. As a project leader, you need to *recognize* and assess the value of accomplishments before you can effectively *reward* them.
- *Make it specific:* Specifically recognizing a meaningful accomplishment is more appreciated than broad compliments. For example, "[Name of team member], thank you for the extra effort you put into that project stakeholder presentation. I think it will help us get the budgetary support we need to successfully finish this project," will be much more meaningful than, "Good job, team."
- *Make it public:* Although there are times when public praise might be inappropriate, as a general rule, you can rely on the phrase *praise publicly and punish privately*. Publicly acknowledging team member accomplishments is almost always appreciated.

The key to recognizing accomplishments without creating a prima donna is to praise when appropriate, and critique when appropriate. If praise *and* critique are administered even-handedly, most project team members will be able to keep their egos in check.

# 2.5 My team doesn't believe in their ability to execute.

By Fran Samaras

## 1. Problem

Your team is generally apprehensive. They have trouble getting started on their task assignments, complain that they don't understand *what* they need to do, and don't *get* the vision of the project. Some of them may have announced that they don't believe in their ability to get the job done.

## 2. Warning Signs

- You are not getting clear status updates in meetings.
- Team members have expressed their doubt in the team's ability, or an individual team member's ability, to achieve the project goals or complete individual tasks.
- The team is unable to articulate what steps they need to follow to complete their assignment(s).

## 3. What will happen if I do nothing?

Ignoring the problem is not a prudent strategy. If you ignore the problem, the following could occur:

- Project could lose momentum
- Missed milestone due dates
- Morale downward spiral
- In-fighting on the team

## 4. Solution

Get to the root cause of the problem(s). Project managers have an obligation to ask themselves the following questions:

- Are the goals of the project realistic?

### A Team That Doesn't Believe

Amy is a project manager who is excited about her new project. She is motivated and ready to tackle it. She can't believe that she has been assigned a supportive sponsor, and has been allocated what she believes will be a sufficient amount of resources needed to complete the job. So, what's wrong?

As Amy starts out traveling around the company, scheduling meet and greets with some of her project leads, they seem apathetic. Soon, she gets complaints about some of her resources assigned to the team and the work hasn't even started yet. She hears things like, "Billy is assigned as the business analyst and he just doesn't always get the full picture on the requirements; Michael, one of the developers, is slow; and look out for Ryan—he is just a trainee."

Still, Amy remains optimistic. Sandy and Matthew are key players on the project, and they seem motivated and ready to dig in.

As the team begins to create their work breakdown, Amy finds some of the resources know what needs to be done and are positive at giving task completion dates to the work assigned, while others seem to be dragging their feet. Team Lead meetings seem productive, but when she gathers the entire project team, there seems to be an air of defeat in the room despite her optimism.

Amy is not sure at this point whether to run for the hills, or dig in and get to the bottom of the problem, since she knows that some of the team seems really ready to go. She's got a million other things to do, and surely a few folks who are in a slump can't bring the whole team down, or can they?

- Is the project implementation date(s) desired by executive management truly achievable?
- Do you have enough money to fund the project?
- Do team members have adequate time to devote to project work?
- Are the deliverables well-defined?
- Are the tasks clear, and do tasks support the deliverables?

If the answer is "No" to any of these questions, you have a responsibility to manage the expectations of your sponsor and paint a picture of reality for your company or client. It is incumbent on you, as the project manager, to articulate what you can deliver given the parameters.

For the remainder of this chapter, we assume that the project actually has realistic goals that the team is fully capable of achieving. So the focus will be on getting the team, or members of the team to believe in their ability to execute.

## 5. What should I do?

You have gotten word that your team feels like they are unable to execute. Your first step is to assess why the team feels inadequate. Engage in conversations with the various leaders on the project. Personally speak to the project sponsor(s), business and IT lead(s), subject matter experts, developers, testers, business analysts, change managers, and others, and gauge their concerns. If it is not possible for face to face conversations, you can create a short survey to gain information, send an email, or simply telephone the team members. If time allows, you can conduct small focus groups with the team to get to the root cause of the problem.

As you can imagine, there could be a plethora of reasons why a team may not believe in their abilities. Here are some tactics to try, based on what your analysis reveals:

### 5(a) Analysis reveals: The team isn't clear on what the project is supposed to deliver

*Remedy:* Share the project vision with the team at the next team meeting. Engage the sponsor to meet with the team. If the vision is too overwhelming, break the vision into phases and work packages. Focus on the immediate deliverables with the team rather than what deliverables you are overall driving to build.

### 5(b) Analysis reveals: The team or individual(s) don't feel they have the skills to perform the tasks outlined in the project plan

*Remedy:* Provide on-the-job training to get the team the skill set they need to succeed. Partner up senior and junior project team members to collaborate on ideas and check or proof deliverables and solutions. Engage quality analysts at each step of the project to check work and educate the team.

If time doesn't allow you to provide training, you may need to take a hard line to remove those project team members who are unable to create the deliverables required, or remove them from critical path deliverables and have them gain experience and confidence with less critical tasks.

### 5(c) Analysis reveals: Only a few members of the team question their ability and are bringing the rest of the team's morale down

*Remedy:* Spend a good part of your day working with the project team members who are struggling. Offer assistance, solutions, and coaching. If you are unable to remove obstacles for them, gain counsel on their issues from your management or project sponsors. You don't have to always know the answer—that's okay. You should however, know who to turn to for assistance.

### 5(d) Analysis reveals: The team feels that they need quite a bit of reinforcement to achieve goals

*Remedy:*

- Celebrate small wins! Reward a team member for solving a problem with a thank you note or public praise; mention their name and accomplishment in the team status report, at the project team meeting.
- Reward a business analyst for meeting with the customer and finalizing a requirement.
- Start a mini-quality program for your project. Highlight deliverables that are completed correctly. Conduct walk-throughs with the whole team or those less confident in their abilities. Provide templates for work, when possible, so a team member isn't staring at a blank page at task startup.
- Award certificates for achievement to team members. This low cost solution can be done easily, and you can find dozens of templates for this purpose online or at a local office supply or stationary store.
- Recognize successful project team members in a corporate newsletter for their achievement(s).
- Write a personalized note to thank the individual for the extra time or effort they put in to meet a date or solve a problem.
- Get a "C" Suite Executive or the project sponsor to write a congratulations or thank you note. I have handwritten notes for some executives and simply brought the note to them to sign, then given them to team members. Be effective when dealing with executive leaders who trust you and are too busy to get involved with the details.
- If your project budget allows, provide small gifts for milestone completions or individual performance achievements. Inexpensive gifts may include a lunch certificate in the office cafeteria or local fast food restaurant ($5–$10 range), movie pass, coffee vendor coupon, or simple catered lunch for the team if there are several people you are rewarding.

Years ago, at a small company I worked for, we had an executive team serve breakfast to a project team that achieved success. The executives pushed carts up and down the cubical rows with donuts and fast food biscuits for the project participants during a *Let the bosses wait on you* day.

The key to rewards is to give the reward when accomplishments are made. Don't just walk into a team meeting and say, "Hurrah for the team," and pass out movie passes. Your recognition must be given in a sincere manner even if you are trying to make it fun.

### 5(e) Analysis reveals: The team feels there are too many obstacles to achieving success

*Remedy:* As the project manager, it is your responsibility to remove the obstacles. Elevate and highlight issues to the team leadership and sponsors, work your issue log, follow up, problem solve, offer solutions, and/or engage subject matter experts to help the team find solutions.

### 5(f) Analysis reveals: The team doesn't believe in your ability as project manager to lead them along the way

*Remedy:* Engage the team—they are your talent. Have team meetings, meet with smaller teams (of like roles), and hold problem-solving sessions. Seek advice from all levels, and be collaborative. Build trust between the team and you. Much of that trust comes from building relationships with the team. Engage the team in building the project plan, and solicit feedback on solutions and project management tactics. Clearly define roles and responsibilities, and ask the team to hold YOU responsible and to not fear bringing to you what they feel is not working.

### 5(g) Analysis reveals: Certain members of the team lack confidence

*Remedy:* Work with team members who lack confidence, or assign more senior team members to bolster confidence. This may mean a bit more micromanaging of the project or tasks in order to make sure that it stays on track. It will be worth your time. Ask yourself, "Was the team *beat up* before on a project and, that, hesitant to start because of a fear of failure?"

Go back to Lessons Learned documents on previous projects. What are you doing differently that could help? Take overt steps to make this experience different from the team's last one. If they prefer to work in the office rather than at home to be less remote and get additional support, let them do so! If the teams need to touch base daily to make sure they are on track, let them do it!

### 5(h) Analysis reveals: The team or individuals have never done project work before, and don't know where to begin, thus, they have fear

*Remedy:* Start at the beginning. Remember when you started in this role. Take the time to explain your expectations. Engage individuals in helping you to decide on task due dates so they are involved with decisions and feel that they have some control of the process. This also builds buy-in.

### 5(i) Analysis reveals: The team can't articulate why they have fear or are doubtful

*Remedy:* Probe into the situation more by asking, "why?" Determine root cause. You cannot let team member feelings fall by the wayside, as those feelings could perpetuate throughout the project and limit your chances for success.

# 2.6 My team doesn't believe in the plan or schedule.
### By Elizabeth Harrin

## 1. Problem

You have a great project plan with lots of detail. The plan is properly documented and you have built a schedule that gets everything done by the date that the sponsor wants. However, the team has now started working on the project, and it is clear that they are sticking to their own schedules and not paying any attention to your masterpiece.

It's very important that the project team get behind the plan and make the commitment to deliver what needs to be done. The risk of a perfect plan that has been built without involvement from the team is that the plan isn't perfect after all. Important tasks will be missed, and the length of time tasks take will be wrong. In the short term, the team may get behind you (even if they don't believe in the plan) and try to make it work. This could mean working longer hours to get tasks completed on time. However, the goodwill won't last long before they start to resent the fact that you signed them up to this plan. It's hard to keep the project going when it's obvious that the team doesn't believe in the plan or the schedule.

### The One-Man Plan

Hans had spent a lot of time working on his project plan. He knew what needed to be done and how long everything would take. Requirements gathering takes a couple of days, right? There weren't that many users to ask, after all.

Hans proudly projected the schedule on to the wall of the meeting room. "Looking at this! We'll be done by June," he said to the team. Their faces were incredulous—and they did not seem pleased that he had saved them so much time by doing all the work for them.

"You've only got one day for budget approval," said Claire from Finance. "You do know that the approval cycle is three weeks? And there's nothing in the plan for training. My department is four hundred people. How am I going train them all on the new system?"

Ouch. Claire wasn't the only one to complain. As they went around the table, each team member picked large holes in his plan. "We absolutely can't do this," Claire said, when everyone had finished pulling the schedule apart. "It's idiotic."

Hans had completely misinterpreted what needed to be done to deliver the project. He realized that he hadn't understood what was involved in some of the tasks, and he had missed some tasks completely. The only good thing was that he hadn't yet shown the schedule to his project sponsor. He needed a new plan, and quickly—he was due to present the schedule to the sponsor that afternoon.

## 2. Warning Signs

- Your project team complains about the deadlines
- Tasks are not being completed on time, if at all
- You are putting your team under pressure to complete tasks by the milestone dates
- Everyone is working long hours
- Tasks are being completed that are not on the plan
- The team's morale is falling, along with their confidence in you

## 3. What will happen if I do nothing?

If you stick with the plan and do nothing, the project will get later and later, and tasks will not be completed on time. You may find yourself putting more pressure on the project team to speed up. Morale and the team's willingness to work with you will fall. Increased pressure means that there is a risk of cutting corners and delivering a low quality product that is not fit for its purpose. The sponsor will become disillusioned with your ability to deliver a good result on the promise of your schedule.

Eventually you might find that no one wants to work on your projects at all, as you have gained a reputation for being a slave driver whose projects always run late.

## 4. Solution

You can't plan in a vacuum. At the end of the day, it's not you who will do all the tasks—that's what the project team members will do. Involve them in working out what needs to be done to meet the project objectives and how long it will take. If your plan and schedule are unrealistic, start from scratch and build new ones, with the involvement of the right people. In summary, you need:

- A complete list of tasks required to deliver the project
- An understanding of the dependencies between these tasks
- Accurate timescales for all of the tasks

## 5. What should I do?

Get the key members of your team together to work out a new, realistic plan and schedule that they can all buy into. Acknowledge that your current working plan is no good and that you need to set a new baseline against which to track progress. Essentially, you are starting to plan this project from scratch, and you need their help.

### 5(a) Create a complete list of tasks

As a group, review all the work breakdown structures and plans you have so far. The person doing the task will have a better understanding of what it actually involves than you ever will. So let them tell you what is required to get the task done. What is missing from the original plan? How does the task break down into subtasks? If you can, delegate the creation of subplans to the workstream leaders.

The aim here is to get a comprehensive list of what needs to be done to achieve the project's objectives. Rely on your experts to help you develop this list—it will help them feel accountable for the deliverables, and more comfortable with the overall plan.

### 5(b) Understand the dependencies

Once you know what needs to be done, it is time to start putting tasks in order and then create the schedule. Dependency management is important here. Again, rely on the experts in your team to help you build the dependencies into the schedule. Take into account:

- What order do the tasks need to be completed in?
- What tasks can be run in parallel?
- What can be started early?
- Who needs someone else to have finished before they can start?
- What needs to finish at the same time as something else?

Once you understand the order of tasks and their dependencies, you can start putting in some dates.

### 5(c) Work out accurate schedules

The team didn't think much of the original schedule you created, so this time around, ask them for input. They have probably spent time carrying out this same type of work. Unless it is a unique project or they are very new to their job, they are likely to have done it before. Given the team members' experience, they should be able to come up with some realistic estimates for timeframes for all the tasks on the plan.

There is no harm in challenging some of the dates when you review the team's input. As the project manager you should find a balance between making up the milestone dates yourself, and allowing the team to define their own dates (e.g., not allowing estimates to go so far into the future that everyone works half days and the project takes ages to complete). Work collaboratively with your team to create stretched, yet achievable, target delivery dates. Also, put some contingency time explicitly into the schedule if you are worried that there is a degree of uncertainty in the estimates.

Finally, it's time to present your new schedule to your sponsor. It is highly likely that the result of this exercise is a project that will finish later than you originally had in mind. It is difficult to tell a sponsor that your initial estimates were wrong. However, what you now have is a project plan that you can believe in and that is backed by all of the members of your team. That's the message to give your sponsor.

# 2.7 My team doesn't believe in me as a manager.

By J. Chris White

## 1. Problem

A problem arises when project team members appear to ignore your requests. You get the sinking feeling that the team members do not respect you as a project manager.

## 2. Warning Signs

- Discussions stop when you enter the project meetings.
- Team members are late to project meetings or cancel at the last minute.
- No one seems to follow the project plan or respond to your requests.
- No one updates you on work progress.
- It seems that a lot of information is shared among other team members, and you are the last to know.
- Your project decisions are overtly challenged.
- Work is not progressing as quickly as it was previously.

## 3. What will happen if I do nothing?

The behavior of the team members will continue to worsen, and you will most likely lose your ability to effectively lead the team. The project may or may not suffer because an informal *project manager* may arise from the team to essentially take your place.

### Is It Me, or Everyone Else?

Alan has always had a problem confronting others and being assertive. This characteristic never caused much of a problem since it usually meant that he overpaid for a meal at a restaurant, or someone else got in front of him in a line at a store. These were all in his personal life. But, at work he now has a wonderful opportunity as the project manager for a high-profile project. He was beginning to notice that this little idiosyncrasy of his was affecting the project and its performance of established objectives.

At first, when team members ignored his requests or were reluctant to share information, Alan wasn't sure how to interpret these actions. He was new to the project team and perhaps they had ways of doing things that were different than what he was used to. Perhaps the distance that he perceived between himself and others was due to the fact that they were still in the *forming* and *storming* stages of team development. "It's only natural," he thought to himself. "It will get better."

In an effort to make things better, Alan backed off a bit and held off on challenging or standing up to team members. He did not want to offend anyone or look like a dictatorial boss. The more he felt the distance and the lack of respect and support from the other team members, the more he fell into a pattern of passive behavior. He thought, "Surely I don't have to remind everyone how important this project is. They'll get it done." Alan remained on the sidelines with the hope that things would get better. He didn't want to upset anyone with a lot of micromanagement of activities.

But, instead, things got worse. The project team missed a third milestone in a row. That never looks good. And the project sponsor was beginning to put a little pressure on Alan and the team.

Alan knew he had to do something. It did not take a genius to figure out that if things continued like this the project would suffer severely, or he would be removed and replaced with someone who could deliver.

## 4. Solution

Sometimes you have to do something drastic to make a point. Now is the time. However, don't do something reckless that will jeopardize the project. Just be assertive with something that already needs to be done. For example, support and defend the team on a key decision that must be shared with upper management to show them that you are solidly on their side. Or, push strongly for additional necessary resources to help the team stay on schedule.

## 5. What should I do?

If your team does not respect you as a manager, you need to change this situation as quickly as you can. There may be several reasons for this, which you should eventually think about so that it does not happen again on future projects, but now is the time for action on this particular project.

You cannot sit on the sidelines when you are a project manager. You have to be in the game. In fact, to a large extent, you control the game. You are like a player, a coach, and a referee all rolled into one. As a *player*, you are an example and work in the manner that you want others to work. As a *coach*, you guide team members on what to do and what the performance expectations are. As a *referee*, you enforce expectations of team behavior and performance. With the particular problem discussed here, the role of the referee sometimes has to come to the forefront.

## 5(a) Theory of situational leadership

Here is a quick, theory overview about human behavior that plays into this dilemma. A spectrum of human behavior ranges from *passive* on one end to *aggressive* on the other end. Sometimes a situation calls for you to be passive, which is often associated with a *participative* style of leadership. Sometimes a situation calls for you to be aggressive, which is often associated with an *authoritarian* style of leadership. Other times, a situation calls for you to be somewhere in the middle, which is called *assertive*. There is no *best* way to act that applies for all situations. Instead, the *best* way to act is situational. This has even been called *situational leadership*.

Maybe, like Alan in the Sidebar story, you *will* need to enter the project soft-handed so as not to rock the boat too much in the beginning. Perhaps it was valid to be passive at that point in time and not jump on everyone's performance or meeting behaviors immediately. It is logical to build consensus. Sometimes, you should opt to be a passive manager throughout the entire project—it depends on the specific conditions.

But, given the current situation on this project, the time for a passive approach to leadership has expired. As the project progresses, you must move to an assertive midpoint in all that you do. If things get bad enough, you may be forced to spend a little time on the authoritarian end of the spectrum to make sure things get done. No one wants to have to do it, but sometimes it is necessary for project success. That comes with the territory.

### 5(b) Take action as a leader

Now that situational leadership theory is in place, here are some suggestions for specific actions to make your team believe in you. You will need to do several things in parallel:

*Make yourself present*

To begin, one way to get people's attention is by being around them frequently. In the past, one strategy was called *Management By Walking Around (MBWA)*. Essentially, make yourself *very* present. Let people see you. Talk with people, even if it's not directly related to the project. This keeps you within their attention span. Plain and simple, you become a regular fixture. One of the benefits of being around other team members a lot is that you pick up additional information that you might not have if had you not been around. Sometimes information is fleeting, and people don't necessarily remember to bring it up at project meetings. When you hear something of interest, you can ask additional questions and gather even more information. Another benefit is building relationships with the other team members, which increases their willingness to listen to you and respond to your requests. Also, it makes it less awkward when you actually need to be present and request a team member to increase his or her performance.

*Make decisions and enforce them*

As you work on *being present*, make some bold decisions, and follow through by enforcing them. The MBWA suggestion can be thought of as a slow, long-term fix. It will help over time. But, you still need a fast, short-term fix to snap things into place now. Figure out some decision that is somewhat important (so people will care), but isn't a make-or-break decision for the project (so the project doesn't fail, in case people are slower to respond than expected). This idea is sort of like the professor dropping a book on the floor next to a student who has dozed off during class. It gets attention due to its boldness and abruptness, but does no harm. As mentioned, good examples are supporting your team on a key decision or requesting additional resources to the project sponsor or upper management. These two problems are fairly common on most projects.

At least for a short period of time, you will have everyone's attention. While you have their attention, make sure they know that you are on their side and that you will run interference, as needed, to allow the team to continue working without distractions. A few bold moves to show support, coupled with the MBWA approach to build relationships, should provide an effective combination for increasing your team's confidence in you as a project manager.

*Communicate with your sponsor*

In addition to quick-and-effective attention from the team and MBWA, talk with your project sponsor or executive. Let them know what is happening and what you are doing about it. This serves three purposes:

- First, it shows the project executive that you are willing to learn and make adjustments. As much as we all want to be perfect, we are not. Of course, don't make it sound like doom-and-gloom or as if the project is dying on the vine. But, you should say something.

- Second, the project executive may have some good advice for you. He or she may have experienced the same situation previously and can give you some company-specific advice to guide you.
- Third, it gives the project sponsor or executive information so that he or she can support you with any heavy-handed or major decisions as you try to get team members back on track.

## References

Senge, P. *The Fifth Discipline: The Art and Practice of the Learning Organization*. New York: Doubleday, 1994.

Wycoff, J. *Mindmapping: Your Personal Guide to Exploring Creativity and Problem-Solving*. New York: The Berkley Publishing Group, 1991.

# 3

# EFFECTIVELY COMMUNICATING

## 3.1 How do I gain my team's trust?

By Dave Prior

### 1. Problem

Yesterday was your first day on site with a new team and a new project. You are good at your job and confident in your ability to get things done. You also have a track record to back up that confidence, but this is a new environment with all new people who know nothing about you.

Earning the team's trust and respect is going to be critical to your ability to succeed in leading their projects, but you need to gain trust quickly if you are going to get this project on track. What are you going to do?

### 2. Warning Signs

- Team members or stakeholders show contempt for project management as a function even before they get to know you.
- Half of the people involved with the project are skeptical about its outcome.
- You feel compelled to make promises and set expectations before being able to develop an understanding of the situation or the state of the project.

**She's Got *Trust Issues***

Sarah has been a PM for a number of years, and considers herself pretty good with people, but she really seems to be having a tough time in a new job. She was hired to reestablish the PMO of an organization that had a reputation for not supporting project management, needing to step in on almost every major project to fix things just a few weeks after the job started. Since the organization had brought her in to fix problems, she could not understand why people wouldn't just give her a few weeks to set up and make things right. Instead, she found every senior stakeholder who she came in contact with wanting to take her under their wing by giving her lots of advice on what she needed to do and how she needed to do it.

And, there was the team. They'd been working nights and weekends on an impossible deadline for two months. Their fatigue was resulting in software code fixes. You'd think they'd be happy to have someone with her level of expertise on board to fend for the team. But when she told the team that she was going to make sure they'd work no more nights and weekends due to last minute scope changes, they had actually laughed at her.

Sarah was really struggling with earning the trust of the team and senior management. What could she do differently that might help her gain trust with more team members and stakeholders?

- Team members and stakeholders voice concerns about the organization's ability to maintain the defined project management process.
- Team members and/or stakeholders are trying to *help* you by taking over meetings and responsibilities, and marginalizing your contribution before they even learn about your experience or background.

## 3. What will happen if I do nothing?

If you do nothing to gain trust, your team may start working around you or not take direction from you effectively. Either of these situations can endanger the project. Sponsors may pull resources away from your project, making it more difficult to succeed. In other words, establishing trust is a huge part of being successful.

First, let's talk about your team. They need to believe that you're looking out for them, removing obstacles, getting them the support that they need to succeed while keeping the organization informed and aware of progress. At the same time, your stakeholders need to be able to trust that you are on top of things, helping the team get the results they are looking for.

If you do not have trust from the team and stakeholders, leading the project is going to be far more difficult than having their trust. If stakeholders do not feel they can rely on you, they may feel compelled to *save* the project by engineering their own solutions around you and the team. They may also start voicing concerns within the organization that will further erode confidence in you and your team. As this makes its way into the team, their trust in you can begin to slip. If the team does not trust that you will be able to get what they need to be successful and keep negative forces at bay enough to allow them to get their work done, then they are unlikely to put forth their best effort. This will result in lower quality deliverables that require a fair amount of rework. Each of these situations increases the potential of failing to meet the defined scope, schedule, or budget.

As an example, Jake, the PM, has asked the team to spend their weekend working because of a critical scope change that must be implemented before Monday in order to keep the project on track. Because Jake realizes that he is asking them to go beyond their usual duties, Jake tells the team how much he appreciates them and that he will work with management to make sure that no additional *critical* scope changes will be introduced before the product launch. Jake tells them that he will protect them and make sure the organization understands that no additional changes will be allowed.

If Jake has the trust of the team, they may be more than willing to put forth the additional effort because they know the project needs it and because they know that Jake will minimize these types of exceptions. If Jake does not have their trust, the team may not believe his promises to protect them and not be inclined to put in extra time over the weekend. Worse, if the level of mistrust in the organization's ability to contain continual changes is greater than their faith in the PM, they may distrust Jake by default.

In dealing with the stakeholders and sponsors, trust is absolutely critical. They have to be able to believe that when Jake says, "We will make this deadline," that they will. What is more important, they have to be able to believe Jake when he says, "If we do not make the following changes, we will *not* meet our deadline." Jake's ability to succeed as a leader of the project is predicated on his ability to get what he needs from the organization. The stakeholders and sponsors control the ability to provide what is needed to succeed. They have to believe that when Jake says, "I need...," that project success is dependent on meeting that need.

To get the best out of the team for the organization, Jake is going to have to find a way to earn their trust. Likewise, he is going to have to quickly build trust with the stakeholders so that they believe what he says, and react accordingly.

## 4. Solution

The solution sounds simple, but isn't. The project manager needs to find a way to build or rebuild trust with the team members and stakeholders. Building trust successfully is not an easy task. The tips below should help you get started.

## 5. What should I do?

Building or rebuilding trust will require different approaches, depending upon the situation. Finding the solution for your particular situation may require a bit of trial and error, and it is largely dependent on your personal experience, management, and social abilities.

Over time, you will end up developing your own set of tools and techniques to employ for building your trust network and personal brand within an organization. Here are ten tactics to help you get started. Used with care, and in combination, they can be very helpful:

### 5(a) Walk the walk

In any situation, one of the best ways to build trust is to demonstrate that you hold yourself to the same set of standards you are asking the teams and stakeholders to meet. Lead by example and show them that your actions speak as loud as your words.

### 5(b) Quick wins

Acting quickly can be particularly effective when taking over troubled projects. In order to rebuild trust, setting expectations that can be met quickly allows you to show both the team and the stakeholders that things have changed, it is a new day, and with you as the PM, things will get done.

### 5(c) Take the hit

As a project manager, one of your biggest responsibilities is to protect the team. As the project leader, one of the ways you can do this is to place yourself in the path of blame directed at the team. When you *take the hit* for the team, it allows members to maintain their focus on the work they have to get done, and demonstrates that you've got their back. This can also show the stakeholders and sponsors that you are not afraid to take responsibility when it means keeping the team focused on the deliverable. This tip comes with a word of caution, however; showing the team that you are willing to stand up for them is one thing—doing it so much that it enables the team to repeatedly underperform is never a good thing.

### 5(d) I'm just like you!

Many people build affinity in order to establish trust. If you are able to establish commonality between yourself and the team, stakeholders, and sponsors, you may get a bit of a grace period during which you get the benefit of the doubt and have some time to establish other, stronger tactics of trust building.

### 5(e) Mr./Ms. Experience

One of the more common tactics for trust building in a work situation is to share your previous experiences. This can be a great way to gain trust and confidence if your stories are able to demonstrate how you have worked successfully through tough situations in the past. If you employ this tactic, do so with caution. If you end up starting stories with, "Back in my day . . .," you may end up losing more trust than you gain, so state why the story is relevant to *now*. Keep in mind that members of your team may also be able to present experiences of their own that can contribute to the conversations that help develop trust.

### 5(f) Ride the pink elephant

One of the most terrifying and exciting things about being a project manager is that when no one else will call out the *pink elephant* in the room, it is your job to make sure everyone not only sees it, but acknowledges it and has a productive conversation about it. If you are able to establish yourself as the one who is not afraid to call attention to the situation or problem that makes everyone uncomfortable, but in a productive way that leads to greater transparency and problem solving, the organization will grow to trust and depend on your ability to step up and call out items that need discussion.

### 5(g) Refer to social tokens

Social tokens are another way to build affinity, which can lead to trust. A *social token* is a reference made to something that may not be directly tied to work, but will help establish that there is a shared interest between yourself and another person. They provide a kind of shortcut to rapport when you are getting to know new people. One very common way to do this is by injecting quotes from movies into normal speech. The simple phrase "Yeah, I'm gonna need you to go ahead and work this weekend . . ." uttered in your very best Lumberg, might not mean much to people who aren't familiar with it, but for those who have seen the movie *Office Space*, it can be a great way to demonstrate that you are able to see irony and humor in office life. Within the IT space, it is very common to have people reference science fiction. Books like *The Hitchhiker's Guide to the Galaxy*, TV shows like *Star Trek*, and movies like *Star Wars* or *The Matrix* can provide shortcuts to establishing rapport, which are gateways to trust. A project management-centered example might include referring to Frederick Winslow Taylor or Karol Adamiecki during a conversation with another PM. If they recognize the references, it would indicate that you are someone who had studied the history of project management. The great thing about social tokens is that if they are used well, they will be recognized by the people you have an affinity with, and you'll gain credibility there. For anyone who does not recognize them, they are not likely to register, and those people, well . . . they probably *aren't the droids you're looking for.*

### 5(h) Mr./Ms. Empathy

Demonstrating that you are empathetic with the people you are working with is a great way to start earning trust. It acknowledges the concerns (whether expressed or not) of the team and stakeholders. In order to be effective, empathy needs to be shown without seeming patronizing or phony. If people feel you are just going through the same checklist with everyone, they are not likely to trust that you are really concerned. Empathy is about finding a way to make people feel appreciated and special at an individual level. Acknowledging them and respecting their situation will usually result in appreciation for your ability to see things from their perspective, which leads to trust as they grow to feel that both of you are on the same wavelength.

### 5(i) The big stick

Part of being a PM is taking the lead with discipline. As stated above, it is important to lead by example, and to hold yourself as accountable as the team and stakeholders. When there are people who require corrective action or need to be removed from the project altogether, not following through will erode trust quickly. Once boundaries are established, maintaining them will first build trust in the new boundaries and then in the person enforcing them.

### 5(j) The enemy of my enemy

When all else fails, one of the fastest ways to build trust is to establish a common enemy. This trust is not expected to last forever, and may be gone as soon as the common enemy is gone, even when the common enemy is the project itself. But until that time, uniting against a common enemy (or problem or struggle) is one of the easiest ways to build a relationship because it allows two or more parties to work together toward a common interest.

*Two ways that don't work*

- *Great expectations:* Some project managers enter an organization with an expectation that they will be trusted, based on the fact that they are the project manager. A job title may grant you the benefit of the doubt for a short time, but unless you can find a way to earn the trust of the people you are working with, what you expected to be trust could become contempt.
- *The miracle worker:* There are always going to be project leaders who like to place themselves in the spotlight, find a crisis (even if manufactured), and then suddenly leverage their expertise and skill to save the day. While the goal of the *miracle worker* is to earn trust by solving problems, this type of heroic approach actually introduces complication and risk into the project, and is not likely to engender trust.

# 3.2 I don't understand what my stakeholders want.

## By Craig Curran-Morton

## 1. Problem

You have the project's scope, and stakeholders have provided you with their requirements. You want your next step to be design then build, but deep down, your inner voice is quietly saying, "I don't really understand what my stakeholders want."

## 2. Warning Signs

- You are lacking the ability to describe clearly and succinctly what your stakeholders want.
- Conflicts appear to be breaking out between project team members and stakeholders as they struggle to determine what they are supposed to be working on.
- Your team and stakeholders appear to have misgivings about misunderstood or improperly prioritized requirements.
- Your stakeholders keep asking you if you understand what they want.
- Your sponsor requests a sit down discussion about the importance of the stakeholder group and to confirm that you understand.
- When you think about the project deliverables, something does not feel right.

### Lost! Have You Seen My Stakeholders' Wants?

Phil was assigned to the project last month. He was new to the company's projects group, having recently been promoted from the field. He looked forward to his new role as project manager and threw himself wholeheartedly into his projects.

Unfortunately, the projects were not going well. No matter how many times he looked at the project documentation, he did not quite understand what he was supposed to be building. It was not like he didn't know the product. He had been working in the area for several years, and thought he had a good grasp on the systems. He just did not feel confident that he understood what his stakeholders wanted.

The stakeholders talked a lot and tended to go off in many different directions. He was trying to corral their ideas, but they were often confusing, vague, or conflicting. How was he expected to understand the mess of information they were giving him?

To make matters worse, Phil's project administrator, Bill, informed him that two of the project's key stakeholders had bypassed him. They were now talking with Debbie, his sponsor, about the project and their objectives. After Phil's last meeting with the two stakeholders, they commented several times how they felt he did not understand them, but he never thought that they would begin to bypass him. Knowing Debbie, if the key stakeholders were meeting with her, she would soon be meeting with him.

Phil looked at Bill and sighed. "Sometimes I wish I was back in the trenches slogging it out. Life seemed so much easier back then." Ring, ring. "That must be Debbie calling me now."

## 3. What will happen if I do nothing?

If you do nothing and proceed with the project, you will have big problems. While there may be various results, two occur most frequently. First, your stakeholders may stay quiet and let you build deliverables that no one asked for, no one wanted, and when the project is completed, no one accepts. Second, the stakeholders may choose the other approach and become very vocal about your lack of ability to manage the project. Either way, the organization, stakeholders, and project team will quickly lose confidence in your ability to manage projects, and you may soon find yourself working in the mailroom.

## 4. Solution

The solution to this problem is multifaceted and involves a combination of both deft, soft skills and hard, practical actions. Each item listed below is an option to consider, and each will get you closer to the destination of better understanding what your stakeholders want. Options include:

1. Asking questions
2. Discovery, validation, acceptance
3. Prototyping

## 5. What should I do?

A good project manager can step into the shoes of the stakeholders and concisely describe what they want, why they want it, and how the project will or will not meet those expectations. Good project managers have an inherent ability to build a rapport with the client, listen to the clients' responses, and understand their needs. These steps help to build stakeholder confidence in the project manager and the project. You can build your rapport with your clients and their needs by using these skills:

### 5(a) Ask questions

When stakeholders start to talk about a project, we often make the assumption that they have a clear idea of what they want. Often, this is not the case. In many instances, stakeholders may have not thought about what they want. This could be because they do not fully understand the problem in front of them; they may not fully grasp the real costs (time, money, resources, effort) of the project; or, they may be afraid of implications of the solution. Moreover, they may know what they want, but are not able to accurately describe a clear idea of what they want to you.

As a project manager, you must ask questions, and lots of them. The challenge is that we are often unwilling to ask questions. In asking questions, we often feel that we are letting inexperience, lack of knowledge, or lack of confidence in our own skills and abilities shine through for all to see. "If people see that I don't know what they want, they will lose confidence in my abilities as the project manager," is one common thought. However, that sentiment could not be further from the truth. You will accomplish two important results by asking questions. First, asking questions allows you to discover new information, validate your understanding, and remove ambiguity. The more questions you can ask, the more you will know, and the more gaps and holes will be filled. Second, through your questions, the client will be able to explore aspects of the project and the product that they may not have thought about before, allowing them to gain more clarity about what they want. With the increase in your and the client's clarity, they will have more confidence in your abilities as the project manager. If it is clear that you *get it*, they will *get you*.

The questions that you ask should be a combination of open- and close-ended questions. Asking open-ended questions (who, where, what, when, why, and how) will allow your stakeholders to provide you with an opportunity to take them on a journey to explore what they really want. These questions open the stakeholders up, and allow you to paint a broad picture. On the other hand, the yes/no nature of close-ended questions may help you to finalize boundaries of the total picture, gain definitive clarification, and understand what your stakeholders are willing and not willing to have included in the scope of the project.

Given this, you may wish to start with open-ended questions and come back to close-ended questions near the end of your exploratory conversation. There is no set rule, and you can mix open- and close-ended questions as your judgment tells you. The following are a list of open- and close-ended questions that can be effective in understanding stakeholders' needs:

*Open-ended question examples*

- What are you hoping to accomplish as a result of the project?
- What are some things that you want the project to do?
- What is out of scope for this project?
- When will you know that the project is complete?
- What does project *success* look like to you?
- What does project *failure* look like to you?
- When must the project be completed? Why?
- Who will own and maintain the final product?
- How will the final deliverables be transitioned from the project to the owner?

*Close-ended question examples*

Unlike open-ended questions, which tend to be generic, close-ended questions are often very project-specific. The following are some examples of effective close-ended questions:

- Do you want training to be included in the project?
- Will you accept the project coming in after your due date of January 31?
- You have said you would like the background to be blue. Do you want royal blue or sky blue?
- Are we able to come in over-budget?

### 5(b) Discovery, validation, and acceptance

A good project manager, after discovering the requirements of the client, will not take those as the definitive requirements and will look to ensure they are correct. The PM will come back to the stakeholders to validate those requirements and gain acceptance. A simple and useful process that you can adopt is called discovery, validation, and acceptance (see Figure 3.1).

- *Discovery:* At this stage, you are a blank slate that needs to be populated. With an open mind, a nonjudgmental approach, and your assumptions in

**Figure 3.1**

check, you meet with your stakeholders in interviews or focus groups, and ask them a series of prepared questions to help better understand their wants. Your focus is to ask questions, document the responses, and capture as much information as you can.

- *Validation:* Once the discovery sessions are complete, take all the information you have gathered from the participants and sift through it. Create a document that outlines all the requirements and information you have gathered from all of the meetings. Categorize the results by functional and project areas. You can further sort out the information based on categories that are appropriate to your project. Spend time understanding exactly what your clients said and did not say. Identify any gaps in your understanding. If you have concerns or questions, document them. Return to your stakeholders to validate and confirm that what you heard and documented is an accurate reflection of their wants. Capture any new or changed information.
- *Acceptance:* Once you validate what you heard, take your documentation and make the necessary changes. Return to the stakeholders one final time to gain acceptance of your understanding of their wants. At this point, you should have an understanding of what they want, and they should know exactly what they are getting.

Your goal with this process is to capture the information, validate your understanding, and gain acceptance from your stakeholders. It can be done throughout the lifecycle of your project from initiation through closing. Moreover, you can use it on a number of different types of documents including product requirements, project requirements, project plans, implementation plans, product reviews, and project close out reports.

The risk of this process is that it can add additional time to your project. It takes time to capture, validate, and gain acceptance on information. However, it may benefit you by minimizing rework and changes in the later stages of your project.

### 5(c) Prototyping

When you are unable to understand the wants of your stakeholders, or they are unable to understand your efforts, turning the words into a picture can help. As the saying goes, "A picture is worth a thousand words." You can use the technique of prototyping to provide examples of what you understand the stakeholders are looking for.

Based on your understanding and keeping details to a minimum, you create an example of what the final deliverable will look like. Your prototype can range from a simple drawing, process diagram, template, layout of a report, or screen mock-up. Use any medium that you feel is appropriate. It is recommended that you don't spend too much time building the *perfect* prototype.

The focus of showing a prototype is to confirm or disprove your understanding of the stakeholders wants. When they see the prototypes, you will be able to tell quickly if you captured the essence of their wants or if you are off base. Given that this is a simple experiment, if the prototype fails, don't consider it a failure. Sometimes it is just as important to understand what stakeholders *don't* want. Prototyping can be used at various stages of the project, but is particularly useful in the early stages of concept and design.

# 3.3 My team members misunderstand or will not follow my directions.

By Jerry Manas

## 1. Problem

You think that you communicated clearly to your team what was needed, but for some reason, team members chose to do things differently. Tasks are often forgotten or being done incorrectly, and extraneous tasks are being added that were not in your instructions.

## 2. Warning Signs

- Your working relationship with your team feels like it lacks depth.
- Deliverables are missing components.
- Reports or forms aren't being filled out correctly or on time.
- Work is being done incorrectly or with poor quality.
- You are feeling frustrated and questioning everyone's ability to perform.

### Moving from Compliance to Engagement

Bill is a hard driving program manager who has nothing but good intentions. His portfolio of projects includes efforts that span the organization and several smaller ones that are related. New efforts often pop up *out of the blue* from various sources. In an attempt to control the chaos, he created a standard methodology for incoming requests and work management. But people aren't following it, and the few people who complete the proper forms don't fill them out correctly. Mark, the VP that Bill reports to, wants to know why nobody is following the methodology, and asks Bill to suggest ways to ensure compliance.

Shelly, one of Bill's team leads, always immediately said *yes* to anything Bill asked. The problem was in the follow-through. There was none. Shelly's *pleaser* personality and supportive approach did not move things forward.

Ralph, another team member, felt like he was Bill's translator. He consistently restated Bill's mandates, so that *people know what they need to do.*

Other team members tended to work in isolation and felt that as long as they did what was right, things would be ok.

Bill called a meeting to talk to the people who were not following the process, and what he learned was enlightening. For one, they never felt engaged in creation of the process, and felt it was overtly bureaucratic. They didn't understand what half of

*Continues*

## 3. What will happen if I do nothing?

If nothing is done, you'll begin to resent your team, trust will break down, customers will be unhappy with the work results, and you'll never really know whether the root cause is due to miscommunication or another issue.

the information would be used for, or why it was needed. Moreover, they had so much other work to do, they felt the information was an unnecessary burden that did not add value.

What should Bill do now? Hitting people with more *orders* doesn't feel right, but he had to find a way to get people engaged, moving toward the right objectives in a positive way.

## 4. Solution

The key is to identify the root cause of the issue. It could be that you are not communicating effectively; it could be that people don't feel engaged in the process; or, other factors could be leading the team astray. Your role as a leader is to identify the possible factors and systematically rule them out, removing any barriers that may exist.

## 5. What should I do?

First, you must find the cause of the problem. In his book, *Fixing Performance Problems* (2005), executive coach Bud Bilanich, also known as *The Common Sense Guy*, proposes that there are eleven reasons why people may not be doing what they're supposed to, and that we need to rule them out in sequence. According to Bilanich (2005), the reasons are:

1. People don't know *what* they're supposed to do.
2. People don't know *why* they should do what they are supposed to do.
3. People don't know *how* to do what they're supposed to do.
4. People think the prescribed methods will not, or do not work, or believe that their way is better.
5. People think other things are more important.
6. People think they are performing in an acceptable manner.
7. Nonperformance is rewarded.
8. Good performance feels like punishment.
9. There are obstacles to performing that the individual cannot control.
10. There are no positive consequences for good performance.
11. There are no negative consequences for poor performance.

The first three reasons deal with communication, specifically your ability to communicate *what*, *why*, and *how*. Be sure that your instructions are clear and simple enough to not cause confusion, yet presented within the context of the big picture. Offer guidance and coaching as needed, commensurate with people's individual readiness to operate independently (i.e., the *situational leadership* model, touted by Paul Hersey and Ken Blanchard in their book, *The Situational Leader*). Milestone lists can help people stay on track of pending deadlines. In addition, people must understand the core concept of the mission, along with guiding principles that can help them make independent decisions. Most importantly, confirm that people understand why they're being asked to do what you want them to do, including particular timing constraints and ties to value for the customer.

Note that reasons 4, 5, and 6—why people don't do what they are supposed to do—refer to instances where people's perspectives differ from yours. It may be beneficial to confirm if they are correct. Being closer to the action, they may have insights you may lack. If necessary, ask them to make a case, stating why their opinion is correct. Sometimes, this gap can be avoided by including them in the planning to begin with.

Reasons 7 and 8 deal with how you leverage people. If they perform poorly and you do nothing or give them easier work, then you are in fact rewarding poor performance. On the flip side, if you burn out your best people by relying on them for everything, you run the risk of making them less effective and possibly causing resentment.

Reason 9 speaks to issues that are outside the control of your team. Few things happen in isolation. Often there are outside variables that create barriers to performance. A systems approach (examining the causal relationship between potential variables) can help you identify and address those factors.

Finally, the last two reasons deal with consequences, positive and negative, for work performance. Good performance should be reinforced through informal and/or formal recognition, and, if possible, financial or other rewards. Ongoing poor performance, once other factors are ruled out and any barriers are addressed, must result in negative consequences, or, if appropriate, removal from the team.

# 3.4 What should my relationships with my team look like?

By Aaron Smith

## 1. Problem

You've just been named the project manager of an important initiative and, as is often the case, the project team was chosen for you, based on available resources. You worked with a few of the same people on previous projects, but many team members are new. It is apparent right away that there are diverse skill-sets and a broad range of personalities on board for this project. Several team members have had problems with project managers in the past, and others are complete unknowns. It is a diverse team mix that could prove to be a tremendous asset—or a thorny burden. You know you'll need to establish a good working relationship with all of the team members in order to maximize their individual and collective value to this important project.

## 2. Warning Signs

You probably need to reevaluate your relationships with the project team if:

- Work feels more like hanging out with your friends than getting things done.
- Team members voice concern to you or each other that they don't know where they stand in terms of roles or expectations.
- Team members rarely, if ever, come directly to you with questions, issues, or concerns about the project.

### Different Teams, Different Relationships

Karen is managing a large, multisite system implementation. Based in New Jersey, the project requires her to manage teams locally, and at a distance in Atlanta, GA, and Montreal, Quebec. Each team's makeup and motivations are extremely different, and Karen is running into different challenges with each team.

The team in New Jersey is filled with people whom she had worked with before, both as peers and subordinates. She knows these people socially and professionally, and the lines are often blurred. Sometimes project shortfalls end up being *okay* when they shouldn't be acceptable. It feels like things are a little beyond her control, but she deals with it the best that she can.

The team in Atlanta is aware that the project, once completed, could make some of their jobs unnecessary. They are understandably tense and far from motivated. Karen doesn't ignore the unpleasant reality or gloss over it. However, she doesn't know how to deal with their concerns. They are distracted in so many ways. What can she tell them that will get them focused on their work in a positive, productive way? She can't make guarantees of employment, and empty promises never help.

In Montreal, the situation is different, but equally challenging, for Karen. A previous on-site project manager had left, but not before weaving a web of distorted expectations in the minds of senior management. The disconnect between the executives' perspectives and the reality of the project is now weighing heavily on the shoulders of the team, which feels betrayed and under intense pressure to deliver features that were unrealistic and poorly defined.

Karen is facing an atmosphere of distrust and resistance. In a group meeting, she tries to lower the temperature by letting team members vent. The result was a confusing mess of complaints, creating an atmosphere of hopelessness and despair. She ended the meeting by letting people know things had to change—the problem was that she didn't know what those changes looked like.

What should she do now?

- Team members resist participating in meetings and avoid project communication channels, such as email, intranet, or voicemail.
- Team members do not seem to be enthusiastic about collaborating on project challenges or suggesting solutions and new opportunities

## 3. What will happen if I do nothing?

Everything will seem ok for a while, then suddenly it will become clear that the project cannot be salvaged. From a career perspective, you will have to battle back from having a reputation for being *green* or *junior*, rather than adding to a successful track record. Without a productive working relationship with the project manager, team members will quickly start to feel lost, handcuffed, or uninspired (sometimes all three, as they can be related). When that happens, project risks and other problems will go unreported and unaddressed. Fresh ideas and potential opportunities will not be discussed. Team morale will suffer, along with teamwork and honest communication. Your project, however promising, is likely to fail.

Any relationship takes a lot of work. In the world of projects, it also takes a focus on goals and the work. Disregarding your team relationships or making them entirely personal is a dereliction of duty, akin to ignoring the project's mission or discounting its strategic goals. You must do something, so what are you going to do?

## 4. Solution

As the saying goes, "No person is an island," and no project team should ever feel like it is working on an island. As the project manager, you should be the face and voice of the project. You need to make sure each team member can clearly *see* and *hear* you; likewise, they need to know that they will be seen and heard.

You must be fair and consistent in your dealings with the team, it goes without saying. But you also need to acknowledge that each team member is an individual, with different strengths and weaknesses, work styles, and motivations. That means you want to try to be flexible and attentive to each relationship as it evolves. A formulaic approach will only garner formulaic relationships. You want more. You want the best that each team member has to offer. The trick is to develop depth in these relationships without making them mostly personal.

The ultimate goal is to find how your team's individual talents can best serve the project as a whole, and how you can *help them* make that happen. This requires honesty, respect, and support from you. In return, you can rightfully expect, and should receive, the same honesty, respect, and support from your team.

## 5. What should I do?

### 5(a) Define your role

Before you can define what you expect from team members, you need to describe what they can expect from you throughout the project. Make it clear, in no uncertain terms, that your eyes are always on *the prize*. From project kickoff to closeout, they should be completely confident that everything you say and do is in the name of project success.

### 5(b) Set expectations

Once you've established your role, you need to set expectations for the team as a whole, and for each team member. Some of these expectations will be universal, regardless of the project or team makeup—accountability for their work and effort, commitment to the goals of the project—and some will need to be tailored to each individual's skill set. This requires time for discussion, questions, and clarification with each team member. Expectations can't just be handed down *from on high*. Yes, you are ultimately in charge as the project manager, but to establish productive work relationships and generate buy-in, you want these expectations to serve as motivational tools, not emotionless dictates.

### 5(c) Be available

From the start, some team members will have no qualms about letting you know exactly what they think and how they feel. Others will be less inclined to speak out in the presence of their peers. Whether your preferred managing style is open-door, walk-the-floor, or more reserved, it is critical that you make yourself available to team members for private, one-on-one conversations. These talks can be much more informative than what results in formal meetings.

With more introverted team members, these *protected* exchanges can reveal ideas or issues that are bubbling under the surface. With more vociferous personalities, one-on-one talks can help lower the volume and clear the air without the drama of a wider audience. In both cases, the earlier and more frequently that conversations happen, the more likely you are to mitigate tensions and avoid unwelcome bombshells deeper into the project.

### 5(d) Be appreciative

Diligent team members are bound to bear down on their daily tasks and responsibilities. When they occasionally look up from the work at hand, they should feel that their contributions are being recognized and acknowledged in relation to the bigger picture.

Appreciation can't be conveyed in monthly status reports. Make it personally meaningful by thanking them face-to-face whenever possible. In addition, make their contributions visible to the rest of the team and sponsors by giving shout-outs to deserving team members in weekly meetings, as well as in formal group settings. Recognition is a powerful relationship-building tool.

### 5(e) Be trustworthy

You can't expect team members to openly share their concerns about the project if there is any apprehension that bad news will affect their standing or be shared in a detrimental way with peers or superiors. If a culture of fear existed on other projects in the organization, make it clear that it won't exist in your project. It might be difficult to convince an individual who has been *burned* before; others may prefer to play politics. But showing that you value honesty over personal calculation will eventually pay dividends—be it uncovering festering problems or encouraging realistic estimates and assessments of current risks.

### 5(f) Be congenial

It doesn't hurt, and can often help, to show interest in your team members' lives outside of the workplace. This doesn't mean you have to step outside of your comfort zone or try to feverishly form friendships with everyone, although that might happen naturally. The point is, professionalism and collegiality are not mutually exclusive.

Knowing that a team member has a parent who is ill, for example, is an important insight into their state of mind, and offers guidance for how you might approach them on a work issue. Knowing that a team member has a passion for classical music or a sport team, on the other hand, provides a comfortable outlet for easy conversation that can go a long way to strengthening your working relationship. In the end, a team that knows you care about them beyond spreadsheets and timelines is a team that will almost always work harder for you and the project.

### 5(g) Be yourself

Finally, there is no substitute for authenticity. You don't want a job that forces you to be someone else. That won't bring you satisfaction, and it won't be effective in leading others. Be yourself, and at the very least, your team will know who they are with in the trenches.

# 3.5 What should my relationship with my sponsor look like?

By Ty Kiisel

## 1. Problem

You ask yourself, "What should my relationship with my project sponsor look like?" You feel like this relationship should be well defined by the organization in the same way that jobs have descriptions, goals, and measures, but that is not the case. Unless you work in a very mature project environment, your sponsor probably doesn't know what he or she is supposed to be doing either. This situation can cause your project to struggle and ultimately fail.

## 2. Warning Signs

Although the following list is by no means all-inclusive, here are a few warning signs that the relationship with your project sponsor is not working and needs attention:

- You can't remember the last time you had a conversation (let alone a status meeting) with your sponsor.
- Direction from management or your sponsor is missing or inconsistent.
- You do not know how your project's goals fit into your organization's goals.
- Project goals are not clearly articulated or understood by management or the project team.
- Every time you see your sponsor, they avert their eyes and head off in the opposite direction.

### One of the Greatest Project Management Successes

Most people agree that the engineering feat of the U.S. transcontinental railroad was one of the greatest projects of the nineteenth century. In fact, many consider it to surpass the building of the Erie Canal in the 1820s and the crossing of the Isthmus of Panama by the Panama Railroad in 1855 (two other great engineering triumphs of the nineteenth century).

On May 10, 1869, when Leland Stanford drove the Last Spike (or Golden Spike) at Promontory Point, Utah to link the United States from Council Bluffs, Iowa in the east to San Francisco, California in the west—travel from coast to coast was reduced from six months to about one week.

The six-year project included hundreds of laborers from the Central Pacific Railroad and the Union Pacific Railroad, and would have even challenged project management professionals using today's sophisticated software and other communication tools. Much like projects today, the Transcontinental Railroad required a dedicated project team, skilled project managers, and committed stakeholders. Here are three traits most successful projects share:

1. The project has a clearly defined business objective, and everyone (project teams, project managers, sponsors, and stakeholders) understand exactly what it is.
2. Executives are committed to seeing the project through to the end.
3. There is a shared sense of determination to finish the project by everyone involved.

Among the reasons that the events at Promontory Point, Utah were possible include a dedicated list of sponsors and stakeholders, including President Abraham Lincoln, who was a big proponent of the Transcontinental Railroad. Without his and other sponsors' dedication, their continuing support and belief in the benefits that a cross country railroad would deliver, the project would never have happened. Any project that doesn't include an active sponsor is like laying the hammer on the ground and expecting it to hammer the spike itself.

## 3. What happens if I do nothing?

Although ignoring sponsor problems and trying to complete a project on your own may seem like a logical option, it probably isn't. Sponsors have a crucial role in successful projects; they likely just don't know what it is. If that's the case, it's up to you to educate them *before* your project fails—or better, before your project begins.

## 4. Solution

A project sponsor's role is one of ally, liaison, and mentor. Their relationship with executive leadership gives him or her an opportunity to promote and champion the project, making it easier for you to complete it. Here are a few suggestions to help you work well with your project sponsor:

- Your project sponsor needs to contribute to a clearly defined business case, including a well-defined business objective.
- You are responsible to ensure that the project has executive commitment to see the project through to completion.
- You and your sponsor need to foster an atmosphere where you can meet regularly together to address status and other project-related issues.

## 5. What should I do?

Your relationship with the project sponsor is about creating a shared understanding of roles and responsibilities. People naturally gravitate toward a situation where they can be critical, but are not responsible for outcomes. This is especially true for sponsors because they are typically in a greater position of power than the project manager. However, the trick can often be finding the place where everyone's interests come together. Then, you can put a structure in place that helps you create the results you want. One or more of the approaches below may help.

### 5(a) Begin well—We Are the Champions, My Friend

Start with an understanding of what you and your sponsor can both get behind in terms of goals and strategy, and then attack together. Like many people who graduated from high school in the late 1970s, our class anthem was *We Are the Champions* written by Freddie Mercury and performed by the rock group Queen. I think it worked. It was never, *I am the champion*; it was always *we are the champions*. I think the same is true for successful project-based work. From team member to stakeholder to executive, we're in it together (whether *we* know it or not).

For project sponsors, *championing* the project starts *before* the project starts. Even in organizations without a project management office (PMO) or formal project evaluation process, savvy project managers understand that helping sponsors start off correctly makes sense.

Ideally, it's the sponsor who identifies the need for the project and therefore understands the *personal impact to them* of the project's success or failure. Without getting into a lengthy discussion, for most projects, the sponsor relationship begins with a business case or at least the identification of the estimated business value gained by a potential project. Ideally, the sponsor is responsible for justifying the project or the business case. Then he or she will need to count on you to help start the project off right. Before a project begins, it is up to the sponsor to identify the following:

- The project's fit with the mission, vision, and values of your organization
- How the project aligns with corporate strategy and financial goals
- The project's risk profile
- The resources required
- The economic benefits and costs (the business value of the project)

Depending upon the sponsor, as project manager, you might need to fill in some of the blanks on the business case. This is good because working with your project sponsor as he or she builds the business case could help your relationship at a number of levels:

- It starts dialog and provides an opportunity to create a healthy project relationship with your new sponsor.
- It gives you input early in the process concerning resource requirements, costs, and potential risks. It also gives you the opportunity to suggest realistic risk mitigation plans.
- It provides a means to evaluate just how committed the sponsor is to seeing the project through to completion.

In other words, part of your relationship with a sponsor is to make sure that there is a good foundation for building the project plan. Working *together* to champion the project to stakeholders and executives helps ensure that they understand the business value of the project and are committed to seeing it successfully completed.

### 5(b) Committing—Well begun is only half done.

A sponsor is an important part of getting a project off on the right foot, but importance doesn't end there. It's not enough that your project team and your sponsor are committed to seeing it through to the end; executives and other organizational leaders need to have the same commitment to ensure that the project environment remains strong. When planning is complete, the role of the project sponsor shifts to becoming the public face of the project to the executive team, keeping them informed and excited about the business benefits that the project will deliver.

That requires the sponsor to remain informed and up to date on the status of the project, to be prepared to answer questions from executive colleagues, and to be able to work with other executives to help secure resources and solve problems as needed.

### 5(c) Have I got a deal for you!

Although the image of a *salesman* might be a little over the top, according to marketer Jay Abraham, "The fact is, everyone is in sales. Whatever area you work in, you do have clients and you do need to sell."

Most project managers and project sponsors would never consider themselves salespeople, but if you are neither seen nor heard, no one knows you are there.

Project managers *and* sponsors have the responsibility to demonstrate how their projects provide business value. If a sponsor is unsuccessful at promoting the values of his or her project to the executive team, a potentially valuable project could be terminated in favor of something of lesser value with a more proactive sponsor.

Similarly, the sponsor needs to be a salesman for the project to the project team. The needs here are different and the sponsor is obligated to recognize those needs. The team may already be aware of *what* the project is doing, but they may not be aware of *why* it is important. If the sponsor is able to sell the team on the importance of the project and what it will deliver, the project manager will have a much easier time in motivating the team to go above and beyond to deliver a quality set of deliverables on time and within budget.

Finally, the sponsor needs to sell the project to the customer. If the *project manager* tells the customer how well things are going, that information provides a level of comfort; however, if the *sponsor* can talk about how much progress is being made, that information carries more weight. It's a fact of business life that information from more senior individuals is perceived as carrying more weight and importance, and that fact is no different when talking to customers.

# 3.6 People say they don't know what is going on.

## By Ty Kiisel

## 1. Problem

P. T. Barnum once said, "Without promotion, something terrible happens . . . nothing." Although he wasn't talking about promoting the goals of a project within the project team, he could have been. Keeping project teams focused on the right things requires that they know what the right things are. When team members don't understand how their role fits into the overall project objectives, there is no way for them to know whether or not what they are working on has any value.

Lack of project promotion inevitably leads to apathy regarding the project, poor morale, and a lack of team cohesiveness, which can lead to project failure. When project teams understand project objectives and know how their role contributes to that objective, they are in a position to do more than simply complete tasks—they are able to contribute to project success.

> **You Want Me to Do What?**
>
> Jeff looked around him at the rest of the project team to make sure that he wasn't losing his mind. No, it wasn't just him; everyone looked confused about what was going on. Jeff and the rest of the team had been sitting there for almost an hour, listening to the project manager talk about an exciting new project. Jeff had heard more details about what each team member was supposed to do than he ever thought possible, and certainly way more than he cared about, and yet he still didn't understand the point of the project.
>
> It seemed like everyone was expected to complete a huge amount of work (with little money and insufficient time), but without anyone knowing *why* the work was being done or *what* the overall purpose was. Jeff supposed that someone in the executive team thought that this was a good idea because they had signed off on it, and he guessed that the deliverables would be useful to someone, but he had no idea who.
>
> Clearly, everyone else in the room who was sitting there listening to the PM go on and on about task assignments was thinking the same thing as Jeff, so this didn't seem as though it was going to be a very successful project. How could anyone expect the team to be committed to getting the work done if they didn't understand why it was important, what the purpose was, or why their piece of work was important?

## 2. Warning Signs

It is easy to see when individual project team members feel like they are *out of the loop*. Some of the warning signs are:

- Team members fixate on things that either don't add value or actually detract from the project's original objectives.
- Team members are confused about what they should be doing, or keep switching between tasks.
- Poor morale and apathy regarding deadlines and milestones cause unnecessary project delays.
- Comments are made or questions are asked about what is being done and why it is happening.

## 3. What happens if I do nothing?

The project may still succeed if team members know enough about the project to at least be able to complete the tasks that are assigned to them at any point in time, but there will be a tendency for people to merely *go through the motions*. Productivity will be lower and the chances of a successful project will be greatly reduced. In addition, the overall project atmosphere will suffer with staff feeling insecure and lacking in confidence. Lower productivity will show up as a lack of focus, greater absenteeism, and more team conflict. The project manager may also likely find that there is less support from their team, and he or she will have less insight into what is really happening on the project.

## 4. Solution

The solution to this problem is straightforward in theory; it's just a matter of making sure that your team members understand the objectives of the project, why it is being undertaken, and what their role is. Of course, the implementation of that solution is more complicated, requiring:

- Explaining the purpose of the project in a way that the team can relate to
- Allowing each team member to connect their role with the overall project purpose and deliverables
- Keeping the project team informed without bombarding them with excessive information that does not help them to complete their tasks

## 5. What should I do?

The key to success is to be consistent throughout the project. Start the project with an explanation of the initiative, the circumstances that led up to the project being approved, and the expected outcomes. Provide the same information to all team members, and provide the same message (subject to changes in circumstances) throughout the project.

### 5(a) Explain the purpose

Historically, management styles used to focus on providing employees with only the information that they needed to complete the tasks assigned to them. In the case of a project team member, an example might be to take a part from person A, do tasks 1, 2, and 3 to that part within three days, and then pass it on to person B. Technically, that's all that the team member needs to know in order to perform assigned tasks, but it's not going to motivate the employee to go above and beyond.

Today, we recognize that employees work better if they have a sense of purpose, if they understand why they are being asked to do what is expected of them, and if they know how their efforts contribute to the overall project and its deliverables.

As the project manager, it is your responsibility to ensure that your project team has that understanding of what the project is expected to achieve, why that's important to the sponsor, the customer and other major stakeholders, what will happen if the project is not completed, or if it is not fully successful (late, over budget, below quality, etc.). You need to allow for questions and be prepared to answer them accurately and fully. In turn, you made need to research the answer and report back to the team.

### 5(b) Connect individual roles to the project's purpose

After you have provided the team with a solid overview of the project, its purpose, and objectives, the team will have a much better understanding of what they need to collectively achieve, and as the project proceeds they will be able to pull together to achieve those goals. However, individual team members may still be struggling to understand how they are expected to contribute to those goals.

If team members don't feel that they are making a relevant contribution to the team, it can be worse than not understanding the purpose of the project at all. They may feel alienated and inadvertently excluded from what the team is trying to achieve because they don't understand how they fit in. However, a team is like a well-built machine—every part plays an important role, and if one part is not functioning correctly, everyone suffers.

The PM needs to ensure that every team member understands how their contribution fits within the project as a whole. At a micro level, *fitting in* consists of ensuring that they understand how their tasks integrate with the overall work breakdown structure—the pieces that come before, and follow from, their work. Once that is established, the PM needs to help the team member see things from a macro level—how their piece contributes to the most visible deliverables of the project. If a team member understands that a major deliverable cannot be achieved without their contribution they will feel a sense of ownership and connection to that deliverable, and hence feel like a valuable member of the project.

### 5(c) The right amount of information

So far, we have looked at the need to provide team members with the context around the project (why it is being undertaken) and how to connect individual contributions to the overall project. We also need to remember that the team exists to complete work on the initiative—the scope of their work is limited to the tasks that are assigned to them.

It is therefore important to balance the amount of information that is provided—enough to allow them to understand how they fit in without drowning them in unnecessary data that they don't care about. This can be difficult because that may be a different amount of information for each individual. Make sure that you ask yourself:

- Does this information help team members to understand the project and its purpose?
- Does this information help the individual members understand how they contribute?

If the answer is, "No," to both questions, you are probably providing too much data.

### 5(d) Always act consistently

Team members look up to the project manager as an authority figure on the initiative. As a result, they hold the information that you provide in high regard. Team members rely on the PM to provide information, and they want to be able to rely on that information to give them practical assistance and to help with their sense of well-being as part of the team.

As a result, it is extremely important that the PM is consistent in the information that he or she provides to the team. If you contradict yourself or fail to explain changes that have occurred, you will be faced with comments along the lines of "But you said. . . ." Not only will that require you to explain the contradiction, it will undermine the trust that the project team has in you and may eventually lead to a drop in productivity and in the team's commitment to the project.

At the same time, you need to communicate when things change. Projects evolve and sometimes the original purpose or priority changes. It is important to share that information with your team, even if they will see it as bad news, but do so within the context of why things are changing, and make sure that they clearly understand that those types of changes are not a reflection on them.

# 3.7 I can't get people to see my point of view.
## By Gina Abudi

## 1. Problem

You can't get others on the project team to see your points of view on the project, such as, the best way to get things done, thoughts on assignment of tasks, how communications on the project status should be distributed, the best ways to approach a specific situation, etc. Because of this, the relationship between you and your team members is strained; they just won't listen to your thoughts and opinions. You cannot seem to influence others on the project to get the things done that need to get done. Your thoughts on the direction the project should take are ignored. It takes longer to resolve issues and make decisions because the team is not collaborative. Your effectiveness as a project manager is slipping.

## 2. Warning Signs

There are some things to look for that will let you know if you are not communicating with others in the best way possible, including:

> **What Am I Doing Wrong? I Can't Get People to See My Side!**
>
> Joe was getting frustrated. He has been trying to tell the project team his point of view on the best way to approach the project, and he can't get the others to listen to him. They never pay attention to his suggestions. It is frustrating for Joe; he has some good ideas on how to move forward with the project that he wants to share.
>
> Abbie has recently accused Joe of pushing his ideas on others and not listening to their suggestions or taking their input! Joe has been doing this job for quite a while, and knew he had the best approach to take to resolve the problem, so what's wrong? Frankly, he was in charge of the project and that meant if something went wrong, he was responsible.
>
> Joe felt that his point of view on a subject should hold more weight than the other team members. He was willing to listen to them—Abbie was wrong when she said he wasn't—but there wasn't time to argue; they needed to keep moving forward. The sponsor wanted the project completed in a short timeframe, so he really needed the team to understand the reason he was trying to get them to change how they were working on tasks. He needed to think about how he was going to get the others to see his point of view. He needed to quickly figure out how to better communicate with the project team.

- Team members seem to *tune you out* by having side conversations, walking out of the room when you are talking, or interrupting you.
- No matter what you say, someone argues the point with you.
- Even when you know that the idea you are presenting is the right one, the team doesn't seem to want to go with your idea.
- You are frequently reminded by team members that they do not work for you.
- Conversations with team members are frustrating; it seems as if everyone always has their guard up around you.

If any of these situations is apparent in your team meetings or in conversations with individual team members, you are having a problem communicating effectively with others to get your point across.

## 3. What will happen if I do nothing?

Poor communication is not a problem that will go away on its own. The team members will continue to be noncommunicative, disagreeable, or combative, and you will continue to be unable to get your point across or communicate effectively with others to help them to see your point of view. The project is likely to fail, and as the project manager, that will inevitably reflect on you, especially as the post mortem will identify communications issues. You will continue to be unsuccessful in getting your point of view across on other projects, and will have difficulty building strong relationships with team members.

## 4. Solution

You need to understand the individuals you work with, and learn more about them and the best way to communicate with them effectively. You are not in an easy situation as a project manager—you just can't tell people what to do, how to do it, and when to do it—they don't report to you. Frankly, even if they did, you still can't be effective in that way.

The most effective project managers know how to influence others to get project tasks completed without having authority over them. This requires an investment in building relationships with your team members and recognizing that they each have different needs. It also requires that you spend the time necessary to ensure that people understand the direction you want to take (your point of view) and why that is the best direction to move in—if it is.

Remember that as a project manager you are not always the subject matter expert; you don't know everything. There are others on the project team who are the subject matter experts in certain areas of the project, and you need to learn to trust their judgment and rely on them to do the right thing.

As the project manager, it is up to you to ensure that the time predicted to accomplish the task(s) fits within the overall project schedule. If it does not, simply demanding a change does not work; you will need to work with the subject matter expert (project team member) to figure out how to best get the work done on time to ensure the project's success.

## 5. What should I do?

Here are the steps you'll need to take to get your point of view across to the team members. Remember that communicating effectively is the key to your success, and ultimately the success of the project. It's important to remember that others on the project team have something to contribute, and their points of view are as valid and important as yours. Sometimes, they have the best approach to the situation.

1. Understand why you are not being effective in trying to get your point across.
2. Start to build better relationships with project team members.
3. Provide details of the direction you would like to take (your point of view).
4. Discuss with the team, listening carefully to others' points of view, and collaborate as a team.

5.  Explain the final decision and how it was made.

Now, let's look at each step in a little more detail.

### 5(a) Understand why you are not being effective

First, you need to understand why you are not being effective in trying to get your point across to the team members. What is it in your approach or style that is failing? Do people feel they are being listened to? Do they have a chance to provide their point of view and have it considered?

You might try talking with a few team members from past project teams to get their thoughts on why you are having difficulty getting your points across to others. Ask them how you might do a better job in communicating. You might also ask others in the organization (or friends outside of work) how effective you are in communicating with others. Ask people what their perception of your communication style is—are you collaborative, or do you try to coerce others to do things your way? If you are coercive—as in bullying others to get your way—you will never succeed as a project manager. Only by being collaborative with others can you succeed. If you find that you tend to be more coercive in your approach than collaborative, you will want to take steps to change your communication style. This change should include being very conscious of how you are coming across to others when you work on a project team.

### 5(b) Build better relationships with team members

Many times, a leading cause of not being able to get others to see your point of view is because you have not established relationships with them; there is no basis of trust from which to start. People need to know who you are, what you are about, and what is important to you. Additionally, you need to understand where they are coming from so trust can be built into the relationship. Too often, spending time getting to know the project team is skipped because the focus is on the project deliverables, timeline, and budget. However, by establishing rapport with others on the project team, you can better understand what is important to them, and that will enable you to better communicate with them.

Establish rapport by asking how the members of your team are doing. Check with them to see if they need support in accomplishing their work. Building an effective project team includes developing strong working relationships. When your team members feel that they are listened to and heard, and that you care about their ideas and who they are as a person, they are more likely to listen to your point of view. This in turn allows you to communicate more effectively and collaborate with them to get done what needs to get done—not through coercion, but through teamwork. Remember that these aren't just your team members, they are also people.

Body language and vocal tone play an important part in what you are saying, and what the team members are hearing, so you need to make sure that the way you present yourself supports the words that you are using. When listening to others, be an *active listener* by showing with body language that you are listening and interested in what they are saying.

Avoid letting your frustration show. If people need to ask questions for clarity, let them do so without becoming upset or insecure, which will serve no purpose other than to alienate them. As a project manager, you are responsible for creating a collaborative environment for the team. By doing so, project team members feel like their opinions matter and their work is of importance.

Remember again that you will not always have the right answer. Through collaboratively working with the other project team members, not only will you be able to get your point across, but you will better understand their points of view and, as a team, choose the best approach to the situation.

### 5(c) Getting across your point of view

Effective communication is key! Prepare for what your message (point of view) is and how you will deliver it. How you communicate with the project team members makes all the difference in the world in effectively getting your point across and getting decisions made to the benefit of the project. You need to be able to *read* people and how they are taking in what you are saying, that is, whether you are being effective or not in presenting yourself and your ideas, and whether you are being clear or if there is confusion among the listeners. Ask yourself, "Am I right? Are there alternatives I am not considering? Am I demonstrating to the team that I am listening? Is what I am doing working, or do I need to try something else?"

As you present your point of view, be clear about the facts you base your information on: due dates, budget requirements, stakeholder requirements, past proven experience, and such. Explain your point of view clearly by including all information needed to make a decision. It is important that everyone on the team has the same information on the project to ensure that points of view can be discussed intelligently and collaboratively. Project team members need to understand what is behind your particular point of view, and you need to understand what is behind their points of view, to ensure the best approach is taken.

To be effective, a *heads up* of what you will be presenting *prior* to the team meeting is of help. There is no need to go into lots of detail, just a high level overview of what needs to be addressed, indicating that you have an idea of how to address the issue but would love to also hear ideas from the team. This enables team members to prepare for how they might address the issue or problem, so that they can share their thoughts. When working to get across your point of view:

1. Provide the project team with an overview of the direction you want to take on the project.
2. Provide the background behind the direction, such as why you believe this is the best direction to take, including information about whether it has worked before and relevant information that you are basing your point of view on. Discuss what resources are required, the time it will take, impact on the project, and so on, from your point of view. Be specific.
3. Watch the project team as you deliver your message: Are they receiving it clearly? Do they look confused or concerned? Are side conversations going on? Frequently ask questions to ensure they are on track with you. You are

not asking them to agree with your point of view, but rather to clarify understanding. If you are not being successful, change your approach.

### 5(d) Ask the team for ideas

Open up discussion on the point of view you presented to the team. Ask them, "What are your thoughts? What are your ideas? Do you think it will work? Do you have any concerns? What ideas might you have? What is the best way to move forward?"

As the team responds to these questions, make sure that you are listening to their ideas and opinions, and demonstrate with your body language that you are listening. Whatever other points of view are put on the table should be discussed by all. Ask again, "Will it work? Will it solve the problem or address the concern? What is required to accomplish it? Will a combination of ideas work?" By opening up discussion with the team rather than immediately making a decision, you lower resistance to your point of view and are more likely to gain acceptance in the end.

If you can't complete the discussion during the meeting, arrange another time and day to continue discussions. You want to be seen as a collaborator, someone who takes the time to consider all options, even if you are convinced that you have the best option to move forward. Even if you are the final decision maker on the path to be taken, you will have built up less resistance by spending time getting the team involved and collaborating with them. The greater the consensus that you can achieve, the easier it is to achieve the goals.

### 5(e) Make a decision and explain it

When you make the decision on the approach to take, explain the decision made and why it was made. Why are its benefits better than the other options presented? If your final decision is a combination of points of views presented during the team meeting, make sure that is clear. Ask for team members' support in moving forward with the decision. However, remember that while consensus is important, responsibility for decisions still lies with you as the project manager—you are accountable to the stakeholders. If someone has concerns, address the concerns immediately, but be prepared to move forward with your decision. Team members will respect your decision when they have had a chance to participate in the process and their points of view have been heard.

# 3.8 Someone on my team has an answer, but I can't get it out of them.

## By Andy Jordan

## 1. Problem

As the project manager, you are completely dependent on your team members to provide you with their expertise. Team members are assigned tasks because of the skills and knowledge that they have, and your job is to manage those activities as effectively as possible. But what if your team isn't contributing, and what happens when you ask for ideas to solve a problem and no one offers suggestions? What happens if the response to specific questions is always, "I don't know"? How can you get your team to contribute to the overall problem solving of the project?

> **Is There Anybody There?**
>
> Natalie sat at the head of the table in complete disbelief. She knew that there must be any number of her team members who had a solution to the problem that the project was facing. As project manager, she had called people together to come up with ways that the issue could be resolved and no one was saying anything.
>
> Natalie had started by asking for suggestions, and everyone had just sat there looking at the desk, avoiding eye contact with her. Then she had specifically asked a few people that she was sure knew what needed to be done, and they had just shrugged or muttered something about not having any ideas. It was so blatantly untrue that Natalie was lost for words.
>
> What was wrong with these people?

## 2. Warning Signs

This problem can be difficult to spot—how do you determine that someone is withholding the answer rather than genuinely not knowing the answer? However, there are warning signs that you can look for:

- Team members are evasive; they don't want to look you in the eye or discuss the matter.
- People start expressing an opinion or idea, but then back down and won't talk anymore.
- The team talks among themselves, but won't discuss the issue with you, ending conversations when you walk by.
- Team members answer questions with, "I don't know," when their knowledge and experience suggests that they should know the answer to your question.

## 3. What will happen if I do nothing?

Doing nothing is not an option in this scenario. If you don't address the issue, then you will not get the answer to the problem that you are trying to resolve on this occasion, and you will establish a precedent that the team doesn't have to contribute towards solving problems that arise on the project. Lack of answers, solutions, and participation by the team will lead to potentially more significant problems later on in the project.

## 4. Solution

To solve this problem, you first need to understand what is causing it. The symptoms that you are observing—a reluctance to answer questions or offer solutions—could be caused by a number of different factors, and the way that you solve the problem will depend on the specific situation that you are facing. To be sure that you are solving the problem correctly you need to:

1. Create a project environment for open communications
2. Understand why there is reluctance to offer a solution
3. Overcome the barriers to communication
4. Reinforce and reassure team members

This chapter shows you how to get there.

## 5. What should I do?

If you have team members who are reluctant to contribute, there is a problem with the environment. Something is leading to a lack of trust or a feeling of insecurity that is coming to the surface through one or more people shutting down and not contributing. This may be because they *can't be bothered*, or it may be that they want the project to fail—but these are both highly unlikely scenarios. It is far more likely that they are either unsure that their solution is the right one, or they don't want to speak out and embarrass themselves. You need to recognize this insecurity and create an environment where your team and individual members can feel comfortable in proposing ideas and solutions.

### 5(a) Create an open environment

If you haven't created the right environment for open communication, you have no chance to succeed at having team members offer solutions and suggestions. You need to make sure that there is an environment where everyone can offer opinions without being belittled or mocked by others. You also need to ensure that suggestions are given appropriate consideration—if someone makes three suggestions that are completely ignored, then they will be unlikely to offer a fourth.

If team members feel that they can't speak up because someone more senior than them in their team is also on the project, then you can also lose a lot of valuable contributions. Create an atmosphere of equality by holding meetings where *job titles are left at the door* and you are a group of equals working to find a solution to a shared problem.

Make sure that you deliver on your promises because that will be the best way to build trust with your team members. If you promise to update people on a meeting with your sponsor, but then don't deliver that update, then you are damaging the likelihood that people will volunteer information on a totally unconnected topic because the relationship is damaged.

### 5(b) Understand the reluctance

If you have created an environment where people feel comfortable sharing ideas and opinions and you are still having difficulty in obtaining a solution, you need to find out why that is the case. You may not know exactly who has a solution, but you should know which two or three people are most likely to know the answer. If they aren't sharing, despite having a safe environment, there are only a few likely reasons:

- They aren't comfortable offering their opinions at the time or in the place that they are being asked. Perhaps they are too shy to speak in a meeting and would be more comfortable in a one-on-one environment.
- They aren't confident that their solution is the right one.
- They feel that someone else on the team should be offering the solution.
- They have talked to colleagues about their ideas outside of the meeting and received a negative reaction.

As the project manager, you need to understand if an issue is causing the reluctance in the current situation, so that you can work to overcome that reluctance. The good news is that you don't need to get it right the first time; you can work through the list above until you find the basis of the problem.

### 5(c) Overcome the barriers

Once you identify the person or people who are most likely to have answers, you need to go through the list of potential reasons for them not offering a solution, and decide which reason is likely. This may be easy—a quiet person may not feel comfortable speaking up in a meeting environment. In other cases, it might not be obvious—there may be a reason that you don't know about. For example, perhaps the person spoke to a more senior colleague about their solution, and received a very negative response.

Next, create an environment where you and the person, or people, can work through the challenge while minimizing the barriers that exist. Even if the person is usually comfortable speaking up in a group, this is likely to be a one-on-one conversation because that will reduce any potential embarrassment, remove any potential problem caused by another team member, and be more effective.

The specific direction that you take to address the problem will depend on what you feel the specific reluctance is, but you can work through some possibilities with a number of different questions. For example, you can ask individuals one of these questions to start a dialog:

- Did you have more thoughts on what the answer might be in this phase of the project?
- Do you have any ideas or solutions as to what might work? It doesn't matter how unlikely it might seem, we really need some ideas.
- Did any ideas come up when you were talking with colleagues about this?
- Did you consider any possibilities that you ruled out?

Think also about the physical environment where the conversation takes place. For example, if you think that the problem may be that colleagues reacted badly, it might be worth arranging a *water cooler* type of conversation, or bringing it up in a scheduled discussion with the individual to cover another topic. In that way, you are minimizing any potential difficulty that the team member experiences.

### 5(d) Reinforce and reassure

When you are able to overcome the reluctance that team members had and can get them to contribute potential solutions to the problems that the project is experiencing, your work still is not done. What you have achieved is to have the team member trust you to a greater degree than they previously felt comfortable with. You need to demonstrate that you deserve that trust; otherwise, you can permanently damage the relationship and be unable to have the individual contribute again.

You need to keep any promises that you make, and be careful what you promise. For example, if the issue was that a senior team member was negative about the individual's idea, it wouldn't be unusual for the junior member to ask you not to mention it to the senior member. That is not a promise that you can keep because, if someone on your team is not contributing to a positive project environment, you need to address that with them.

Do not make a bigger deal of the issue than necessary. If the reluctance was simply a case of someone not being comfortable speaking in a group, there is no real problem to solve. You don't need to "force" someone to speak up in a meeting, but make sure that they are comfortable approaching you individually if they have some ideas on solving problems.

# 3.9 How do I deliver bad news?

## By Andy Jordan

## 1. Problem

Maybe you have finished a status meeting and discovered that the project is not going according to plan. Or maybe you came out of a meeting with the customer or sponsor, and they have told you that there are some fairly major changes needed on the project. However it has come about, you now have some bad news to deliver to your team, and you know that it's not going to be well received.

You need your audience to focus on what needs to happen next, not get stuck on the emotional reaction of how unfair the news is, or how something could possibly have happened. How do you do that?

## 2. Warning Signs

Any project problem or change has the potential to be perceived as *bad news*, and you need to be prepared for any eventuality. Signs that the audience may see or are seeing the news as bad include:

> ### I Can't Believe This Is Happening...
>
> Have you ever had one of those days? You come to work in the morning and everything's great, but as soon as you sit down at your desk with the first cup of coffee, the project sponsor sticks his head around the corner and asks, "Have you got a minute?" Fifteen minutes later you suddenly find that the customer wants to move the schedule for delivery up by four weeks. They are offering good money to do it, but that's a month's less time to get the project completed, and the team isn't going to like hearing this request.
>
> Just as you are wondering how to deliver that message to a team that's working to their maximum, there's another visitor. Your senior developer walks in with a long face and tells you that the technical team has hit a major problem. The first set of performance tests show that the system isn't capable of coming anywhere close to the performance figures that the project calls for, and the only solution is to completely redesign the software. It's going to delay you by at least two weeks.
>
> You look at the clock. It's not 9:30 yet, and already you are having a nightmare of a day. You stare at the phone wondering which piece of bad news to deliver first. Either way, there are going to be a lot of angry and upset people who will doubtless blame you for the news. Maybe you should just leave things for a while before telling people what's happened.

- The news will have a significant negative impact on the project and cause more work for your audience.
- The news will impact the ability to meet the triple constraints of time, budget, and scope.
- The person or people with whom you need to communicate have been very definite about their expectations, and the expectations are different from what you need to tell them now.
- The audience has been working in a stressful environment where one more thing could prove too much.
- Before you have finished delivering the news, the audience is pushing back and the questions all start with, '"Who?" or "Why?"

## 3. What will happen if I do nothing?

Bad news does not go away just because you don't tell anyone about it. Instead, things tend to get worse and you are left with not only the original bad news to deliver, but also having to explain why it took you so long to communicate the news in the first place. At best, you delayed the ability of your audience to assist in resolving the problem or adapting to the change under the circumstances. At worst, you have lost your credibility with the key people with whom you have to work, and are faced with managing a project where neither the stakeholders nor the project team trust you.

## 4. Solution

Projects rarely go exactly according to plan, and you shouldn't expect them to. That means *bad news* is a fact of life for project managers. You need to be able to deliver it in an objective way that allows the news to be heard and understood, and then allows everyone to focus on how to deal with the problem and keep the project moving forward. You need to:

1. Ensure that you fully understand the problem yourself.
2. Consider how your audience is likely to respond to the news and create an environment that will help ensure that you get them to focus on the facts and the required actions, rather than on emotional reactions.
3. Work with your colleagues to identify alternative solutions and actions that will allow you to get past the problem.

## 5. What should I do?

Let's start with what not to do: panic! When you hear some bad news, there is a natural tendency to think of the consequences, and human nature being what it is, we tend to think about the worst case scenario. You are the project manager, and people will be looking to you for guidance to correct the situation, which can be a good thing. It gives you a chance to control the situation, but first, you have to understand what is going on. It doesn't matter whether bad news is as a result of a tightening of the schedule, additional scope, delays, or any other reason—you need to stay calm and focused.

### 5(a) Understand the issue

You can't deliver bad news unless you understand it yourself. The team will have questions and you need to be able to answer them. When you hear bad news, you need to go through the following steps:

1. Make sure that you have heard and understood the message. If the bad news is in writing, reread it until it is clear; if the bad news is in a conversation, don't be afraid to ask the speaker to repeat what they have said.
2. Ask questions for clarification or additional information. You need to make sure that you completely understand what you have heard and have the full picture. Try to avoid written exchanges, as they can leave too much up

to interpretation. However, if you received the news via email, try to reach the sender in person or on the phone. As an obvious example, if stakeholders are asking for the project to be delivered a month early, make sure you understand whether the scope or the budget are also changing and to what extent—you will need that information to move forward.

3. Consider the audience to whom you need to deliver the message. Think about what the news will mean for them, the areas that concern them, and the questions that they are likely to have.

4. Decide how you are going to deliver bad news. Can you meet face to face with everyone with whom you need to talk? Should you deliver the message to the group all at once? Do some people need to know earlier than others?

When you are sure that you thoroughly understand the news, the impact it is likely to have, and the way it needs to be delivered, only then are you ready to deliver the bad news.

### 5(b) Create the environment

Wherever possible, avoid using written forms of communication. It may sound appealing because it is more convenient, but you can't control the way that people will interpret it, where and when they will read it, or how they will react. It also makes it harder for people to ask questions, and it doesn't allow people to support one another as they hear the bad news. Most importantly, it may come across as an attempt to avoid the issue on your part.

If you deliver the message individually, you run the risk of repeating yourself and answering the same question over and over. Additionally, getting everyone together in a group means that they will all hear the news at the same time, preventing rumors from starting. Everyone will hear the same message, and the same questions and answers, and they will be able to support one another.

On the other hand, some messages need to be delivered in a one-on-one setting. For example, if the news involves people losing their jobs, then you need to sit down with people individually and explain the situation to them. That is not a message that should be delivered to a group.

Consider what will be expected of you. Do you have to deliver bad news to your team or to a customer, sponsor, or group of stakeholders? Different groups will look for different things from you—your team is looking for leadership and confidence that you can help them get through this, and stakeholders are looking for evidence that you are on top of the issue and that you have a plan of action to solve the problem.

### 5(c) Deliver the message

Bad news is difficult to deliver, and it won't get better over time. You need to deliver the message as early as possible (bearing in mind preparation) so that you can start working with people on getting past the news. There are a number of things that you need to bear in mind when delivering the message:

- *Be positive*: People will gauge their reaction based on the way that you deliver the message. If you make it sound as though the situation is hopeless, then your audience will react hopelessly.

- *Don't beat around the bush*: You are there to deliver bad news and spending five minutes avoiding the topic or talking around it is not going to help—it just raises the anxiety level of the audience.
- *Don't play down the issue*: You know how bad the news is, and pretending that it isn't a big deal isn't going to work. People won't believe that the news is not serious, and you risk losing credibility.
- *Don't deflect the blame*: We all know that there can be a tendency to shoot the messenger, as done in ancient Greece, but trying to get away from your responsibility by blaming other people is not the right approach.
- *Don't take sides*: Phrases such as, "I can't believe that they are doing this to us," will not make the message any easier, and it can easily make enemies of a group of people that you rely on to get the project completed.
- *Don't assume that you know how people feel*: Everyone reacts differently to bad news and phrases such as, "I know how this must make you feel" don't help—you do not know how each individual feels.
- *Give people time to process the news*: Significant events take time to be processed. You need to give people a chance to start to come to terms with the news before you try and get them to focus on the solutions or next steps.

### 5(d) After delivering the message

Once bad news is delivered, provide your audience time to come to terms with it. Depending on how bad the news is, and to what degree people are going to be impacted, that may take a few minutes or several days, but people will need that time and you can't force them through it or away from it.

How you can make the biggest contribution is by helping the team to move forward. The time that you are delivering the bad news is not the time to start talking about the action plan to recover because your audience won't be paying attention. However, you need to help people see that this isn't the end of the world and that they can be part of the solution to the problem. Regardless of whether the audience is composed of stakeholders or team members, you need to help them work to identify and implement a solution. That will allow them to focus on moving forward, rather than getting stuck on the problem.

You may need to deliver the same message several times as people process the news, and it may take some people longer to accept it as real. That's okay, people react differently. However, if you are consistent in your messaging and focused on the steps necessary to move forward, people will believe it.

For example, if you have just told stakeholders that you can no longer deliver the project on time, within budget, and within scope, you need to present recommendations as to how to move forward based on your understanding of the priorities. If date is the main driver, then present the stakeholders with options for modifying scope and modifying budget. Discuss the pros and cons of each option and work together to agree on the best approach.

If your audience keeps reverting back to the bad news, then it is an indication that they may not be ready to move forward yet, and they may need more time to come to terms with the situation. As the project manager, you have to make sure that people focus on the solution, not on the unfairness of the problem.

# 3.10 I can't get management to resolve an issue or dispute.

By J. Chris White

## 1. Problem

Your project has major issues and everyone knows it. But, when key issues have to be decided, upper management either takes too long to make their decision or removes themselves from the decision-making process completely. As the project manager, you feel like you have been abandoned to resolve everything yourself.

## 2. Warning Signs

This problem is fairly easy to recognize, and as project manager you are likely to be the first person to experience the problems. The warning signs include:

- Team members will often *wait around* for decisions to be made before they can move forward with work.
- Many decisions that need to be made on the project are *above your pay grade*.
- Project deliverables are sometimes late because of delays in issue resolution.
- The end customer is starting to get frustrated with decision delays.
- Decisions that need to be made keep getting passed around in upper management like a *hot potato*.

### Who Is the Boss?

Elaine's frustration was reaching an epic level. She had been handed a new product development project midstream that was known to have several critical issues that might have a significant impact on the success of the project, as well as the happiness of the customer. She was assured that, even with all these issues, the rest of the management team would support her and make sure she had everything she needed to get the project back on track. With a nod of approval from upper management, she accepted the job.

That kind of supportive talk quickly turned sour. Elaine found herself stuck on several occasions because she was waiting on upper management to resolve some issues that were beyond her level of authority. The delayed decision making caused a few features on the new product to be delivered late. Two new features even had to be removed from the plan and put on a *future upgrade* plan. Not good.

Elaine was accustomed to pushing decisions up the chain of command for new product development projects because these types of projects tend to pave new ground. There are always problems that need higher level resolution. However, the lack of timely support she was receiving was extremely problematic. Yet, she didn't feel that she could demand answers from upper management. They signed her payroll check. She definitely did not want to *bite the hand that fed her*.

Elaine felt like she was between a rock and a hard place. If she continued to get no response or a slow response from upper management on issue resolution, her project would continue to suffer severely. But, she didn't want to put her job in political jeopardy by pushing too hard on her superiors. Should she just go ahead and resolve the problem herself?

## 3. What will happen if I do nothing?

If upper management does nothing and the situation continues, progress on the project will slow down and possibly come to a halt. Even if your project limps across the finish line and both you and your team survive this one, the delays along the way will cause your end customer to have doubts about the future performance of both you and your company. Even though it may not be your fault, the fact that you have your name attached to a late project will not look good for you professionally.

## 4. Solution

You have an administrative bottleneck. You either have to get management to resolve the issues that need attention in a timely manner, or remove the need for those particular managers to get involved. You need to:

1. Review the role that management as a group is playing—establish whether they are necessary for the issues that are present
2. Evaluate specific managers who are causing problems—establish whether they can be removed from the decision making process
3. Eliminate the problem or issue requiring a decision, if possible
4. Appeal to upper management for better support
5. Approach the customer

## 5. What should I do?

Nothing is more frustrating in the project management environment than waiting for someone else to make a decision related to your project. You no longer have control, and you have placed the project's fate in someone else's hands. In this particular case, upper management (or the level of management above you and your project) is the culprit causing delays.

### 5(a) Review the role

Before taking any rash action, the first thing to do is to review the issues or decisions that upper management is making to ensure that their involvement is really necessary (see Figure 3.2). Are they being brought in on the issue for political reasons? Is it an upper manager's pet project and does he or she like to micro manage? If there is justification for keeping these upper managers out of the decision loop (or at least out of a few of the decision loops), talk with your project sponsor or project executive on how to take action to reduce their involvement. You might get lucky and find out that upper manager actually doesn't want to be involved. He or she may have been brought in out of respect, rather than necessity.

Your project executive may be able to help you understand the original purpose of upper management involvement. More importantly, your project executive should be able to give you advice on how to handle the political side of things, so that no one is offended or feels slighted if you discuss changes to the approval process.

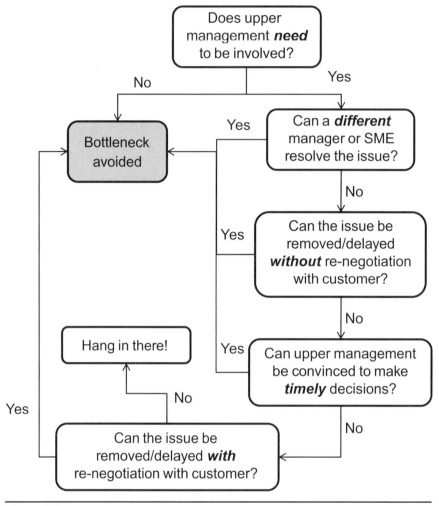

**Figure 3.2**

### 5(b) Evaluate the manager

If you find out that upper management involvement is necessary and adds value to the project, the next step is to find out if that *particular* upper manager is necessary or if there are other managers who may be able to fulfill the decision making role. As stated above, this situation can be treated as an administrative bottleneck. If you cannot remove the bottleneck, the next best thing is to increase the *capacity* or *throughput* for the bottleneck. Thus, if you can find another upper manager to fulfill this role, the new upper manager may have more available time (i.e., capacity) to help with the project. As an alternative, you may be able to find another subject matter expert in the organization who can make the necessary decisions, removing the need for the original manager to be involved. If the issue is a technical issue, it is often the case that the upper manager is not the most knowledgeable source, and that another technical person is better suited to resolve the problem or answer questions.

### 5(c) Remove the issue

If the involvement of upper management is necessary and the specific decision maker cannot be replaced, another option is to see if it is possible to remove the *decision* that needs resolution. This does not happen often. Most of the time, the decision or issue is there because it is necessary for the project. However, occasionally, a review of the scope of the project and its deliverables shows that some *decisions* that require upper management attention are not value-added.

Another option is to delay the resolution. Of course, the resolution is already taking too long (or else you wouldn't be reading this). This is a good move, however, if the issue is officially pushed to a later date on the project schedule so that it does not disrupt or delay other tasks.

### 5(d) Appeal to upper management

If you cannot find another upper manager to take over issue resolution role, and you cannot remove the decision from the project or delay it to allow other tasks to proceed, your last resort *within* the confines of your organization is to make a stronger plea to upper management that these decisions are crucial to project success, and that they need to be made in a timely manner to maintain sufficient productivity on the project.

Another discussion with your project sponsor or executive would help here, to see if he or she has any advice on how to make this demand a little more palatable for upper management. You definitely do not want to make enemies or offend anyone, especially when your project relies on them. This is an area where sponsors should be providing you with active support, especially since it is possible that the sponsor is a colleague of the managers who are causing problems.

### 5(e) Approach the customer

If the key upper management decision maker is not responsive and your project is still experiencing issues with late or incomplete deliverables because of slow issue resolution, the absolute last resort is to approach the customer to see if the deliverables or issues can be removed from the project, delayed, or pushed to a future project (e.g., next release of a set of software). If deliverables or dates cannot be renegotiated, then you must endure the project the way it is. Sorry!

# 3.11 My boss won't listen to me.

## By Luis Crespo

## 1. Problem

Regardless of what you have to say, your boss will not listen to you. It seems as though most of the time he or she is not interested in the project or what you have to report on it, and when they do take an interest, it is simply to instruct you on changes that have to happen. They don't seem interested in discussing anything, and there is no consideration for whether their instructions can be carried out within the constraints of the project.

## 2. Warning Signs

Lack of interest or listening from a boss is a problem that is fairly easy for a project manager to recognize and a problem that the project manager takes the brunt of. Some indications that you may have this problem include:

- Your status reports are not read.
- Your requests for actions or decisions are ignored.
- Your boss does not attend status meetings when required, or skips and reschedules meetings that you have scheduled with them.
- Conversations with your boss make it obvious that he or she is not aware of, or interested in, your concerns—the boss just wants the instructions carried out.

### Are You an *Invisible PM*?

It's 5:30 p.m. and status reports are due by end of the day. With the projects that Debbie is managing, it will take her at least until 9:00 p.m. to complete them all. Each weekly status report will be at least 5 pages long and emailed to a distribution group of more than 20 people, including her boss.

To Debbie's continued dismay, no one reads the status reports and most immediately delete the email. Her manager, who is the person requesting the weekly status reports, opens her report, but only glances at it and disregards the call to action where it states that there is a resource need on the project.

Later the next day Debbie sends a long email to her manager summarizing her status report in order to request the additional resource. The manager sees the email and reluctantly opens it. He sees the first of seven paragraphs and closes the email quickly. Unfortunately, he doesn't see the last paragraph requesting the resource.

During the next weekly status meeting to which the manager is a required invitee, he is a no-show. There is no management representation and the only attendees are Debbie and her QA and Dev team. Considering that the project is now in danger of slipping its date, Debbie had hoped for a better turnout.

Debbie needs to escalate the resource matter to her manager, so she sends him a meeting invite for later in the day. Determined to be as clear as she can, she puts in her invitation subject *Resource needed*. Her manager, seeing yet another email from Debbie, just ignores it. Debbie shows up to the meeting, but it's just her in attendance, as her boss is a no show.

Debbie has become the *invisible PM*, affecting her project and ultimately her job.

## 3. What will happen if I do nothing?

Not improving the situation will undermine your authority as a project manager. Your team will perceive that your boss does not listen to you and soon they will do the same. Another aspect of the situation is that stakeholders often observe which project managers have the respect of their supervisors and take that as a sign of how they should relate to the project manager. In their view, if the perception is that your supervisor will not listen to you, then why should they entrust their projects to you or trust your guidance and authority?

## 4. Solution

You need to understand why your boss is not listening to you. A solution should address the following areas:

1. An honest, open self-assessment of your communication style (or an assessment aided by someone who knows you)
2. A list of all the possible reasons as to why you may not be listened to
3. A meeting with your boss to solicit feedback regarding the matter
4. Formulation of a plan as to how to improve the situation
5. Follow up, including a review of progress and adjustments to the plan for improvement, if required

## 5. What should I do?

As the project manager, you need to formulate a plan that allows you and your manager to work together to get the project completed successfully. You don't need to be best friends with your boss, but you do need to be able to work together.

As with any plan, you will need to have certain deliverables to be successful. These will be: your self-assessment, your reasons list, a meeting with your boss, and your plan for going forward.

### 5(a) The self-assessment

When it comes to self-assessment, many of us balk because we either feel we know ourselves well enough or believe that there is nothing that needs to change. However, when we encounter a situation, such as when someone is not listening to us, it is critical to start with ourselves to ensure that we are doing all that we can do to promote sound communications. Communication problems are rarely the fault of just one person.

Since a self-assessment may be daunting, and since we may not be as honest with ourselves as we should, we should refer to someone who knows us or spends a considerable amount of time with us, such as a close friend or family member. The key is to be able to gauge whether or not our communication style is effective. If the boss is not listening to you, chances are that others may not be listening as well. However, bear in mind that people act differently in the workplace than in their personal lives.

You need to ask yourself the following questions:

- Would I listen to what I have to say?
- If I would not listen, what are the reasons?
- Is the tone of my communications appropriate?
- Is my style of communications effective?

- Do I tend to overdramatize my statements or exaggerate facts?
- Is it my vocabulary, or lack of it, getting in the way of communicating?

Based on your honest answers to this self-assessment, you should be able to identify some changes that you need to make. You have taken your first step to better communication.

### 5(b) The reasons for not listening

There are a number of reasons why your boss may be disinterested or not listening to you. It is just as important to review these possibilities as it is to complete the self-assessment:

- *The disinterested boss:* First, recognize that one of the reasons that your boss may not listen to you is that he or she is disinterested. They may be disinterested in your opinion, their job, the project, or any number of things. Be cautious of that disinterest because it is contagious. Make sure that your boss's disinterest does not rub off on your or your work effort. Your team still needs to feed off of your example and energy, so it is important that you keep a high level of interest.
- *The misunderstanding:* One common reason why communication fails between individuals is due to a misunderstanding. When a misunderstanding occurs, it usually causes one or both of the two parties to become less receptive to incoming communications. The misunderstanding could have been caused due to a variety of reasons, stemming from personality conflict to a perceived lack of knowledge or expertise. It is important to realize that this may be a reason why your boss may not be listening to you. Can you trace it back to a specific occasion or situation where there was a rift between you and your boss? Is it something you can resolve by apologizing or owning up to a misstep that you took? Can you *forgive and forget* a mistake that your boss made? Although this may bruise your ego, forgiveness may go a long way to improving your relationship and subsequently mending any communication lines that were broken.
- *Information overload:* Sometimes we tend to think that over-communication is good communication. However, the key is the right communication at the right time. It is possible that you are not being listened to because you tend to over-communicate. You ramble on in emails that never end, your status reports read like novels, and when you call a meeting people need to block off their entire day. This kind of communication style tends to close off people, especially supervisors, from listening to what you have to say. It may be that you said something important or something that required an action item, but it was buried in pages or hours worth of over-communication. In this scenario, you need to ratchet down the communications. The numbers here may be an exaggeration, but the point is to target communications appropriately in style, substance, and volume. As a project manager you need to stick to the communication plan you established, and ask yourself the following questions:

○ Would I have time to read a status report that is multiple pages long if I am responsible for a whole department and multiple project managers?

○ How do I feel when I get invited and have to sit through long meetings that should have only taken an hour or less, at most?

○ Do I truly read every email that I receive, and how do I treat emails in which I need to scroll down?

Once you empathize with your receiver, your communication style will change.

- *Your communication tone:* The old adage, "It's not what you say, it's how you say it," could not be any truer. You need to target your communication style to the needs of your audience, and the fact that this is communication with your boss does not change that. Some questions you can ask yourself:

  ○ Do I adapt my style to my audience?

  ○ Am I aware of my tone and body language?

  ○ Am I able to distinguish between enthusiasm and aggressiveness or uncertainty and timidity?

Based on the self-assessment and the reasons list, you should have more perspective before you move on to the next step, which is the meeting with your boss.

### 5(c) The meeting with your boss

When you are sure that your boss does not listen to you, you need to tackle the situation head on. If your supervisor finds your communication lacking, he or she will be impressed by the fact you are, at least, prepared to talk about the subject and have not only brought forward a problem, but also a likely solution. Your supervisor may have a preconceived impression of your abilities and skill set, so it is important not to reinforce any negative perceptions with negative behavior or attitudes during the meeting. Comments such as, "You never listen to me!" or "Why does no one listen to me?" will not gain you much favor or respect in a professional environment. Instead, begin with, "I have noticed lately that I have a challenge in trying to communicate my ideas to you, and I was hoping that we could use this time to help me with this. I have some ideas, but first, I would like to solicit your feedback—if there is something specific you see in my communication style or if you even feel that communication is an issue."

Make sure that you remain objective and provide tangible evidence of the problem that you are experiencing. For instance, you may let your supervisor know that you alerted him or her that your project was suffering from a resource shortage, which would cause project slippage. These alerts and requests went unanswered, and when the project slipped, your supervisor asked you why. In this case, you provided concrete evidence of a specific time when miscommunication may have occurred.

An important outcome of the meeting will be getting your boss's feedback on your communication style and substance. Your supervisor may tell you that the reason that he or she is not listening to you is that your ideas or your feedback is inaccurate or perceived to be baseless. Try to get your supervisor to provide you with some examples without sounding like you are performing an interrogation. Instead of saying, "Yeah, prove it!" try something like, "I really appreciate the feedback; could you provide me some examples so I know what to look out for in the future?" This may help turn around the perception of your supervisor about your communications. Although it may not make him or her begin to listen to you more, it will at least help you understand if there is some basis for their actions.

### 5(d) The plan

Although you walked into the meeting with your boss with a plan, you may have walked out needing to revisit it. Once you figure out how to fix your situation, or if there truly is a situation to fix, then you can put a plan in place. What does *a plan* mean? Through this process of self-assessment and feedback from your boss, if you found out you were an overcommunicator, your first order of business needs to be where to trim back. Is it your status reports, meetings, emails, face-to-face, or all of the above? Let's take the status report as an example. Most managers, especially at an executive level, will tell you that they will only read the first page of any status report. Knowing this is critical, especially if you know executives are part of your report's audience. Even if they are not, the rest of your audience will appreciate your placing all important or new information at the top of a status report. If you need additional detail on other pages, plan to not bury a call to action or an important risk at the bottom of page 5.

### 5(e) Moving forward

Having the meeting with your supervisor and formulating a plan does not mean he or she will start listening to you right away; it's going to take some time, especially if the reason was due to mistrust based on previous performance issues or a lack of communication skills. It is imperative that you take the feedback that was provided to you and put it into practice immediately.

Don't expect immediate changes on your supervisor's side, but make sure that if he or she felt that there was something lacking in your development, this is something which you can track and discuss at your next review. The worst thing is to have something to work on and not follow up and track progress on your plan. If it was a mix up, then there is no need to rehash, but watch out for warning signs that it may be happening again.

Communication is the most important aspect of your job as a project manager. You should see yourself as the chief communication officer of your projects. How you communicate, and how others receive your communications, greatly impacts your project success and overall career success.

# 3.12 I can't get the team to talk to each other effectively.

By Ed Evarts

## 1. Problem

My team members don't communicate well with each other. It seems that team members either don't talk to each other or when they do talk, the conversation doesn't move the project forward. Sometimes it feels as though talking makes things worse—members get distracted, tempers flare, and productivity drops.

## 2. Warning Signs

This *ineffective talking* problem can creep up on you. You likely won't find that it happens overnight, but occurs gradually. You only notice it when you compare today with the situation several weeks ago. Some indications that you might have a problem include:

- Team members are not engaged during meetings.
- Confusion reigns regarding deliverables, due dates, and core responsibilities.
- Team members are stressed when interacting with each other.
- Negative emotions and comments permeate team meetings.
- Relationships between team members are frayed.

### To Tell or Not to Tell—What's a PM to Do?

You made a decision to speak to your team about communication issues that you have seen and have heard about from others. Team members are not talking to each other effectively and team meetings feel like siblings squabbling at dinner. Some team members behave worse than others. Some team members seem to handle criticism well, while others crumble at the first sign of trouble. Some are aware of communication issues, while others remain oblivious.

As you plan for the meeting, you are suddenly struck by a question: Do you tell team members in advance of your desire to speak with them, or do you say nothing until the meeting itself? You find this question challenging due to the varying degrees of team members' participation in, and awareness of, communication challenges.

You don't want to risk people not showing up because they don't want to talk, but you also don't want people to be shocked at the start of the meeting and not be able to focus on the issues being discussed.

You also know that people will have time to think about what they want to say if you tell them ahead of time, but at the same time it also allows people to prepare *defenses* or negative comments.

You're not sure what to do.

## 3. What will happen if I do nothing?

Not addressing communication issues will result in continued deterioration of relationships and progress. Negative perceptions of peers will become further engrained, impeding the ability of your team members to speak openly. If reliable team members are not able to talk and share openly, others will fill in the gap with their own stories and information, which is often erroneous. Team members will become frustrated, which could lead to hurtful statements. The energy-fueling team spirit will be drained, and the success of the project will be in jeopardy.

## 4. Solution

Fostering effective communication among team members is a key accountability for a project manager. While there is no *one size fits all* solution when it comes to effective communication, two solutions exist that create an environment unique to your team, and where members can talk with one another in open and candid ways:

- Create a *Team Communication Commitment* document which states *rules of the road* which are generated and agreed to by team members.
- Build awareness of personality preference differences that determine how team members take in and share information.

## 5. What should I do?

If you have concluded that your team (not just one or two members) is not talking to each other effectively, you need to evaluate the situation immediately. To proceed with the project, without taking action, will make matters worse. Rationalizing that members are having a bad day, need to work it out on their own, or that the issue will go away, will not make this problem go away. You are responsible for getting relationships back on track before the project collapses.

So, where do you start? Follow this three step model to give a communication jump-start to your team (see Figure 3.3).

### 5(a) Step 1. Call a time-out

You need to declare to the team your concern regarding how members are communicating with one another. This isn't always easy or comfortable to do, so here are some ideas on how to build your comfort and confidence in taking this first crucial step.

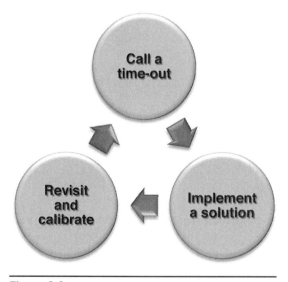

**Figure 3.3**

*Develop your message:*

How you say what you want to say is very important. Take time to think about how you want to convey your observations and practice your delivery. Find an individual in whom you trust to help you develop your message and provide you feedback on your delivery style. While the message doesn't have to be perfect, you don't want to shoot from the hip on this topic! Your team needs to see and feel the importance of the issue you are presenting to them. A well-crafted and well-presented topic will demand more attention and respect than an ill-crafted, unpracticed message. By being clear and candid, you have an opportunity to model the communication behavior you desire in others.

*Craft current state, impact, ideal state, and benefit statements:*

A key piece to your message, in addition to being clear and candid, is communicating the current state of the situation, the impact of the current state on the team, the ideal state which you believe will benefit the team, and the benefits of working in the ideal state.

1. *Current state statements* describe the situation as you see it. Your observations should be clear and to the point, supported by examples. Give examples that will help team members see what you are saying, help them relate to the situation better, and be part of the solution. Make sure your statements answer the following questions:
    ○ What are the behaviors I am observing?
    ○ What is a specific example of each of these behaviors?
2. *Impact statements* explain the positive or negative effects the behavior is having on the team. Impact statements describe the effects certain behaviors are having on the current team state, with examples to which members can relate. These statements typically answer the following questions:
    ○ What is the impact of this behavior on the team?
    ○ Why is this important to the team?
    ○ What are the consequences to the team of not changing this behavior?
3. *Ideal state statements* describe the best case communication scenario for the team. It can't hurt to aim high with respect to your expectations as long as your expectations are realistic. Ideal statements help members build a vision of what should be. Ideal statements are visionary and inspiring. Like ice cream to an eight-year old, team members should say, "I want that!" These statements typically answer the following questions:
    ○ What is the best way in which team members can talk to each other effectively?
    ○ What strategies can we use to enhance communication?
    ○ What do we do to get us back on track if one of us is not communicating effectively?
4. *Benefit statements* describe how positive modification of behavior will help the team. Benefit statements provide team members the reason—the

incentive—to talk to each other effectively. Benefits help members under-stand what is in it for them by actively supporting ideal state strategies. These statements typically answer the following questions:
   ○ What are the benefits to the team in addressing this issue?
   ○ Why are these benefits important to the team?
   ○ Why are these benefits important to me?

*Plan your timing:*

*When* you say what you want to say is very important. Take time to think about when to best deliver your message so you can plan ahead. A vacation week or a week when a significant milestone is due is not a good time to get everyone's at-tention. Devote a full meeting to the topic or, if you can only find a portion of a meeting, share your concerns at the start of the meeting. This way, the significance of your concerns will be clear, as if you are saying to the team: "This is important enough to discuss first." If you start to feel like no time is a good time, consider host-ing a special meeting, in a relaxed atmosphere, to focus solely on this topic.

*Request recommitment:*

Once you have successfully delivered the message, it is important to ensure that everyone is on board. The level of commitment needed in order to create your ideal state can be high. Follow these three easy steps to obtain commitment:

- *Ask* if any team member has additional questions, observations, or ideas.
- *Restate* your understanding of the ideal state and benefit statements.
- *Request* verbal commitment by each member, in front of the team.

Calling a time-out requires professional courage as it will impact the team. Certain areas of progress may be slowed, some members who talk to each other effectively may be surprised or confused, and valuable time may be lost. By crafting effective ideal state and benefit statements, you help your team focus on a future they can affect instead of a past they cannot change.

### 5(b) Step 2. Implement a solution

Now that you have clearly articulated the ideal state for, and the benefits of, effec-tive team communication, it is time to implement a solution for team member com-munication issues. Strategies exist in addition to the two solutions described earlier in this chapter, which are also very effective. Let's look at these two solutions again in detail:

*Solution #1: Create a Team Communication Commitment document.*

Communication challenges arise when team members are not clear on objectives, roles, responsibilities, timing, and expectations. To make matters worse, teams don't understand how to handle communication issues that arise on a day-to-day basis, and relationships and progress deteriorate quickly.

One solution that you can apply is the development of a *Team Communication Commitment* document. This document clearly details how team members will communicate with each other, and how team members will handle deviations from the communication plan. This solution is effective at the kick off of a project or at that point when you have determined that the way team members are interacting with each other is hindering the progress of the project.

A *Team Communication Commitment* document is easy to build. To be effective, make sure that it includes the following elements:

1. **Name the project:** Since some members may be on multiple project teams, create a project name so team members have a consistent label to be used when discussing the project. By doing so, all team members will be clear on which project you are referencing.

2. **Identify project team members:** If team members are going to be asked to commit to a set of communication agreements, you need to be clear on who is committing to them. By listing the names of the team members, each member's stake in the team increases. Statements such as, "I didn't think that applied to me" can be avoided.

3. **Create alignment statements:** You and your team will craft statements that describe the preferred methods for communicating with one another. This allows team members to openly share their ideas and feelings, as it relates to how team members should speak with one another. Sharing ideas and feelings openly enhances buy-in and clarity around expectations. Typically, this part of the *Team Communication Commitment* document is comprised of:

   a. Team meeting communications
   b. Email and texting communications
   c. Phone communications

These statements do not have to be numerous or complex. Here are some examples from each of these areas to help get you started:

**Team meeting communications**

- "I will speak only after a team member is done speaking."
- "If I disagree with a team member, I will respond in a respectful and constructive way."
- "If a topic of discussion is pulling the team meeting *into the weeds*, I will suggest that the key parties discuss the topic off-line."

**Email and texting communications**

- "I will use email only to share information. If I have an issue or concern with a team member, I will speak with him or her directly."
- "If I need to respond directly to a team member, I will ensure that I do not use *reply all*, resulting in team members receiving emails that are of little value to them."
- "If an email includes an action item or a need for an immediate response, I will highlight this on the subject line."

**Phone communications**

- "I will call or be available at the time scheduled."
- "I will be respectful of a team member's calendar and ensure that our conversation stays within the time scheduled."
- "If a conversation becomes heated, I will suggest to my team member that we meet face-to-face, invite the project manager to join our conversation, or defer the call to a later point in time."

4. **Create realignment statements:** In this section of the *Team Communication Commitment* document, you and your team identify remedies for behavior that is not consistent with the agreed upon communication guidelines. Not knowing how to handle deviations to your team agreements is a common reason for the deterioration in both communication processes and team relationships. By taking time to establish responses to communication challenges, your team has a tool kit for getting team members back on track. Using this tool kit will result in reducing emotion, sharing feedback candidly and professionally, and ensuring project success. Realignment statements are generally comprised of three areas:

   1. The *issue* you want to address with a team member
   2. The *impact* his or her communication style has on the team
   3. The *desired behavior* you expect to see going forward, consistent with previously agreed-upon alignment statements

The following are examples of alignment and realignment statements for you to consider:

**Alignment statement:** "I will speak only after a team member is done speaking."

**Realignment statement:** "I've noticed in our meeting today that due to your passion for the topic, you are jumping in and cutting off other team members before they are done speaking" (the issue). "When you interrupt another team member, you are not showing respect for his or her point of view. You may cause a team member to get frazzled and possibly lose a good thought" (the impact). "As a reminder, we agreed as a team that each team member would only speak after another member was done speaking. While I appreciate your passion, please give other members an opportunity to voice their perspectives before jumping in" (the desired behavior).

**Alignment statement:** "I will use email only to share information. If I have an issue or concern with a team member, I will speak with him or her directly."

**Realignment statement:** "I saw in an email you sent this morning that you are frustrated with the pace of work of one of your team members" (the issue). "Whether or not your frustration is valid, including emotion in an email risks significant misinterpretation by a team member" (the impact). "As a reminder, we agreed as a team that each member would not use email to express emotion. Speak to the other member directly if emotions begin to enter the conversation. Take some time to connect directly with team members if you find yourself getting emotional on a particular topic" (the desired behavior).

A *Team Communication Commitment* document creates a strong foundation upon which to build effective team communication and standards of communication behavior. When you develop this tool alongside team members, you will see a *sigh of relief* as issues that are problematic for other teams are discussed openly and solved collegially on your team.

*Solution #2: Build awareness of personality preference differences.*

Anytime that team members talk with one another, an opportunity to create a successful outcome is created. Whether team members are communicating to share information or brainstorm, communication has the potential to move a relationship and the project forward in a positive and healthy way.

When communicating with others, you spend most of your time practicing what you are saying, how you are going to say it, and when or where you are going to say it. Our focus tends to be on ourselves. Less attention is paid on understanding whom you are speaking to and how the listener will understand the information you are sharing.

A solution to help you understand the communication style of yourself and your team more effectively is personality preference. Each of us possesses personality preferences which act as default tendencies when interacting with others.

These preferences may illustrate themselves, for example, as extraversion or introversion. Extraverts tend to be more expressive when listening to you, by possibly smiling and nodding their head frequently. Extraverts think aloud and share openly in meetings. Introverts tend to be less expressive when listening to you, as introverts are processing internally the information you are sharing. Their reaction may come less expressively, or later. Introverts think quietly and share when they are ready.

Assessment tools such as the Myers-Briggs Type Indicator (MBTI), Majors PTI, Golden Personality Type Profiler, and Kiersey Temperament Sorter allow you to understand the personality preferences of team members, which will provide you insights on how individuals process information. When team members talk with one another, regardless of the topic, understanding their own personality preferences and the personality preferences of their peers will provide opportunities for a successful outcome.

## 5(c) Step 3. Revisit and calibrate

Now that you have called a time-out and have crafted either a *Team Communication Commitment* document or implemented a personality preference assessment, put into place a process for revisiting how the solutions are working. Just because the solution was crafted by the team and worked initially, does not mean it will always work. Players change, priorities shift, and time passes. On a recurring basis (not less than monthly or longer than quarterly), take time at a team meeting to ask team members how the commitment to the ideal and benefit statements are going, or if the strategies identified by increased awareness of personality preference are making a difference. Don't be afraid to suggest modifications to calibrate team energy and focus. Sticking with the original plan if multiple team variables have changed will return you to the point where you started. Revisit the team communication strategies and calibrate these strategies to ensure the team continues to build on success. You may find a need to call a time-out again, and you are now well positioned to handle how team members are talking with one another.

## References

Bilanich, B. *Fixing Performance Problems: Common Sense Ideas That Work*. Charleston, SC: Book-Surge Publishing, 2005.

Rath, T., and Harter, J. *Wellbeing: The Five Essential Elements*. Washington, D.C.: Gallup Press, 2010.

# 4

# NAVIGATING PEOPLE CHALLENGES

## 4.1 The office politics are killing me.

By Andy Jordan

### 1. Problem

You have enough challenges as a project manager without having to deal with office politics. When you find yourself caught between groups with different agendas and priorities, there is the potential for your project to be derailed. People put the needs of the project second, behind their need to establish and reinforce their political alliances and position within the organization. You can't be successful if people aren't focused on the work.

### 2. Warning Signs

This problem can manifest itself in a number of different ways, and it may not be immediately obvious that you are dealing with a political situation rather than any other type of people-related problem. Look for the following signs that may indicate that you are dealing with a political challenge:

- Actions are being taken by team members or decisions are being made by stakeholders that don't make sense from an objective project standpoint.
- People are focused on positions, opinions, and beliefs rather than the concerns of the project.

---

**If I Wanted to Be in Politics, I Would Have Run for Office!**

Sean sat down heavily into his chair and sighed deeply. He had just come from what must have been the worst status meeting of his project management career. It was clear that this project had fallen victim to office politics.

The design team had deliberately come up with the most complicated solution that they could in response to what they saw as an insult from the build team who had claimed that they were short staffed because, "there were too many high paid designers." The end users of the product were doing everything in their power to kill the project entirely because they were afraid that it would mean job losses, and Sean was pretty sure that the resource owner for the quality team was withholding people because she was upset that her project had been turned down in favor of this one. How would Sean drag the project (and his career) out of this mess?

---

- People are focused on groups to which they belong (such as organizational departments or geographic offices) rather than the project team.
- People are deliberately ignoring or acting against the project plan and your requests.

## 3. What will happen if I do nothing?

While a certain amount of office politics is inevitable, if you allow politics to take over your project, you will end up with different factions focused entirely on their own self-interests and the project will suffer. The best that you can hope for are significant delays and lost productivity; the worst to expect are attempts to sabotage the project by groups who don't believe it should be happening.

If political conflict is not dealt with early, it will only get worse and prove to be almost impossible to recover from. Not only will the delays be insurmountable, the damage to relationships will linger and destroy any trust that existed.

## 4. Solution

In order to solve political problems you need to first understand what they are about. You need to recognize that everyone has their own agenda, and that agenda doesn't always coincide with the needs of the project. You need to remain objective and not get caught up in the politics yourself, and you also need to recognize that you don't have to personally solve every problem yourself. There are a number of steps that you can follow:

1. Identify the political positions, the person or people holding those positions, and the reasons behind them.
2. Work with all parties to try to remove politics and identify appropriate channels for concerns to be raised and addressed.
3. Monitor for improvements, taking more formal actions if things are not getting better.

## 5. What should I do?

We all know that politics are inevitable in the workplace, but we shouldn't allow ourselves to view them as helpful in any way. By their very nature, office politics undermine organizational priorities because they force people to position themselves for their own advantage, not the best interests of the organization.

A project can be a political hotbed because it involves implementing change into an organization and that will always result in the potential for people to be *winners* or *losers*. You may find people who don't want the project to be implemented, want changes made so that the project is more useful for their group, or want the project deferred because it will take resources away from their own initiative. You may even observe people trying to oversell the project to make it sound more important than it really is in order to secure more resources. You need to deal with all of that.

### 5(a) Analyze the problem.

Before you can solve anything, you need to understand exactly what the challenge is that you are dealing with. Politics is a multifaceted problem. You need to establish:

- Who is causing political difficulties?
- What is their position, and what are they trying to achieve?
- How is the project being affected?

You might think that the people causing the problem are fairly easy to identify—they are the ones who are playing the political game. It's not always that easy, though. If you are having problems with team members from a certain functional area, is it because they are playing politics, or is the issue with their manager? This is an important distinction. If the problem is at a management level, you can't use their manager to solve the problem, and dealing only with the team members won't solve the problem.

Once you have identified the sources of the political activity, the next step is to try to understand what the individuals are trying to achieve. Political games are all about improving the outcome for the players, so as project manager put yourself in the shoes of each of the players and ask yourself what they want. Sometimes it's easy to tell. For example, if the implementation of a new system will result in a series of job losses, it's easy to understand why some people may be looking to sabotage the project. At other times, you need to dig deeper to identify the real agenda, such as another project that the disruptive stakeholder is championing or that a team member wanted to be assigned to. It's important to understand the true issue before trying to solve the problems.

The final piece of the analysis is to identify how the project is being affected. This can seem obvious, but be careful not to jump to conclusions. At one extreme, you may have a team member who is being openly hostile, freely claiming that another project should have been approved instead of the one that you are managing. The impact seems clear, but if everyone else on the project is ignoring them and getting on with their assigned tasks, the impact is minimal, so don't make it into a bigger issue than it really is. At the other extreme, you may have a very savvy politician who is undermining your project in a more sophisticated and subtle way. You need to make sure that you fully understand how far reaching they are, so that you can be certain that you understand all of the potential issues that you are facing.

### 5(b) Remove the politics

Once you are confident that you understand all of the players in the political games, what they are trying to achieve and what the impact on your project is, you need to act. You can't allow yourself to be drawn into political games, but you do need to act decisively and demonstrate that you are in control of the project. You need to remain objective at all times, and wherever possible you need to be sensitive to the positions that the political players hold. In many cases they are feeling insecure or threatened.

Take the following steps with each *ringleader* that you identified in the section:

- Speak with them directly and discuss:
  - The project and how it may be making them uneasy

- ○ The impact that their actions are having on the initiative (often the source of political games is unaware of how significant the impact is)
- ○ What you can do to try and ease their concerns (arrange for a conversation with the sponsor, provide additional information, etc.)
- Arrange follow-up actions and a review schedule to revisit how the individual feels and whether the project situation is improving.
- Document all instances of political interference between the meetings so that they can be further discussed and corrective actions taken.

It's important to confront people directly and to let them know that you are aware of what they are trying to do. Make sure that they understand that the project is suffering as a result. The meeting shouldn't be aggressive; it needs to be tackled in a constructive and objective manner. However, there needs to be a clear understanding that the disruption needs to stop or there will be further consequences.

You may be dealing with individuals who are more senior than you in the organization, but that can't alter your behavior. You are working to manage an initiative that has been formally approved by the organization and any political interference is counter to the organization's expressed wishes—you have the moral high ground.

In many cases, the open discussion with the individual concerned is all that is necessary, especially if it is combined with attempts to ease any anxiety that person is feeling. When the individual is acting through other people it can sometimes take time for the improvement to be noticeable, but because all parties know that their political actions are not aligned with the organization they will often improve their behavior when they are called on their actions. If they don't, you need to move to the next step.

### 5(c) Escalate as necessary

You are the project manager and responsible for implementing a project that was approved by others. You need to be able to explain the project's purpose and objectives, but you don't have to defend it. If you continue to experience political difficulties after trying to directly address the issues with the people involved, you need to escalate for others to deal with them. If the person is on your team, talk to their manager and explain the situation and the steps that you have already taken to address it. You don't necessarily want the person replaced, but you need to demonstrate that you are in control and you won't stand for people trying to undermine you or the initiative that you are leading. If the issue is with a resource owner or stakeholder, ask the sponsor or other senior stakeholder to step in. It's not your place to determine whether the disruptive influence has a valid point—others can make that determination while you continue to deliver the project that has been assigned to you.

This isn't a case of admitting defeat; rather, it is recognition that you have a job to do and can't allow people to detract you from that focus. If you do, then the political games were successful.

# 4.2 My sponsor doesn't trust me or give me the authority I need.

By Peter Taylor

## 1. Problem

The one person you would expect to support you doesn't seem to be able to place the necessary trust in you as a project manager or provide you with the correct level of authority that you need to deliver the project. You feel that your sponsor is second guessing your every move and it's starting to feel as though they don't believe that you can manage the project.

## 2. Warning Signs

This is a problem that can be fatal to a project's chances of success. As a result you need to be very sensitive to the early warnings, which include:

- You are spending an excessive amount of time in reporting back to your sponsor on micro-details of the project.
- You both *double up* on meetings instead of you representing the sponsor, or worse, you are not involved in meetings at all.
- You are being kept out of the *decision loop* on key matters relating to your project.
- Your project team members are bypassing you for decisions and answers.
- You spend your time trying to catch up with what is going on with your own project.

> **When You Know You Are Outside the Loop**
>
> Brian walked towards the coffee machine; he really needed caffeine to keep him motivated and alert. This was turning out to be one difficult project. In 10 minutes he had yet another meeting with Joyce, his project sponsor, and these meetings never went easily.
>
> His thoughts were interrupted by Justin who was already stirring freshly brewed coffee. "Hey," said Justin. "How are things?"
>
> Brian replied that things were good, thanks, and asked what was new. Justin was on the technical team for the underlying business system that Brian's project was interfacing with.
>
> "Good call from Joyce," continued Justin. "We are going ahead with the new release, so your team will have to adjust your specifications to take this in to account, but hey, that was the right decision, of course. Have a good one." And he left.
>
> Brian knew that he and his team had more work to do. Great! More replanning and with who knows what impact, all thanks to his sponsor, Joyce.
>
> He sighed, took his coffee, and headed off to Joyce's office for their scheduled meeting.
>
> Fifteen minutes later his smartphone alerted him to a message from Joyce, who had not yet appeared. "I'm running late, sorry, wait for me. I'm attending a meeting with the hardware suppliers about the loan equipment. Update you on decision when we meet."
>
> Brian shook his head and decided that things had to change, right now. But how?

## 3. What will happen if I do nothing?

Eventually, the project team will learn to bypass you completely as they see the decision maker as being solely the sponsor and that you are merely a delay in the decision process rather than a key player.

Your role will become questionable and, potentially, unnecessary.

## 4. Solution

It is critical that you learn how to control your sponsor. He or she can be your greatest asset, but can also become the biggest threat to your success.

Critical to any project's success is having a good project sponsor, but, as the saying goes, "you can choose your friends, but you can't choose your relatives," and the same is true of project sponsors. We all end up with the project sponsor that we are given, rather than one that we have handpicked.

So what can you do? Break it down and take yourself and your sponsor through three steps (see Figure 4.1).

## 5. What should I do?

### 5(a) Discover what's in it for them

A little bit of history can go a long way here. What do you know about your project sponsor? How did they get the role of sponsor in this particular project? Have they had issues in the past with projects going wrong or difficulties with previous project managers? Have they ever had any training in being a sponsor? Understanding the sponsor's background can help you understand why they are behaving the way they are. Insight is a great thing.

Warning! It is often said that a recent ex-project manager makes a very bad project sponsor. It is hard to stop *getting your hands dirty*, and there is always the tendency for the sponsor to feel that they can do a better job because they have more experience. They may even feel that they are helping out a less experienced project manager.

When you research the background of the project sponsor, set up a meeting to reestablish the purpose of the project and the sponsor's expectations of you as the project manager.

Here's a tip for when you meet: Don't ask *hard* questions, such as what, why, or when, but rather ask *soft* questions. Ask what their hopes are for this project, and

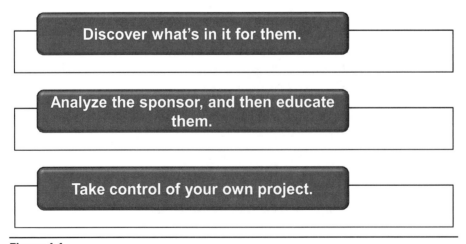

Figure 4.1

what their fears are. You will get a lot more feedback this way to help you understand what drives the sponsor, and therefore, how you can work more effectively
and efficiently with them.

Okay, what next?

### 5(b) Analyze the sponsor, and then educate them

Now, do some careful thinking about sponsors, how they currently work, and why.

Use the power grid (see Figure 4.2) as one tool to assess your sponsor (or for all
stakeholders). It may turn out that what you have now is a high interest sponsor
(almost certainly true if they are actively involved in this project and find it hard to
trust you or hand over authority to you) and probably a high power sponsor. This
combination means some hard work for you in managing them effectively.

Now you need to educate them. What do they understand their role as project
sponsor to be, and what do they believe it entails? Since the project has already
started, they should have completed the following; how have they done?

Identify each item in Table 4.1 with a Yes, No, or Maybe. It is up to you.

What should their job now be? Again, identify what the reality is (see Table 4.2).

Based on this analysis, you must now spend time educating your project sponsor
on what the project and organization needs from them in order to support you as
you try to deliver a successful project. Use the checklists given to talk them through
what they have been doing right and what they have been doing wrong. Sensitivity
is obviously critical, but that doesn't mean that you don't say what you need to say
clearly. Get the message across!

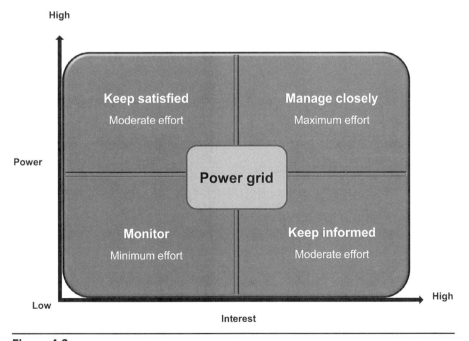

**Figure 4.2**

**Table 4.1 What should your sponsor have done for you (and your project)?**

|  | Status |
|---|---|
| Provided direction and guidance for the strategy that this project supports |  |
| Negotiated funding for the project |  |
| Actively participated in the initial project planning |  |
| Identified the Project Steering Committee members |  |
| Worked with you to develop the project charter |  |
| Identified and quantified the business benefits to be achieved |  |
| Made the project visible in the organization |  |
| Advised you of relevant protocols, political issues, potential sensitivities, etc. |  |

**Table 4.2 What should your sponsor be doing for you (and your project)?**

|  | Status |
|---|---|
| Reviewing and approving change requests |  |
| Gaining agreement among the stakeholders when differences of opinion occur |  |
| Assisting the project when required by exerting their organizational authority and ability to influence |  |
| Assisting with the resolution of inter-project issues |  |
| Chairing the Project Steering Committee |  |
| Supporting you in conflict resolution |  |
| Encouraging stakeholder involvement and building and maintaining their ongoing commitment through effective communication strategies |  |
| Evaluating the project's success on completion |  |

It is possible that they will score well on the things that they should have been doing but, with some help from you, will also be able to see things that they have been involved in that cross over into your world, the project management activities.

List what your sponsor shouldn't have been doing for you, (and your project) as well.

### 5(c) Take control of your own project

Armed with this new intelligence, it is time for you to take back your own project:

- Have a final, clear-the-air meeting with your sponsor and summarize what you have both discovered and, hopefully, agreed on.
- Re-kick off the project with your key project team to make them aware of the clarity of roles and the expected communication channels.
- Plan your own and your project sponsor's activities over the next two weeks.
- Assess those two weeks later to see how you have both performed and whether or not matters have improved. Go back to the checklists to see how you are doing now.

# 4.3 My team members pad their estimates.

## By Jennifer Russell

## 1. Problem

You need to come up with an accurate schedule for your project—well, as accurate as you can—but you suspect your team members are adding extra time to their estimates. How can you overcome this and get to a realistic, reliable schedule?

> **The Poetry of Schedule Estimation**
>
> As we know,
> There are known knowns.
> There are things we know we know.
> We also know
> There are known unknowns.
> That is to say
> We know there are some things
> We do not know.
> But there are also unknown unknowns,
> The ones we don't know
> We don't know.
>
> —*Donald Rumsfeld, Feb. 12, 2002, Department of Defense news briefing*

## 2. Warning Signs

Be careful with this problem—if you fail to spot it then it may be too late to do anything by the time that it becomes obvious. Some things to look for include:

- The estimates seem to be longer than similar tasks on previous projects.
- Objective calculations used to check estimates seem to suggest that estimates are too high.
- Your team gives you estimates, and then schedules long vacations during the project.

## 3. What will happen if I do nothing?

If a little padding is added to this task, and a little is added to that task, pretty soon it adds up to a real significant change to the schedule!

The problem with padded estimates is they are not treated as a contingency. Fred thinks he can do his task in 3 days, so he tells me it will take him 5 days. Instead of starting his task on Monday, he starts it on Wednesday, since he has extra time. Once Friday comes, he realizes that there are other conflicts, and he's unable to deliver on time.

Estimates are only as good as the estimator is at predicting the future, and most of us aren't working as psychics on the side. The situation can be even worse with junior employees, who have less experience in estimating. If your schedule turns out to be wildly inaccurate, it will cause others to question your estimates in the future, and you'll find your budget and schedule cut.

## 4. Solution

You need to get to reliable, consistent estimates. How do you get there?

1. Use accepted tools and techniques to develop estimates.
2. Build consensus on project estimates with the whole team.

3. Request a range of estimates from each team member, rather than a single estimate.
4. Instead of asking how many days the task will take to complete (total duration), ask for a number that represents the actual time spent on getting the task done (effort).

## 5. What should I do?

Your team members want higher estimates, so that they have as much time as they need, and even a little extra. You want to get your project completed as quickly as possible, to make all your stakeholders happy. Here are a few ways to get around this conflict, and develop accurate (not padded) estimates:

### 5(a) Use accepted tools and techniques

One big reason that estimates are padded is because team members have a lack of confidence in the accuracy of the estimates that they are developing. Knowing that they may be wrong, they add a *safety net* to the numbers to try and avoid estimates that are too low or too short.

To help avoid padding, you can provide your team with a number of different tools that they can use when developing estimates. These don't need to be particularly sophisticated, and while some of them have complex names, you can ignore those and focus on the tools themselves. Here are some examples:

- *Historic estimates:* Are there similar tasks that were completed on previous projects that can be used for comparison purposes?
- *Expert estimates:* Are there people in the organization (even if not on your project) who are experts on how long the task should take or how much it should cost?
- *Calculated estimates:* Can you use industry or vendor numbers? For example, if you need to buy 1000 square feet of tiles, and tiles cost $6 per square foot installed, you can estimate $6000 for the task.

### 5(b) Build consensus on project estimates

If you work with your project team for a while, you will get a feel for how each individual modifies an estimate, and can be prepared to adjust it if necessary to get an accurate result. For example, if you know that Jerry is always overly optimistic, you may need to lower his estimate, whereas you may need to raise Floyd's estimates because he is overly conservative.

For a brand new team, with whom you haven't worked before, you don't have that knowledge. You don't know how to modify each estimate in order to get to an accurate schedule.

You can avoid the problem of chronically padded estimates by having the team reach a consensus on their estimates in an open meeting, where team members would be less likely to pad the numbers. In that meeting, team members can go over assumptions and risks, and feel more confident in the numbers they're providing, especially if those numbers are backed by the tools described above. This approach also ensures that the project requirements are clearly understood by the people doing the estimating. A well-informed team will *always* produce better estimates!

If possible, arrange for another person to facilitate this meeting, as you will be needed as a participant. You may have a perspective that some of your team members do not, about project priorities, constraints, and assumptions, and you need to be part of the decision making process.

In this case, more experienced estimators on the team can help figure out where an estimate provided by others might be inadequate, and adjustments can be made at that time.

### 5(c) Use a range of estimates

Another way to help your team members feel confident in giving you accurate commitments is to ask for a range of dates for delivery.

A range of estimates doesn't mean you adopt the latest date to be on the safe side. Parkinson's Law says, "Work expands so as to fill the time available for its completion." If you give more time than needed to do a task, people will often use that extra time to make the task *better*, by adding features, doing additional testing, etc. While obviously well intentioned, this kind of *gold plating* makes the project take longer than it should, and may introduce new issues and risks.

The best way to get a range of estimates for a task is, instead of asking Carol when her task will be completed, ask her for a best-case scenario, worst-case scenario, and most likely scenario. Discussing the rationale behind her numbers will bring up risks and issues. Also, now that Carol feels like she doesn't have to deliver an estimate at the first opportunity, or be safe and find the last possible date, she will feel more confident committing to a reasonable date, with something like a 90 percent confidence of achieving it.

In order to get a good range of dates, allow each team member enough time to think through the problem before getting a commitment. If you ask a team member to estimate a task on the spot, he or she might make up a number quickly to make you go away. Giving people the time to come up with a careful estimate will pay off in greater accuracy in delivery.

### 5(d) Ask team members for task effort, not duration

If you ask your team members, "When can you get this task done?" their answers will vary, as they calculate other projects they might be working on or other issues that might come up. Instead, consider asking, "Okay, pretend you can work uninterrupted, nonstop, on this task. What's the number of hours you need to get it done?" Once you know the amount of effort required, it allows you to add in all the variables to come to a real duration. Your team members shouldn't have to do that calculation on their own. Be sure that the estimate you develop together takes into account the skill level of the folks doing the work. Just because it might take a normal person three days to complete this task, doesn't mean that it will take every team member three days. It might take someone one afternoon, because he or she has specialized skill, or it might take a week , because she needs to get up to speed on some underlying concepts before he or she can really get going.

No one works 100 percent of the time. By acknowledging this in the estimation process, we can get to more accurate duration estimates.

By explicitly examining and working through all the buffers needed, you get the information you need to estimate as accurately as you can during planning—the more uncertainty, the greater the buffer. You can have contingency amounts for a particularly risky work package, or for the project as a whole.

The size of the contingency, and whether it is at the work package or project level, is entirely dependent on the risk inherent in the project at the time the schedule is developed.

Help your team start each of their tasks as soon as possible in the schedule, as this will also reduce risk and uncertainty.

And above all, make sure that an externally mandated date doesn't drive the thought process for your team members! You need to understand what it really takes to deliver on tasks, not drive your people into a death march. This can be tough, as some shareholders may assume that everyone pads estimates, so they may want you to cut the commitments you've made. This is not a game you want to start playing! Be ready to carefully defend your schedule if challenged.

If estimates for some tasks are still fuzzy, it might be a sign that you need to break that task down into lower level tasks, to get to a clearer estimate. If your work breakdown structure is flawed, your estimates will be inaccurate, so it might be a good time to check whether or not you need to refine things a bit.

# 4.4 Some team members lack the skills they need.

### By Mark Price Perry

## 1. Problem

Your organization has a lot of important projects going on and resources are spread thinly across the initiatives. Your project seems to have really suffered and a lot of the resources assigned to the initiative don't have the skills that they need to complete their tasks successfully.

## 2. Warning Signs

If you have a lot of background information on your team, this problem may be obvious right from the start, but in some cases this problem may be hidden until the work actually gets underway. Some of indications that you may have a problem are:

> **You Want Us to Do What?**
>
> Alan sat at his desk and reviewed the new project that he had been assigned to manage. It looked like he had also been assigned a full team, which made a nice change, but Alan was worried. He had worked with all of the team members before and they were all good, strong contributors, but they didn't have the skills or experience necessary to complete this initiative.
>
> Alan's sponsor had explained that there were a lot of high priority projects underway and resources were tight—everyone had to make compromises. That was to be expected, but there were compromises and then there were lost causes, and this felt like the latter.
>
> Alan knew that at least some of the team members knew that they had been assigned to the project and having just seen a couple of them in the lunch room, they looked nervous. He could imagine how they must feel: nervous about what was expected, but not wanting to admit that they didn't really know how to do this type of work. Alan wasn't sure how he was going to deal with this one.

- The team seems to be unprepared or confused about the project's purpose.
- The background and experience of the team doesn't match with what is required to complete the work.
- The team seems to lack motivation.
- There are a lot more task and requirement based questions than usual.
- Early work items suffer from delays or quality issues.

## 3. What will happen if I do nothing?

People won't magically gain necessary skills if you ignore the problem. Instead, the project will continue to struggle, missing deadlines, experiencing problems with incorrect or low quality deliverables, and suffering from low team morale. The project will inevitably be seen as a failure that will reflect on the people involved in its execution.

## 4. Solution

This isn't a problem that can quickly be solved, so you need to recognize that one way or another the project is going to be impacted. The solution will have to consider the needs of both the team and the project in order to identify the right approach:

1. Establish the importance of this initiative relative to others within the organization.

2. Create and execute a plan to address the skill shortfalls.
3. Replan the project to accurately reflect the situation.

### 5. What should I do?

This is obviously a significant issue, but don't panic! Just like every other problem, there is a solution that you can develop and implement. Before we start looking at the step-by-step solution, there is one important, additional consideration to bear in mind.

Your team doesn't have the skills to be successful at this project, but that's not a reflection on them. I don't have the skills necessary to fly an aircraft, play professional sports, or perform open heart surgery. That doesn't make me a lesser person, and you can't let your team feel that they are incompetent just because they don't have the precise skills needed for this project.

### 5(a) Establish importance

The fact that the resources who have been assigned to you seem to be the ones who were *left over* from higher priority initiatives will tell you something about the importance of this project relative to the others, but that doesn't mean that no one cares. It also doesn't mean that the project will continue to be low priority over time, so you need to ensure that you fully understand the organizational priorities:

- What is most important: scope, schedule, budget?
- Are there non-negotiable elements such as a regulatory deadline or a fixed price contract?
- Are there dependencies on other initiatives that the project contributes to, or does it consume deliverables of another project that is currently underway?

This will help you to understand how (or if) you can rework the plan to make allowance for a skills shortfall. You also need to discuss the matter with your sponsor and other senior stakeholders, including the PMO, to establish what options you have available to you, such as:

- A budget to hire outside experts to assist with some elements of the work where specialist skills are required.
- Training scheduled to develop the skills that the team requires.
- Internal expert resources freed up from commitments to other projects at some point during the project, and made available to you.
- Adjustment of the project to reflect what the team can achieve.

Once you have answers to these questions, you will be able to develop a plan to address the skills gap that exists.

### 5(b) Create and execute a plan

Once you understand the relative importance of your project compared to the rest of the project portfolio, and you have an appreciation for where flexibility exists within the project constraints, you can build a plan to address these issues. This isn't the project plan at this point; rather, it is a case of establishing how you can get your project team to the point where they can deliver the project. This can include a combination of approaches based on the information that you collected:

- Additional team members from other projects or operational areas who can bring the skills required
- Budget to bring in external consultants who either have the skills or who can develop the skills in the team
- Training of resources
- Informal mentors and ad hoc assistance from organization or industry experts

In some cases, it may be possible to undertake these items in parallel with some project tasks; in other cases, it will be necessary to put the project on hold until these items are addressed. Either way these tasks need their own plan and as the project manager, you need to manage the execution of these tasks just as much as any other project plan.

One of the biggest mistakes to make, at this point, is to focus only on the work necessary to get the project executed. It is even more important to provide the individual team members with the skills development that they need to allow them to feel confident with the work—the benefits of that will last far longer than this one initiative.

### 5(c) Replan the project

Once you have a plan to address skills shortages on your project, you can revisit the project plan as a whole. At this point, you know what the most important constraints are, but you need to be realistic. Just because the sponsor tells you that time is the most important factor does not mean that the original schedule can be met, especially if the same sponsor isn't prepared to provide any experts or pay for training.

You need to provide a realistic plan based on the skills development approaches that you have put in place and are now executing. You should try to resequence tasks where possible to allow for experts becoming available or for training to be provided, but where that cannot occur you need to realistically build in delays or extend the amount of time that a task will take—failing to do so will not allow the project to deliver any sooner!

You also need to plan for the changes in budget that will be necessary, not just the additional costs incurred by tasks taking longer or being delayed, but also the costs associated with training, consultants, etc. These costs are attributable to the project.

If the sponsor agreed to a change in scope, you need to clearly identify the functionality that is being removed and if possible provide preliminary information about when it will be provided.

# 4.5 Other projects keep stealing my resources.

By Fran Samaras

## 1. Problem

You have assembled a project team and you're moving along executing the plan. Recently, you have noticed that your project resources are becoming unavailable and are resurfacing on other projects. It is pretty clear that your resources are being stolen by other competing initiatives.

## 2. Warning Signs

This should be a fairly black and white issue—either your resources are working on your project or they aren't. The difficulty is in recognizing when small issues turn into dangerous trends. Some things to look for are:

- You are not getting clear status updates in meetings.
- Task completion dates are frequently slipping.
- Meeting attendance is always unpredictable.
- You hear by means of *hallway* talk that there are new or other projects that are a drain to the company.
- Your project team openly communicates to you that their time has been reallocated by their superiors to other projects or other tasks.

## 3. What will happen if I do nothing?

Some of the signs of an impending problem can be very subtle and as the project manager you have to be alert to them. If you ignore the problem,

---

### Here Today, Gone Tomorrow

Angie is a project manager assigned to what she believes (and her sponsor believes) is a high profile, important project with the company. With her sponsor's approval, she forms a steering committee and engages leaders in the company to provide resources for her project. The leaders seem especially happy that someone, finally, is going to work on the project, so she's feeling confident.

Bob, an executive in Operations, met with her and expressed that he would be happy to allocate resources, but they have a lot on their plates. Angie maintained her enthusiasm, thinking that if Bob is releasing staff to work on the project, it should be fine.

Angie checks her list of assigned resources after the meeting again. She has been given *the best of the best* from the company to support her project. She is beaming.

That week, Angie attends a PMO meeting. Her colleagues are actively working their projects. Some of the project managers mentioned that their dates are slipping and they casually mention team members are working on too many projects. Angie remains confident—this won't happen to her project as she has been assigned a full team.

After the meeting, Angie meets with Jules, who is another project manager. Jules told her that he heard there are a series of new compliance changes that need to be implemented as soon as possible. She feels that this will probably impact legal, but certainly not her project, so she carries on.

Angie plans her kick off meeting, sends the invitations, and notices that some key project resources are unable to come to the meeting. "It's summer," she thinks, so one or two people being on vacation makes sense, but this many? The kick off meeting is a success despite the no-shows. She works with the people who did show up to determine work packages and they assign resources to work the tasks. She's happy and has a good realistic plan.

The following week, she has her team meeting. She's sure everyone will attend. She's checked and rechecked schedules and everyone looks free yet—you guessed it! More no shows! Plus, the work that she anticipated being completed this week hasn't been touched. Should she have seen the writing on the wall?

your remaining project team becomes overwhelmed with extra work that they need to pick up. Critical path tasks are not completed and your project will not be completed as projected or may simply be put on hold.

Potentially worse, if your project team sees that you aren't addressing the problem they may see it as confirmation that the project is no longer a priority, and they will start spending more of their time on other projects or operational work.

## 4. Solution

Let's face it—corporate priorities can change more than we like. Executives have been known to make a decision to support a project with resources one day, then have crises arise or new initiatives come up that take precedent. Optimism, a good project plan, and a full roster is no guarantee that the work will be done and your project will be implemented.

You need to take a structured approach to managing this issue and progress through the following steps:

- Assess your losses: who are you losing, and for how long?
- Research and document: Find out what is causing the loss of your resources.
- Reforecast the plan or negotiate the return or replacement of your resources (or both).

## 5. What should I do?

In the Sidebar, note that Angie may have missed some real indications that her project resources could be dwindling. Let's outline those indications:

- Team members not attending meeting(s)
- Hallway *buzz* about new critical compliance project
- Bob, the operations executive, said they have *a lot on their plates*
- Colleagues mentioning that dates are slipping due to conflicting projects

When should she have reacted? Right away!

### 5(a) Assess your losses

The first step is to begin to assess what critical path items are affected with the loss of resource(s). You need to understand whether the impact is minor and temporary, or whether there is a potential delay to the project to the extent that recovery becomes impossible. If the impact is material then immediately make this transparent to your sponsor(s) or steering committees, and elevate to your boss. If your company or client is serious about delivering the project, they need to know what is affecting progress and make serious prioritization decisions.

As the project manager, you cannot work in a vacuum. Angie should have probed at every opportunity mentioned. She should have spoken with her colleagues to understand the conflicts and asked Bob what they were working on, not automatically assume the compliance project would be limited to the legal department. She should continue to assess the *lay of the land* to identify risks and document them in her risk plan.

### 5(b) Research and document

Once you establish that your team resources are being stolen, reallocated, or re-assigned, the next step is to start doing your homework. Begin reaching out and digging deep to figure out where your resources are going. What projects are they working on? Have the stakeholders changed the priority of your initiative relative to other projects? Document what you uncover.

Next, document who is assigned to what projects and for what percentage of time. What new priorities were added of late that supersede your project? Actively communicate with your project team to understand their commitments and other responsibilities if their work on your project is not their only responsibility. If a team member goes to another project, find out which project it is and probe to see if their commitment on that project is indefinite or for a short period of time. Communication is key—speak to the team members individually and speak to stakeholders. Then, create a simple summary of this information to be shared with your project leadership.

Document this problem in your issue log. Elevate the problem again, using this forum. Look for and recommend solutions: Are there other resources within the company that you can use to complete the tasks? Can you outsource tasks to a consulting firm to assist?

### 5(c) Reforecast or negotiate?

If you find your stolen resources will only be used for a limited time, or have found solutions to the resource gaps through replacement resources or resequencing of tasks, replan your project to reflect these changes. Ensure that this revised plan is reviewed and approved by your management, project sponsors, and your steering committee.

You may also be able to resolve the issue directly with the other projects, or through the PMO. It may be possible to negotiate with the persons who *stole* your resources to share that resource's time to—split time between initiatives based on critical path items. That plan may require further changes, but if it allows for a critical resource to complete work on multiple projects without impacting the constraints, then it is well worth it.

Sometimes you may find that there are simply too few resources to complete the work in the desired timeframes. If this continues to be an ongoing problem with your organization and not an isolated incident, encourage your leadership to create enterprise-wide or portfolio-wide dependency and impact tracking sessions, and enterprise-wide or department-wide resource planning.

# 4.6 My *team* isn't really a team.

## By Harlan Bridges

## 1. Problem

Your team doesn't seem like a team at all. Rather, they act like a group of individuals with differing agendas and goals. Disagreements are frequent, and communication is ineffective or lacking entirely. Everyone seems to be more focused on themselves and their own needs than they are on the project and its needs.

## 2. Warning Signs

This problem can manifest itself in a lot of different ways, and as the project manager you need to be able to identify the warning signs early and act swiftly. Some of the common indications that you may have issues include:

- There are disagreements or conflicts between team members.
- There is a lack of cohesion.
- Team members are clearly not communicating.
- There are *silos* and work is being done in isolation.
- Team members have other priorities that are interfering with project work.
- There is a significant lack of respect for team members.
- The team does not agree on the goals and objectives of the project.
- Team members seek individual recognition rather than recognition for the team.
- Team members are unsure of their role.
- No one seems to be confident that the team can deliver.

### Do You Feel Like a Referee?

Jeremy sat at his desk wondering where it had all started going wrong. For the third time this week, Jim and Curtis were in his office shouting at each other. Each accused the other of not being a team member and not getting their work accomplished.

Jeremy is the project manager of a large web development project, a project that the company is expecting to increase its market share through an online ordering capability. Jim is the technical lead for the project and Curtis is the subject matter expert (SME) assigned from the business unit. He also represents the customer. This latest argument was over project goals.

As Jeremy reflected over this project, he realized that the conflict between Jim and Curtis was only one symptom of a lack of team work from his project team. The team was not functioning as a cohesive unit. The programmers were not communicating well, and individual components of the application often failed when integrated as a whole. Deliverables were late because some team members were placing a higher priority on their "regular" jobs. It appeared that the team did not understand the importance of the project and how it fit into the company's strategic goals.

Certain team members felt they were doing more than others and weren't getting any recognition for their efforts. Others felt that certain people were hogging all the attention. Team morale was nonexistent and the team was at risk of falling apart.

Jeremy spent so much of his time refereeing fights among the team that he was unable to meet his obligations as project manager. He realized that this has become a significant risk to the project.

What could he do to turn things around?

## 3. What will happen if I do nothing?

Teams that do not work well together put any project at great risk. Chances are increased that project goals will not be met, or that budgets will be overrun, or that schedules will not be met. Relationships between coworkers may be permanently harmed. Careers may be ended. There are no good outcomes that can occur by doing nothing; these problems don't solve themselves.

## 4. Solution

As the project manager, you have the responsibility for developing and leading cohesive teams. Remember that you are not so much managing a project as leading a team of people who must come together to achieve the goals of the project. Often, people are part of a functional unit within the business and do not directly report to you. You will have to establish yourself as a leader and mold the individuals into a team. What can you do to create cohesive, successful teams?

First, you need to understand the characteristics of a successful team. Then, you can create an environment that helps the team take on those characteristics. These characteristics include:

- The right people on the team
- Respect for every member of the team
- Well-defined roles and responsibilities
- Clear and honest communication
- Understood and agreed upon project goals
- Team ownership of project goals
- Team responsibility for the success of the project

## 5. What should I do?

As project manager, you need to start laying the foundation for effective teamwork by creating an environment where people can work together effectively.

### 5(a) Get the right people

To get the right people, you need to develop a resource plan. A resource plan requires that you identify and understand the work to be done, at least at a high level. This will identify the type of personnel required and will help you to recognize skills and abilities required to complete the work. Use the resource plan to begin identifying the resources for your team.

Effective teams require the right people. There are many factors to be considered when choosing team members, such as:

- Do they have the skills required to complete the work?
- Do they have the capacity to work on the project, and do they have the time?
- Do they have the ability to effectively work with others?
- What is their position within the organization, and do they have the right level of influence?
- Are they results oriented?

In most organizations, project team members are part-time teams. They usually have to split time between their regular job and project work. In order to reduce conflicts between their different responsibilities, work closely with the team member's functional manager. Come to an agreement with the functional manager on terms such as availability, dealing with emergencies, and time away from their usual duties.

### 5(b) Create a team identity

Project team members are often from different functional areas or departments within the organization. They identify themselves as members of that organization and that team. A project requires them to leave their *home* team and play for someone else's team. Who is that new team? If they do not know, it is difficult to feel loyal to, or be a part of, that new team.

Once you have identified your team members and brought them together, begin creating a team identity. Involve the members in this. Here are some activities that can help:

- Choose a team name, perhaps the project name or a nickname
- Develop a team logo
- If budget allows, order team shirts, coffee mugs, or similar items
- Announce the new project team to the organization; be sure to list the team members
- Create a project web site on the company intranet

Once you have established the team identity, use it often. Refer to the team by the team's new identity.

### 5(c) Develop a team operating agreement (TOA), aka team charter

Once you have determined your team identity, it's time to create the team operating agreement (TOA) or team charter. Include the entire team in the development of the TOA to ensure that everyone buys into it and has ownership. The TOA provides the ground rules and guidelines the team will use to work together in an effective manner during the project. It can include anything the team believes must be addressed in order to work together. Some typical items included are:

- Team communication rules and expectations
- Decision-making procedures
- What meetings will be held and ground rules for conducting meetings
- Roles and responsibilities
- Personal courtesies and how the team interacts with each other

Upon completion of the team operating agreement, every team member as well as the project manager should sign it, indicating their agreement. The TOA is a living document and should be revised as needs arise.

### 5(d) Define project goals and objectives

The project goals and objectives are defined in the project charter. You have one, right? The project sponsor and the project manager usually develop the project charter jointly. They will work together to define the goals and objectives of the project, as well as the project success criteria. This document is what drives the scope of the project.

Use the project charter to help the team understand what is expected of them and of the project. As project manager, it is your responsibility to ensure the team has a clear understanding of project goals, objectives, and scope. Your team must know what success looks like in the eyes of the project sponsor. The project charter should also clarify how the project fits into the strategy of the organization. This will help the team understand the importance and relativity of the work they are doing.

### 5(e) Use leadership strategies

The most important aspect of team building is effective leadership from the project manager. The project manager is ultimately responsible for creating effective and successful teams. Some project managers are naturally charismatic, and people seem to want to do their best for them. Most of us do not have that gift. So how can the rest of us be effective leaders? Fortunately, although leadership entails many skills, these skills can be learned.

- *Practice effective communication:* Become an effective communicator and always be honest in your dealings with the team. Learn to listen. Communication is your most effective tool in dealing with people. A simple rule is to tell your team everything about the project unless there is a valid reason for not doing so. Don't manage with a *need to know* attitude but rather a *why shouldn't they know* attitude.

    Organize the team's work in such a way that team members are mutually dependent and recognize it. This will produce a strong impetus for the group to become a team. Encourage a problem solving orientation in the team. Associate project success with teamwork and lack of teamwork with project failure.
- *Create rewards and recognition:* Set up a system of rewards and recognition for your team. A good technique is to create a way that team members can nominate other members for rewards or recognition. This fosters camaraderie and avoids the perception of favoritism. Present rewards and recognition at team meetings and consider inviting the team member's functional manager to present the award. Post it on the project's web site.
- *Manage conflict effectively:* It is not possible to eliminate conflict from projects. How the project manager deals with conflict will determine whether conflict is harmful to the team and the project. In fact, controlled conflict can result in beneficial effects, such as thinking in a new way, coming up with novel solutions, and encouraging creative thinking. But unmanaged or unresolved conflict usually leads to problems.

    Often you will have to become a negotiator between the team members in conflict. This requires good listening skills and a bit of detection on your part. You must find the root cause of the conflict before you can address it. Work with all parties in the conflict to create a solution. In other words, help your team members find a solution. Don't solve their problem, but support them in finding a resolution.

- *Empower your teams:* Empowering others requires a level of trust on your part. Encourage the team to make decisions and find solutions to problems. It is your job to support the team in its work. Project managers with strong leadership skills trust their teams to do what's right. Micromanagement is a team killer. You have selected a team for their expertise and ability to do the work. Trust them to do so. Your job is to clear their path of obstacles to project success and to provide them with all they need to do their jobs.

# 4.7 My team spends more time arguing than working.

## By Gina Abudi

## 1. Problem

The team is not working well together:

- They are not getting along with each other.
- They won't communicate with each other.
- They blame each other every time something goes wrong.
- They stubbornly refuse to help each other out.
- They are constantly bickering with each other.

Or, the team was working well together and all of a sudden something changed. There are many reasons this change might have occurred, including:

- A new member joined the team in the middle of the project.
- A team member has personal issues that are affecting his or her performance.
- Significant changes to the project occurred that changed how the team works together.

### Oh, No! This Team Is Not Getting Along!

Anne was sure this was going to be a great team when she was assigned as project leader. The project was exciting—it was launching a new product for the company. She knew some of the individuals on the project team already and had worked with a few of them before. Certainly this was a different project than any of them had ever worked on, and some of the team members were new to the company. She thought that would be exciting for everyone—a challenge ahead!

She found out that she was wrong. Anne saw there were some issues in the beginning when the team first got together on the project, but she assumed they would all work it out. That never happened. Anne thought about the last team meeting: Howard complained that he was the only one doing any real work; Sara said she had enough to do and didn't need to be working with people who didn't appreciate her; Jasmine, as usual, showed up late to the meeting; and Don hadn't made any progress on any of his tasks. Other members refused to even open their mouths and talk during the status meeting.

Certainly, the project was at a standstill. What was going on? How was Anne going to get this team moving in the right direction? Could she possibly *start again* with the same group? Something had to be done—and soon—or this project was never going to succeed. To top it all off, she had a meeting with the project sponsor in a couple of weeks about progress. What was she going to tell him about the team? Could she fix the issue before then?

Whether the team has not worked well together since day one, or it's a situation where they were working well at some point and now that has changed, it's essential that you get the problem resolved and the team working together effectively and efficiently as soon as possible to ensure a successful project conclusion. You find you are trying to manage a project with a bunch of people who seem to be working against you. If you can't turn the team around quickly enough and get them to work well together, the project is likely to fail.

## 2. Warning Signs

There are some things to look for that will let you know that the team is not working well together, such as:

- Team members are working in silos, not sharing information or pitching in to help others.
- Team members are not showing up for team meetings, are late, or are non-participative.
- Frequent conflicts occur among team members.
- Missed deadlines or minimal progress on tasks hold up tasks of other team members and increase the risk of the project failing.
- There is a lack of communication among team members.
- There are frequent negative conversations among team members about other team members outside of meetings.
- Open antagonism against other team members is prevalent.
- Team members are trying to move off the project and onto other projects.

If any of this is apparent on your team, you have a problem with team members not working effectively together, which will affect your project timeline and the overall success of the project.

## 3. What will happen if I do nothing?

For any project to be a success, the team needs to learn how to work together—supporting each other toward the successful conclusion. If nothing is done, the situation will continue to worsen; it will not just go away. Unless you intervene in some way, the team members will not resolve the problem themselves and will continue to grow further apart. The project is likely to fail. Managing a project team and the interactions among the team members is a key part of the project manager's role. You need to understand the basics of team development to learn how to manage your team as effectively and efficiently as possible.

## 4. Solution

You need to figure out how to get the team to work together This is a key priority for you at any point where the team has trouble with communications or functioning. You will need to pull the team together to work through their issues; it may even mean some *time out* from the project. By improving how the team works together, you can get the project moving in the right direction and avoid a failed project. To get the team moving in the right direction, you need to determine what is preventing them from working well together, and what will help them to resolve the issues.

## 5. What should I do?

### 5(a) Understand the stages of team development

First, step back and consider the five stages of team development. The first four stages were known as *Tuckman's Stages*. The stages were developed by Bruce Tuckman and published in 1965. In 1977, Tuckman and Mary Ann Jensen, added a fifth stage, *Adjourning*. Let's discuss the first four stages, which is what you need to understand in order to get your team working well together:

- *Stage 1—Forming:* The team first meets each other in this stage.
- *Stage 2—Storming:* Team members begin to work together and compete with each other for status and acceptance of their ideas.
- *Stage 3—Norming:* The team begins to work effectively as a team, no longer focused on their own goals, but rather on developing a way to work together effectively and efficiently.
- *Stage 4—Performing:* The team is functioning at a high level and is focused on reaching the goals of the group as a whole.

By understanding how teams work together and move through these four stages to reach high performance, you will be better equipped to get your team working together. Figure 4.3 depicts movement of teams through the stages of team development. Remember that some teams never make it to Stage 4, high performing, but stay at Stage 3, norming. Additionally, changes on the team could move a team that is performing in the *norming* stage back to *storming*. The project manager will

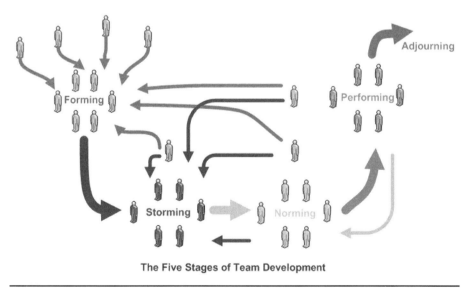

**The Five Stages of Team Development**

**Figure 4.3**

need to be aware of changes that move a team back, and help them move forward as quickly as possible. Understanding the stages of team development enables you to be more effective as a project manager.

As can be seen in the figure, teams may move back and forth between stages as changes occur that affect how the team works—for example, new members join, someone leaves, the project scope changes, a team member develops personal problems, or other reasons occur. A team may move from norming back to storming, performing back to storming, norming back to forming, etc. In many cases, the team can get back to where they were fairly quickly. As the project manager, it is your responsibility to understand how teams function, and where you are needed to step in and assist them to keep moving in the right direction.

### 5(b) Resolve your team problem

Take these steps to resolve your problem of the team not working well together.

#### 1. Step back so the team can begin to build relationships with each other.

You may already have individual relationships with some of the team members based on working together on past projects. If you do, use what you know about the team members to understand what is going on within the team. Use those relationships to call on team members to understand what is happening.

This team needs to spend some time getting to know each other and learning about each other so they are comfortable working together. It is possible that, prior to the project starting, the team did not have the opportunity to meet and get to know each other. This should be done now, but not in an hour or two; the more difficulty that exists with the team working together, the more time needs to be spent in team building. Consider an entire day for a team that is working together poorly. You need to do some serious team building and issue resolution. This is important and needs to be fit into your schedule. You and the entire project team need to be together to start to build relationships and work together. Think about:

- Have any team members worked together before? If so, get them together and ask them what they found helpful when they first worked together.
- Are some members trying to reach out to the others? If so, get them involved in getting the team to work well together. They may have some good ideas!
- What are the personalities of the various team members? Are they shy and quiet? Outgoing and loud? This may help you understand some of the issues you are facing.
- What are your options for getting the team together face-to-face for a couple of hours for a team-building event? If not possible, when the team is virtual, think about your options for getting them together virtually through Web conferencing or other means. Ideally, you may have access to a virtual platform; if not, use a conference call, but definitely get everyone together. Some possibilities to consider are:
  - Breakfast or lunch get-together (if the team members are all in one location)

- ○ An *after hours* get-together (if the team members are all in one location)
    - ○ A virtual get-together where the team is still able to see each other via cameras on their computers
    - ○ A conference call get-together
- Even if the team is getting together via a conference call, a team-building event is possible. Some possibilities to consider include:
    - ○ Presentations by team members about themselves: backgrounds, past projects, hobbies and interests, etc.
    - ○ Use of the Myers-Briggs Type Indicator
    - ○ Various team building exercises—there are many team-building exercise books available, along with lots of information about team building exercises on the Internet

Think about who you may want to bring from outside the project team to direct the team building. Maybe the project sponsor or a client could run a session? Maybe a neutral party, like a team-building consultant could help facilitate team building exercises?

Prior to the team meeting, ask the team to bring to the meeting their concerns about the project. What are the issues they are facing on the project, or otherwise, that is making it difficult for them to work together well? Do not short change the team building event as it will help strengthen the team, but also include discussion around team issues as they must be resolved to ensure success on the project. Make sure that problems and issues are brought to the forefront so they can be addressed and resolved. Prior to the get-together, make sure the team is aware that one discussion will be focused on the fact that the team is not working well together, and you want ideas from them as to how to improve the team as a whole. That way, team members can prepare to bring their best, positive ideas forward and make the most of their time together.

## 2. Come prepared on the day of the team meeting.

You have seen how the team is not working well together. In addition to team building exercises, devote sufficient time to listing all of the team issues (no names necessary) that are having a negative effect on the project and focus discussion on the resolution of those issues. If others brought issues to your attention outside of the project, bring them up. However, this is not the time to point fingers or blame. As the project manager, it is up to you to keep frustrations at a minimum and keep the group moving in the right direction. This isn't easy. You may find bringing in a facilitator will help greatly here.

If problems are related to the scope of the project, disagreement around the project goals, etc., you may want to bring in your project sponsor to assist. It is important that the team works well together, so do not be afraid to call on others to help you get the team back on track. If issues are around individuals not pulling their weight and completing their tasks, or not showing up for team meetings, get the issue out on the table.

Make sure you have someone available to capture information to share after the meeting (note taker).

Once all issues are voiced, and the team has agreed those are the issues, the meeting should focus on discussions around why the issues are taking place and what can be done to resolve or move past them. At this point, ask the team, "What would help to get everyone to the meetings on time? What would help to ensure you can complete tasks in a timely manner?" Be sure to capture all information. You may need help from others. For example, if you find out that some team members cannot complete their tasks on time because their immediate supervisor pulls them to work on other projects; that is an issue that will need to be addressed with someone other than the team member. Your sponsor can help here.

The key is to be sure that *all* issues are on the table. A plan must be developed to address each issue, with another plan to address issues that arise going forward, before they grow into larger conflicts that are detrimental to the project.

### 3. Follow up after the team get-together.

Gather the notes from the get-together and share them with everyone soon after the meeting. You want their input on the notes, so ask for team members' responses and acknowledgement of acceptance of the get-together notes:

- Is anything missing from the list of issues?
- Is anything missing from the steps to resolve them?
- Is anything missing from how to monitor progress and address issues going forward?

If issues need to be addressed by others outside the project team, or by the sponsor or other stakeholders, be sure to get a timeline from them for resolution on the issue.

The goal is to have everyone buy in to what happened at the meeting and the agreed-upon output from the get-together. At the next team meeting, reserve some time on the agenda to see how things are going after the team building session. Ask the team if there are other issues that have come up that should be discussed. Likely you will find the team more apt to speak up, or to tell you about issues they addressed already and which are now resolved.

Teams that have spent some time up front getting to know each other are much more likely to be able to handle issues that arise, in a timely manner.

### 4. Next steps and monitoring the team.

As a project manager, you need to guide your team as they move through the stages of team development. Remember that issues will arise, and that they may need your guidance in working through them to get back on track and work well together. Anything could change and set the team back from, for example, Stage 3, norming, to Stage 2, storming. As the project manager, you need to give the team the space they need to work through issues, but also be available to guide them, or jump in and resolve for them, when necessary.

# 4.8 There is too much finger pointing.

## By Andy Jordan

## 1. Problem

You are managing a project that is experiencing several problems at the same time. They are serious issues, but nothing that you haven't seen before and you know that problems are to be expected on projects, which never go according to plan. However, it seems like the team and the stakeholders are more focused on *the blame game* than they are on trying to complete tasks or resolve the issues.

The first question from a stakeholder is always, "Whose fault is that?" or "How did you let that happen?" Your project team is more concerned with showing that the problem is someone else's fault.

As the project manager, it feels like you are isolated. You are trying to get the project completed on time, within scope and budget, and with high quality, but everyone else is undermining your ability to do that by focusing on the wrong things. You know that you have to do something, but you aren't sure what or how.

> **The Project Manager Did It Again!**
>
> "You aren't going to believe what Nancy did now! She's got that elevator design wrong again. There's no way that Sharpe will sign the contract now—she cost us that customer for sure."
>
> James cringed in his chair as Ted yelled this accusation across the room. Ted always seemed to be trying to look better than everybody else by telling tales about other people. Didn't he know that as project manager, James did not care who had or hadn't made a mistake. James just wanted to get the project completed successfully.
>
> Ted certainly didn't understand how difficult it was for Nancy to get the design perfect. She was restricted by the building construction company, the customer had very specific needs, and the latest state regulations imposed a lot more controls on this project. But Ted didn't care; he wanted to show how great he was, and that usually meant trying to show how inadequate everyone else was.
>
> James knew that he had to speak to Ted, but what should he say? Ted had a critical role to play on the project, and James couldn't afford to upset him. At the same time, everyone else seemed to resent Ted and had started to come to James, pointing out any small mistake that Ted made. That was making Ted's accusations of others worse, turning into a battle of wills with no one winning and the project losing.
>
> Sometimes James thought that it was easier to deal with his twin five-year-old boys at home than it was to manage his project team at work. Why couldn't they all just get along and work on getting the project completed?

## 2. Warning Signs

You may have a problem with finger pointing on your project if:

- Stakeholders are more concerned with assigning or deflecting blame than they are with helping you solve a problem.
- You end up having to talk to multiple people to find out the real problem because everyone refers you to someone else.
- Instead of coming to you with problems, your project team members come to you with complaints and issues about other people on the team, and those complaints are focused on the person, not the issue.
- You spend a lot of time in status meetings talking about people and not about tasks.

- People are *playing politics*, trying to make sure that they look good in the eyes of people who matter in the organization, rather than trying to get the work done.

## 3. What will happen if I do nothing?

When people start blaming one another, negative actions can escalate quickly. People will inevitably take it personally and become angry and frustrated. Team members will lose motivation and be tempted to respond by making accusations of their own, which makes the situation worse. The trust between people involved in the project will be destroyed, and the focus will switch from the tasks to individuals' own needs. You can end up with open conflict where the underlying work becomes secondary.

The loss of focus on the project tasks will lead to delays and a drop in quality, which in turn will lead to more occurrences of people blaming others. If the issues aren't dealt with early, relationships may be permanently damaged and the project may never recover. The impact on the customer will be disastrous and may have impacts far beyond the current initiative.

## 4. Solution

You need to be decisive and act quickly:

- Create an environment where the team and stakeholders respect one another, understand the priorities and challenges of their colleagues, and work together as a cohesive unit. Strive to create a culture of respect and encouragement within the team.
- Be objective, and always treat everybody equally, never taking sides. Lead by example.
- Address finger pointing as soon as it occurs, and draw team members back to the issue, not the people.
- Don't ignore accusations. Acknowledge the comment and turn it into a learning opportunity for the team.

## 5. What should I do?

Finger pointing is not the kind of issue that can be addressed simply by dealing with the problem itself. It is a symptom of a lack of trust and respect between team members. To address the issue completely, you need to treat both the symptoms and the underlying cause of the problem. Throughout, you must be prepared to deal with issues head on, making sure that you remain focused on the issues themselves and not the people; be objective at all times. Recognize that some people enjoy *playing politics* and if they can draw you into a debate full of opinions instead of facts, then they will have achieved their goals.

### 5(a) Create the right environment.

Although the ideal time to build your team is at the start of the project, it's never too late to build a team atmosphere. A group of people working on the same project are not automatically a team; they are just a group of people. To become a *team*, they need to build relationships and trust with one another, and make a commitment to work together to achieve the common goal of delivering the project. That means getting to know one another as individuals, learning about the roles that each person plays on the project, and deciding what some of the challenges might be. Work with the team to agree on some values. Values could include such things as agreeing that everyone will encourage one another, that all communications will be respectful, or that members will contribute to the agenda.

It's a lot harder to assign blame to someone that you know and respect than it is to a stranger. If your team starts to work together as a true team rather than a collection of individuals working on their own tasks, you will notice that they develop more respect for one another and accusations will reduce.

The action on your part does not need to be a complex series of formal team building exercises. A simple kick off meeting with lunch, and everyone given the opportunity to talk about themselves, their background, and what they have to do on the project, will go a long way.

The situation is the same with stakeholders and vendors. Project managers who see a lot of finger pointing between the project team and stakeholders, or the team and a vendor, will often find that the two groups were treated as separate entities. Treat them all as one team and work to include them.

### 5(b) Be objective and deal with issues early

Blaming people for things that go wrong on a project is extremely contagious. It can spread remarkably quickly as people try to deflect the blame from themselves and *score points* against other people. As the project manager, you need to deal with it as quickly and firmly as possible.

When you are faced with finger pointing, you have to remain totally objective. If a team member or stakeholder is coming to you and blaming other people for problems, it can be very easy to sympathize with them. This can easily be construed as agreeing with their perspective and effectively condemning the person that they are blaming for the issues. You have to make sure that you separate the issue that is causing the problem from the people involved.

You also have to make sure that you never resort to making accusations yourself. The project manager has to be totally focused on:

- The problem that needs to be addressed
- The steps necessary to correct the problem
- The root cause of the problem and the steps necessary to ensure that the issue does not occur again

It is possible that the root cause of the problem is a mistake by an individual, but this needs to be addressed through training and helping the individual understand the importance of accuracy, not publicly blaming them for problems.

Try to engage all impacted parties in coming up with alternative solutions to get past the problem, not only the two individuals or groups who are either engaging in, or subject to, accusations. You don't want the issue to be about only those two people because it seems like a contest, which will ultimately result in a *winner* and a *loser*. Instead, you want the entire team to come up with the best solution to a challenge that the entire team is facing, which helps build the positive team environment.

The language that you use can also go a long way toward creating a team atmosphere. When people are looking to blame others, they are focused on themselves, so you will hear them using *I* when referring to themselves and you/he/she when referring to other people. To bring the focus back to the team you need to make sure that you are using *we* when referring to how things are going to get resolved. You make it everyone's problem, not just the problem of a single individual.

You need to have a conversation with anyone who is being accusatory on your project, but make sure that the conversation is held in private, not in front of others. Make sure that the conversation is as positive as possible, focusing on:

- The problem at hand, not the people
- The need to work together as a team if the project is going to be delivered on time, and within scope and budget
- The need to look forward toward solutions, not backward at who to blame

### 5(c) Don't ignore accusations

If you don't acknowledge accusations when they are made, you may be condoning the action. Instead, acknowledge that a point has been made, but turn it into an opportunity for the team to solve a problem. For example, a comment that, "Engineering completely misunderstood what we had to do," can become a discussion into how we can produce clearer requirements and design documents for engineering.

# 4.9 People around me have hidden agendas.

By Dave Prior

## 1. Problem

Managing the project is always challenging, but trying to keep everyone focused towards a deadline or deliverable can become difficult when faced with interference from someone's hidden agenda, which can get in the way of your project.

## 2. Warning Signs

Recognizing that team members have hidden agendas can be a real challenge, and if you don't spot the signs, you can be in big trouble. Some things to look for in hidden agendas are:

- Individuals who regularly offer praise, encouragement, sympathy, and support and then inadvertently but repeatedly pull the rug out from under you, a task, or your project.
- Individuals who agree to provide support in front of superiors and then continue to pursue work that is not in line with the project.
- Stakeholders who demonstrate behavior that suggests that they need to *make things happen* in order to keep their project at the top of the priority list.

## 3. What will happen if I do nothing?

### Jim Is Speechless . . . Again!

Jim has received the signed contract for the new project he is starting, and once again, Lenny has delivered a signed contract that does not include a timeline, deliverables that are measurable, or any real cost information. Lenny is highly respected throughout the company because he is the best salesperson the organization has ever had. When the contracts are created, Lenny usually brings in a PM to make sure the contract is determined to be sound before he takes it to the client.

Unfortunately, Lenny's chief *negotiation* tactic seems to be adding scope, shortening the timeline, and removing cost from the contract. No wonder he is able to get so many contracts signed. Sometimes Jim feels like Lenny has some secret agenda that includes having Jim fired for inability to deliver these impossible projects or quit out of sheer frustration.

Lenny is feeling great. He met his numbers for the quarter and received a lot of praise from his boss. Sure, he had to give in on a few points during negotiation, but that's the nature of the business. He is going to qualify for that quarterly bonus he needs to pay for his 10-year old daughter's braces. He knows it may be a little tough on the project team, but those guys are the best in the business and they always manage to get it done. It is also why their base salary is so much higher than his. For Lenny, having a job where he is incentivized on commission is a great fit that motivates him to do well in sales.

Jim's frustration is totally justified. The project is probably going be incredibly tough and his tendency to see Lenny as having a hidden agenda is natural. But is Lenny driven by the opportunity to cause Jim grief, or is he really motivated by the praise from his boss and ability to earn enough commission to pay for his daughter's braces? If Jim was able to understand Lenny's motivator, are there things he could do to encourage Lenny to make the contract more viable from a delivery standpoint?

Unless you can read minds and control people's thoughts, no action you take is going to prevent people from having hidden agendas. However, if you do not take steps to become aware of the hidden agendas, people's motivators and goals, and learn when and how to leverage that information, you are allowing your project to remain in harm's way. The project may become the victim of those hidden agendas being put into play.

## 4. Solution

"Everyone has a hidden agenda. Except me!" according to Crichton (2010). If you are a project manager, you are already dealing with hidden agendas. Coping with them is as much a part of the job as creating and managing schedules. You cannot prevent hidden agendas any more than you can prevent it from raining outside, but you may be able to influence the degree to which the hidden agendas of others have a negative impact on your project. The goal is not to try and prevent people from having their own agendas, but learning to understand what they are, how they might positively or negatively impact your project, and what steps you need to take to protect your project.

With careful observation and analysis, you can hypothesize what the hidden agendas are, and from that point, the steps become similar to traditional risk management. You will need a structured approach:

- Acknowledging the existence of a hidden agenda and accepting that it's not personal.
- Listening, observing, and understanding to ensure that you comprehend each hidden agenda that you are facing.
- Analyzing and responding to each agenda, turning threats into opportunities and minimizing project disruption.

This chapter will show you how to get there.

## 5. What should I do?

With a little practice, a few key steps can help you get past the threats imposed by hidden agendas, but first, you need to become comfortable with the idea that people on your team will have their own reasons for doing what they do. That doesn't mean that they aren't committed to the project; it just means that their priorities may be different than for you or the organization. Your main function in managing these agendas is to ensure that these different priorities do not impact their work and the decisions that they make.

### 5(a) Step 1: Acknowledge and accept

If you happen to be a project manager who becomes offended and disturbed when you find out that people are motivated by things other than making your life and work run as smoothly as possible, then accepting that fact is your first step. It is also one we all need to remind ourselves of periodically, no matter how long we've been in the profession.

Become comfortable with this—everyone is driven by different motivators, even when they are working toward similar end goals. For example, you may be leading your project because successfully managing work is how you measure your success as a PM. Another PM might be driven by praise from superiors, the adoration of team members, or a bonus after final delivery. Whatever the end goal for each individual, he or she is likely to be working out a plan to bring a desire to fruition. The degree to which your goals are sympathetic to theirs may be beyond your control.

### 5(b) Step 2: Listen, observe, and understand

Even after you accept that hidden agendas exist and are not something to fear, they still present risk. If you can't tell what the hidden agendas are, you will not be able to analyze them or determine what to do next. Ask yourself:

- Why is this person saying certain things?
- Why does this issue seem so important or unimportant to this person?
- What is in it for them if the decision goes their way?
- What is motivating this person on this project?

Look at the way that people are communicating with you. Does their body language support the words that they are using, or is it sending a different message? This disconnect might raise additional questions about why they seem to be trying to deceive you.

Dr. Paul Ekman is a recognized expert in facial expressions and body movement. In Ekman's approach to reading people, the critical first step is to determine a baseline of behavior: "We each have our own behavioral style, our own mannerisms. If, for example, someone always talks hesitantly, then hesitant speech is his or her baseline. If such a person were to be hesitant when asked about a crime, it doesn't mean anything. But if it were not the person's baseline, then hesitant speech would raise the possibility of deceit. I usually ask people to tell me about the best and worst experience they had in the last month to discover their usual behavioral repertoire."

As you develop this understanding of how to read the people around you, your ability to spot the clues and understand the motivators that drive their hidden agendas will become clearer.

### 5(c) Step 3: Analysis and response planning

Once you are confident that you understand each hidden agenda that you are dealing with, you can plan and implement a response. Your response should be based on traditional Planned Risk Response Tools & Techniques (*PMBOK® Guide*, 2008).

For example, we've all worked with those people who suddenly find terrible disasters where there are none, and then magically resolve them. This usually happens when they are in the view of senior management and their solution often involves tossing a few key people under a bus. These *heroes* tend to be motivated by either the approval of senior power figures or the lure of achieving some type of higher power or authority. Knowing this, or hypothesizing this, allows you to assess what risks this might present to your own agenda that you need to avoid, transfer, or mitigate. In the best possible situation, it might give you the information that you can exploit by reframing the situation and building a *golden bridge across the chasm* (Ury, 1993), so that their hidden agenda actually supports your own.

Of course, you don't have only one hidden agenda to deal with, and at times the agendas may be conflicting. Try to look at agendas collectively, and build risk response strategies to deal with multiple issues where possible. Also, recognize that you need to *choose your battles*; consider that not every project risk needs to be actively managed, and acceptance is a perfectly reasonable strategy for dealing with the agendas that are likely to have minimal impact on your project. Be prepared to revisit the agendas in the future if necessary.

Everyone has a hidden agenda, but they do not have to impede your project. With careful analysis and planning you can turn what appears to be a weakness, into an advantage.

# 4.10 I do too much work to manage anything.

## By Jerry Manas

### 1. Problem

You have an open door policy, but people come to you all day long with issues. You are so busy with your own work that you can't really give others the attention they need. There's not enough time in the day to do your own work, plus manage your team. You want to spend more time on management and leadership, but if you do, you'll never get your work completed and that will delay the project. What should you do?

### 2. Warning Signs

You would think that this problem would be easy to spot—you don't have enough time to do everything. Reality, though, creeps up until you suddenly realize that things have gotten out of hand. Look for the following signs:

> ### Are You Too *Nice*?
>
> Nancy has an open door policy for her team members to come to her at any time with problems. She's cheerful and always willing to listen and offer advice. But lately, she's been under a lot of stress. She's been working late hours finalizing the budget, doing paperwork for three new hires on the team, and writing performance evaluations for four other team members. Plus, Nancy is supposed to submit her monthly status report to management on the project's accomplishments and other metrics.
>
> In the middle of all this activity, everything seems to have gone wrong on the project at once. Several major milestones are in danger of being missed, one of the vendors has been delivering poor quality results, and her star team member announced his resignation.
>
> With all of this going on, she just doesn't see how she can effectively lead the program, get her work done and keep her open door policy. She needs a better way of getting her job done, but she's not sure how.

- You are increasingly frustrated when people come to you with problems.
- You work late to catch up on the work you were supposed to do during the day.
- Your team feels that they aren't receiving the guidance and leadership that they need.
- You find yourself taking accountability for additional items on the project plan.
- Your deliverables start to slip and you miss deadlines.

### 3. What will happen if I do nothing?

If you do nothing, you will burn out, which can lead to serious health problems. Plus, you'll become resentful of your team members, which they will sense and begin to avoid you, resulting in a breakdown in the relationship. You will start to miss deadlines or quality targets as you take on more work, which will lead to you working even harder to try and address those issues.

Outside of the office, you will have less time for family and friends, which will create additional tensions. Even when you are with them, your mind will still be on the job.

## 4. Solution

On airlines, flight attendants go through their standard safety routine, telling adult passengers with small children that if the oxygen masks deploy due to an emergency, they should give themselves oxygen first in order to care for their child. The same concept applies to managers, support personnel, and anyone in business. We must *give ourselves oxygen first* by setting time aside to get our work done. This must be balanced with the need to be available to those who need us. As a manager, this is even more vital.

You also need to recognize that you cannot be the single solution to project problems. If tasks are falling behind or you are short of resources, the solution is not for you to take responsibility for those tasks—you already have a role to play as the project manager. If you take responsibility for other project aspects, you are effectively saying that project management isn't important.

## 5. What should I do?

In order to give yourself room to breathe, yet remain available to people, there are several changes you can make to help you manage your time and priorities and to avoid over committing.

### 5(a) Create planned downtime

Create time in your schedule to get your work done. Make people aware that this is scheduled work time for you and that you should only be interrupted for true emergencies during this time. Be sure to specify what constitutes a true emergency. By creating a set time each day or week to focus on your own tasks, you are effectively scheduling your work just as you do for team members. Arrange this time based on your needs, not what is convenient for the team—time to work on the status report the day before it is due for example.

### 5(b) Schedule appointments

Require people to schedule appointments with you for issues that need discussion and are not emergencies. Many issues can be addressed in this planned fashion, and can be maintained in a master list and prioritized. You would be amazed at how much productivity is lost through *drop-ins*, which are unplanned meetings or conversations that take you away from your work. If you aren't able to control drop-ins, then take more formal steps—if you have an office, shut the door. You may want to try working from home on days that you need to focus on individual tasks, but not on evenings or weekends.

### 5(c) Hold The doctor is in *hours*

Some people will need to come to you with issues and questions that cannot wait until a scheduled appointment. Only allowing people to see you by appointment could come across as rigid and antisocial, not a good message for a manager to send. Schedule certain times, regularly spaced throughout the week, when you are available for questions or to help people who have challenges or problems. For most issues, people will be able to wait until that time window. Tell people, "I have an open door policy, but not all day long." Let them know the hours you hold open for drop-ins. Emergencies, of course, are an exception.

### 5(d) Create a prioritization system

Any effective manager needs a time management system for prioritizing and scheduling the work that must be done each week. A good system to follow is David Allen's *Getting Things Done*. Allen advises listing all tasks that must be done, putting aside that which isn't yours or can be deferred to a later date, grouping related tasks, and always focusing on the *next action*, provided it is still relevant at that time. Most of all, be open to reprioritizing regularly.

### 5(e) Delegate

Sometimes, managers feel compelled to do it all themselves. Don't fall into that trap. Try to identify work that can be delegated to another team member. Plan to spend a little time up front training someone, but in the long run, this effort pays dividends. Perhaps what seems tedious to you could be a stretch goal for someone else. Likewise, teach them your newly found time management skills. They'll need it too.

### 5(f) Assign work appropriately

If your project is suffering from a lack of resources then you need to flag that to your sponsor and identify the increased risk that will result. Of course, you should attempt to keep the project on target with the resources that you have, which will inevitably mean increased workloads across the team. Make sure that you focus on having the right people assigned to these tasks—and that's usually not you! You may think that you are helping by taking responsibility for some work package items, but you likely aren't, and your important project *management* will suffer.

### 5(g) Establish decision-making principles

Help your team members help themselves. By establishing guidelines and principles for decision making, you can empower your team to make more independent decisions. This way, they won't have to come to you for every little thing. As a side benefit, it will distribute responsibility throughout your team—just recognize that you remain accountable.

In the short term, this may cause you additional work as team members look to you for validation that they are making the right decisions, but it's a valuable investment in the future benefit of the project, the team member, the organization, and yourself.

## References

Allen, David. *Getting Things Done*. New York: Penguin, 2002.

Tuckman, B.W. *Developmental Sequence in Small Groups*. Psychological Bulletin, 1965; 63(6), p.249-272.

Tuckman, B. W. and Jensen, *M. A. Group & Organization Studies*. (pre-1986) Dec 1977; 2,4 ABI/INFORM Global p.419.

# PART B

## Management—The Science of Project Management

# 5

# DEALING WITH CONSTRAINTS, ASSUMPTIONS, AND SCOPE

## 5.1 We took on too much.

By Alexander Matthey

## 1. Problem

In the initial euphoria of being assigned the project management of an important corporate initiative, less experienced project managers nearly always overlook the precise perimeter of that assignment. A clear scope statement is often not established, reviewed, and compared within the timeline and for the budget provided.

Overlooking the preparation of a scope statement is certainly not intentional, but whatever the justification, failing to establish the precise scope remains detrimental to the organization from customer satisfaction, functionality delivery, budget overrun, and schedule delay points of view. The PM does not necessarily collect honors, either.

## 2. Warning Signs

- The stakeholders, who are the major impacted parties to the project, do not agree on what

### Are You Sure You Will Deliver It?

Tino was happy to receive a program management offer from a multinational telecommunications company. To be part of a world-wide program, in his area of double expertise and passion—telecom and program management—within a ten-minute drive from home was the right next step in his career.

The euphoria he had before starting rapidly subsided on the first day. A debriefing with his new boss revealed that the program was already behind schedule. Tino was expected to drive the implementation team over five continents to roll out an AirPort telecom infrastructure for 100 airport line connections from August to December, equaling 1500 connections by next July. In the past 18 months, only 35 had been done. Now, how did those numbers compare?

There was another challenge that Tino was facing: the detailed technical design was incomplete even though roll-out was underway. How much rework would be generated by this risk, which was almost certain to cause issues? "Hmmm," Tino thought to himself. "Who will supervise the engineering team? Who will drive these *experts* to come out with a solution in 2-3 months, when in the last 18 months they could not do it themselves?"

He discovered four months later that the decentralized sales division, which was in charge of *selling* this solution, was losing commission revenue on

*Continues*

165

the project has to achieve or what the major deliverables are.

- No scope statement is yet produced for the project.
- If there is a scope statement, it is not aligned with the needs of the project stakeholders.
- There is no work breakdown structure (WBS) produced during early planning.
- The person footing the bill (the sponsor) does not give clear limits as to what needs to be achieved first or later, and for how much, in writing or orally.

numerous airline accounts by proposing this new solution. Right now, the hurdles were how to motivate over the phone 12 sales managers reporting to another VP and spread over five continents, and to plan scope-wise how to get them on board today.

Tino felt the pinch after two days. Isn't it far beyond the capacity of himself and the eight regional representatives reporting in dotted line to him, to roll out this new world-wide AirPort telecom infrastructure solution in 150 airports and 1,500 terminal connections in 11 months?

A program with floating perimeters, and many dimensions for breaking down the work, had led to too many things to do! Tino had no idea where to start.

- All targets are flexible; the only common point is that everybody talks in superlatives about the result of the projects once it is finished.

## 3. What will happen if I do nothing?

If you don't recognize and address that you are taking on too much because of an unclear or ill-defined scope, then you will see an ever-increasing list of things to be accomplished (scope creep). This will result in dissatisfied stakeholders, who aren't seeing the results that they expect, and unhappy resource owners who have provided members of your team and see those assignments getting longer and longer. Scope creep will leave you demoralized and feeling that you haven't been able to achieve what was expected.

## 4. Solution

Even if not told so, you must clarify what needs to be done with the sponsor, customer, and any stakeholders. The earlier you do this, the better. You should proceed methodically, through iterations of meetings and analysis, which slowly build the complete and approved scope:

- Create a narrative description of what will be delivered—the scope statement—to define what the project will and will not deliver.
- Create a WBS to have a visual representation of what needs to be delivered with increasing levels of detail.
- Compare the actual project deliverables with the scope and WBS, and get stakeholder agreement that you have delivered all of the elements (and nothing else).

## 5. What should I do?

When you realize you took on too much scope, you need to quickly clarify what will be delivered, when, and for what cost. You need to ensure that you reset all stakeholders' expectations. You need to get all major players (sponsor, customer, team, you) on the same page as quickly as possible.

Your starting point is your sponsor. He or she should be able to provide full details of what is expected of the project, when it must be delivered, and how much has been budgeted for the project's execution.

### 5(a) Apply common sense

Remember that the problem with common sense is that it isn't very common! So apply the principle expressed by the following Q&A, often used by trainers when talking about a huge quantity of work (scope) to be covered (delivered): Q: "How to eat an elephant?" A: "Piece by piece." Apply common sense to break down the work into manageable pieces.

You need to combine your common sense with a solid knowledge of the project deliverables (from your project team) and a solid understanding of project management (which you bring), which allows you to identify the major project elements that can then be expanded into the full work breakdown structure. At this stage, you will include major project elements and perhaps major milestones, but identification of scope will immediately bring clarity to the project and provide something tangible for stakeholders to review and discuss.

### 5(b) Not yet started or at an early stage—apply one process

After detailed consultation with the sponsor or customer, and once you are in agreement, draft an easily understood description of what needs to be delivered in the scope statement. From this, develop the following (in this order):

- Detailed description of what needs to be done, broken out into packages in a top-down manner that gets progressively more detailed (WBS).
- Sequence the lowest level breakdowns of the WBS in a network of activities (network diagram).
- Estimate the time and cost of all necessary activities to determine the schedule and budget—the amount of time and money needed to do the identified work. This may be different from the timeline originally proposed by the sponsor and amount of money set aside for the project.
- Work with the sponsor and customer to refine the plan through various iterations until all aspects are approved.
- Once approved, refocus all your team members on what has been agreed to and manage their execution of the tasks.

### 5(c) Advanced stage—apply another process

If the project is further along, it doesn't make sense to replan the entire initiative. Instead you want to focus on the work remaining. You can't change work that's already been completed, but you can work with the stakeholders to make sure that there is agreement on what elements need to be added to the already completed items in order to complete the project satisfactorily. If some scope creep items have already been completed, that reality has to be accepted, but you can prevent further scope creep from occurring.

You also need to work with the sponsor and customer to understand whether the budget or schedule is more important—are they prepared to spend more money to preserve the delivery date, or would they rather accept a delay in order to avoid a cost overrun. Once that is agreed upon, you need to:

- Repeat the process for developing the WBS and estimates, but focus only on the remaining required scope items
- Revise the existing schedule and budget to reflect the revised deliverables and their costs
- Refine the schedule and budget as necessary to account for the preference of preserving delivery date or cost
- Work with the sponsor and customer until the revised plan is approved
- Once agreed, re-focus all your team members on the revised work and ensure that no one is working on items removed from scope

The essential element in the list is the word *focus*. Use all other usual PM techniques, such as teambuilding, motivating, tracking against WBS, schedule, and budget (collectively called *baselines*) to achieve the newly clarified and fixed objectives.

### 5(d) Assistance—know when you need to ask

Managing scope creep can be a daunting activity, but you don't have to do it alone. Don't be afraid to ask for help from your project team and stakeholders, and from other areas of the organization, if available. As the project manager, you need to recognize scope creep and move to stop it, but that doesn't mean that you have to do it alone.

# 5.2 Everything has changed. I need to reset goals and expectations.

By J. Chris White

## 1. Problem

The conditions that were present at the beginning of the project changed so drastically that the project doesn't make sense anymore. You can't simply incorporate a few changes and proceed; rather, this is a fundamental shift that requires the entire project to be reset.

## 2. Warning Signs

Sometimes this problem occurs all of a sudden. There is a dramatic shift that suddenly changes the project entirely. However, this problem can also come about slowly, such as when a large number of changes gradually make it harder to continue with the project until you find that it needs to be reset. Some things to look for include:

- The project champion or sponsor announces a new goal or objective for the project.
- Previous milestones no longer seem logical.
- The skills of the assigned resources no longer fit the work that needs to be done.
- The atmosphere on the team seems frantic and panicky.
- You feel like you are back at square one.

## 3. What will happen if I do nothing?

If you do nothing, the project will not meet its objectives. Once you recognize that the goals and objectives are no longer aligned with the team's tasks, you need to address

### Everything Started Great, and Then . . .

It had been a long time coming, and everyone hoped it would never actually happen, but now the writing was on the wall: the key governmental regulations around which Pam's project were formed had just been overturned by a regulatory oversight commission. Pam wondered to herself, "Some high-paid lobbyists must have gotten to those people."

Regardless, this meant an overhaul of the project: new goals, objectives, deliverables, schedules, perhaps new resources, and so on. Everything had changed. In fact, in many ways the project now needed to go in the *opposite* direction than before. Even though she was an experienced project manager, Pam felt paralyzed.

Up until this point, Pam had done a wonderful job of managing the project: on time, on budget with 100 percent of deliverables met. This was one of her best performances so far. Now, with these regulatory changes, she was basically back to square one and needed to reset the project. Well, *reset* was perhaps not strong enough, in her opinion; the need was more like *destroy and rebuild*. So many changes were necessary.

As she arrived at work that day and walked in the front door of the main office, she felt people staring. Everyone knew the situation. She felt like she was getting the *dead man walking* look from everyone in the lobby. She turned down her hallway and it seemed that people were moving out of the way, purposely avoiding her. "Wow," she thought to herself. "This is worse than I thought."

As she approached her office, her assistant gave her the bad news: Mr. Harris, the VP of her group and her project executive, was in her office, waiting. As she walked in, the first words out of his mouth were, "Yes, the regulations changed, but that is only half of it. Wait until you hear the rest of the changes that impact your project." At that point, Pam's only response was, "I'm going to need a bigger cup of coffee."

the situation. If not aligned, the project will inevitably fail; in addition to being associated with a failed project, you will have to explain why you didn't act when it became obvious that the project wouldn't succeed.

## 4. Solution

While this isn't technically a new project, for all intents and purposes you need to treat it as such. The changes to the project or its goals are so fundamental that you need to step back and replan the initiative. It is similar to a builder who has to *snap the guide line* every once in a while to see a straight line that should be followed when constructing a wall. You need to:

1. Understand the circumstances that necessitated a reset, and work with stakeholders to confirm the revised expectations
2. Build the new work breakdown structure (WBS), estimates, resource allocations, and schedule
3. Gain approval and implement changes
4. Manage performance against plan

## 5. What should I do?

There are a lot of similarities between this solution and the building of your original project plan at the start of the project, but the key difference is the need to ensure that everyone—sponsor, customer, team members, and other stakeholders—understand the need to step back and conduct this reset.

### 5(a) Fully understand the changes that necessitate this project reset

Understanding what happened and why will provide insights into how to move forward, or at least what to consider. There are two distinct goals:

- Let your stakeholders know that you still have the project under control and that you have a plan to move forward.
- Ensure that you understand from the sponsor and customer exactly what the changes are and the implications that they have. This includes both the tangible changes to the project (scope, budget, timelines) and changes to the expected business benefits (goals and objectives).

### 5(b) Build the new plan

Before entering into a project reset, make sure that your sponsor and customer understand that you cannot commit to being able to meet their timelines, budget, or scope until you have completed the planning. You understand what they need after completing the work so far, but you don't yet know if it is feasible. You also need to ensure that your sponsor recognizes that the changes that you are implementing may require additional or different resources, that there may need to be compromise on the constraints (larger budget to meet a more aggressive timeline, for example), and that you need their support to make these changes happen.

The building of the revised plan is similar to the original planning exercise. Use your team to develop the WBS, estimates, resource allocations, etc. You will be able to reuse elements of the original plan, but they will still need to be assessed and validated. Ask yourself: are the estimates, resource allocations, dependencies, and so on, still accurate?

### 5(c) Gain approval and implement

Once your revised plan is complete, you need to review it with stakeholders to get it approved. Make sure that you highlight:

- The key changes from the original plan in terms of scope, cost, and time.
- Any variations from the requested scope, time, and budget targets. (Be prepared to discuss ways that the targets could be met with additional changes.)
- The resource changes that you need in order to execute the plan, along with the implications if that doesn't happen when required.

There will inevitably be discussion and negotiation during this process, but once you have stakeholder approval you then need to implement the plan just as if you were starting the execution of any other project.

### 5(d) Aggressively manage performance against the plan

In theory, performance management should not be different from other types of management, but in reality you need to be even more alert to problems.

- Team members need to adjust to the revised work.
- The pressure of having to replan mid project may have led to planning errors that need to be recognized and addressed.
- Resource changes may have impacted team performance.
- The project may have higher visibility because of the changes.
- The project already has a track record of significant change, so you need to be prepared for more changes in the future.

# 5.3 We don't have the resources we need.

## By Fran Samaras

## 1. Problem

You have been assigned a project within your company. You work with the sponsor and find that your team roster is woefully short. Your existing team tackles the WBS, and you simply don't have enough resources to get the work done.

## 2. Warning Signs

Maybe more than any other problem, lack of resources needs to be recognized early. The sooner you recognize and accept that there is a resourcing problem, the less severe the issue will be, the easier it will be to fix, and the more time you will have to be successful in implementing your solution. Here are some things to look for:

- Your project team communicates to you that their time has been reallocated by their superiors to other projects or tasks.
- You know up front that your project is missing key resources.
- You thought you had enough resources, but now tasks and milestones are slipping.
- Your company had layoffs and some positions were not backfilled. You are tapping the same people for project work who are already assigned to multiple projects or initiatives.
- Your project team has been working with excessive, unplanned overtime.

### Mountains of Work, But No Resources

Bill is a project manager at a small company. The executives at the company are excited about the possibility of growth, and want to make sure they are positioned for the volumes of new work expected and the resulting increase in a long list of projects that will follow.

Bill was recently assigned to manage three medium-sized projects. He worked with each project sponsor (from different functional areas) and was getting the same resources over and over again being offered to him to staff his projects. He can't believe what he heard: each sponsor has named virtually the same resources for their respective projects.

Bill called together his project team to begin to create the work breakdown structure for the first project and resource plan. He saw that the project team would be allocated at least 50 percent of their time to work for this project. The next day he had a project meeting for project #2. Many of the same folks were back again for this project.

They successfully identified the tasks and created the work breakdown structure. They were able to assign resources to this project, using the other 50 percent of their available time, but there were gaps.

The following week, Bill was ready to begin the third project planning. Again, most of the same folks were there. They created the work break down structure and were ready to assign resources. As Bill expected, no one in the room had capacity. They were assigned a few other roles, but for the most part, they did not have the resources to get the project done. What was he going to do?

## 3. What will happen if I do nothing?

If you ignore the problem, your remaining project team members will become overwhelmed with extra work or tasks that are not handled. As this problem worsens, critical path tasks will not be completed, and your project will fall so far behind that it is impossible to recover. You have a commitment as the project manager to be transparent about issues affecting your project.

## 4. Solution

There are several potential solutions to this problem. You may be able to secure a transfer of resources from other projects, use temporary staff or outsource some of the work packages, use a different approach to project execution to try and trim down the time taken on each task, remove some functionality from the project, or extend the schedule to give yourself more time. However, you can't do any of these things on your own. You need to work with your stakeholders and follow a series of steps:

1. Understand the acceptable options and analyze the impact of each
2. Select a strategy, communicate it and replan accordingly
3. Manage the plan

## 5. What should I do?

It can feel lonely as a project manager, but remember that you aren't alone. Your stakeholders are there to support you. In this instance, the sponsor and the customer in particular need to be heavily engaged in helping you manage this problem.

### 5(a) Understand the options.

In some ways, you are lucky to have a resourcing problem because there are many potential solutions that can be implemented:

- Add resources to the team from other projects, organizational areas, or other areas of the company to address the shortfall
- Hire temporary staff—bring in outside contractors to address the need for more resources
- Outsource some of the work; break off some of the project elements and have a vendor complete the work for you
- Use a different approach to the work—agree to take shortcuts and use less formality, effectively accepting increased risk in order to achieve faster progress
- Reduce the scope by eliminating some of the deliverables
- Extend the timeline by delaying the project end date

Of course, these are all fine approaches in theory, but in reality most of these options will be unavailable. You need to work with your major stakeholders, especially the sponsor and customer, to determine which strategies can be used on your project.

If the delivery date is set in stone, then the only options are to increase the budget (add resources in some manner) or reduce scope. Which of those options is more acceptable to the stakeholders? These decisions can't be acted on in isolation—you will need to gain other stakeholders before you can move resources from other projects or departments, and work through procurement for approved vendors.

Once you have a short list of potential solutions, you should analyze the impact of each of them. The specifics will depend on which options are under consideration, but they may include consideration of these questions:

- What kind of skill sets will help the most, do we have those skills in the organization, and if so can they be made available?
- If skills need to be *bought in*, how easy are they to obtain, and can we afford them?
- What elements of the project are the easiest to outsource, and is there a vendor who can do the work for us at a price we can afford, and within our time constraints?
- What elements of the scope can be removed with the least impact on other deliverables, and are those acceptable pieces to remove?
- How much more time do we need to deliver the project with our current resources, and can we reduce that delay if we get additional resources?

### 5(b) Select a strategy

Once you have reviewed the options with your stakeholders, and have considered the advantages and disadvantages of each approach, you should determine a course of action and act decisively to implement it.

Communicate the decision to all of those impacted—stakeholders and team members—and ensure that everyone understands the reasoning behind the decision. Explain the fact that other options were considered before making the final choice. Be prepared for questions, and warn the sponsor to expect questions, also.

Work with your team to replan the project based on the decision made and re-baseline the plan as soon as it is completed. You will need to consider if estimates were recalculated to reflect different resources, any new tasks that have been added, which elements have been removed, and so on. Make sure that you understand the impact of the change on all aspects of your project:

- You need to revisit project risks.
- You may have additional stakeholders (resources, purchasing department, vendors, and so on).
- Your deliverables and success criteria may have changed.
- You may have different constraints.

The possible impacts are plentiful, so use your team to help identify them.

### 5(c) Manage the plan

You have done a lot of work to get to this stage. Now, you must execute the plan that you have developed. Having completed a lot of analysis, you have come up with a solution that will address the resource shortfall on your project, and you have rebuilt the project plan around that solution. It's now up to you to ensure that the team can deliver by executing that plan, and while that is theoretically no different from managing any other plan, there are a few things to be aware of:

- Stakeholders will be on edge and likely concerned about minor variance. They have had to compromise the original plan in order to get the project complete, and that's going to worry them.
- Your team may have lost focus or be demoralized about the changes. They will be learning how to work with new and different team members.

- There may be an atmosphere of *it doesn't matter*—a perception that, because the date was pushed or resources were added before, it will happen again if there are problems.

# 5.4 We're fine, but over budget.
## By Andy Jordan

## 1. Problem

Your project is humming along exactly as you planned. It seems like the perfect project, and so far your work estimates have been spot on. Each week your status reports are showing that you are right on schedule. There's just one little problem—those same status reports keep showing that you are over budget. In order to stay on schedule, you are spending more money than you had planned, and the situation isn't improving. You are becoming concerned that the project isn't going to come in on budget, no matter what you do.

## 2. Warning Signs

You would think that the warning signs for this problem would be easy to spot—you spent more money than you planned for. While that's true, you should expect some minor variances from your budget—the key is to distinguish between those minor variances and more significant problems with your costs that will impact the overall budget. You should be looking for:

> **It's Only Money, Right?**
>
> Scott was really pleased with how his project was going. The team was several weeks into the work and almost every task was coming in on schedule. Suppliers were delivering when they said they would, and the team was completing their work on time. Scott was really looking forward to the project meeting in a few minutes with the sponsor and customer to give them the good news.
>
> There was one nagging doubt at the back of Scott's mind because everything seemed to be costing more than planned, and the budget was starting to look like it was too low, but no one was going to worry about that when he was able to report such great progress on the schedule, were they?
>
> Two hours later...
>
> Scott felt like he had been run over by a train! The project meeting was a nightmare. He tried to explain how well the project was going by distributing the stellar status report and a schedule showing everything was right on track, with no issues and all risks under control. The sponsor and the customer didn't seem to care—they just wanted to talk about the budget. They wanted to know why the project was overspending, how Scott was going to get it back on track, and why things had gotten so bad without his escalating it. Scott didn't know what to do next.

- One or more major unplanned costs
- One or more work areas that are coming in significantly over budget
- A consistent cost overrun on the majority of your tasks (minor expected variances should be approximately equal above and below budget)

Note that although we are talking about terms like cost and budget, the situation isn't restricted to cash overruns. Some projects don't track money spent, they track *effort* spent—the number of hours or days of work required to complete the project.

The principles discussed in this chapter will apply equally to all situations, where the effort required is greater than planned—that's a different type of budget, but just as significant.

## 3. What will happen if I do nothing?

If you do nothing, the situation will get worse; it's as simple as that. Even if the project doesn't become more over budget, the time left to recover is reducing, making it harder to bring the project back on track. Usually, the problem that caused the first cost overrun will also affect future work items and if not addressed the project will become further over budget. That might lead to the project scope being cut, may force the schedule to change in order to try and reduce costs, or in the worst case scenario, may lead to the project being cancelled.

## 4. Solution

Cost overruns are common, and needn't be seen as insurmountable problems. However, you need to take a structured approach to the problem that involves understanding why the problem has occurred, how you can recover, and what you may need to change going forward. Also, consider that theoretical cost overruns may occur—a situation where the costs of the work planned exceeds the budget assigned to the project—a sign of future *real* problems. You need to:

1. Fully understand the cause of the cost overrun and the extent of the impact
2. Take steps to prevent the underlying problem from affecting other tasks on the project
3. Apply strategies that will help the project budget to recover

## 5. What should I do?

When you are planning your project, you work with your team to assign a budgeted cost (in effort and money terms) to each work area. There are many different ways of estimating those costs, but however you do it, you end up with an overall project budget that is essentially the sum of the costs of all of the work elements. This is a fairly straightforward exercise at a basic level. If your actual cost when executing the project wasn't what you planned, then either:

- Your planning was inaccurate
- Something happened that changed the reality from what you could reasonably expect

Before you do anything, you need to know which situation occurred, with the implication that you have to manage budget at the work package level in the same way that you manage your schedule. Whether it is dollars or effort, you need to know how much each task should cost, so that you know early on if you have a cost overrun and need to take action.

### 5(a) Understand the cause and extent of the problem

Sometimes things change after we have made our plans. The cost of equipment may suddenly increase, a supplier may have problems that force you to find an alternate supplier, or other such things. Foreseeable problems should have been identified during the risk planning exercises that you conducted with your core team, and you may have a contingency reserve to offset additional costs (but that's not a free pass for you). On the other hand, a mistake may have been made during planning. For example, you assumed that you would only have to pay $5 per square foot for tiling but in fact it is going to cost $7 per square foot.

Whatever the cause, it should be fairly easy to identify as long as you work with your team members to understand what is happening at the task level, but the harder part is to determine the extent of the problem. Some questions that you need to consider are:

- If equipment costs have suddenly changed, where else in your project do you need similar equipment?
- If a supplier is unavailable, what future tasks are dependent on the same supplier?
- If your estimate was wrong, where else on the project might you have made the same mistake?

When you or a team member first identifies a cost overrun, the numbers may be fairly small. Perhaps the equipment issue has cost the project $1000 more than planned. However, if you have other tasks later in the project that require the same equipment, you may be facing a total overrun of $20,000, and that's what you need to start managing to now. You can't wait until those costs have actually been incurred; that is like waiting until a risk becomes real rather than trying to manage it before it happens.

### 5(b) Take steps to prevent the problem from getting worse

Once a cost has been incurred, you can't *unspend* the money. What you can do is prevent the over-budget problem from getting worse. In our equipment example, you may have time to find an alternate supplier before some of the future equipment needs occur. Alternatively, you may be able to work with your team and stakeholders to agree on a different approach that removes the need for the equipment entirely. Of course, that approach will have its own associated costs, but you are looking to minimize the impact of the overrun, so if the revised approach is cheaper than the more expensive equipment, then it is worth it.

If the problem is due to a mistake during planning, you need to try and find ways to lower the costs to a level closer to your budget. You may be able to find a lower cost resource to complete the work or lower cost materials.

### 5(c) Apply strategies to help the project recover

It is never completely acceptable to be over budget, but sometimes it is more acceptable than other problems. Before you can apply strategies to try to bring the project back on track, you need to understand where the project cost sits in relation to other project constraints. If we think of the three main constraints of budget, scope, and schedule, one of those has to be the most important, least important, and in the middle.

Your project sponsor can help you understand the priority of those constraints, and where budget sits in that priority list will determine what you are able to do to help the project recover. For example:

- If budget is the most important constraint, you can change the scope and schedule in order to keep the project on budget.
- If budget is least important, you must accept a budget overrun if the alternative is to change the scope or the schedule.
- If budget is the second most important constraint, you can change the third most important constraint to preserve the budget, but you must accept an overrun rather than change the most important constraint.

Any changes to scope or schedule still go through your formal change management processes and must be approved by the stakeholders, but the priority of the constraints can provide you with the authority to make those changes.

It is possible that you may be able to reduce the overall cost by eliminating one piece of work entirely, thereby effectively offsetting a cost overrun by not incurring other costs. Alternatively, you may reduce the resources assigned to the project, or negotiate for a longer delivery date from suppliers. This could extend the completion date, but will lower the costs.

These are dramatic steps, and as the project manager you should be looking for other opportunities to help recover from cost overruns. The advantage that you have with budget is that a cost savings that you make in a totally unrelated area to where the problem occurred will still help; it is not like the schedule where things such as the critical path cloud the issue.

There are many things that the project manager can do to help reduce costs on upcoming tasks:

- Assign less expensive resources to tasks, especially ones that are not on the critical path
- Negotiate discounts from suppliers for prepayment or better payment terms
- Find alternate solutions, suppliers, or parts—perhaps using outsourcing to someone who can do the work more efficiently, or the reverse, which is bringing work in house rather than use higher cost suppliers

You need to ensure that the impact on other aspects of the project are acceptable to the stakeholders—lower cost parts may mean lower quality parts, which in turn may have an impact on the overall quality of your product, for example.

### 5(d) A note on reserves

When you are doing risk planning, you identify that there may be a budget impact if the risks become real; this is called a *contingency reserve*. Additionally, there is recognition that some things may happen that you can't see coming, and so a fund is put aside for those situations—this is called a *management reserve*. Collectively, the contingency and management reserves should be between 10 and 25 percent of your total project budget.

In reality, sponsors are very reluctant to formally assign reserves as part of your project budget. That's okay, but there needs to be recognition that not assigning the reserves does not make the risks any less real. If the reserves aren't formally assigned to the project, there will likely be cost overruns on the project as a result of risks, and they may not be recoverable without dramatic project changes.

# 5.5 We're fine, but short on time.

## By Andy Jordan

## 1. Problem

You have a great understanding of the project deliverables, the team is progressing through their tasks, and there are no major issues. Even the budget seems under control. However, there is a problem with the schedule—everything is taking a little longer than planned and now you are faced with insufficient time to complete the outstanding work before the due date. The date is important on this project, so you can't simply ask for more time; instead you have to find an alternate solution.

## 2. Warning Signs

The challenge with this problem is recognizing the warning signs early enough. By the time the more obvious signs are showing themselves, you may have a situation that will be difficult to recover from. You should be looking for:

> ### What Do You Mean It Won't Be Done for Two Weeks?
>
> Everything was going well on George's project. There had been no major issues, the team seemed focused and motivated, and morale was good. Going into the status meeting, George was looking forward to another round of good news. However, just ten minutes into the meeting, George's world fell apart. The IT team reported that they needed another two weeks to complete their work—and it was on the critical path. Suddenly, George was faced with a two-week delay on a project that could not be late.
>
> He didn't understand it—the estimates were completed properly, the resources were assigned as they were supposed to be, and the resources seemed to be working well. Yet, the project was behind schedule and George had a meeting later this week with the sponsor and customer. George needed to take steps quickly to stop the delay from getting worse and bring things back on schedule, but what exactly could he do and how should he go about it?

- Float or slack time (tasks that had plenty of time suddenly being up against deadlines) being used up on early work packages of the project, possibly as a result of resources being moved onto critical path activities (tasks that have to be finished on time or the project will be late).
- Contingency or reserve time being used up at a faster rate than the project is progressing, due to risk events occurring.

- A drop in confidence from your team when they are providing status updates; they seem less sure that the tasks are going to finish on time than they have been previously.
- Failure to meet scheduled completion dates for tasks, after allowing for any float or slack.

## 3. What will happen if I do nothing?

Schedule problems don't cure themselves. They can be caused by any number of reasons, but they all need to be acted upon as early as possible. If you don't deal with schedule issues when they first appear, not only are they likely to get worse, you will have less time left to resolve them. Falling three days behind with three months to go is a manageable problem, but the same delay with only two weeks left is a lot more difficult to resolve.

Additionally, if you don't act quickly to address schedule problems, you will be sending a message to your team that the delays don't matter, and the team will not feel a sense of urgency to correct the situation.

## 4. Solution

Running short of time is common, but doesn't have to be the end of the world. There are a number of things that you can do to recover the situation. The key is to make sure that those actions are working together as a unified set of actions, rather than a series of disconnected steps. You need to:

- Fully understand the situation and your options for attempting to recover
- Implement appropriate steps to avoid a schedule overrun
- Understand the reasons for the schedule difficulties and try to prevent them from recurring or getting worse
- Replan the project (or some elements), if necessary

## 5. What should I do?

When you have a problem with schedule, there are a number of things that you need to do. You need to address the problem that exists now, while at the same time trying to prevent the problem from getting worse, or creating other schedule problems with the actions that you take. At the same time, you need to understand how the problem came about and determine if it's likely to happen again (and if so, how you can try to prevent it). Before that, though, you need to understand your options.

### 5(a) Understand your options

Every project has constraints, most typically time, scope, and cost (money and/or resources). If one constraint is falling behind, you can potentially correct the situation by adjusting one or both of the other constraints. However, you need to know how those constraints are prioritized. If you do not already have this information, talk to the project sponsor to discover the priority.

The priority of the constraints will guide you in the steps that you can take. Let's assume that scope is the most important constraint, followed by time and cost. What this means is that you must do everything possible to avoid changing scope. Once you have done that, you need to ensure that the schedule is met, and then, make sure the budget is achieved. As a project manager, it is acceptable to increase budget in order to preserve the schedule—schedule is more important than budget. However, changes cannot be made to scope to get the schedule back on track because scope is the highest priority constraint. Remember that any change to constraints needs to go through the project's change management process and be approved by the appropriate stakeholders.

If schedule is the most important constraint, you can potentially change budget and scope in order to get the project back on track. You should start with the lowest priority constraint and then move to the second priority if you are not fully successful by adjusting the priority constraint alone.

If schedule is the third priority constraint, it doesn't mean that you don't have to do anything to bring the project back on track with dates. Rather, it means that you have to take steps that will not impact scope or budget.

### 5(b) Make the necessary changes

Regardless of the relative priority of schedule against other constraints, you should look for the most efficient way to bring your project back on schedule. You should not change budget or scope unless you absolutely must do so. That's difficult because it means that you need to compress the work into a shorter timeframe to bring the project back on schedule without reducing scope. In order to avoid increasing the cost in terms of money and/or resources, you have to look at better utilizing the resources that you already have.

If the project is suffering delays, it is likely that some of your resources are unable to work full time on their tasks. Their work has been planned, but delays elsewhere in the project are preventing them from completing that work. Here are some ways to use resources to get the schedule back on track:

*Fast Tracking*

One way that you can utilize resources is through a process called *fast tracking*. This involves taking two tasks (usually on the critical path) that have a finish to start relationship (task B starts when task A is completed) and overlapping them. An example may be to start the product design before the requirements are complete. This isn't ideal, but if there is enough of the requirements document completed to let you start designing, it can help the schedule.

This approach won't work for every situation, and it does increase the risk on the project. You are more likely to make mistakes in the design if the requirements aren't complete. Additionally, it may take more overall effort, including a need to redo some of the design work when the requirements are completed.

However, if the designer would otherwise have been unable to start while they were waiting for the requirements, then fast tracking is worth considering. You just have to make sure that the total duration of the two tasks combined is less than it would have been by leaving the second to start when the first was completed. If you can achieve that goal for tasks on the critical path, you have saved some time on the overall schedule.

### Crashing

Where fast tracking utilizes resources that you have already assigned to tasks, *crashing* is a technique that involves either reallocating resources from other tasks or adding more resources. As a project manager you need to recognize that crashing may increase the cost of your project if it involves adding resources.

Crashing involves taking work that has been allocated to one person or a small team and adding additional resources to the task. This approach can't be used for every task; for example, you can't speed up the time it takes a piece of machinery to produce a part by adding a second machine operator. There is a limit to the benefit, as when a painter needs a week to paint a building and it's likely that three painters can get the work done in a couple of days, but 100 painters won't get the work done in half an hour.

Crashing often increases the amount of effort required to complete the work. You can't generally double the resources and halve the time. There is some loss of efficiency in crashing, but it can generally be used to reduce the duration of a task. If crashing is applied to critical path tasks, it can help to bring your project back on schedule.

If you can crash tasks by reallocating your existing resources from tasks that are not on the critical path, you need not increase the overall project cost. But, if you need to bring additional resources onto the project, you need to formally increase the budget through the change management process.

### Formal project changes

Work with your core project team to identify a number of ways that the project can be completed more quickly. It may be as simple as fast tracking or crashing a few tasks, or it may require more significant changes. Examples of formal, significant changes include:

- Replanning the project based on a larger number of resources
- Outsourcing part of the project work

- Reducing the scope of the project to eliminate some of the requirements or defer them to a later release
- Lowering the quality standard and removing some of the work associated with ensuring quality
- Increasing risk tolerance and allowing for riskier work practices

Some of these may not seem like good options, but they should be considered if schedule is considered more important. All of these are formal changes, and you need to follow the projects formal change management process as if the customer had asked for a change.

As the project manager, you should analyze the likely impact on the schedule of making the change, as well as implications elsewhere on the project. The responsibility for approving a specific course of action will lie with the change review board, which should include your sponsor and a customer representative.

### 5(c) Understanding why the problem has happened and replanning is needed

Once you implement steps to bring the project back on track, there is more work to be done. You need to understand what caused the schedule problem in the first place, and if necessary, take steps to correct the situation. Some problems are genuinely unforeseen events that cause delays, such as a snowstorm that causes flight delays and means that a part is late in arriving. While the impact is real, these don't require detailed analysis as they are unlikely to recur, but these are, by far, the minority.

Much more common are issues with either execution or planning. Execution issues occur when resources are not delivering on the tasks assigned to them. This may be because of lack of focus, conflicting priorities with other initiatives, a failure to recognize the importance of the work, or other reasons. These issues require you to use your management and leadership skills to help the team members who are having difficulties to refocus on the work that they need to complete.

Planning issues come down to incorrect estimates. The work takes longer than expected, for example. In this case, you need to revisit future estimates and see if the same planning mistakes were made for them. Using your core team, you need to analyze the assumptions that you used in creating the estimates, and then compare them with the reality that actually happened. If you need to reconsider future estimates based on what you now know, do so as soon as possible and communicate any new estimates with your stakeholders.

Stakeholders need updated information to make the right decisions about the project, and you need an accurate plan to understand how best to change the project and bring it back on schedule.

# 5.6 We can get everything done on time and under budget, but not very well.

By J. Chris White

## 1. Problem

With the purpose of meeting the cost and schedule targets of the project, you have been aggressively managing your team members and it seems to have worked. However, the team has ended up *cutting corners* and the quality of deliverables has suffered. As a result, the customer is not satisfied that the deliverables meet their standards, and is rejecting some of the work.

## 2. Warning Signs

Quality failures can be *hidden* during the process of completion. It is easy to see when a project is over budget or behind schedule, but *under quality* is tougher to see. There is also a tendency for people to think that *the quality will be okay*." Things to look for in quality control include:

- The quality of the work being done by project team members is beginning to decrease.
- Milestones are being approved, even though they are not complete, in an effort to *keep things moving*.
- Everyone seems to be rushing.
- Everyone appears to feel overwhelmed.
- Team members are putting in extra time without charging it to the project.
- A key stakeholder found a poor quality project deliverable in the quality assurance process.

## 3. What will happen if I do nothing?

Simply put, things will continue to get worse. If you don't address quality issues as soon as they arise, then you are subconsciously telling your team that quality isn't as

---

**Two Out of Three Ain't Bad**

Elisha ran the earned value (EV) numbers one more time just to make sure. If she was going to tell her customer some bad news, she knew she had to be absolutely positive. According to the EV calculations, the project was on time and slightly under budget. That was the good news.

The bad news was that some of the work was not getting done. "Well," she tried to convince herself, "it's not that the work is *not* getting done. It's just not getting done at the level we all originally thought it would." Elisha could recall several project team meetings where certain customer requirements were removed in order to meet the schedule and budget constraints of the project. "De-scoped" was the term they used in the meeting. "De-pressed" is how she now felt.

This was a great customer. They always wanted additional features to the product line, which meant a stream of projects for Elisha to manage. However, on this feature upgrade project, the work was not quite up to snuff. She didn't want the company's reputation (along with her own reputation) to diminish in the customer's eyes. Fortunately, the customer was not yet aware of the situation. All the customer knew was that the project was on time and on budget. And, it was indeed. Unfortunately, not all the feature requests were making it into the final upgrade. The original list was too much to do within the schedule and budget constraints.

This wasn't the first time that Elisha had experienced this problem. Many times she had seen the three-way tug-of-war among schedule, cost, and scope (i.e., quality). It seemed that there were always trade-offs to be made. Was this normal, or did she fall asleep during the part of the project management class that discussed *quality*?

important, and quality will continue to decrease. When quality problems are discovered, as they inevitably will be, you will have a dissatisfied customer, and potentially a rejected product. The team could get labeled as not having enough experience or expertise to get the job done, which can reflect negatively on future career paths. Depending on the deliverables of the project, the impact could be far more severe—does anyone like low quality medicine, cars, or buildings?

## 4. Solution

Welcome to the world of trade-offs. The do-nothing scenario is to accept losses in quality or scope to keep within cost and schedule targets. When this option is not acceptable, there are three choices:

- Make sure you exhaust all options for getting all the original, required work done within the original time and cost constraints for the project.
- Renegotiate with the end customer or project sponsor to decrease scope or quality requirements, so that all the newly defined work can adequately be done within the original time and cost constraints.
- Renegotiate with the end customer or project sponsor to increase the time or cost constraints, so that the original scope of work can be accomplished at the desired quality level.

## 5. What should I do?

Schedule, cost, and scope (i.e., quality) form the Bermuda Triangle of constraints for any project. Consider the example of a carpenter making a three-legged stool. The first two legs can be made imperfectly, and the third leg is then just altered to make up for the imperfections of the other two legs to achieve the "level" balance for the stool. This metaphor is useful because you can visualize the tension among the three competing constraints.

### 5(a) Exhaust all options

The first option focuses on ensuring that you are making the most of the resources that you have and that they are as effective as possible. For instance, do you have the right resources on the team? Are other projects stealing your key resources? To get more information and ideas on this, look at other chapters in this book because they cover these in more detail. Here are a few good sections of the book to review:

- 4.4: Some team members lack the skills they need.
- 4.5: Other projects keep stealing my resources.
- 4.6: My *team* isn't really a team.
- 5.1: We took on too much.
- 5.3: We don't have the resources we need.
- 7.12: Oops, I forgot a chunk of work that needs to be done.
- 8.4: I may not have the right team.
- 9.6: Costs are much higher than we thought.

### 5(b) Decrease scope or lower quality

Before making any rash decisions which involve trade-offs between scope and quality, find out if your project is ahead of schedule and/or under budget. You may be able to ease one or both of these constraints a little and still meet your original quality targets. You (or your project sponsor or customer) may be putting unnecessary pressure on the project beyond what it needs. For instance, the project may be one week ahead of schedule. You could let the schedule slip a week and still be on schedule. This little bit of slack time (or budget slack) may be enough to improve quality.

If you reviewed your schedule and cost status to find they are at or behind your targets and the scope or quality is still suffering, then you need to look at decreasing scope or lowering quality in more detail.

If you simply have way too much work to do for the project, not enough schedule/cost to do it, and no flexibility to increase scope or budget, you need to prepare the customer and your project sponsor to either reduce the scope or accept a lower quality deliverable set. Once they know your situation, they may be willing to voluntarily remove some scope or quality requirements to bring those requirements more into line with schedule and cost targets. Just kidding; this rarely happens! Everyone usually wants all original requirements met (and probably some additional requirements, too). If you get lucky and they bite on this suggestion immediately, count your blessings. It's still worth asking. Just don't be surprised if they don't budge. If they don't initially accept your position, you have just entered into another requirements negotiation phase, much like at the beginning of a project. However, in this case, something has to budge. That's all there is to it. It's a matter of *what*, not *if*.

At this point, a strong customer relationship really pays off because you will know what is truly important to the customer and can use that as a bargaining chip. For example, you may say, "I know you want both features $X$ and $Y$. But feature $X$ is the real driver because it is a competitive differentiator for your product. Feature $Y$ is nice to have, but not absolutely necessary on this first release. We can make sure it is the first feature that we add on the next project," and so on. The key is that the customer and/or project sponsor must be made aware of the situation and the potential final results. The more warning you give them the better; as time progresses, the options for response decrease significantly.

### 5(c) Increase schedule or budget

The third option is to renegotiate with the end customer or project sponsor to increase the time and/or cost constraints so that the original scope of work can be accomplished at the desired quality level. Implicit in this option is the understanding that neither scope nor quality can suffer. That means that scope and quality are a higher priority than schedule or cost. As in the second option, when you negotiated for scope and quality requirements to be decreased, you will now be negotiating at a *higher level* and trading off schedule and cost requirements to make way for additional scope and quality. It's the same concept as the second option, but with the inclusion of requirements from all three elements of the Bermuda Triangle tossed in for consideration. As with the second option, something *has* to budge. It's just a matter of *what*.

### 5(d) No changes

In reality, there is a fourth option: the customer or project sponsor does not renegotiate and instead demands that everything needs to be done as originally planned with the original cost, schedule, and scope goals. If they do not budge on anything (and you've exhausted all other options for changing team members, etc.), the last resort is to somehow convince project team members to work extra time that is not documented on the project.

This is probably one of the toughest challenges a project manager can face. You have no way to compensate the resources because they cannot add cost to the project. And, you need them to work additional time to meet the scope and quality requirements without exceeding the calendar targets. Plain and simple, more work has to be done each day. If you have good relationships with the team members, you can probably get away with a little bit of this. They may be willing to give you a little extra time, and, this may be all you need. If you need more extra time, you'll have to get creative. There are no *standard* solutions to this problem. Failure may be the only option.

### 5(e) The project post mortem

Regardless of which option you choose (or is chosen for you), examine why and how the project got into this situation. Perfect projects don't experience these types of trade-offs. But, no one has the luxury of the perfect project these days. So, look at the conditions that made this current project imperfect. Was it because the original estimates were too low with regard to actual labor hours? Was it because a new technology or approach didn't pan out the way everyone expected, so rework was needed? Was it because something outside of the project changed and necessitated a new plan (e.g., a change in a specific regulation or product certification)? Did the team simply bite off more than it could chew because it was too optimistic?

When doing this detective work on lessons learned, be brutally honest with yourself and your project team. It is very easy to point the finger somewhere else. If it was a bad estimate to begin with, own up to it and understand the ways in which the estimate was bad, so that it won't happen again. If members on the project team were not performing at the expected level at the beginning of the project, identify it and let them know about it, so that they won't do it again on another project. If the learning curve at the beginning of the project was longer than expected, figure out why.

Other chapters in this book deal with how to correct some similar situations (e.g., add *buffers* to the project to accommodate cost and schedule risks). The point being made here is to do a thorough reflection on the project. If you're not learning from each project and seeing opportunities for improvement, then you're fooling yourself.

# 5.7 My project's end point is a moving target.

### By Cicero Ferreira

## 1. Problem

When the project began, you knew the deadline. However, time has gone by, and now you feel that the project will never end. There is always a major new demand or change in scope, and the end date is postponed, again. Additionally, estimates always seem to be too low and deadlines are missed

## 2. Warning Signs

You would think that this was an easy problem to spot, especially when the deadline moves out. However, there are a number of valid reasons why that might occur. You need to distinguish between a onetime delay and the beginning of a trend that could lead to the project that never ends. Here are some things to look for:

- Multiple delays to the project occur because decisions are not being made promptly or the sponsor/customer continues to change their minds.
- There are a number of scope changes, especially additions to the feature set.
- Your budget or resources keep being reduced and compensated by extending the timeline.
- Estimates are consistently inaccurate on the low side; work always seems to take longer than planned.

### Is This a Project or a Process?

It was a brisk fall morning in New York City and a light rain was falling. Shannon was in her office dreaming about her upcoming vacation in Rio de Janeiro when her manager entered the room. He had just come from a board meeting, and there was a new urgent demand.

They needed to redesign the main process of the manufacturing company they work for, the Order to Cash (O2C) process. The board had defined the following two objectives of reduction: (a) the process cycle time, and (b) the need for working capital.

Now they needed to start this twelve month project as soon as possible. Two weeks later, the project team was working, and Shannon was happy to have been appointed as the project manager. However, at the time, she did not foresee the multiple timeline problems that would arise from the project.

The problems began four months later when Shannon's company acquired a competitor, who had the best O2C process in the market. That caused Shannon's team to reschedule their project's work in order to learn about the new O2C process.

As if that were not enough, in the coming months, there were changes in tax regulations as well in the technologies for process workflow, and business process management. These changes were the causes of a schedule redesign, which led once again to a new work plan.

Eighteen months later, Shannon was again in her office, not so happy now, looking out the window at the Manhattan skyline and contemplated: "My project's end point seems to be a moving target."

## 3. What will happen if I do nothing?

If you don't address the issues that are causing the end date of your project to push further out, you are sending a message that you are okay with what's happening. If you don't push stakeholders for timely decisions, they will assume that there is no hurry. If you don't question the constant changes, the assumption will be that you can accommodate them. You can't take the perspective that *there's nothing we can do about it* because it will result in further delays, worsening morale on your team, and ultimately lead to project failure.

If the cause of failure is within your team, either with planning or execution, and you do nothing, your team will question the point of producing estimates if they don't mean anything. The team will also start to ignore deadlines, which clearly don't matter.

## 4. Solution

The solution to this problem will depend upon the cause of the constant delays coming from one of two categories:

- External factors—scope changes, delays in making decisions by stakeholders, resource reassignments, and such
- Internal factors—problems with planning estimates or with the execution of the work by the project team

However, there are a number of similarities to solving both problems. They both require consideration and resolution of:

1. Understanding why the problem is occurring; the root cause of the issue
2. Exploring alternative approaches to solve the problem and recommending a course of action
3. Implementing the solution and monitoring for improvement
4. Recovering from the delay that has already occurred

## 5. What should I do?

This problem can be a challenge for project managers because the reason for the problem may be beyond your control. You, therefore, need to ensure that whether the problem is external or internal, the people involved understand the impact of the delays and the importance of eliminating and correcting them.

### 5(a) Determining root cause

The reason for a delay may seem obvious, but you need to look beyond the obvious and understand why the problem is occurring. For example, if delays are occurring because of a failure to make decisions, is it because the stakeholders don't understand the need for timely approvals, or is it because something has changed and there is doubt about what the decision should be?

For external issues, you need to discuss these reasons with your stakeholders and find out what is going on:

- If we are making lots of scope changes, is it because the original scope is wrong? Do we need to step back and build a new set of requirements rather than subject the project to constant change requests?
- If we keep losing resources, is it because the project is no longer a priority? Is it because an unplanned project has come up that needs to be

addressed? If so, we need to reset expectations and formally replan the project (or potentially put it on hold or cancel it).

- Are decisions slow because the urgency isn't understood, because the project manager hasn't communicated when decisions are needed, or is something else going on that makes the decision harder to make? If so, let's get all stakeholders together and discuss the issues and potential courses of action.

For internal issues, the matter is easier to deal with because there are usually only two reasons why delays consistently occur:

- We planned badly and did not accurately identify how long tasks would take. That may be because we didn't fully understand the work, or our work breakdown structure was incomplete, and we are now having to complete work that wasn't on the plan. Maybe we were too optimistic in our planning.
- We are executing poorly against the plan. The plan numbers make sense, but we aren't meeting the targets because team effectiveness is not where it needs to be. The team is not working together well, or is not committed to the project, but is working on other things that are not formally assigned to them. Maybe they are the wrong resources for what we need.

### 5(b) Exploring solutions

Once we understand why the problems are occurring, we can do something about it. The first step is to engage with the people who are responsible for your delays and make them part of the process of developing a solution. Any actions that you take to correct the problem will require commitment from them, so it is important to make them a part of developing those actions.

Use inclusive terms in the discussions. For example, say, "How are *we* going to better control scope?" rather than, "How are *you* going to reduce the number of change requests?" Always remain focused on the ultimate goal of reducing project delays.

Recognize that there may not be *perfect* solutions. If the issue is that your project planning was flawed, then the only solutions would be extending the schedule, increasing resources, or reducing scope. This isn't really a delay, but more an inaccurate delivery date, initially.

Once you identify various courses of action, you need to work with stakeholders to determine the plan that will actually be implemented. This may be simple, if stakeholders commit to make decisions within two days of receiving the request. Or, it may be a more complex solution that involves significant change to the project.

Once the decision has been made, it needs to be communicated to everyone on the team.

### 5(c) Implementing and monitoring

The agreed upon solution needs to be implemented immediately, which may have a major impact on the project. A major replanning to address faulty estimates may require progress on the project to slow down or stop until the revised plan is complete. A reconsideration of the project scope and requirements may have the same impact, or at least a refocus onto tasks that the team is sure will remain in scope.

Regardless of the solution, you need to closely monitor how successful it is and act immediately if:

- *A stakeholder misses a deadline for a decision*: Chase them aggressively as soon as the deadline has passed.
- *A change request is received a few days after the revised scope is approved*: Call a stakeholder meeting to discuss the matter.
- *You find that a team member is being pulled off to work on another project after you have confirmed your resource assignments*: Talk to your sponsor and their functional manager to understand why this is occurring.
- *A team member misses the revised date for completing a task*: Talk to them to understand what the problem is and try to address it immediately.

## 5(d) Recovery

Even though you have implemented solutions to address the cause of all project delays, and you are monitoring the success of those solutions, you are not done. This problem started because the project didn't seem like it was ever going to end, and the deadline was getting pushed further and further out. Now that you have solved the problems that were responsible for the *never ending* project, you need to examine whether you can recover from some or all of those delays.

Depending on the nature of the problems, recovering the delay might not be possible. If your project changed fundamentally as a result of major scope changes, revised estimates, or a different staffing model, you need to rebaseline and establish a new delivery date. But if the delays were caused by bad execution or slow decisions, you may be able to recover at least some of the lost time.

You need to work with your team to identify areas where recovery can occur and then execute plans to achieve that recovery, although, of course, the estimates need to be realistic.

# 5.8 Part of my project has no end to it.

### By Fran Samaras

## 1. Problem

Your project team is driving to create their deliverables, but you begin to notice that some tasks are repeated again and again. You look at the project plan and you keep adding these same tasks with no end in sight.

## 2. Warning Signs

This problem requires attention to all aspects of the project. If you only focus on the high-level aspects, you are likely to miss this problem as it gets buried in the details. Look out for:

- Planned tasks that are being repeated over and over
- Production support, customer conversion, or similar tasks being included in the project without defined end dates and status
- Loose ends that don't seem to be cleaned up near the end of a project
- As project manager, you keep getting tapped to fix or look at problems from your last project
- Your project scope was never really clearly defined, and enhancements or problems keep getting added to your project plan
- One task keeps getting extended while everything else is moving forward as planned
- A resource seems to be spending a lot of time on a fairly straightforward task

> **I Thought I Was Helping . . .**
>
> Jennifer and Nick are the project manager and business lead on a project, respectively. They have recently been tasked to implement a new system and associated process changes. While they had to narrow down the scope to achieve a date required by their sponsor, they did implement on time and have celebrated their success.
>
> Barbara, in Operations, was excited about the new system, but didn't know where to turn as she began to have problems from time to time on the system.
>
> Jennifer and Nick were now working on the enhancements to the new system, so Barbara reached out to them. Nick and Jennifer had that "team player" attitude, and had the developers make quick fixes to Barbara's problems as they came up.
>
> Next thing they knew, the occasional one off, here and there, resolutions they were providing did not seem to end. Barbara's requests were endless. The extra fixes started to get in the way of the other enhancements.
>
> Nick and Jennifer's "team player" attitudes were waning. There was no end in sight. What did they do wrong?

## 3. What will happen if I do nothing?

If you ignore the problem, your remaining project team becomes overwhelmed with extra work that they need to pick up that may not be associated to new work assigned. Critical path tasks may not be completed and your project will not be completed as projected or it may simply be stopped or put on hold. Worse yet, your company may see the project as a failure even though something was implemented, due to your inability to segment ongoing activities.

## 4. Solution

To deal with this problem successfully, you need to be able to identify the potential problem areas, and then plan and execute strategies to prevent them from becoming a problem, or undo any damage that has already been done:

1. Identify tasks or activities that have the potential to cause you problems.
2. Build comprehensive transition plans into your project with customer sign-offs confirming acceptance.
3. Look for additional items that may be problematic during project execution, and develop additional strategies to address them.
4. Execute a transition plan and formally end the project.

## 5. What should I do?

To manage this problem successfully, you need to plan for potential problems at the start of the project, and monitor and act on any issues that occur during project execution.

### 5(a) Identify potential problems

Start by looking at the project scope to ensure that all elements are appropriate for the project. If the scope includes tasks that should be part of another function within the organization—professional services, production support—the scope may need to be modified to remove these tasks. The work can still get done, but it's not a project task.

Some items won't show up in the scope and will need to be picked up from the project plan. Look for tasks that are scheduled to be repeated constantly and pay them special attention. Are they actually contributing to a deliverable, or are they really operational tasks that should either be removed from the project or transitioned to an operational team during later phases of project execution?

### 5(b) Build transition plans

Work that should not be part of the project can't simply be ignored. It still needs to happen so your project needs to include formal transition and hand over. To be successful you need to:

- Identify the transition tasks
- Identify who they need to transition to
- Build the plan for transition
- Establish the measures/indicators that will confirm that transition has been completed

This may require the involvement of your human resources or organization design staff to help determine how this new work load will affect your organization. In some cases, new departments or responsibilities will need to be formed to deal with the new work. Additionally, you will need to identify where, in existing processes, the work would best be integrated, if appropriate.

Once you target an area where the work most appropriately may be handled, engage that group's leadership as soon as possible. You don't want to make a recommendation without giving this stakeholder some heads-up.

Work with the operational areas to create procedures and how-to guides for the staff taking on this new work. Create new job descriptions, if appropriate. Create production standards or success criteria for the tasks, especially if you have that frame of reference from your project experience and/or documented it in your project plans. Next, outline a transition time frame including job training, if needed.

### 5(c) Identify additional issues during execution

When you are in the project's execution phase, there is still the potential for never ending tasks to crop up. At this point, you need to be careful—problem task transition activities can get missed, or they might be legitimate project tasks that are just dragging on and never seem to be completed. If it's the latter, there are other areas of this book that can assist you. It may be a symptom of one or more of the following issues:

- Inaccurate planning
- The wrong resources assigned to the work
- Unclear requirements

If you identify additional transition requirements, repeat the steps previously mentioned, being conscious of the point where the project stops doing the work and the ongoing operational function takes over. This needs to be an identifiable milestone where there is no confusion over where the responsibility lies.

### 5(c) Transition

As part of the project closure you need to execute the transition plan that you developed earlier. This will include procedure review, training, customer acceptance testing, and so on, and may involve a number of iterations. It is imperative that you get sign off from the staff or department that is assuming the work, so you can officially close the repeated work off of your project plan.

# 5.9 The requirements keep changing.

## By Elizabeth Harrin

## 1. Problem

At the start, you thought it was great that people were so enthusiastic about making sure that the project delivered something which was fit for its intended purpose. If that meant a few changes here and there, so be it. Now the changes are piling up, and it looks as if you'll never get finished, since the goal posts keep moving.

Changes to requirements are common on projects. After all, when you started out, you may have had a clear vision of what needed to be done, but as the project progressed, users started to realize what is possible and asked for more features. Or perhaps the client keeps changing her mind. Whatever the reasons behind requirement changes, you are facing a project suffering from major scope creep.

## 2. Warning Signs

Don't get hung up thinking that changes are bad, they aren't. However, if you are seeing some of the following issues, you are going beyond normal changes and may have a problem:

> **Everything Changes . . .**
>
> Emily was nearly at the door when her sponsor said, "Oh, and you know that invoicing module? Will you make sure it does currency conversion for our international accounts?" Emily smiled tightly. This was the fifth change to the requirements for the invoicing module this week, and it was only Wednesday. Last week, her sponsor had told her that the module only had to cope with national accounts. "I'll see what I can do," she said.
>
> On her way back to her desk, Samantha from Sales stopped Emily in the corridor. "We've done some focus groups with customers," she said, "and here's what they want from the database." Samantha handed her a long list. "Mostly new stuff, but these two are just rewriting some reports. You can do it all for the launch day, can't you?"
>
> "I'll see what I can do," Emily said. The reports had already been written. How could she tell the development team that they would have to do it all again? The changes didn't even look that important. All the requirements for this project were changing on a daily basis and at this rate they would never get everything done by the launch date.
>
> Emily knew she couldn't carry on like this. She was being a doormat, saying yes to everyone although there was no way it would all get done. The requirements were too fluid and she needed a new approach to keep the project, and its stakeholders, on track.

- People are changing their minds about what they want.
- Requirements that were agreed upon are now different, or removed entirely.
- You are spending a lot of time chasing people for agreement, or just chasing people in general.
- Your plan is out of date as soon as you update it.
- The project is running late because you have to schedule rework to cope with the changing requirements.
- You can't see the end of the project.

## 3. What will happen if I do nothing?

The project will drag on if you do nothing, as constant changes to requirements mean nothing is ever completed. Eventually, the project will be cancelled or you will be asked to step down. The project will be taken over by someone who will be able to deliver what is needed. Your credibility as a project manager depends on being able to complete projects and ensure they deliver business value, so there is a risk that you'll end up being seen in the organization as someone who can't control a project, which is not good for your career.

## 4. Solution

Changes aren't necessarily bad; they just need to be handled in a controlled way. You need to stop the scope creep and make sure that everyone signs up to the current list of requirements. You need a way to make sure that if there are changes in the future, everyone understands what the impact is of making those changes. In summary, you need:

1. An agreed set of current requirements
2. A clear understanding among your project team and stakeholders of the impact of making changes
3. A change control process

## 5. What should I do?

When the requirements keep changing, it is important to nail them down as quickly as possible to get back on track. Establish where you are now, and how you will handle changes when something else changes—because it will!

### 5(a) Clear set of requirements

Go back to your scope document. What is this project trying to achieve? This forms the underpinning structure of your requirements. List all the requirements you currently have on the project and make sure they all tie back to the project's objectives.

Ask all your stakeholders to review the list and confirm that it presents the current view of what they want the project to deliver. If there are conflicting requirements, these need to be resolved. Organize individual sessions with each of your stakeholders to understand their point of view and exactly where the points of difference lie. Then, get the relevant people in the same room to discuss the requirements—what's in and what's out. If they fail to reach an agreement, you might have to get your sponsor or other outside help to arbitrate and make the final decision.

This exercise will give you a comprehensive view of the project's requirements. Any changes after this point need to be assessed and taken through the change control process that is detailed later on in this chapter.

### 5(b) Set expectations

As part of talking to all the project's stakeholders about their requirements and the definitive list, take the time to explain to them that there is always a cost associated with making a change. If they change their minds in the future and want to add or modify a requirement, there will be a price to pay. It's not always a financial price—as a result of the change:

- The project could take longer, or finish earlier.
- More resources could be required.
- The result could be a different quality outcome than what was previously agreed.
- The project could cost more.
- The project may be exposed to a different level of risk.

Changes can be desirable, so stakeholders should know that they have the option to make changes if required. However, they should do so in the full knowledge of what the impact could be, and with guidance from you about how possible it is to make the change. For example, it is easier to accommodate changes early in a project. If you are building a hotel, it is not going to be easy to change the layout of the bedrooms when the decorators are finishing up. Any smaller changes that cannot be accommodated now could be packaged into a Phase 2 or other project in the future.

### 5(c) Change control process

Now that you have a baseline of project requirements, you need to know what to do, should you be asked to make another change. A change control process establishes how requests are handled for new requirements, or modifications to existing requirements. You may have a formal change management process, or you may choose something less formal. Either way, the steps are the same:

1. A request to make a change to the requirements (scope) baseline is received.
2. The change is assessed against set criteria, typically the impact on:

   - Schedule
   - Resources
   - Other requirements
   - Budget
   - Project risks
   - Objectives and project as a whole, if the change is not done

3. A decision is made whether to implement the change or not (see Figure 5.1):

   - If yes: document the change, update the plans and schedule, and let everyone know.
   - If no: tell the person who requested the change that the work will not be done, and the reasons why.

Make sure that project stakeholders and, in particular, your sponsor, understand and agree to the change control process that you will be using.

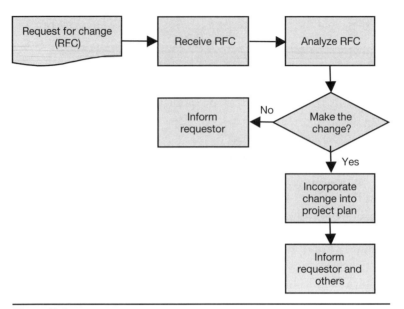

**Figure 5.1**

# 6

# BUILDING AND DELIVERING ON REQUIREMENTS

## 6.1 My sponsor told me what to do, but there's not enough detail.

By Michael Wood

### 1. Problem

You want to get started on your new project, but you feel your sponsor's expectations and direction are incomplete and lacking in detail. How do you facilitate more detail from your sponsor and other key stakeholders regarding the specific outcomes a project is to deliver?

### 2. Warning Signs

Perhaps the most telling warning signs are feelings of uncertainty, fear, and doubt regarding your preparedness for starting the project. However, knowing how to recognize vague objectives does not have to rely on feeling. Instead, be sensitive to the use of terms that require interpretation to quantify. For instance, while a project objective

> **Sponsor Vagueness Syndrome**
>
> When Lucy got her first project management assignment, she felt lost at first, and didn't know where to start. Lucy was suffering from Sponsor Vagueness Syndrome. She thought that she had to take whatever direction was provided and run with it, and she did just that.
>
> Lucy wasn't very confident about exactly what the sponsor wanted, but she worked with her team to come up with a plan that she hoped would meet the sponsor's needs, and started executing it.
>
> Unfortunately, a month into the project after reviewing the first few status reports, the sponsor became disenchanted with Lucy's efforts. The sponsor began questioning Lucy's actions and that resulted in more specific details about what was expected of the project. Lucy had totally missed the mark and, for all intents and purposes, had to restart the project.
>
> Time lost, monies lost, and Lucy's future prospects were not looking good, how could she have managed project startup differently?

to *streamline the sales processing and fulfillment systems to improve sales and sustain competitive margins* might seem clear to the sponsor of the project, it lacks any actionable information. There is a need for clarification of what is meant by *improve sales and sustainable competitive margins*. Specifically, watch for:

- A lack of objective measures
- Use of phrases like *details to follow*
- References to functionality in other systems or products without providing the details

## 3. What will happen if I do nothing?

Starting a project with vague or incomplete objectives and guidance exponentially increases your risk of project failure in false starts and in implementing erroneous solutions. Therefore, it is unwise to begin projects with anything less than well quantified and actionable objectives. The last thing you, as a project manager, want to do is to guess at what the project's sponsor's expectations are, or what they mean by terms such as *better, faster, competitive, or improved*.

## 4. Solution

As a project manager, you must learn how to facilitate the sponsor and others as to what outcomes are to be achieved and in what timeframe. Moving sponsors from the vague or abstract toward the specifics of a project so that it can be accurately framed and scoped requires strong interpersonal communication skills, patience, and acceptance that people rarely know what they want at a specificity level that can be acted upon. Instead, most people communicate broad areas of desire, frustration, or need, with the expectation that during the course of the effort their needs will become more completely defined.

The real issue isn't so much that the sponsor is vague, but more that project managers are not trained on how to ferret out specifics related to expectations and ground rules (project protocols, requirements, and the like). Even more so, project managers must know how to prove and validate that the requirements identified are functionally accurate and correct. Thus, an almost instant disconnect is created if the project manager and team flounder in a sea of vagueness, and the sponsor's frustration grows as the project stalls or runs amuck.

To move the sponsor and key stakeholders from vague to quantifiable and actionable objectives, consider the following steps:

1. Drill down on the stated objectives in order to understand them in more fundamental operational terms.
2. Vet the project's objectives against the organization's business plan and strategies to ensure alignment.
3. Document and obtain sponsor approval for the revised *quantified* project's objectives.

## 5. What should I do?

One way to avoid the predicament of vague objectives is to engage the sponsor and other knowledgeable stakeholders with the goal of establishing a clear set of project objectives that can be expressed in quantitative terms. In the author's book, *The Helix Factor*, a case study is used to illustrate how a typical a project sponsor might state core objectives in terms that are not actionable, even though somewhat specific. In this case, those objectives were as follows:

- Increase sales about 20 percent a year.
- Stabilize workforce at current levels.
- Increase cash flow by $15 million a year.

Given these overarching goals as a starting point, the project manager was tasked with finding ways to improve operations and underlying IT systems in a way that would contribute to achieving the objectives. The obvious challenge is how to get started, who to involve, in what timeframe, for what budget, etc. While not all projects are so far reaching in expected outcomes, this example shows the point that with little more than a gleam in their eyes and broad expectations, sponsors can initiate projects that require the project manager to organize, mobilize, and define in great specificity how to proceed.

Working with sponsors to quantify project objectives is best done in the form of facilitation work sessions where you can gather the sponsors and other knowledgeable stakeholders into one room and collectively shape the project's objectives—building consensus on a go forward strategy.

### 5(a) Drill down on the stated objectives in order to understand them in more fundamental terms

Given a set of detailed objectives, the project manager will want to understand how a 20 percent increase in sales, stabilizing the workforce at current levels, while increasing cash flow $15 million a year fit together with one another. In addition, the project manager will want to establish any budgetary and time line expectations of the sponsors and management. Finally, the project manager will want to elicit guidance as to who in the organization has the requisite knowledge needed to shape the improvements needed to achieve the identified objectives.

Below are a few clarification questions that might have been asked of the sponsor(s), given those same objectives:

- What changes does the sponsor think must be made in order to achieve 20 percent growth?
- What percent of the growth will come from industry growth versus increased market share versus acquisitions?
- Who in the organization (people or groups) should participate in identifying and shaping ways to achieve a 20 percent rate of growth?
- Does the current workforce have the capacity to support the growth objective?
- Will the achieving of a 20 percent growth in sales provide the desired $15 million in additional cash flow?

- What areas other than sales and marketing might contribute to increasing sales and cash flow to the levels desired?

These and other clarifying questions help the project manager develop a better context for pursuing the project and provides the rationale and insight needed to help the project team appreciate the importance of the project. Hopefully, through this exploration, the project manager will establish a set of additional expectations and objectives that provides a roadmap into the functional areas being impacted by the project's goals. What is critical is that the perceptions of the sponsor(s) be expanded and quantified into meaningful operational terms.

When completed, the project manager will have a clearer understanding of the project's scope, what operating units should be involved, the timetable for achieving results, any budgetary constraints, and more. With this information, the project manager should be able to organize the discovery phase of the project, the goal of which is to identify the improvements (changes) needed to business processes and systems in order to achieve the sponsor's goals.

### 5(b) Vet the project's objectives against the organization's business plan and strategies to ensure alignment

Just because you have quantifiable project objectives doesn't mean they are right for the organization's goals and needs. The savvy project manager, with these newly developed objectives in hand, will take the time to cross reference them against the organization's business plan and long-term strategies. This step is not only a due diligence best practice, it also ensures that the project is aligned with the overall organization's objectives and reduces the risk of producing outcomes that create disconnect throughout the enterprise.

The results of this step should be documented in a way that reflects the relationship between the organization's objectives and the project. This can be done using a simple matrix as shown in Table 6.1. In the intersecting cells, place a short explanation of how the project objective supports and achieves the organizational objective. Each project objective should contribute to at least one organizational objective.

**Table 6.1** Organizational and project objectives

|  | Project Objective 1 | Project Objective 2 | Project Objective 3 | Project Objective 4 |
|---|---|---|---|---|
| Organizational Objective 1 |  |  |  |  |
| Organizational Objective 2 |  |  |  |  |
| Organizational Objective 3 |  |  |  |  |
| Organizational Objective 4 |  |  |  |  |

### 5(c) Document and obtain sponsor approval for the revised, quantified project's objectives

Once you have completed the correlation of project objectives to the business plan, you should review the results with the project sponsor and obtain their approval for going forward. At that point, you will be set to convert the objectives into detailed business requirements that will ultimately drive the project plan.

# 6.2 We ended up with the wrong design.

### By Michael Wood

## 1. Problem

What happens when you end up with the wrong design? Most likely a wrong design is a symptom of the wrong requirements, which in turn could be the outcome of a defective requirements discovery process (the actual problem). Unfortunately, learning this usually happens in the course of implementation (training, testing, etc.), and not during design. Because *wrong* designs typically don't reveal themselves until late in the project, management, sponsors, and stakeholders view the effort as a failure, questioning the competency of the project manager and the supporting team. This is the last place any project manager wants to find themselves.

## 2. Warning Signs

The first sign that something is amiss with design specifications should surface during the design reviews where each design specification is compared

> **Follow Bob Mackie's Approach for Design Success**
>
> Dress designers who make custom dresses for stars like Cher and other headliners, go through a design process. Bob Mackie, who designed many of Cher's bejeweled gowns, followed a process to ensure he designed the right dress for Cher (one that would provide Cher with a dress she was delighted with). His process involved:
>
> Step 1. Develop a drawing of the gown and obtain Cher's approval.
>
> Step 2. Pin up a dress on a mannequin with Cher's dimensions, using faux jewels, and get Cher's approval.
>
> Step 3. Create the dress (again with faux jewels) and have it modeled by a model with Cher's dimensions for another approval by Cher.
>
> Step 4. Fit the prototype dress to Cher and have her approve for production.
>
> Step 5. Produce the dress with real jewels, and deliver.
>
> When asked what happens if Cher still doesn't like the dress, Mr. Mackie replied (paraphrased here), "Well, I guess Cher just bought an expensive dress she didn't like." He could make this declaration because of the due diligence he took to validate that such an event would never take place.

to the underlying requirements. When found at this point, corrective action is relatively easy. The warning sign is clear that you have a flawed design at the design review stage of a project—when the design does not agree with the underlying requirements specifications.

However, should the design conform to the requirements and still be wrong later, the requirements gathering process may be flawed, representing a more systemic problem.

Unfortunately, when design flaws are not found during the design review, they are usually not found until development is complete. Thus, when finally discovered, causing expensive rework, missed deadlines and blown budgets. The warning signs at this stage include:

- Stakeholder rejection of the final product or program
- Immediate volume of change requests during implementation
- Identification of usability or suitability defects

## 3. What will happen if I do nothing?

Implementing the *wrong* design is not something that goes away with time. Doing nothing is not an option. (Whether you will be allowed to fix the problem is an altogether different question. Unfortunately, implementing the wrong design means the proverbial horse has left the barn, so closing the barn door after the fact will not help much.) What are some of the impacts of doing nothing? That depends upon how mission critical the project is to the future prosperity of the organization. At the extreme, the impact could include:

- Loss of revenue
- Loss of jobs
- Lawsuits
- Reduced stock prices
- Loss of market share
- Business failure

At the lower end of the *wrong design* spectrum, you might experience things like:

- Costly rework
- Budget overruns
- Missed implementation deadlines
- Loss of personal and team credibility

It is clear to see the importance of getting the design right and, when defects are discovered, why it is critical that they be addressed quickly and with full transparency. While you can't fix the mistakes that produced the wrong design on the project, you can learn and take steps to ensure you never end up with a wrong design again.

## 4. Solution

There are a number of ways to ensure that you never end up with the wrong design. The best way is to build in *proofs of correctness* into your development lifecycle methodology, so that as the project progresses you are required to correlate:

- Requirements to business processes
- Design to requirements
- Applications to design

These check points ensure that defects, anomalies, and departures from stakeholder needs are detected as early as possible to their introduction into the project's process.

In addition, the use of prototypes can help stakeholders understand how well the effort is progressing toward producing the desired project outcomes. Whether system simulations, scale models, or a new dress for a superstar, prototypes improve the visualization process, and thus help avoid missteps and miscommunications that can lead to a wrong design.

Adding check points to the project process does not have to add cost or time to the project. In fact, done correctly, they can save time, money, and more.

## 5. What should I do?

While there is no guarantee that a design once implemented won't be flawed, steps can be taken to minimize the possibility. As systems become more complex and central to enterprise success, it is increasingly critical that the level of due diligence followed to ensure alignment between the organization's needs, its operational practices, and supporting systems is defect free.

### 5(a) Align requirements to business processes

The first step to building safeguards into your process is to build in tests during the discovery phase (that's right, discovery, not definition) that correlate the identified requirements with how they will be utilized once deployed. These correlations are most often referred to as *use cases*.

Simply put, a use case is a scenario or set of scenarios that describes the *who, what, when, where and why* aspects of how a function or set of features will be used. Use cases come in many flavors, from narratives to complex diagrams, to simulations and prototypes. In general, the simpler the use cases presentation, the better its chance of being understood by stakeholders.

Based on experience as an information technology professional, here is an example of an effective approach to developing use cases, using a layered process. The first layer of the process is an *end-to-end workflow diagram*. This diagram depicts the lifecycle of a workflow in terms of each phase the object of the workflow travels through from its origination (birth) until it no longer changes or transforms. For example, a simple end-to-end sales process might have the following phases:

1. Customer request for quote
2. Quote sent to customer
3. Customer placing order
4. Order approved
5. Order shipped
6. Order billed (invoiced)
7. Order paid

Within each phase of the process, the required procedures are identified to move the object of the workflow (e.g., the order) from one phase to the next. For each identified procedure, the system interactions (technology touch points) are defined in terms of the inputs, processes (business and processing rules), and database updating rules needed to support the procedures. This information can be presented in a narrative format, a modeling language like UML (unified modeling language), or a diagrammatic model. A best practice in this area is to break the business case down to individual requirements packets consisting of the following components:

- Requirements overview
- Requirements specifications (layouts, rules, etc.)
- Design specifications (I/O models, process logic diagrams)
- Estimates for design, programming, testing, training and deployment

Since each packet can be traced to a specific workflow (via cross indexing) to the procedure level, a context is established along with a reliable level of certainty that the requirement is functionally correct and deployable.

### 5(b) Align design with requirements

The next step is to use high level process simulation and/or prototyping tools to build a testable version of the requirement that users can use to validate that the formats, business rules, user interface, and such are correct. At this point there is little chance that the requirement is flawed, and therefore if designed and built to the specifications contained within the packet, the design should be correct.

There are many design workbenches available that will accelerate the design programming process. Whether using a workbench or manual design technique, be sure to include a traceability process. *Traceability* is the process of mapping design specifications back to the driving requirements. A cross indexing scheme can accomplish this, or use the requirements-design packet approach as previously discussed (which included indexing).

### 5(c) Align applications with design

The final step is to use the requirements and design documentation to create testing criteria and scripts that can be used to exercise the application once programmed. If you developed a comprehensive set of use cases, this task becomes straightforward: what is needed is to create test data that adequately exercises the use cases process, options, and alternatives.

Developing test scripts requires that all functional possibilities are tested to ensure the application can handle every logical eventuality. Hopefully, the design specifications provide these rules down to the field level.

Another example of a layered process can be found in the Sidebar story on the process Bob Mackie used to ensure the right dress design for Cher.

Regardless of the subject matter of the project, the work plan should incorporate relevant checkpoints that test how well the outcomes being produced align with the expectations of the stakeholders.

# 6.3 We have the wrong technology for the job.

## By Michael Wood

## 1. Problem

What happens when your technology is not sufficient to support the information processing requirements of the organization? Usually, unplanned capital expenditures happen, that's what! The good news is that the cost of updating platforms and infrastructure is less expensive than it was even a few years ago. Today, it is very rare that IT groups have an underpowered environment. Gone are the days of managing CPU cycles and disk space (DASD). Ironically, in a world focused on *lean*, when it comes to platforms and infrastructure, most savvy CIOs go *fat* on technology. Why? In order to optimize people's effectiveness and productivity, it makes sense to reduce the need to compete for processing resources.

> ### Everything's Slowing Down
>
> Like many CEOs, Greg had a tendency to exaggerate a bit. "Nothing is working anymore!" However, it was a good wake-up call. Charlie, the company CIO, knew at that point that his economizing on technology investments over the years was no longer appreciated by management. He had been feeling the stress of constant down time due to platform capacity and outdated technology for some time and his competencies were now frequently called into question along with his "penny wise, pound foolish" approach to leading the company's IT organization.
>
> It felt like everyone was complaining about systems taking too long to process their transactions and IT staff taking too long to fix problems. IT support is always a thankless job, but Charlie's organization seemed to be taking it to a new level.
>
> Charlie is stuck with too little budget to really upgrade services and overwhelming demands for the basic services already in place. What can he do now?

So, what can you do when you find yourself in an embarrassing situation where your platform and technology are not aligned with the processing expectations of your stakeholders? In general, the answer depends on what the impact is at the time this revelation becomes evident.

## 2. Warning Signs

We are all familiar with some of the symptoms of IT problems. However, erosion of the platform's ability to support the needs of the organization can happen over time, and it may not be until you find yourself in crisis mode that you realize that you have a problem. Monitoring system performance against a minimum performance baseline on an ongoing basis will provide you an early warning mechanism for knowing when improvements to the infrastructures are warranted. Look for it to show you:

- Increases in downtime or outages
- Declining service levels
- Increased response and resolution times
- Increased user complaints

## 3. What will happen if I do nothing?

When you learn that your platforms, infrastructure, and technologies are no longer appropriate for the needs of the organization, you have little choice but to take action to bring things back into alignment. Doing nothing can change the meaning of CIO from Chief Information Officer to Career Is Over in very short order.

## 4. Solution

There are two basic approaches to addressing technology problems, and the right solution will depend on the circumstances of your individual organization. The two options are:

- Catch up all at once
- Use an incremental approach that spreads the cost of catching up over future projects

## 5. What should I do?

To determine the right solution, consider the current IT situation, the needs of the business today, and the needs that will be driven by upcoming initiatives. When you implement a solution, you need to be sure that it truly is a solution and you don't have problems after its completion.

### 5(a) Catch up all at once.

Fixing technology shortfalls in one fell swoop is usually the option of last resort, and is required when the lack of capacity is so dire that operations are failing to the point of impacting sales and customer relations. Typically, this situation is career threatening, and potentially business threatening. The good news is that given the excessive organizational pain level, getting the needed funds is fairly easy. (However, once the crisis is past, the ensuing inquisition might spell *career over.*) Make no mistake about it, the risk here is retribution as the leadership questions how you allowed the organization to fall so dreadfully behind. Of course, the reasons are many and often out of the control of the CIO.

Often, over the years, management has refused IT requests for upgrades and investments to keep IT current. More often than not, the problem was caused by the CIO's mistaken belief that keeping things lean and mean will be appreciated and rewarded. Not true. CIO 101—at a minimum you are expected to provide everything needed to support the IT needs of the organization all the time, no matter what.

### 5(b) Catch up incrementally via future projects

Hopefully, infrastructure shortfalls can be resolved in a less crisis-driven mode by factoring infrastructure investments into every project. This more incremental approach allows the capital investments associated with new platforms and other technologies to be matched with the value added by the project they support. For example, a new customer relationship management project (CRM) implies more than just new software; it also includes the requisite equipment and related technologies.

One way to accomplish the embedding of needed infrastructure into projects is to assume that zero infrastructures exist to support the initiative. Under this assumption, the project would then require the requisite technologies to support the implementation. Granted this is overkill, but it provides a worst case scenario.

With this knowledge, you can determine the incremental technologies needed. The difference represents an efficiency benefit to be realized from existing infrastructure. Now the judgment part comes into play. How much of that benefit do you want to use in additional investments in order to improve the overall infrastructure needs of the organization? Here, you will want to look closely at the ROI (return on investment) the project promises to deliver. A good rule of thumb is that projects should yield at least 20 percent ROI. So, any returns over 20 percent might be candidate for some added infrastructure investments.

Consider a simple example: assume a company's minimum threshold on project ROI is 20 persent (see Table 6.2). You are tasked to budget a project that has a potential return of $1.295 million, thus, to attain a 20 percent ROI the project could cost up to $6.475 million. Your best case estimate is $3.5 million which would provide a 37 percent ROI (1.295 million/3.5 million), way beyond the threshold.

However, your current platforms and infrastructure need a $2.3 million overhaul. Given that you never want to budget a best case scenario for a project, you could take this opportunity to budget around $6 million ($3.5 + $2.5 million) thus providing monies needed to improve the infrastructure while providing some contingency for overruns that might occur while staying below the $6.475 million to achieve the needed 20 percent ROI.

Using this approach, it looks like everyone wins. You deliver a needed project, you fix the infrastructure, and the organization gets a stellar ROI.

Even if you only recover half the infrastructure shortfall, you are ahead of the game.

**Table 6.2** Example of using high-yield projects to finance infrastructure improvements

|  |  | ROI % | ROI $ |
|---|---|---|---|
| Best estimate (given) | $3,500,000 |  |  |
| Expected ROI (given) |  | 37% | $1,295,000 |
| Budget assuming 20% ROI (the value if $1,295,000 is 20%—the most you can spend to achieve required ROI) | $6,475,000 | 20% | $1,295,000 |
| Potential available for infrastructure investment (the difference between your estimate of $3.5 million and the maximum spend of $6.475 million) | $2,975,000 |  |  |
| Overall investment needed to bring infrastructure in line with enterprise needs (given) | $2,300,000 |  |  |
| Revised project budget including infrastructure improvement needs (best estimate plus infrastructure shortfall plus $200,000 contingency) | $6,000,000 | 22% | $1,295,000 |

# 6.4 The design meets the requirements, but does not satisfy the project's goal.

By Michael Wood

## 1. Problem

Your worst nightmare comes true. You diligently defined the project's requirements, then faithfully designed those requirements along with complete traceability, and built the application in accordance with the design. Now you discover that when the solution was deployed, it failed to meet the project's goals. In short, you spent the money, used the time and resources allotted, produced the result, and it was the wrong one. An ultimate failure.

How could this happen? What went wrong, and where did the methodology fail?

## 2. Warning Signs

More likely than not, the seeds of failure were sown due to a flawed requirements discovery process that did not use business process analysis to drive requirements identification.

| Avoiding Nancy's Nightmare |
| --- |

Everything was going right with Nancy's ERP enhancement project until things started to unravel during the testing phase. It became apparent that the design, while aligned with the requirements, wasn't going to satisfy the goals of the project. Completing the project, only to learn the outcomes delivered failed to achieve the expected objectives, would be a nightmare come true.

How should Nancy proceed now that she knows that the project is in failure mode? How will this failure impact the organization? Whose jobs might be lost? How much time, money, and effort would be squandered? Clearly, Nancy now carries a heavy burden, one that she and others can learn from going forward.

Should Nancy get a project to manage in the future, perhaps she should consider using business process analysis to ensure that the solutions being developed properly correlate to the outcomes desired.

Correlating project objectives to the changes in business processes needed to achieve those objectives, and driving the underlying IT requirements based on process changes identified, will keep you from sharing Nancy's nightmare.

Even today, there seems to be a lack of clear understanding of how to develop provably correct requirements. Perhaps it is the main reason IT applications are often criticized for not aligning with the needs of the organization.

When the design meets the requirements developed but do not meet the project's goals you have a serious problem brewing. Wrong requirements result in wrong designs, programs, and outcomes. This is a very expensive proposition. When you produce flawed requirements you most likely have a defect in the requirements discovery and/or definition process. Unfortunately, the *warning signs* of this usually happen very late in the project or after the project has been implemented into production. Things to look for include:

- Stakeholder complaints
- Customer refusing to accept the product
- End users claiming that the product doesn't meet the need
- Data conversion issues

It may be too late to save this project, and you certainly can't undo all of the damage caused (wasted time, money and resources) for this initiative, learning from the failure to improve the requirements discovery and definition processes can prevent future such mishaps.

## 3. What will happen if I do nothing?

There is little if anything in the world of project management that can be ignored when failure occurs. Doing nothing in the face of project failure usually exacerbates the situation to the point of crisis at which:

- Reputations could be ruined
- Jobs could be lost
- Stakeholders could be damaged

Implementing projects that fail to deliver the value expected is perhaps the greatest fear of project managers. While there is little that can be done to salvage failure, there are lessons to be learned that can avoid an encore of future failures.

## 4. Solution

The project landscape varies, depending on the project. Whether building a bridge, developing new medicine, or implementing new systems, the solution to ensuring that the requirements align with the needs and expectations of the project's stakeholders requires a discovery process that provides adequate maps, correlation, and checkpoints.

It is a good idea to ask yourself, "How can I prove that the solutions I am implementing are correct for the organization?" Perhaps this question was the primary motivation behind the author's development of *The Helix Methodology*. This top-down/bottom-up approach engaged client management in a comprehensive, stakeholder value focused process. Before one single IT requirement or specification was developed, time was spent validating project objectives against stakeholder needs, alignment with strategies and business plans, and operational realities.

The project's objectives were then recast into operationally measurable terms. The business processes affected by these objectives were also identified and subsequently analyzed to identify what changes in processes, policies and technologies would need to occur in order to achieve the objectives specified. Thus, a complete map was developed that traced the project's requirements from the top of the organization into operations—a map that would be used to drive IT requirements discovery.

At the time I had no idea, but I had developed one of the world's first *Lean* business process improvement methods. Back in the 1970s, there wasn't a language for discussing things like process maps, value gap analysis, value delivery systems, and the like. It wasn't until the early 1990s that workflow management started to get attention. If not for the emerging popularity of TQM (total quality management), reengineering, and GE's success with Six Sigma, we could still be in the stone age of process improvement.

The evolution of business process analysis, improvement and management has resulted in the creation of a connective tissue that binds stakeholder needs to strategy;

to business objectives; to operations; to supporting IT. Best of all, it has led to a general acceptance that IT requirements are best derived as a by-product of business process analysis. As a general rule, the process of identifying IT requirements for business process analysis is as follows:

- Define every requirement in terms of how it supports project goals and affected business processes.
- Develop use cases for each requirement or cluster of requirements.
- Develop standard definitions for explicit input, update and output requirements as evidenced by touch points within the process workflows, and use cases.

## 5. What should I do?

In general, whether you are a project manager of construction projects or IT projects, the first thing you should do, when you become aware that the outcomes of the project will fail to satisfy its goals, is sound the proverbial alarm. The sooner you let management know of the problem, the better the chances for corrective action.

Going forward on future projects, you will want to build in safeguards and early warning systems to alert you to a misalignment at every stage of the project lifecycle. The best practice would be to implement a requirements discovery process that is stakeholder needs driven and provides the context and maps needed to provide the level of traceability that is required to ensure that the right requirements are defined, designed, developed and deployed.

Within the world of information management this discovery process takes the form of business process analysis and is summarized as:

### 5(a) Define every requirement in terms of how it supports project goals and affected business processes

Driving requirements from process analysis documentation is perhaps the only sure way to prove that the requirements developed will align with the needs of the people and processes they leverage. Every requirement defined should be documented in terms of how it supports the project goal and processes affected. This level of traceability is rare in development efforts, yet is virtually fool proof in terms of ensuring that the requirements developed are functionally correct.

### 5(b) Develop use cases for each requirement or cluster of requirements

The next step in proving that the requirements support a project's objectives is to develop process-oriented use cases for each requirement or cluster of requirements. Each use case presents the rationale behind how each requirement will contribute to solving specific business challenges or needs. Think of these as *proofs of correctness* that create a context between what is going to be developed versus what is actually needed by the enterprise. Where practical, each use case should be accompanied by a prototype of the requirement. Prototypes allow the user of the requirement to experience it in *real* terms and can provide the final assurances that the requirement, as specified, does indeed fulfill the intended need.

### 5(c) Develop standard definitions for explicit IT input, update, and output requirements.

Standard definitions are evidenced by IT touch points within the process workflows and use cases, and as implied by the data model. In a 2007 article, the author presented a comprehensive overview on how to drive provable, correct requirements from models and other documentation produced during a business process improvement (BPI) initiative. As a primer, those seeking to improve their requirements discovery skills can find suggested standards for uncovering implied requirements from process and data model maps. In addition, the article details an approach for creating standard estimating metrics for each type of input, process, and output of an application (Wood, 2007). The approach presented has been successfully deployed over a host of projects of all sizes.

# 6.5 Beyond being *done*, how do I measure quality?
### By Michael Wood

## 1. Problem

The project is complete. You came in on budget, on time, and even achieved the expected outcome. Yet, you are feeling uneasy; something just isn't right. While congratulations abound, no one is smiling. What's going on?

Projects are like air travel. Just because you arrived at your destination doesn't mean you enjoyed the trip. If the experience was bad enough you might not want to board another plane and do it again, no matter how great the paradise that awaits you; the means doesn't justify the ends. Maybe it is time to consider the quality of the project process in terms of its ability to produce the right outcomes in a way that is as pain free as possible.

**Is Your Project Like a Trip to the Dentist for Stakeholders?**

You have an impacted tooth and it hurts. You go to the dentist and learn that you need a root canal. The procedures, cost, number of visits, etc. are explained, and you book an appointment.

The work is done, the pain gone and your smile saved. The dentist seeks to book your next visit, a cleaning, but you resist. Why?

Assuming there isn't a financial component to your decision, what caused your resistance? Could it be that, even though the procedure was successful and the result stellar, the process was too painful to risk a repeat experience?

In projects, as in going to the dentist, the outcomes have to be worthy *and* the process painless if true success is to be achieved. Achieving positive outcomes that were painless to attain can wash away the sins of budget overruns and missed deadlines.

## 2. Warning Signs

The first sign that the quality of your project process may need improvement may not come until the next project when the project's stakeholders (management, users, project team, sponsors) appear reluctant to engage after their previous experiences. When the process is too painful, regardless of the outcome achieved, people steer clear of repeating the experience. By being sensitive to the behavioral clues that people exhibit during the course of a project, you can be forewarned that the approach being taken is either easy to digest or causing pain to those involved. Early warning signs that the process is running amuck include:

- Poor status meeting attendance
- Lagging project status reports
- Unreturned phone calls
- Emotional detachment by those who logically should be very engaged

## 3. What will happen if I do nothing?

Believe it or not, most projects are not pain free. What is frightful is that project process quality is rarely part of a project's post implementation review (PIR). As a result, it is rare that improvements to the project methodology in terms of cultural fit, interpersonal relationship management, and other soft skill factors are ever improved upon. Instead, organizations rely on the temperament of the project manager and project team members to set the pace for how communications and people issues will be handled. In short, doing nothing appears to be the norm when it comes to improving project process quality. Instead, most changes to project methods and frameworks center around increasing compliance to:

- Project paperwork standards
- Tracking protocols
- Issue management
- Status reporting requirements

Since pain is associated with projects, it is accepted as *the way it is*, akin to visiting the dentist.

## 4. Solution

With the advent of major investments in ERP (enterprise resource planning), CRM (customer relationship management), BI (business intelligence), and other major IT application environments, project portfolios have grown larger and more complex. To combat this complexity, project management frameworks like Agile and Scrum have grown in popularity to the point of being a distraction in some cases. Yet, with all these advancements, it seems that improvements to the *human equation* aspect of project management have seen little or no improvement at all.

Adding an assessment of project process quality to the post implementation review process offers one way to identify improvement opportunities in this area. Specifically, this process should include an evaluation of how stakeholders would rate the experience. Ideally, the data collected would be captured in a way that could be evaluated over time and across many projects so that trends and improvements could be monitored.

## 5. What should I do?

Perhaps the fastest way to incorporate an assessment of project process quality into the post implementation effort is via a stakeholder survey. The challenge is to develop a survey that will readily allow you to contrast desire versus expectation versus experience—in short, to quantify stakeholder satisfaction with the project process. The goal of the survey is to identify gaps between these three areas. The wider the gap, the more improvement that is needed; the narrower the gap, the more mature the process quality during the project.

Using a three-pronged approach to each question can result in overtly large surveys, and thus the number of areas to be assessed should be kept to about 5 to 12 subjects.

The last area that the PIR needs to explore is one of *stakeholder satisfaction* with the project process. Often, the project ends up successful, but stakeholders seem unreasonably negative toward the project manager. The budgets were met, the project delivered on time, every deliverable achieved, every objective attained, and every expectation met except one—the process was too painful.

During this phase of the PIR, a survey usually works best to take the pulse of the stakeholders in terms of how painless or painful they found the project experience. However, the survey needs to be structured correctly. It is not sufficient to just have stakeholders rate the project's *pain level* on a scale of 1 to 10. Instead, the survey needs to test gaps in expectations. For example, instead of having stakeholders rank their satisfaction with the length of status meetings, you might ask them the following:

How long should project status meetings be?

1. Less than 30 minutes
2. 30 to 60 minutes
3. As long as they need to be

How long were the status meetings you attended?

1. Less that 30 minutes
2. 30 to 60 minutes
3. Greater than 60 minutes

How satisfied were you with the length of status meetings?

1. Dissatisfied
2. Satisfied
3. Pleased

Using this three question approach, the expectation gap can be quantified and correlated with satisfaction levels. Contradictions can be evaluated. For example, if a stakeholder answered (1) to the first question, (2) to the second and (3) to the third, a contradiction arises. How could the expectation of less than 30 minutes with an experience of more than 30 minutes result in a positive satisfaction level? Clearly, there are other dynamics in play.

More important, though, is the knowledge gained in relation to what stakeholders define as the right duration for status meetings in contrast to their experience. With this knowledge, you can fine tune future communication plans and meeting procedures to provide a better stakeholder experience.

While this example is simple, it makes the point that understanding stakeholder satisfaction levels requires the quantification of expectations and experience so that meaningful baselines and metrics can be established and acted upon.

# 6.6 The team is frustrated with rework based on changing requirements.

By Michael Wood

## 1. Problem

A project that is beset with change requests often means the team will need to rework or redo deliverables that are already completed. Change requests that lead to rework can happen for a number of reasons; some occur due to changing needs and requirements, while others occur as a result of defects in the requirements discovery and definition processes. Substantial requirement changes encountered during the construction phase of a project suggest that either the requirements capturing process is flawed, or that the change management process is in a chaotic state.

## 2. Warning Signs

Luckily, the warning signs that something is wrong are relatively easy to spot:

> **Where Did We Go Wrong?**
>
> The only thing that can upset your development team more than having to build applications to exacting specifications is when they do so only to be besieged with rework requests because of defects found in the requirements or design blueprints provided them.
>
> Such was the case on Glenn's ERP improvement project. After spending months defining and implementing a strict set of requirements and design specification processes and documentation rules, he found that the level of rework situations was worse than ever. Now with the programming staff at his throat and IT's credibility with management and the user community at stake, Glenn needed to fix the problem or risk a mass revolt.
>
> Luckily, Glenn took a logical approach, pinpointing where and why things were running amuck. In so doing, he found a flaw in the design review process that didn't adequately correlate the design specifications to the underlying requirements documentation. While the fix to his defective process didn't make the changes in process any easier to digest, Glenn stopped the bleeding and soon the volume of change requests was back to a normal level.

- The volume of rework or change requests being experienced is greater than expected.
- Stakeholders begin changing their minds regarding previously approved requirements.

If the need for rework occurs during testing, it could be a sign of flaws in the specification and development process. However, if change requests are flowing during the design and construction phase of the project, you can be sure that the requirements discovery phase failed to identify a complete and comprehensive set of requirements, ones that the stakeholders feel comfortable with. Be sensitive to the volume and nature of change requests that impact requirements before they are in a testable state.

## 3. What will happen if I do nothing?

If requirement changes abound during the construction phase, the rate of change can exceed the rate of progress. Development staff can begin to feel victimized by the process because they are tasked with having to redo work already completed due to no fault of their own. Allowing this to continue can hamper staff morale. Even worse, it can sow the seed of failure for projects, as milestones fail to be achieved on time and on budget, or are not met at all. For project leadership, it is imperative that a runaway change process be corrected and resolved.

## 4. Solution

In an ideal world, requirements would be frozen before design commenced, and likewise the design would be frozen before the first line of code was written. Unfortunately, the one constant that we can expect to be with us always is that of change, whether due to people changing their minds or defective definition processes.

To cope with the constant presence of changing requirements, the savvy organization integrates a formal change management process into its project management practices. The process needs to provide a mechanism for vetting the request to determine its functional contribution to achieving the project's objectives. Each change should be organized into a set of categories; each category implies how crucial the request is to the project's success, as shown in Table 6.3.

A mature change management process alone will not fix issues related to defects in the development lifecycle process. When experiencing large change volumes, you need to take time to assess what is driving the change request volume. High volumes of change requests that surface after the definition phase is completed are often symptoms of a flawed definition process. To better understand what is driving high volumes of change requests, each request should be analyzed to determine to what extent the development process is flawed. Basically, changes in requirements can be driven by one or more of the following reasons:

- Defect in the requirements discovery process
- Defect in the requirement definition process
- Defect in the design process (design does not align to the requirement)
- Defect in the building process (program does not follow the design)
- Stakeholder preferences change, not based on a functional need

To be able to establish the necessary corrective actions, you must understand where the problems are on your project.

## 5. What should I do?

Once you analyze the process and understand the phase of the project lifecycle responsible for introducing defects into the specification, steps can be taken to improve the underlying processes.

**Table 6.3** Requirements and scope

| CATEGORY | DISPOSITION |
| --- | --- |
| New core functional requirement | Change scope (time and budget) and include |
| Correction to functional requirement | Change scope and include |
| New simple, nonfunctional requirement | Add to scope, time and budget permitting |
| New complex, nonfunctional requirement | Consider for next release |

### 5(a) Defect in the requirements discovery process

Defects in the requirements discovery process will typically yield missing requirements. Once discovered, correcting this situation usually introduces brand new requirements into the scope of the project, and could possibly require changes to related requirements in order to affect the change. With any luck, your design walkthrough process will identify the missing requirement prior to the commencement of construction.

A missing functional requirement is the worst situation you can encounter, especially when identified during the testing and training phase of the project. The ripple effect of this type of situation can profoundly impact the credibility of the team with stakeholders and the credibility of the discovery team with developers. Most of all, it can obliterate delivery and budget expectations.

To fix this type of defect, you will need to improve the requirements analysis function in a way that ensures that all requirements identified can be mapped back to the processes, project objectives, and strategic goals they support.

### 5(b) Defect in the requirement definition process

After a defective requirements discovery process, the next most serious problem is a defect introduced into the specification during the requirements definition process. Here the definition team understood the need for a deliverable, or set of deliverables, but failed to define that deliverable correctly. When these types of defects make it through to the testing phase before detection, the rework needed will ripple back to the definition process and back through design and construction. Again, the budgetary and delivery date impact can be severe.

To fix this process, consider improving the requirements review and walk-through and inspection processes. Be sure that during these reviews, each requirement identified has supporting definition documentation, that the documentation conforms to established standards, and that the stakeholder of the requirement fully understands the associated trade-offs, options, and business rules.

### 5(c) Defect in the design process (design does not align to the requirement)

A flawed design process usually means that those developing the design specifications are not paying close enough attention to the requirement's layouts, business rules, or established standards and protocols. More often than not, defects introduced into the specifications during the design phase are systemic to either noncompliance to established standards, or defects in those standards.

Typically, a mature design review process will identify design issues and minimize rework efforts. Design issues that go undiscovered until testing and training, or after deployment, can have devastating effects on the organization and its stakeholders beyond the project level. Again, a mature design review process that correlates all aspects of the design to the underlying requirements should safeguard against any major design defects making their way into production.

### 5(d) Defect in the building or construction process (deliverable does not follow the design)

Perhaps the biggest reason for excessive rework of deliverables occurs when the builders of that deliverable do not faithfully follow the design specifications. Instead, they view the specification as a suggestion or example of the kinds of things the stakeholder wants, and then proceed to craft their own view of the solution. This can result in inconsistent user interfaces, budget overruns, and more problems. When this situation is encountered, it is imperative for the PM to correct the behavior and ensure that all team members understand the importance of adhering to established rules and standards.

### 5(e) Stakeholder preferences change, but are not based on a functional need

While it is impossible to stop people from changing their mind about a requirement, it is possible to implement a change request review, validation, or vetting process that protects the specifications from nonfunctional, nonessential changes. This vetting process needs to be comprehensive enough to ensure that requests can be fairly evaluated in terms of the value they add to meeting the project's objectives. Clearly, there is no end of good ideas, but those ideas also have to be evaluated in context to the trade-offs in budget, time, and windows of opportunity that their inclusion into the scope of the project represent.

# 6.7 Our specifications are unclear.

## By Michael Wood

## 1. Problem

The only problem with unclear design specifications is the results they produce. Leaving the interpretation of application blueprints up to the discretion of programmers can produce outcomes that are inconsistent, erroneous, and misaligned. Unfortunately, these issues usually don't surface until testing begins and you learn that the programmers used the specifications and guidelines, but not technical blueprints.

## 2. Warning Signs

The first sign that specifications are unclear typically occurs when the programs produced do not reflect the intent of the designer. Since programmers are notorious for forging ahead on their programming efforts even if

> ### What Part of Specifications Do You Not Understand?
>
> Joyce was feeling good about the progress being made during the design phase of the Business Intelligence system development project, that is, until she discovered that due to a lack of detail in the specifications, the programming team did their best at building something close to what they thought was needed.
>
> Unfortunately, the programming staff got it wrong. Making matters worse, many of the programming staff took emotional ownership of what they produced and became very defensive over making any changes.
>
> Thus, a blame game began with the programmers blaming the designers for being vague and not appreciating the solutions generated. The designers blamed the programmers for not asking questions and seeking more clarification.
>
> All of this infighting and failure could have been avoided by implementing design protocols and standards that were monitored during the design process.

the specifications are ambiguous, it isn't until the results they produce are reviewed that you learn about the problem. If the results of early testing are serving up inconsistent user interfaces and processes, you should be forewarned that your design specifications may need to be tightened up and that the implementation of design and programming standards may be needed.

## 3. What will happen if I do nothing?

Not righting the unclear specifications ship can sink the success of a project as resources are wasted and the results thrown out, and the massive rework runs the project's due date and budget aground. Doing nothing is a form of capitulation, which can lead to career stunting results. Professionalism demands diligent stewardship and taking action.

## 4. Solution

Design specifications are akin to construction blueprints and should leave nothing to the imagination during the programming (construction) phase. Developing detailed specifications does not have to be costly or time consuming if properly approached, using standard protocols and reusable design structures. Through a collaborative effort between designers and programmers, a set of standards and structures can be developed in relatively short order. This process can yield results that both groups support, which in turn improves compliance and the predictability of the results produced across the breadth of all development projects. The benefits derived from this approach include:

- Improved traceability between design specifications and the applications produced
- Improved supportability of design and code
- Improved uniformity and consistency in the user interface (look, feel, flow)
- Improved time and cost estimating
- Reduced design time
- Reduced programming time
- Reduced testing time
- Reduced training time

Getting the process started doesn't have to be an *all or nothing* proposition. Instead, starting with some basics and evolving the standards and structures on a continuous improvement basis can provide a better end product in the long run. However, at minimum, the first version should include the following rules and standards for:

- Contents of each design packet—inputs, processes, outputs (IPO)
- Data naming conventions to be used in schemas
- Objects and controls (dates, drop down lists, grids, use of tabs, etc.)
- Test scripts
- Training materials
- Implied components for table maintenance (i.e., add, change, delete, inactivate, audit trail)
- Estimates by type of IPO based on complexity, format, and such

## 5. What should I do?

The first step is to conduct a series of work sessions with senior design and programming staff in order to indentify the strengths and weaknesses of the current design and build process. Through these sessions, it is possible to create a consensus as to what would constitute the ideal framework (best practices) for standardizing the development process, along with a phasing strategy that capitalizes on the strengths, and addresses key weaknesses in a logical and cost effective manner. In addition, it is quite likely that during these sessions you will find that informal standards are in place within some teams, which might provide some *low hanging fruit* opportunities for making rapid improvements.

Before beginning these work sessions, you might find it helpful to review the development methodologies that are commercially available in terms of their depth and appropriateness for your organization. Often, these methods can be easily adapted into the IT culture and can offer a way to accelerate the process. However, a word of caution; do not go into the work sessions with the intent of selling the group on a predetermined solution—doing so could be met with a strong push-back by designers and programmers alike, and doom the effort to failure.

Consider a two to three day off-site retreat for the first set of work sessions. The goal of this retreat is to identify the attributes and components to be included in the specification and programming standard. The output of the retreat should be specific and detailed enough to drive the next steps of defining each standard in terms of rationale, format, use rules, training materials, and so on.

At the end of the retreat, individual and group assignments (statement of work along with expected deliverables and due dates) can be made to produce recommendations for each component of the standard. Every one to two weeks, bring the team together to review and shape the progress being made. Using an Agile project management approach for this initiative will help to keep it on track and improve your chances of releasing the first version of the standards in two to three months.

Once an initial version is ready, select a small but reasonably complex project to exercise the new standard against. The project should be short in duration and pursued with two goals in mind: the first objective is to achieve the project's business objectives, and the second is to assess the standards used in terms of:

- How well the applications produced agreed to the design specifications
- Efficiencies experienced by use of standard design structures, objects, controls, and the like
- Inefficiencies and shortfalls encountered in the use of the standards
- Improvements and recalibrations of the standard for use in subsequent projects

# 6.8 We spend too much time on documentation.

### By Michael Wood

## 1. Problem

The lament of project stakeholders that too much time (and money) is being spent on documentation is all too familiar to most project managers. Whether perception or truth, the value of what is being produced is not being seen as needed or worth the effort. It could be that bureaucracy is creeping into your project or that your terminology needs a facelift.

When documentation is not part of the integral work product being produced by a project, it is often deemed as overhead and not worth the effort. Imagine if architectural blueprints were developed after the house was built. Would it really ever get done? Would spending the money to produce them be seen as a waste?

Value-driven documentation provides a means to an end and, thus, integral to the development process. However, perhaps we should stop referring to it as documentation and instead revise our language to use terms such as specifications and blueprints.

### Did Sam Spend Too Much Time on Documentation?

Sam was quite emphatic about making sure the requirements and design specifications for the new ERP system were correct and complete. After all, he had seen far too many projects run amuck due to incomplete specifications, and he was not going to have that happen on this project.

Imagine Sam's surprise when his sponsor was critical of the project's progress and started raising concerns that too much time was being spent on creating documentation versus getting important things done. Sam was dumbfounded. Didn't the sponsor understand that creating accurate blueprints from which to build was crucial to success?

Sam's mistake was a simple one. In all status reports, he constantly referred to specifications as *documentation*, not realizing that the sponsor interpreted that word to mean *paperwork*, and that paperwork was akin to bureaucratic waste. Sam learned that the word choice can often frame the perception of others.

Sam, being the wise and savvy project manager he was, followed up with the sponsor stating, that there will be no more time spent creating needless documentation, and that the focus will be to ensure that design blueprints are accurate and complete, to avoid errors during application construction.

The sponsor was pleased that Sam got the message.

## 2. Warning Signs

There are a number of warning signs for this problem with some of them more obvious than others:

- Stakeholders and/or team members are complaining about the time and effort spent on documentation.
- Delivery of project specific documentation is late or incomplete.
- People *go through the motions* of completing document templates without actually providing the value that was intended.
- Sign-offs take too long.

## 3. What will happen if I do nothing?

Under specifying requirements and design blueprints is fraught with ugly paybacks. Not only can the project's success be put at risk, but the future supportability and ability to deploy systems that are developer independent is hampered. When faced with claims that too much time is spent on paperwork and documentation, it is inferred that there isn't a valid value proposition in play. When this happens, it is imperative to streamline where possible, but not to shortcut the specifications needed to ensure a successful development effort.

## 4. Solution

The first step in resolving the *too much time on documentation* lament is to eliminate all documentation that does not advance the project or add value to the final outcome. Once that is done, start referring to inputs and outputs to the development process as specifications, blueprints, and work products. The distinction may not seem important, but labels matter and convey value. In truth, terms that better describe the nature of the item will improve communications and the ability of lay people to comprehend the value being produced. The following steps should help you align your specifications, blueprints, and work products being produced to the needs of your specific development projects:

1. Eliminate non-value added paperwork
2. Standardize contents and formats of all work products
3. Adopt new language for referring to work products (lose the term *documentation*)

Keep in mind that the goal of specifications is to accurately reflect the needs of the organization in a way that is free of vagueness or in need of further interpretation. This holds true whether the project is about software development, construction, infrastructure improvement, or a flight into outer space.

## 5. What should I do?

While it is possible to allow needless paperwork and documentation to clog the path of productivity on projects, it is rare that this problem exists related to the development of thorough specifications. More likely than not, the requirements and design documents produced are on the skimpy side; thus, the volumes of rework and poor testing functions are out there. Examining your application blueprinting disciplines can help you fine tune the specification process.

### 5(a) Eliminate non-value added paperwork

When looking at any process, it is always good to eliminate paperwork that does not contribute to the value of the intended results. This goes for specifications as well as general project documentation. General project documentation includes sign-offs, charters, change requests, and so on, and should not be confused with requirements and design specifications. By eliminating needless steps and paperwork, efficiencies are gained and progress is more readily discernable.

Challenge every type of document being produced in context to how it helps propel the project forward or prevents the injection of defects into the final product. Where the value added is not sufficient, consider eliminating the item from the process.

### 5(b) Standardize contents and formats of all work products

One way to streamline the specification process and ensure consistency and portability of designs is to standardize the contents and formats of the work products to be produced. All work products should be consistent and complete. However, you should carefully consider what to produce, given your particular situation. You want to be sure that all document types are reusable and consistent. One way to do that is to create a standard template for each document type produced (across all projects). Standardizing documents in this way makes it easier to distribute work among project staff and for staff members to pick up where others left off. Here are a few examples of documentation you may be called upon to produce.

*Project Documentation*

Are you working for an organization that may do this type of project again? Will they want to know what was done on your project so they can learn from it? If there is a central repository for this sort of material, contribute only what is asked for. The rest will likely never be used. However, it is important to understand what will be required before starting your project so that:

1. You can produce this documentation as a by-product of your work rather than as a separate effort.
2. You can understand the format and composition of each document up front so that you do it right the first time.

For example, your idea of a project plan and the company's idea of a project plan may be two entirely different things. If you start off understanding the standard, you will only have to build one plan.

Project documentation can include:

- A project charter
- A project plan
- An issue tracking database
- Resource assignments
- Estimates, revisions, and actuals
- Change orders
- A lessons learned document

Your organization may require more or less than the above. The important thing is to know what is required up front.

*Training Materials*

Significant projects nearly always produce something that people use. Those *users* often need to be trained. There are a variety of training materials you can develop to ensure that the product you have produced will yield the results you are aiming for. Consider each of the following:

- Workbooks are used in training sessions to provide basic information, examples, and exercises for students in a classroom setting. Develop and provide a workbook only if you need to train people, in person, on the product you are producing.
- Self-paced guides are designed for trainees to work through on their own. Develop and produce a self-paced guide if the information is fairly brief and can be clearly conveyed using only printed material.
- Reference manuals contain detailed information on processes and procedures. Develop and provide a reference manual only if you are dealing with information that is rarely used, but critical when needed.
- Job aids provide step-by-step instructions to be used in the workplace. Provide a job aid if you changed the way people work and it will take some time for them to adjust to a new process.

*Technical Specifications*

If you are working on an IT project of any size, specifications are crucial. At a minimum, technical specifications should contain:

- An overview
- Use cases
- References and cross indexes concerning related workflows, policies, and procedures
- Samples of layouts and formats (for screens, reports, displays, etc.)
- Business and process rules
- I/O (input/output) models
- Mapping to data dictionaries
- Process logic diagrams

Given that these document types are built based on standard templates, each can be worked on independently of other deliverables. Therefore the development work can be spread across as many individuals as you can afford to employ without fear of material deviations across the quality of the programs produced. Remember to engage the PMO and other governance and oversight groups to ensure that improvements made to each document can be utilized, as appropriate, enterprise wide.

### 5(c) Adopt new language for referring to work products (lose the term documentation)

Most of all, to avoid the perception that you are spending too much time on documentation, adopt specific language when referring to requirements and design specifications and blueprints. Be sure to educate lay people about how quality specifications can reduce cost, allow for accelerated programming efforts, and ensure a supportable and maintainable application.

# 6.9 Sponsors complain that documentation and training are insufficient.

By Michael Wood

## 1. Problem

All the good work that went into designing and building a business application can be placed in jeopardy when the supporting training process is insufficient. Whether due to poor materials or proper instruction, the result can be the same. All too often, users reject new or improved systems that are too difficult to learn.

## 2. Warning Signs

The problem with training issues is that they can appear late in the project, so action has to be taken promptly to avoid major difficulties. Look for:

- Boredom or inattentiveness during training
- Missing processes or features in documentation
- Questions that aren't answered in any of the end user or technical material

**So Close and Yet So Far**

Simone was tasting success on her recent warehouse management project. The project seemed to go as smooth as could be expected. All that was left was user training and deployment into production.

But something went terribly wrong and the project was almost terminated because the operational users of the application found it too difficult to learn.

It seems that in the process of meeting budget expectations, little or no monies were set aside for quality training materials and formal classroom training.

Instead, users were expected to learn the new application on their own by playing with it on the test system. The development team believed that the user interface was so intuitive that no formal instruction was needed. They were wrong.

Simone learned a valuable lesson on this project. She learned that the cake isn't finished until iced. The *icing* on a project is the training and implementation support provided. Cutting corners on this critical phase of the project can make the difference between a smashing success and a dismal failure.

## 3. What will happen if I do nothing?

This late in the project, doing nothing or even being slow to act can cause project failure. Customers will lose faith, and while the problem may be a simple omission from a printed manual, the perception will be that the product has problems and cannot meet the customer's needs. Instead, quick and decisive action is needed.

## 4. Solution

The most expedient course of action when there is a breakdown in the training process is to collaborate with stakeholders (sponsor and key users) to reengineer the training course(s) and supporting materials as quickly as possible. This can be done via the following steps:

1. Conduct work sessions with the sponsor and key users to identify shortfalls and defects in the current approach to training, course design, course materials, and related user manuals.

2. Jointly develop new courses, materials, and manuals.
3. Conduct pilot training course(s), using qualified trainers to test and validate the quality of training and materials.
4. Conduct formal training.
5. Provide ongoing on-the-job training (OJT) to reinforce classroom learning.

## 5. What should I do?

Reengineering faulty user documentation and training materials is not necessarily easy to do. However, when needed, you will only get one opportunity to make things right, so you need an approach that secures sponsor and key user support. By engaging the sponsor and users in the reengineering process, you can ensure their buy-in and acceptance of the outcomes produced.

### 5(a) Conduct work sessions with the sponsor and key users to identify shortfalls and defects in current approaches to training, course design, course materials, and related user manuals

Engaging the sponsors and key users to fix the problems with documentation and training communicates your openness and willingness to cooperate, and turn a bad situation around. Facilitating work sessions that identify and document the issues of sponsors and key users demonstrates your ability to listen and comprehend their expectations.

### 5(b) Jointly develop new courses, materials, and manuals

Since you only want to rework the user documentation and training once, you would be wise to let the sponsor and knowledgeable users shape the materials so that they have a personal investment in the final result. In addition, their inclusion in the process ensures that you produce a result that is in accordance with their expectations, stated or not.

Of course, you want to make sure the materials are as complete as possible and conform to established guidelines. Where possible, engage knowledgeable users to also participate in the teaching of the courses. This will add to the overall acceptance and credibility of the newly reengineered materials.

### 5(c) Conduct pilot training course(s), using qualified trainers to test and validate the quality of training and materials

Before rolling out training to all users, conduct pilot sessions with a select group. You want to ensure that not just the materials are complete, but also that:

- The instructors are providing a good training delivery (style, knowledge, and so on)
- The timing of the course works—the right amount of content in the right timeframe
- There is the right mix of lecture, discussion, and practical training

A pilot group allows for easy feedback and refinement of the material prior to a wider delivery.

### 5(d) Conduct formal training

When conducting formal classroom training, keep the number of attendees to a minimum. This will allow for high quality, personalized attention. In addition, keep the training sessions to under a half day each. Trying to cram too much new knowledge into elongated training sessions dilutes the learning and knowledge retention process.

Set up a lab or breakout room where users can go to practice their newly learned skills, as well as get one-on-one tutoring as needed. Be sure to have knowledgeable support staff in the labs to facilitate a quality learning experience.

### 5(e) Provide ongoing OJT to reinforce classroom learning

Formal classroom training is important, but can only go so far in preparing users on using new systems productively. The larger and more complex the system being deployed, the greater the need for OJT. A best practice in this area is to station support personnel around the operational areas affected. In addition, issues and support requests should flow through a central clearing location so that support can be logically dispatched. If you have a help desk function in place, consider dedicating one or two people to field the extra support needs. However, don't compromise the service levels of normal help desk functions by funneling this process in competition with other support needs.

If need be, set up a separate phone and texting number to handle support during the application's first week or so of production use.

## References

Wood, M. *The Helix Factor: The Key to Streamlining Your Business Processes.* Marmora, NJ: Natural Intelligence Press, 1998.

Wood, M. September 2007. "*Identifying Requirements from BPI Documentation.*" Gantthead .com. http://www.gantthead.com/content/articles/237951.cfm

# 7

# PLANNING

## 7.1 I don't understand why we need to plan so much.

By J. Chris White

### 1. Problem

It seems as though you are never done with planning. You are constantly required to provide updated plans to senior management, the project executive, and the end customer for your project because things have changed.

### 2. Warning Signs

There are many potential indications that the problem of perpetual planning may exist. It doesn't automatically mean that planning is out of control, but you need to understand what is happening:

- Things may happen that alter the project scope from the initial baseline plan.
- Progress on current work activities may be slower than expected and the project is falling behind on schedule.
- The project might be over budget.
- You might be getting an inordinate amount of calls or emails from the project sponsor asking for progress updates.

**Plan, Plan, Plan**

Things were getting busy. Monthly status meetings became biweekly, and then came weekly meetings that became a meeting every few days. For each status meeting, a revised plan was expected and needed. At first, Eric looked on this favorably.

"As a PM, that's just job security," he surmised. But, now that the frequency of meetings had increased and been going on for awhile, Eric began to wonder if this would reflect poorly on him and his team.

The first thing Eric tried was to *put his foot down* (metaphorically) and demand that plans had to remain in place for longer periods of time and could not change so quickly. This proved to be difficult because there were plenty of justifications for the changes. When he started to take a case-by-case approach, everything seemed to be a special case. So, this didn't really help, and he decided to let the changes happen.

The next change that Eric did to cope with the emerging situation was to try to do everything himself. He was the PM. He had control. However, he quickly got overloaded and was not able to keep up with the work. He assigned a couple of the group leaders on the project team to update their parts of the overall plan, as required, and then Eric would combine them and roll them up to the total project level. This worked much better because the knowledgeable people were involved and it allowed him to observe from a global perspective.

But, the problem still remained: Why was the need for planning and replanning so high? What could be done about it?

- The end customer might not be happy with project deliverables to date.
- It seems like this plan is on everyone's radar, but not in a good way.

## 3. What will happen if I do nothing?

If you do nothing, the project may get so off-course that it doesn't meets its objectives. The purpose of replanning is to get the project back on track, and you can't just stop those activities because they are taking too much time. Without replanning, all the negative aspects of a project failure may come into play—a poor reflection on your career, an unhappy end customer, lost resources, and such.

At the same time, you can't just accept the problems that are creating the need to replan. You need to understand and address those underlying issues as well.

## 4. Solution

For whatever reason (which you'll eventually need to look at), the current project has not kept up with original goals and deliverables that were established at the baseline. If you want the project to meet its original goals and deliverables, then constant replanning is a necessary evil. It's not fun, but think of the alternative—project failure. The best that you can do moving forward is to get a disciplined approach to the replanning process. This requires a structured process:

1. Understand the causes behind the planning and replanning
2. Develop and implement a consistent project status review process
3. Implement a communication plan

## 5. What should I do?

Like a pebble dropped into a still lake that generates many ripples that propagate outward, small differences at the beginning of a project can have wide reaching impact later on. Consequently, for projects that are not well-defined or for which customer requirements were not completely specified and negotiated, a great deal of planning and replanning is often necessary to keep the project on course.

### 5(a) Understand the causes behind too much planning and replanning

If you find yourself doing a lot of planning and replanning throughout a project, one of several things has happened:

- You and your team did not do a good job at the beginning of the project in identifying, understanding, and clarifying the objectives and expectations of the project. This can be from several perspectives: the end customer, project sponsor, project team members, or a company executive. So, now that the train has left the station, it's up to you to figure out what is *really* supposed to be accomplished on this project.
- Things changed drastically from the beginning of the project due to emerging or previously unknown or unstated project requirements, which results

in a new set of work activities. For example, the market conditions that warranted the project may have changed significantly.

- The project started with some requirements purposefully unfinished. Now, the end customer or project sponsor cannot make up their mind(s) on what the project should accomplish.
- You are being micromanaged by your boss, project sponsor, or an executive. (Yikes!)
- Different resources were involved in the planning or proposal phase, and now a new set of resources have been assigned to implement the project, perhaps with a long delay in between proposal and project initiation.

You need to know what happened that created the current situation so that you can address the underlying problem on this initiative and avoid the same thing on future projects. Always make sure you learn from your current project. There is rarely a time when the experience on one project does not come in handy for handling a similar situation on another project. You may also want to review other chapters in this book to understand how to prevent different types of situations. Some relevant chapters include:

- 3.2: I don't understand what my stakeholders want.
- 4.2: My sponsor doesn't trust me or give me the authority I need.
- 5.2: Everything has changed. I need to reset goals and expectations.
- 5.7: My project's end point is a moving target.
- 5.9: The requirements keep changing.
- 6.7: Our specifications are unclear.

### 5(b) Develop and implement a consistent project status review process

For whatever reason, you must now do a lot of planning and replanning to get the project back on course and headed productively toward its objectives. What you need now is a disciplined process, as well as a solid communication plan for keeping everyone informed. Your first course of action is to develop and implement a consistent project status review process, if you do not already have one. *Consistent* means that the process is repeatable and the members on the team can become familiar with the steps in the process, as well as the information expected of them, and the output results they can anticipate. *Status review* means that there will be a comparison of what was supposed to happen within a certain period of time and what actually did happen in that same period of time.

The status review may consist of activity status, cost, resource assignments, availability, and due dates. To help with consistency, it is useful to employ a standard document or form that has specific question and answer sections, status inputs, names of responsible team members, and such. As the weeks progress and the documents are collected (either in hard copy or electronically), they form a project history and documentation trail. A key piece of information that should be included in the document is the expectation for the next time period (i.e., what activities will be accomplished, what deliverables will be completed, which resources are involved).

Where there are variances between what was supposed to happen and what actually did happen, you need to understand why, and this should help you identify some of the underlying issues of any replanning. The status review will provide the first indications of where items differ from the original plan, and the causes of these differences are the likely seeds of future replanning.

### 5(c) Implement a communication plan

This leads to the next thing you need to do, which is implement a communication plan that shares status information with all relevant stakeholders, including the full project team, project sponsor and executive, end customer, and perhaps several functional areas of the company that are involved (as in a matrix organization). The key is to ensure that the information is shared with the right people in a timely manner. This will help to establish expectations and requirements for the next time period, and perhaps in several future time periods. This alone will help to define future expectations and will go a long way towards alleviating some of the replanning.

Where your status reviews indicate that there are new items that may lead to replanning—delays caused by unclear or incomplete requirements, suggestions that deliverables don't meet expectations, new change requests, and the like. You need to specifically flag this with stakeholders to ensure that they are aware of the issue and any potential implications, early in the process. That will allow stakeholders to make decisions about how they want to proceed with an awareness of the potential impact.

# 7.2 How do I break a project down into smaller parts?

### By Josh Nankivel

## 1. Problem

You have been trying to figure out how to manage a huge project. There are so many moving pieces that the complexities are becoming confusing. The path forward is murky and there's a sense of unease about what is coming up. You don't think that you can manage this project without splitting it up, but you don't know how to do that.

## 2. Warning Signs

You might think that the signs of this problem are simply a feeling of unease in your own mind, and you certainly shouldn't ignore that feeling, but look for the following signs:

- The team is uncertain of what they should do, even though you have told them the grand vision many times.
- Although you are employing good scheduling practices, your schedule keeps changing as you add more work that was not in the original plan.
- You find your team members doing tasks that are not on the schedule because they know these things need to get done when they pop up—some of them are even emergencies.
- You don't have a good view of the project status as a whole, and you aren't sure how to answer the question "How is it going?"

## 3. What will happen if I do nothing?

You could continue to *keep the faith* in your project schedule, even though it seems to be changing weekly with additional tasks that really need to be done, but that were not in the original plan. You could tell yourself that this always happens on projects and there is no way to avoid it. Blind faith in a project schedule is not virtuous though—it is insanity.

---

**Is Fire Fighting Inevitable?**

Lisa came to the project late. Taking over for the previous project manager, she tried to listen and learn as much as possible about the project before making any changes.

Soon after she came on board, Lisa was gathering status from various team members and almost everyone had at least one task they had been working on that wasn't in the schedule. They were falling behind because hours planned to work on scheduled tasks were being cut into by *extra* tasks.

"Wow, I'm going to have to hire a scheduler to keep up with all these changes," Lisa grumbled. She was concerned about the amount of work that she had to do on this schedule. Perhaps she could start a new schedule and put big blocks of tasks on there instead. That would ensure the schedule wouldn't have new tasks added all the time.

But that was not a good solution. For some reason, new work kept popping up out of the blue. Is this some kind of conspiracy plot led by that evil mastermind from Sales to drive Lisa crazy? "OK, maybe I'm being paranoid now. I guess *fire fighting* is just part of the job of a project manager," thought Lisa. "It's always going to happen, right? I just wish it didn't happen every day."

The problems will get worse over time, and eventually management may lose confidence in your ability to manage the project. You won't be able to produce confident estimates to completion due to all the uncertainty and change. They may decide to replace you with someone else, or shut down the project entirely.

## 4. Solution

This is what happened: you tried to define how your project would get completed before you were clear on what you were doing. What you need to do is define clearly what you are delivering. Delivering—that's catchy. You will also need to break these deliverables down into manageable pieces, so this isn't so overwhelming and confusing.

## 5. What should I do?

Breaking down the work in a project works best with a process designed to keep you from messing it up. Be sure to include your project team, key stakeholders, and other subject matter experts in this process.

### 5(a) Start with big nouns

Start with the high-level requirements of your project. These are the objectives that describe the *end state* you are trying to achieve. There will be a handful of major deliverables, not verbs but nouns. For instance, a task might be *build system X* but the deliverable is *System X*.

You can do this process in outline form, with an organizational structure-like hierarchy, using mind-mapping, or whatever works best for you. The key functionality you need is to build a hierarchy of all the deliverables. This hierarchy is called a *work breakdown structure*.

### 5(b) What makes up the big nouns?

Next, take each of the high-level deliverables and ask, "What are the smaller pieces that make up this big task?" Notice we did not ask, "What work will it take to produce these?"—that question comes later on. Get crystal clear on what you are delivering before thinking about how you will do it.

For instance, System X is probably composed of several subsystems. Let's call them Subsystem A, B, and C. Each of these subsystems has a unique functionality, and System X needs all of them to do its job.

### 5(c) Keep going!

Each subsystem is likely made up of a collection of modules or packages, which in turn are made up of procedures or functions. The specific products and subproducts are going to be context-sensitive to what you are creating with your project.

Stay focused on nouns and what these deliverables are made of. It is human nature to jump right into *how*, so be careful to redirect the team towards nouns when this happens. Keep them focused on *what*.

### 5(d) When do I stop?

It depends. Wherever you stop, the lowest points on each branch of your work breakdown structure are called *work packages*. This is the transition point where the product (what) helps shape, and is integrated with, the schedule (how, who, when, where).

For discrete deliverables that have a clear start and finish within the life span of the project, you will get to a logical stopping point, which is usually in the 20 to 80 hours of effort range. If your breakdown, at any step, seems to be arbitrary and not a true reflection of the product(s), it may be a sign that you have gone too far.

For activity-related deliverables of a service of some kind, there is a different approach available. For instance, configuration management is a service you will provide in some way throughout the life of your project. It doesn't have a discrete start and completion within the project life span. In this case, break the *configuration management* service deliverable down into the individual or groups of services provided. In this case, some examples may include Configuration Management Board, Document Management, and CM Process Improvement.

### 5(e) Then what?

Now that you have a clear idea of what your product is, you can tackle the other questions with confidence, such as "What work will it take to produce these?" Depending on the type of project, you probably want to allocate the high-level requirements down to lower levels in your new work breakdown structure. Then, with a clear idea of what *finished* looks like, it is time to identify the tasks that will be completed to deliver each of the work packages.

# 7.3 Everything is *top priority*.

## By Andy Jordan

## 1. Problem

You have built your work breakdown structure (WBS), and have a good understanding of what work needs to be done. Now you need to plan out the way that the work needs to get done, but it seems as though everything is the top priority—you aren't sure which work to do first or how to assign the resources to the work.

## 2. Warning Signs

There are a number of signs that you may be experiencing this problem, but the good news is that they are fairly easy to spot:

- Every task seems to need a specialist resource.
- Every task seems to need to start immediately.
- You have more tasks happening in parallel than you have resources to do the work.
- Critical resources are assigned to multiple concurrent work items.
- You don't have a view of interim milestones on your project.

> **Where Do I Start—There's So Much to Do and It's All Important!**
>
> James thought that he must look like a deer in the headlights—that is, awe struck. He had been looking forward to his first project management opportunity. All the way through the building of the work breakdown structure, things had gone fairly well. Even during the estimation, he had felt like things were under control.
>
> Now, though, they had to start building the plan and James wasn't sure where to start. Everyone was telling him that their part was the most important, needing to be done first. Stakeholders were pushing for the parts that they wanted, resource owners wanted their resources scheduled first so that they could be freed up to go back to their teams, the customer was pressing for a prototype urgently, and the sponsor expected everything to happen at the same time.
>
> James was confused; he didn't know what to do first—everything was top priority, so how was he supposed to figure out the right project plan?

## 3. What will happen if I do nothing?

If you don't address this problem, your project will revert to a chaotic mess. Your team members won't be clear as to what they need to focus their attention on, you won't have any idea on how (or if) the project is progressing, and sponsors and stakeholders will quickly lose faith in your ability to deliver the project successfully. From that point, things can only get worse.

## 4. Solution

There's a reason why everything on your project seems to be a top priority task—it is. If you built your WBS correctly, then every piece of work needs to be completed successfully to achieve overall project success. However, that's not the same as saying that everything needs to be done now and given to the most skilled resources. You need to build a sequence of tasks that will come together in the final solution, and you need to allocate all of your resources across those tasks to make sure that people are as productive as possible without being overworked. To do that:

1. Identify the tasks that are dependent on one another, and build sequences of those tasks with the relationship between them defined.
2. Assign resources to the tasks ensuring that all team members are used.
3. Adjust the sequencing of tasks based on the resource assignments.

## 5. What should I do?

Remember that you aren't alone in this exercise. Engage your core team members to assist you. They will better understand how some of the technical tasks fit together, and they can also assist in determining who can work on different tasks.

### 5(a) Identify how tasks relate to one another

When you built the WBS you focused on *what* had to be built and gradually broke it out into more detail until you got to the bottom or work package level. Then you figured out the tasks needed to build each of those work package items—the *how*.

Those *hows* offer great starting points to sequence the work because you already have the work broken into bite-sized chunks. Suppose you are building a wall—there are a number of things that you have to do, such as framing the wall, putting up drywall, and applying the finishing treatment. There are some gaps, but you get the idea.

There is an easy sequence to these events—you can't paint until the drywall is done, and you can't do the drywall until the wall is framed. This gives you a string of tasks for building your wall:

1. Frame
2. Drywall
3. Paint

You can apply the same logic to the tasks that make up each work package. Every task is important, but they can't be done in parallel. There is a need to do some tasks before others if you are going to be successful. Work with your team to go through the work packages and create that sequence. You may still have some choices, and some things that can happen simultaneously, but you now have at least some of your work sequenced.

Next, go up one level in your WBS and start looking how work across the related work packages should be sequenced. In the wall example, you can't start the wall until the floor is complete. Once you have done that, go up another level and repeat the process. Keep going until you get to the top of the project.

What you will end up with are a bunch of task *string* sequences of the order that work needs to get done. There may well still be a lot of strings, but you are starting to make progress. Already things are looking better than when everything seemed to have to get done at once. Now, think about who needs to do the work.

### 5(b) Assign resources

Your sequences of tasks are no good until there is someone to do the work. You need to assign people to the tasks that you have sequenced, considering a number of factors:

- Who is the best person for the job?
- Who else is capable of doing the work?
- If multiple people can do the work can one of them be more valuable elsewhere?

Start by assigning people to the tasks where only one person can do the work—those are your critical tasks where you have no flexibility. You'll find it a lot easier if you put all of your task sequences together. A project management tool can help you here, but flipcharts or a whiteboard will work as well. Don't worry yet about how long tasks will take; you'll get to that later in planning. For now, you are only concerned with the sequence.

Once you have assigned your *only choice* resources, take a look at section 5(c) and apply those rules. Then come back here and repeat this exercise with the tasks where there is a *preferred* resource out of your options. Then go back and repeat section 5(c).

Guess what, when that's done, come back here and apply resources to the remaining tasks based on who has the most availability to do the work. Then go back to section 5(c) one final time.

### 5(c) Adjust the sequencing

As you assign resources to the various task *string* sequences you will identify some problem areas. These are task sequences where the same person is supposed to be working on more than one thing at a time. While that might be theoretically possible by splitting the individual's time between those tasks, you can't do that for free. Tasks will take longer that way, and there will also be some lost productivity as the resource shifts focus between multiple tasks. If possible, try to have the resource assigned to their tasks sequentially.

This will create an additional relationship between strings of tasks—you now have two previously independent strings that are connected by the fact that they both need the same resource. The need to sequence the work is driven not by the fact that the work itself has to go step by step (as in the wall example), but rather because the person working on it needs to go step by step.

Your work strings are starting to get more complex. Suppose that Task A is to be completed by Steve. Task B follows Task A, and Steve also has to work on Task C. Our tasks now split: Task A leads to both Task B (the work relationship) and Task C (the resource relationship).

Unlike with sequencing work, resource relationships can be harder to figure out because the order is not always obvious. We know that we have to frame a wall before we drywall it, but how do we know which task a resource should work on first?

The later planning stages may cause some adjustment, but initially, consider the following:

- Which task has more work dependent on it? That task should probably be sequenced first because it is holding up more work.
- Which task is holding up the project? If people are sitting around waiting for work to be done, it should be completed as quickly as possible.
- Which task is simplest? Get the easy stuff out of the way as quickly as possible.

You will revisit sequencing later on in the project when you have estimated and built your schedule through a process that analyzes the critical path, which is covered in a later chapter.

As you repeat this cycle of assigning resources and adjusting the sequencing, you will build your entire project task sequence. There likely will be some independent sequences of tasks, and that's fine—you aren't trying to get to just one.

What you will have achieved when this exercise is complete is a logical progression of tasks that allow the project deliverables to flow from one another and consider resource needs. More importantly, you have built a structured approach to all of the important tasks on the project. This will allow you to move on to the next steps of planning and build a formal schedule with dates and milestones.

# 7.4 Someone must have done this before. Where do I find more info?

By Cornelius Fitchner

## 1. Problem

You have been assigned a project that takes you far outside of your comfort zone. Whether you are an experienced project manager or not, you may find yourself in uncharted territory. This is clearly a stretch assignment for you, but the sponsor and stakeholders are counting on you to deliver results. You understand the goals of the project, but you have never led a project like this and are uncertain where to begin.

## 2. Warning Signs

This is a *pit of the stomach* problem: you know that you have a problem when you feel uncomfortable about what's going on. Be aware of the following feelings and behavior:

- You are confused or overwhelmed, and don't know how to tackle the project.
- You don't feel you've been given the tools needed to complete the project.
- You are procrastinating or avoiding stakeholders.
- You fail to write regular status reports or gloss over the issues.
- There are various technologies with which you are unfamiliar, and you think a lot about the technology.
- People, perhaps your team members, begin to doubt your ability to succeed.

> **Real Project Managers Ask for Directions**
>
> Sam heard the reliable clank of the closing door behind him and a long, resigned sigh—his own—and thought back to another time when he'd walked out of someone's office with a new project and no clue as to how to complete it.
>
> Then, as now, he was new to the company and the technology, and was overwhelmed by the task he faced. Back then, he was a junior project manager way out of his league. Then, as now, it was the largest project he had ever been asked to lead and there were huge risks involved. To top it all off, Sam had no experience with that type of project.
>
> At the time, he was asked to lead a project in which one of the stakeholders was a large, international nonprofit organization, and he had felt unable to meet the expectations of both the individual stakeholders and the sponsor. One influential stakeholder in particular, Mr. Vargas, who headed a section of the nonprofit, could easily have made the project fail, and he had voiced his concern about Sam's capability to lead a project of this scale.
>
> Sam had never dealt with such powerful people, nor with a team as large as this, which needed to be coordinated and guided. As he was new to the organization, he did not really know where to turn. He wondered how to begin the journey without a map. Sam thought to himself, "Someone must have done this before."
>
> Now, years later, hearing that door close followed by the feeling of being overwhelmed brought it all back to him. The difference between then and now is that Sam has lived through this before, and he knows what to do to get the information he needs in order to complete the project successfully.

## 3. What will happen if I do nothing?

If you try to lead a project without the necessary experience or resources, or fail to reach out to others who can help, you will overlook vital aspects of the project that need addressing. You will deliver a mediocre project that neither serves your stake-holders' implicit and explicit needs, nor is in the best interests of your sponsor. Your team may lose faith in you and be reluctant to invest time and effort into the project. You would be missing an excellent opportunity to further your own development as a project manager and increase your skills by learning from others.

In the end, remember that you are not doing the project for yourself, but for your sponsor. It takes a certain level of maturity to recognize your own limitations and seek help. That is when you start to grow as a project manager.

## 4. Solution

While each project is unique, it may not be a new *type* of project. Think of projects like the Olympic Games. The first one was literally the first project of its kind, and you can certainly consider putting on the Games as a project. Since then, it has been done every four years. Each successive Olympics was unique, but was based upon the experience of previous Games.

What does this mean to you? It is a given that many projects like yours have been successfully completed before. All of those project managers had to go through what you are now facing. In order to succeed on this project, you must reach out and get the tools and information you need. You have to know:

- Where to look for information
- Who to ask
- What resources are available to you

## 5. What should I do?

The *first* thing you must do is something referred to as the *prime question*, the basis from which to begin your search.

### 5(a) Who do you know?

You must first ask yourself, "Who do I know who has done this before?" If you do know someone, that's a great start—although it is unlikely to be your only source—and if not, the process does not end there. Following the prime question, you must continue and then ask yourself, "Who *else* do I know who has done this before?" or "Who do I know, *who knows someone* who has done this before," and so on. Continue to drill down until you find someone (or a group of people) who has experience that can help you out.

While it may seem obvious, it is surprising how often project managers fail to dig deeper and fully take advantage of the resources at hand by forgetting the ideas of the six degrees of separation—we are all only six connections away from any other person on the planet. The information you need may already be available, and closer than you think.

### 5(b) Inside sources

In addition to the people you already know who come to mind immediately, you may be able to get information about an unfamiliar type of project from several sources. Your first contacts should be your:

- *Sponsor:* Has the sponsor supported a project like this before? The sponsor has a lot at stake, so he or she will try to help, but may not be able to. Ask him or her to refer you to someone else, in keeping with the prime question.
- *Team members:* What is the experience of your team? Have they worked on similar projects for this company or their previous companies?
- *Customer:* Has the customer requested similar projects? Can they put you in touch with the business lead in their company who worked on that project?
- *Project managers (internal):* Your current colleagues may have worked on a comparable project or know someone who has and can put you in touch with them. Ask for Lessons Learned files, project stories, and templates.
- *Project management office:* Your company's PMO may have documentation and processes available that can help you tackle this project, and chances are good that someone there may have experience on a similar project or know where to get information.
- *Document control and quality assurance:* If your company is in a controlled industry, the Document Control (DC) department may be able to provide completed project documentation for similar or related past projects. They may be able to give you standard operating procedures (SOPs) for completing some of the documentation. Make friends with DC personnel. The same holds true for Quality Assurance (QA). Your friends in QA will know if there are templates that *must* be used, and they will gladly share the information.
- *Other stakeholders:* Have some of the stakeholders been involved with similar projects? The stakeholders want this project to succeed, so they likely will be glad to help.

For each of these, you should ask for a description of the project, and find out where and when the project was completed; ask whether the resource has sample documentation or templates and Lessons Learned (post mortem) files. Ask them to share experiences and provide other contacts you can talk to who will be helpful.

### 5(c) Secondary sources

In addition to the sources mentioned who are close to you, a great deal of information is available when you cast your net a bit wider. Being mindful of confidentiality agreements, security concerns, and careful not to disclose trade secrets, there are many other resources that you may be able to call upon.

- *Former project management colleagues:* Be aware that colleagues who are now in other positions in the same company could offer some advice.

Colleagues who are at other companies may have nondisclosure agreements or competitive clauses to honor, and so may be unavailable to you.

- *Other external project managers and consultants:* If you cannot find a project manager with experience through the ordinary channels, consider hiring a consultant to get you started, either an expert at managing this type of project or an expert on the subject itself. You probably only need the basics to get pointed in the right direction.

- *Professional associations:* National, international, and local chapters of professional associations can be good resources. These organizations host events for networking, offer training courses, and are valuable sources of information. Many local chapters also have their own Web sites with helpful resources. Some of the major associations include:
  - Project Management Institute (PMI)
  - American Society for the Advancement of Project Management (ASAPM)
  - International Project Management Association (IPMA)
  - The International Association of Project and Program Management (IAPPM)

- *Communities of practice (formerly called specific interest groups or SIGs), through PMI.org:* These specialized forums allow members to interact and share knowledge. Each community is focused on a single subject area, for example, Agile, project risk management, retail, and others.

- *Internet sources:* Don't forget the Internet. Use it to search for the type of project, (e.g., software), and add keywords such as project management, project schedule, project plan, and templates. It is surprising what can be found if you are creative. For example:
  - Project management-related general interest Web sites and forums, of which there are hundreds. Here you can post questions to experts and fellow PMs, and search for articles and white papers on subjects of interest.
  - Industry Web sites and professional associations (related to your project's industry).
  - Social media and new media offer the newest ways of making connections and getting information. The trends in communication are ever evolving, so keep up with the latest technology and Web sites.

- Social media sites such as *LinkedIn, XING, Facebook,* and *Gantthead.com* have groups dedicated to project management where connections can be made. In fact, these sites demonstrate the prime question best by creating networks based on professional connections or friendships.

- New media like podcasts present listeners with the opportunity to get the information they need at the time of their choosing. Shared experiences and lessons learned that you can tap into are available on a variety of topics in podcasts, which are usually free. Because they are time shifted, you can access the archives and listen to the podcasts relevant to your project.

- *Library:* Your library or local chapter of your professional organization may have project management books to lend.
- *Training:* While much information should be available to you by consulting the sources listed above, sometimes outside training is required, either in the classroom or with online seminars and courses. Talk to your boss or the sponsor and make the case for training, but make sure you impress him or her with the steps you have gone through to try to obtain the information already.

Never be embarrassed by what you do not know if you are trying to grow as a project manager. Good project managers are not born knowing what to do. They become great by constantly learning, asking, and doing.

# 7.5 I have no idea how to estimate how long this will take.

## By Andy Jordan

## 1. Problem

You are in the midst of planning your project, and you have been working with your project team to build the work breakdown structure. You now have a good understanding of all of the work that needs to be completed, and the dependencies between tasks. Now you need to estimate how long the project is going to take and you aren't sure where to begin. Several members of your core team have ideas about different aspects of the project, but it seems more like guess work than real estimation. You need to be able to come up with reliable estimates that accurately reflect the time needed to complete the work, and you need to be able to do it in an efficient way.

### How Do I Know How Long It Will Take?

Laverne was confused. She had always wanted to be a project manager, and now she had finally been given the opportunity. However, she was at a complete loss about what to do next. Her team had been great in working out what tasks had to be completed and the work breakdown structure (WBS) looked great. Laverne knew that she now had to take that WBS and build a comprehensive project schedule, but that meant completing estimates and she wasn't sure how to do it.

Some of the team said that there was a similar project a couple of years ago and that maybe the estimates from that would help. Laverne knew that there were some people in the company who knew a lot about the tasks that had to be done, so maybe she could ask them for help with the estimates. That wouldn't help with everything though, and then those estimates had to be turned into a proper schedule, and she wasn't sure how to do that either. Laverne needed some help.

## 2. Warning Signs

The warning signs for this problem may be easy to spot, but they may also be harder to see. Often your team will provide you with estimates that are nothing more than guesses, showing that no one knows how to estimate the work, and you need to identify those situations. You may have a problem estimating if some or all of the following are happening:

- Team members are unable to explain the logic behind the estimates that they provide.
- Team members tell you that they have insufficient information to estimate the work.
- Estimates are inconsistent or have gaps in them.
- Team members lack confidence in their estimates.

## 3. What will happen if I do nothing?

You can't manage what you can't measure. If you don't have accurate estimates, you will never be able to determine how well the project is progressing against the schedule. Worse, if you have inaccurate estimates, you will be managing the project against incorrect targets, and your team may be working to unrealistic expectations. Inaccurate estimates will also make it impossible to accurately communicate the status to your stakeholders and can easily result in a lack of confidence in the project manager.

If you don't have estimates at all, then work will be proceeding without anyone knowing when it needs to be completed, you won't know when resources will be freed up, or when other resources will be needed. You won't be able to manage your team's workload and you won't be able to provide stakeholders with any objective information on the progress of the project.

## 4. Solution

There are a lot of different techniques for estimating work and it needn't be a difficult undertaking. There are a number of steps that need to be taken to come up with an accurate estimate of how long the project and its different parts will take.

1. Determine the correct method(s) for estimating effort for the project and engage the right people to develop the estimates.
2. Assign resources and calculate durations after allowing for adjustments.
3. Build the overall schedule by creating dependencies, joining the tasks together, and resolving resourcing problems.

## 5. What should I do?

Estimating effort and duration needs to be a systematic process. You need to have a plan for the estimating process, and then follow through on that plan, completing all of the steps in the right order. If you don't do that, you can make serious mistakes with your estimates, and may not even know that mistakes have been made until it is too late.

Before you start developing the estimates themselves, you need to make sure that everyone involved in the process is clear on two concepts—effort and duration. *Effort* is the amount of work needed to complete the task; *duration* is the amount of time that it will take. As a simple example, if there are five days of effort needed on a task, it will take one person five days of duration, but will take five people working together only one day of duration. Either way, it is still the same amount of work (effort), but the timeframe (duration) differs depending on the number of resources.

We'll look at duration in more detail later in this chapter, but for now let's focus on effort. You need to make sure that everyone involved in estimating is approaching the task consistently:

- Effort estimates should be just the work needed to complete the task; time spent on other tasks should be ignored (it will be factored in later).
- Estimates should not be *padded*, but should reflect the true work estimate.
- Estimates should use consistent units; you don't want half of your team providing estimates in hours and the other half providing estimates in days.

Once everyone involved in estimating is aligned on those points, it is time to start the actual estimating.

### 5(a) Methods for estimating resources

The success or failure of estimating can often be traced to the decisions taken about how to estimate the project. The most common estimating methods are:

- *Analogous or comparison estimating:* involves comparing the work that you have to do with similar work that has been done in the past. Historic projects can be a great source of information as you will have data about how long the work actually took. You need to adjust time to allow for the differences between that work and the current initiative, but it provides a very good starting point for your estimate. If you are lucky, you can use this method to estimate the whole project, but more commonly it is used for a subset of the project work.
- *Parametric or unit based estimating:* involves calculating how long it will take to do a specific task and then multiplying it by the number of times that the task has to be completed. For example, if it takes two hours to paint a wall and there are seven walls to paint, you can calculate that it should take fourteen hours. You have to be careful using this technique to ensure that you don't make incorrect assumptions—the size of each wall, the amount of time needed to clean up after painting, and such.
- *Three point estimation:* asks people who know about the work to be completed (experts) to look at a task in three different ways—the best case, worst case, and most likely estimates. These three estimates are then averaged for the estimate that you will use in the project. In this way, you factor in how things going well or things going badly could impact the estimate.
- *PERT estimation:* which stands for Program Evaluation and Review Technique, is an extension of the three point technique. It still uses best case, worst case, and most likely scenarios, but adds *weighting* to the most likely estimate in order to reflect that it is more likely to happen than the best case or worst case. The formula for PERT is:

$$(\text{Best Case} + 4x(\text{Most likely}) + \text{Worst Case})/6$$

Choosing the right method is important, but you also need to ensure that the right people are involved in the estimation process. You cannot assign the task of estimating the complete project to one person because they won't have the skills and expertise to build reliable estimates. Instead, you need to assign different aspects of the project to the different resources on your team based on their skill sets. In addition, you may need to go beyond your project team and seek expertise from other parts of the organization, or even beyond.

As an example, if you are using analogous estimating for some of the tasks on your project, then resources from the project that you are using as a comparison will be good resources to assist in estimation. For parametric estimates there may be some standards that you can use, for example, established union rates for certain tasks, that allow you to use an industry standard without having to calculate estimates internally.

Whenever you have to rely on expert opinion you should try and engage as many people as possible. If you can have multiple experts developing estimates, you can develop an average that is likely to be more accurate than just one opinion. This can be particularly true if you have the experts produce PERT estimates individually, and then work together to discuss variations in their estimates (a process known as *wideband Delphi*).

Finally, in deciding on estimation methods and resources, you have to consider how you are going to break the project up for estimating purposes. It is unlikely that you can take the project as a whole and estimate the time that you need, but you may be able to group some tasks together to simplify the estimating process. Analogous estimating is often done this way. The alternative is to use something called *bottom up estimating*, where estimates are completed for every task and then added together to come up with the overall effort estimate.

### 5(b) Calculate task durations

Once you have been through this process, you still only have effort estimates. Before you can calculate how long your project will take, you need to calculate durations. There are three variables that you need to consider to do this:

- *Any fixed timeframes that you will be faced with:* Some tasks may not be much effort, but they can still take considerable time. For example, ordering equipment from a third party manufacturer may only take a few hours of effort, but the delivery time could be several months.
- *The resources assigned to each task:* Although you will probably need to revisit this step in the next part, you need to determine who is going to be assigned to each task. This decision will be based on the number of resources available for the project, their skill sets, their availability,and such. Some tasks may have multiple resources assigned while others may only have a percentage of someone's time if they have to work on multiple tasks, or are only available to your project on a part-time basis.
- *The degree of adjustment that you need to make for time spent on non-project work:* Even if a resource is assigned full time to your project, you won't get a full working day from them on project tasks. People will have to deal

with email, phone calls, team meetings, and the like that will take up time that they are assigned to project work. Additionally, there are always distractions from work that cannot be avoided, such as water cooler conversations, or personal business. Some estimates put the total time lost to these two factors at greater than 30 percent. In other words, in an eight hour day, a resource is able to complete less than six hours of project work.

Once you have made these adjustments, you will have effort and duration estimates for each of your tasks or groups of tasks.

### 5(c) Build the schedule and resolve resource problems

You almost have enough information to build your schedule. The only other information that you need are the dependencies between tasks—which tasks are related to other tasks on the project. (As an example, you can't install floor tiles until the floor tiles have been delivered.) There are three types of dependency:

- *Finish to start:* This is the most common type of dependency. Task B cannot start until Task A has finished.
- *Start to start:* Task B cannot start until Task A has started.
- *Finish to finish:* Task B cannot finish until Task A has finished.

Additionally, you may have lead or lag time. *Lead time* reflects something able to happen before a significant event, and *lag time* reflects something that will not be able to happen until an amount of time after a significant event. For example, a start to start relationship with two days of lag would be *Task B cannot start until two days after Task A has started.* A finish to start relationship with three days of lead would be *Task B cannot start until three days before Task A has finished.*

Once you have this information, you can build your project schedule, generally using one of the many project management tools. This involves laying out all of the tasks considering their dependencies to create different sequences of tasks, all of which have to be done in order to complete the project. The sequence of tasks that has the longest duration is the project's *critical path*—the group of tasks that determines how long the overall project will take.

Once you complete this schedule, you need to go back to your resource assignments and see whether you need to make any changes. It is likely that the sequencing of tasks has created some situations where resources are over-allocated and other situations where resources are under-utilized. You need to try and balance this by *resource leveling*, which is minimizing the variation in the amount of work each resource has from week to week, and removing any over-allocations that require resources to complete more than a day's worth of work in any given day.

In making decisions about the resources, you should always try to protect work on the critical path. Removing resources from here will delay the completion of the project. It is always better to reschedule tasks or reallocate resources from tasks that are off the critical path.

Once all of your resources have been leveled, you will have a reliable schedule that clearly shows how long each task and the entire project should take to complete.

# 7.6 The project management software is not helping me.

## By Andrew Filev

## 1. Problem

You understand that the company has established a project management tool as the standard that has to be used, but you feel that it's useless. You seem to be constantly battling the tool to enter information and maintain data, and still the numbers don't come out the way that you think they should. You aren't even sure if you can trust the dates that the tool is giving you.

Working with the tool isn't making your life easier Instead, it is creating more administrative work that takes away from the time that you have to manage the important elements of the project. Whether it is a bad tool, or whether you need to better understand how to use it, you have a problem.

> **What Is Wrong with This Software?**
>
> Jeremy slumped back in his chair, completely frustrated with the project management software on his computer. Uncaringly, the software continued to blink its cursor. Jeremy had spent hours entering every last piece of the schedule that his team had built—all of the dependencies, resource assignments, estimates, and the rest. He had taken care to get everything right—everything.
>
> Instead of providing an accurate view of the project tasks in a structured Gantt chart, the software kept changing Jeremy's estimates, moving start dates, or throwing meaningless error messages. The first few times Jeremy thought that maybe he had done something wrong, but no—he had entered everything correctly.
>
> A few minutes ago, Jeremy had seen the software change a value on him that he had just corrected—it was becoming a battle of wits between him and the software. It was clear that the software was possessed, and had it in for Jeremy!

## 2. Warning Signs

Sometimes you know that the tool is causing you problems, but many times PMs don't realize that they are having tool problems until it's too late. It's crucial that you recognize the signs of this problem or you will be relying on a tool that is not providing reliable data. Warning signs to look for:

- You minimize the amount that you use the project management tool, preferring other tools wherever possible.
- You only use the most basic features of the tool, and you aren't sure what a lot of the functions are.
- The tool is an administrative overhead rather than something that assists you in efficiently handling project administration.
- The information in the tool is out of date because you can't stay on top of all of the required updates.

## 3. What will happen if I do nothing?

This is not a problem that will solve itself. At best, you will learn to work around the limitations (real or perceived) of the tool, but there will likely be a number of ongoing problems, such as slips in the schedule caused by a misalignment of the plan with the real work required, work being forgotten, or misunderstandings of what should be worked on. All of this will likely lead to serious problems on the project, inevitable delays, overruns, and a loss of faith in you and your team.

## 4. Solution

The solution that you implement will depend heavily on the reason for the issue—is it actually the tool that is the problem, or is it the ability to use the tool that is causing issues? Are you in a position to know the answer to that question? To address the problem, you need to:

1. Analyze the problem and understand the real issue
2. Address the issue by either:
    a. Improving your skills with the tool
    b. Securing a more appropriate way to solve the problem
3. Monitor for improvement

## 5. What should I do?

The project management tool is fundamental to the success of the project. When things are going right, it provides a valuable support that handles much of the administrative burden leaving you free to manage the actual project. When things are going wrong, it can be a monster that you spend most of your time fighting. If you see the monster on your project, then you need to kill it swiftly.

### 5(a) Analyze the problem

Project management software is extremely powerful, and offers a huge number of features that can assist project managers—everything from earned value management to critical chain analysis. The problem is that many project managers don't use those techniques in managing their projects, let alone use software for it, so it is just *noise* that makes it harder to get what you need from the tool.

At the same time, tools can't do everything. Depending on which tool your organization uses, and how it is implemented, your ability to complete functions may be limited. You need to understand whether you are struggling because you don't know how to get the best out of the tool, or because the tool can't do what you need. Sometimes it's obvious and you know that a project management tool can support a project schedule with dependencies, but sometimes it's less obvious, such as if it can support team members providing updates directly into the project file.

To try to establish where the problem lies, use all of the following sources:

- Speak to experienced project managers and the PMO within your organization to make sure that the tool is capable of doing what you need. Review the help files and user manual to ensure that the functions you need are provided
- Search online resources for information

These should give you some idea as to whether the problem is with the tool or your ability to use it properly, which will then allow you to move on to the next step and solve the problem.

### 5(b) Address the issue

You are in the process of managing a project so you need a solution that is quick and effective. Remember that, as we look at the options.

#### Improve your skills

The most likely scenario is that the tool is capable of doing what you need, but you don't have the skills to make the most of it. That can be addressed through formal training courses, and you should take advantage of courses whenever possible. However, a course can take time to schedule and may not be available instantly. Therefore, try to find yourself a *tool coach*, who is someone familiar with the tool that you are using and who can assist you in building the plan. This may be someone in the PMO or a more experienced project manager. There may even be documentation from a similar exercise that was completed in the past and which you can request.

You don't want this person to build your plan for you; that won't teach you anything. But you do want them to be able to provide tips and best practices that will help you to improve your abilities to the point where you are working with the tool rather than against it.

Make sure that you capture all of the advice in writing and make it part of the project documentation, so that it is available for future project managers to refer to.

#### Find a better way

It's possible that the tool can't do what you need it to do. If that's the case, no amount of training is going to help, so you need to find another solution. That may ultimately involve replacing the project management software or upgrading it, but that's not a feasible solution in the middle of a project when time is your enemy.

Instead, look at another way to solve the problem, either another process, a different tool, or another way to get what you need. Suppose, for example, you want to have your project team update the status of their tasks themselves, but the project management tool doesn't support it. You are faced with a compromise solution, but you can still drive efficiency into the process:

- Create a template so that everyone is providing updates in the same format and you aren't searching out information.
- Establish a schedule for updates to be provided so that all of the updates come in at approximately the same time, and it's easy to see if something is missed.
- If your organization has some form of collaboration software, make the template available there and create a task with a deadline in each team member's email and scheduling tool for them to update it each week.

You can't let tools control you as a project manager. There is too much work to do, and far more important areas for you to spend your energy. In reality, you may need to implement a little of both approaches, and you may need to refine the approach during the course of the project—the work is not going to wait.

### 5(c) Monitor the impact of the changes that you have made

You cannot assume that the work you completed in 5(b) will work. You have to confirm the success, which means monitoring for an improvement. There may be objective measures that you can use—a reduction in the amount of time that it takes to update your project plan, for example—but you will also have to rely on subjective measures, such as your comfort level using the different functions in the tool, for example.

You need to be honest with yourself. Convincing yourself that you are now comfortable with the tool because you don't want to bother your *tool coach* anymore is not going to work if you are still fighting the software. You won't become a master of the software overnight, but you need to be able to be confident with the basic elements and recognize what the tool is telling you about the state of your project.

# 7.7 My schedule is totally unrealistic.

### By Cornelius Fitchner

## 1. Problem

When you started this project, you used forward scheduling to estimate duration, taking into account the project constraints. Now however, your sponsor has given you a new fixed end date. After reviewing your initial time estimation, you determine that with the current scope and resources, it is unrealistic to complete the project by the deadline.

Often, this problem occurs when customers have little experience estimating time or they set an arbitrary completion date due to an industry trade show or budget cycles, or for other reasons. They may not understand the consequences of changing project constraints, and this makes your job that much harder.

## 2. Warning Signs

We can all recognize this problem, and we are all experienced with it. Look for the early signs that this problem is about to make your life a misery:

- Your customer admits that the schedule is aggressive or tight.
- Your sponsor says, "I have a challenge for you," when discussing the delivery date.
- Your senior engineer says the new deadline is not attainable.
- You look at the schedule and know it's not possible because your duration estimates are longer than the deadline.
- Commonly heard phrases are "Overtime," "Make it happen," "Can I rely on you?," "Do or die," and "Are you a team player?"
- Team members use words of doubt when referring to the schedule.
- You have been given a typical project with a typical schedule!

### Is This Schedule Achievable?

It was Rohit's dream project: a small but talented team, an adequate budget, management support, a realistic schedule, and a cutting-edge product. Everything was on schedule for the new wireless, high-definition computer monitor to be completed and introduced at the International Consumer Electronics Show in January.

It had been a miserable two years economically, and the company was counting on this product to get it into the black for the year. If it didn't appear at the top trade shows, there was no way that was going to happen. Rohit's sponsor, Sharon, who headed Sales and Marketing, realized one of the up-and-coming electronics trade shows in Asia was scheduled for October. Because the product's exposure at these shows was critical, she asked Rohit to get the product finished in time for the Asian show—three months earlier than scheduled.

When Rohit went back to his team and explained that the schedule would have to move up, his head engineer laughed and said, "No can do." His team, which had been so fired up, suddenly seemed demoralized and negative.

Although Rohit knew immediately that the pushed up schedule was unrealistic, he hadn't been ready to discuss it with Sharon until he was prepared to offer options. Finally, Rohit went back to Sharon and told her that the schedule simply was not possible without modifying other project constraints such as budget or scope.

"Absolutely not," she said. "The monitor has to do everything we said it would do or our customers and stockholders will bolt. We don't have any more money for this project, and we have no more time." Sharon came closer to Rohit and said, "Look, I know it's going to be a little tight, but we need you to make it happen."

## 3. What will happen if I do nothing?

Trying to meet an unattainable deadline without changing any of the other project constraints is the fastest way to give yourself an ulcer. If you have done your estimations and know how long it will take with the current resources, scope, etc., then fooling yourself into thinking you can meet the deadline won't help anyone—not you, your team, or the sponsor. If the project is not an outright failure, at best, the quality will suffer, and at worst, a last-minute forced compromise will have to be found. Your team will be demoralized and conflicts will arise. If it doesn't end well, your reputation will also suffer.

If you don't deal with the issue head on, you will have to deal with it later. If you do it as soon as you see a problem, you still have the opportunity to deliver something good. Otherwise, you will deliver a half-baked solution and have an unhappy customer who says, "Why didn't you tell me earlier?" Those are words a project manager never wants to hear.

## 4. Solution

Early and proactive *expectation management* is the key. By showing your sponsor today what a realistic schedule looks like, and giving options for moving forward, you can usually find a good solution.

It is not unusual for project schedules to be unrealistic at the beginning because so little is known about the project and people have high expectations. They are excited, but don't know what it will take to achieve, and that is where expectation management comes in.

Of course, the best solution to an unrealistic schedule is to convince your sponsor to extend it by presenting an accurate, realistically estimated schedule. If changing the end point is not possible, something else has to give, and that something would be one or more of the other project constraints such as scope, quality, budget, resources, or risk. These project constraints are where you can give options to your customer in order to achieve the required deadline. Your customer has to decide what the most critical constraints are, and it is your job to guide them.

## 5. What should I do?

If your schedule is unrealistic, there is usually a good reason for it. Find that reason and use it to manage your sponsor's or customer's expectations. For example, is there a trade show or are there budget considerations?

There are two ways of handling an unrealistic schedule:

1. The schedule can be changed—work with the sponsor to develop a new realistic schedule.
2. The schedule cannot be changed (date of delivery is the primary constraint)—one or more of the other project constraints have to change (usually a combination). Help your customer and stakeholders decide what the most critical constraints are and develop a new approach based on that.

# Project Constraints

### 5(a) Schedule

The ideal solution is to extend the schedule. For example, you tell the customer that by extending the project schedule without changing the scope or any other constraint, he or she will defer $XXX on this year's budget, which can be added to next year's budget (see Figure 7.1). By deferring the project budget, the customer is able to stay within the company's current budget targets and is able to preserve the scope of the project.

Barring extending the schedule, other project constraints *must* be changed.

| | Year 1 | Year 2 |
|---|---|---|
| Current | $100,000<br><br>(= Scope reduced or other constraint changed; schedule maintained) | |
| Proposed | $80,000<br><br>(= Scope maintained; budget & schedule deferred) | $20,000 |

**Figure 7.1**

### 5(b) Scope

You can reduce scope, make it less complex, or defer it. Often deferring scope is an acceptable option for customers because they are not saying that they won't or can't do it, which are negative words. However, they are able to say that they don't have time to do everything right now. Deferring scope is usually a good first step to suggest. Sponsors don't really like to *give up* or reduce scope as a first option (after all, they want their requirements fulfilled), but they understand the direct connection between scope and schedule, so discussing how to defer scope to future phases is something they can follow. For example, in a software project, propose implementing the main functionality first and deferring the reporting and exporting functions to a later stage because they are not needed initially before the data has been entered.

### 5(c) Budget

To meet a fixed project deadline, budget is often one of the most difficult constraints to change. You can either increase or defer the budget. It is usually very difficult to get more money out of the sponsors because they are working under a corporate structure with its own constraints, and they also have to divide their money between several competing projects. Ask your sponsor if he or she can get money out of another bucket, that is, from other projects or categories, such as capital expenditures. If the budget is maxed out for full-time employees, is there a budget for consultants (or other resources)?

If no money is available, that leaves an opportunity to guide your customer back toward deferring the budget and, consequently, the project, or toward changing additional constraints.

### 5(d) Resources

One way to meet an unrealistic deadline without changing the scope is by adding resources; this is called *crashing*. You can hire more, cheaper, or better-experienced resources. All of these have financial consequences. Hiring more resources results in hiring costs and more administration, and could cause team issues, so your leadership skills will be critical.

- To hire additional *regular* resources, a budget increase will be required, or the sponsor must look for money in other budgetary pools, such as, for consultants.
- Hiring cheaper resources may be one way to shave time off the schedule without increasing the budget. You may, for example, consider offshoring.
- Hiring resources that have more experience (including consultants) will cost more up front, but because of their knowledge, they should be able to get their tasks and deliverables finished in less time.

In all cases, on-boarding is an issue and has to be weighed against the expected gains.

### 5(e) Quality

Can the customer accept less quality in order to meet the deadline? Find out what the customer's tolerance is to a result or an end product that is less than acceptable or agreed upon. Find out what the critical specifications or features are and work to that. Example: you deliver the fully functional prototype robotic arm on time. It meets all finished product specifications; however, one of the non-critical internal components does not meet a dimensional specification by 0.02 cm. The sponsor has agreed to accept the out-of-specification part in order to meet the deadline because it does not affect the performance of the machine. He has in effect accepted less quality.

### 5(f) Risk

We perform risk management (RM) proactively as a basis to understand areas of our project where things can go wrong. It is required to avoid, mitigate, transfer, or accept negative risks. While risk management helps us to stay within our schedule, the activities consume both time and resources, so the only way to gain any time in RM is to do one of two things:

*1. Implement a simplified RM approach.*

- *Fewer RM activities:* Ask your customer, "Which risks can you accept?" Your customer may wish to have fewer risk management activities, and you can offer ways to mitigate the associated risks. For example, if the sponsor is willing to cancel the weekly technical reviews to speed up the schedule, thereby increasing the risk to the project's objectives and quality, you could suggest changing it to a bi-weekly or monthly review instead.

- *Higher-level risk management:* Follow the standard RM processes in the *Project Management Body of Knowledge (PMBOK® Guide)*, but only on the highest levels. For example, typically you would list every possible risk (hundreds) and drill down to analyze each in detail. Instead, keep it at a higher level. This is not for the inexperienced or the weak of heart. For this, you will need a thorough knowledge of and experience in risk management in order to know which to focus on and which to put onto the watch list.
- *Rolling risk management:* Rolling risk management would be an ongoing, focused review of the project with a view toward looking ahead. Schedule regular meetings in which you review the status and risks of the project. Focus on the midterm *future* of the project and ask, "What could go wrong?" Continually posing this question should help keep you and your team thinking about risk management and mitigating risks along the way.

There is a great deal of literature available to help you develop simplified or alternate approaches to risk management.

*2. Do not avoid formal risk management.*

Avoiding RM is the last thing you should consider because if you do not know and manage your risks, something will go wrong, and the schedule end point will not be met.

There is, however, one circumstance where you may be able to forgo *formal* RM activities, and that is on a small-to-medium project where the project manager has a great deal of personal experience with the same type of project. If you are that project manager, you will know the issues, pitfalls, and risks already. You have seen it all; you know what is coming and are aware of the possible dangers ahead of you. You will need to listen to your instincts and be mindful of risks as you go along.

Both approaches are inherently risky and could lead you to miss your deadline because you may overlook risks or fail to deal with them appropriately. Any changes in risk management activities must be discussed with your customer because the ultimate goal of getting the project done on schedule is put in jeopardy by not dealing with risk at an appropriate level.

# 7.8 It's hard for me to tell what is important (the critical path).

By Andrew Filev

## 1. Problem

You have read and heard so many times that efficient project planning is key to your project's success. But when dealing with a complex project, it can be difficult for you to identify the tasks that need special attention. It also can be a challenge to differentiate between the tasks that should be completed first, and assignments that can be delayed without delaying the whole project.

> ### There's a Lot of Work—Which Parts Are Most Important?
>
> Leo was confused. He was pleased with the progress that he had made so far, and the team had really come together in building the plan. However, now Leo had to try and figure out how to schedule the work and he wasn't sure how to do it. It seemed like everything was important, so how did he decide what to do first and what to postpone? Were there some tasks that needed special attention, and if so, how could he identify them?
>
> Leo's team had lots of ideas, but there didn't seem to be any consensus on the best way forward, and Leo didn't want to *guess* on the right approach. He needed a structured approach to figuring out what work to do first and what to delay.

## 2. Warning Signs

There are a number of indicators that you are experiencing this problem. They include:

- You are unsure which tasks should be completed first, and which can wait a little longer.
- You don't know which tasks you need to prioritize, and you keep changing priorities on the go.
- Your team is unsure about what tasks they should be working on and complete first, so they try to do everything simultaneously. This leads to unproductive multitasking and a lot of stress in the group.
- Parts of your project get delayed, and this jeopardizes your project's success.

## 3. What will happen if I do nothing?

When you cannot identify the most important tasks, you'll end up focusing on the wrong parts of your project work. While you're busy with things that are less important, critical tasks will be missed, and your project will be late. Project delays may need budget extensions. Your stakeholders will be unhappy and they will see it as your fault.

## 4. Solution

You can solve this problem by using standard methodologies to define the most important tasks. One of them, critical path analysis (CPA), is a popular method and a powerful tool that helps you schedule and manage complex projects. Building a CPA will help you identify the tasks that should be completed on time, and the ones that you can delay without jeopardizing or delaying the whole project. CPA also allows you to identify the minimum length of time needed to complete a project.

## 5. What should I do?

A critical path acts as the basis for schedule preparation and resource planning. During management of a project, it allows you to monitor the progress toward meeting the deadlines. It helps you to see where remedial action needs to be taken to get a project back on course. Another benefit of using CPA within the planning process is to help you develop and better understand the constraints and dependencies in your project.

To maximize the benefit, use critical path analysis together with a Gantt chart, as this chart clearly visualizes your project schedule. Leverage the latest project management technologies to build your critical path and create a structured plan. Software applications that have Gantt charts with task dependencies can be extremely helpful in defining clear task sequences. They also will save you time when you need to adjust your schedule due to changes in the project.

### 5(a) Understand the critical path

The critical path method (CPM) is a mathematically based algorithm for scheduling a set of project activities. The essential technique for using CPM is to construct a model of the project that includes all of the following:

- A list of all activities required to complete the project
- The dependencies between the activities
- The estimate of time (duration) that each activity will take to complete

Using these values, CPM usually calculates the longest path of planned activities to the end of the project, and the earliest and latest points that each activity can start and finish without making the project longer. This process determines which activities are *critical* (i.e., on the longest path) and which have *total float* (i.e., can be delayed without making the project longer).

As an example, let's take a simple real-life project: hanging a picture on the wall. What should you do to complete this project successfully? First, define and list all the tasks that have to be done, so that the whole project is completed (see Table 7.1).

**Table 7.1**  Task list

| |
|---|
| Choose a place on the wall |
| Buy the screws |
| Choose the picture |
| Drill a hole |
| Screw in the screws |
| Hang the picture |

When we think of these tasks, we realize that some of them cannot start before the others are finished. That is, some tasks are dependent on the others (see Table 7.2).

**Table 7.2** Dependencies

| Task | Dependent on |
|---|---|
| Choose a place on the wall | — |
| Buy the screws | — |
| Choose the picture | — |
| Drill a hole | Choosing a place on the wall |
| Screw in the screws | Buying the screws and drilling a hole |
| Hang the picture | Screwing in the screws and choosing the picture |

The actions *drill a hole, screw in the screws* and *hang the picture* form a sequence of tasks that must be performed in a specific order, one right after the other, to ensure a successful result. Such tasks are called *sequential* activities.

So these three tasks in the example, together with the start of our project (choosing a place on the wall), are the most important critical steps that must be taken to arrive at the proper solution to our problem. These actions will be placed on your critical path for this project. The essential concept behind critical path analysis is that you cannot start some activities until others are finished. These activities need to be completed in a sequence, with each stage being more-or-less completed before the next stage can begin.

Here's what a sample schedule can look like (see Figure 7.2). The critical path consists of the longest sequence of activities from project start to end that should be started and completed exactly as scheduled to ensure the project is completed by a certain date in the future. The activities on the critical path must be very closely managed. If jobs on the critical path slip, immediate action should be taken to get the project back on schedule; otherwise, completion of the whole project will slip.

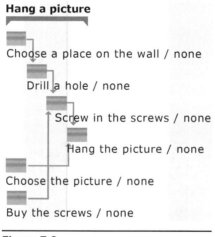

**Hang a picture**

Choose a place on the wall / none

Drill a hole / none

Screw in the screws / none

Hang the picture / none

Choose the picture / none

Buy the screws / none

**Figure 7.2**

Imagine that you have a project that will take 300 days to complete. If the first activity on the critical path is one day late, the project will take 301 days to complete, unless another activity on the critical path can be completed one day earlier. So the critical path is simply all the tasks that determine the end date in your project schedule.

There can be more than one critical path in a project, so that several paths run in parallel. For instance, in our case, *choose a picture* and *hang the picture*, as well as *buy the screws*, *screw in the screws* and *hang the picture*, form other task sequences that also are important for us to complete the project.

The critical path may contain all the important activities on the project, or not. In fact, sometimes the activities on the critical path are not the most important parts of the project. At the same time, there will be tasks that are not on the critical path, but still determine your project's success. Understanding the critical path involves determining which activities are critical to complete on time. But other activities, lying outside of critical path, may also be important and require extra diligence and focus.

### 5(b) Understand the resource constraints

Traditional critical-path-derived schedules are based only on causal (logical) dependencies. We've already marked these dependences in our plan (e.g., it is impossible to drill a hole before you choose a place on the wall). However, a project can have resource limitations, which should also be taken into consideration. These limitations will create more dependencies. These dependencies are often called *resource constraints*.

So, if you work on a team, your project work can be split between the team members. In our case, while you're choosing a place on the wall and drilling a hole, one of your friends can go and buy some screws, and your spouse can choose the picture. The tasks can be done in parallel, as demonstrated in Table 7.2.

However, if you're the only person responsible for the project, you have a resource constraint (i.e., you cannot drill a hole and go shopping for screws simultaneously). In this case, your critical path will look different (see Figure 7.3).

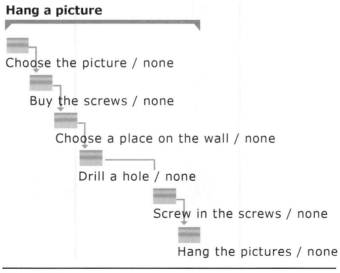

**Figure 7.3**

In Figure 7.3, we assume that you first need to choose the picture, and only later can you buy the screws. However, depending on the project conditions, these tasks can be performed in a different order.

Such a critical path is called a *resource critical* path. This method was proposed as an extension to the traditional CPA to allow for the inclusion of resources related to each activity. A resource-leveled schedule may include delays due to resource bottlenecks (i.e., unavailability of a resource at the required time), and it may cause a previously shorter path to become longer. This is what you see in Figure 7.3.

### 5(c) Calculate the length of your project

In project management, a critical path is the sequence of project activities that add up to the longest overall duration. This determines the shortest time possible to complete the project.

Getting back to our example, let's assume that you have to do everything by yourself. For each activity, show the estimated length of time it will take. Also, you determine the approximate start time for each task on the critical path. Here's how it can be done in our example (see Table 7.3).

Now, if we add up all the critical task durations, we will get the approximate time that is needed for the whole project to be completed. In our case, 2 hours and 26 minutes. Add the duration to the start time, and you'll be able to calculate the earliest project completion time (10:26 in our example).

**Table 7.3** Resource critical path

| Task | Duration | Start |
|------|----------|-------|
| Choose a picture | 30 minutes | 9:00 am |
| Buy the screws | 30 minutes | 9:30 am |
| Choose the place on the wall | 5 minutes | 10:00 am |
| Drill a hole | 15 minutes | 10: 05 pm |
| Screw in the screws | 5 minutes | 10: 20 pm |
| Hang the picture | 1 minute | 10: 25 pm |

### 5(d) Understand the flexibility in the critical path.

The critical path method was developed for complex, but fairly predictable, projects. However, in real life, we rarely get to manage such projects. A schedule generated using critical path techniques is often not followed precisely. As mentioned, any delay of an activity on the critical path directly impacts the planned project completion date. New requirements may pop up, new resource constraints may emerge, and so on. Let's have a look at that scenario (see Figure 7.4):

Let's say you're planning to redecorate the living room together with your spouse. Your tasks will include:

- Getting rid of the old furniture
- Painting the walls
- Fixing the ceiling
- Installing the new furniture

Your spouse will be responsible for:

- Choosing the new curtains
- Hanging the new curtains

**Hang a picture**

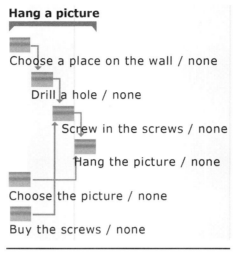

Choose a place on the wall / none

Drill a hole / none

Screw in the screws / none

Hang the picture / none

Choose the picture / none

Buy the screws / none

**Figure 7.4**

The curtain tasks form a sub-project and can be treated as a noncritical path. Your spouse can *choose the new curtains* and *hang the new curtains* any time before the end of your project. So these tasks do have flexibility in the start and end date, or *float*. These tasks are parallel, and they will not be placed on the critical path. The whole project can be seen on a Gantt chart (see Figure 7.5).

However, if any of the parallel tasks get significantly delayed, it will prevent your whole project from being completed on time. Therefore, you should always keep an eye on parallel tasks. Now, let's assume that choosing the curtains took your spouse longer than you initially expected. This will delay the end of the project (see Figure 7.6).

Your redecoration is incomplete without the new curtains, so the path that previously was noncritical becomes critical for the project's completion. The initial critical path changes.

**Redecorating the living room**

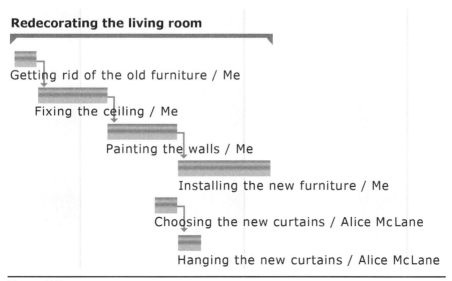

Getting rid of the old furniture / Me

Fixing the ceiling / Me

Painting the walls / Me

Installing the new furniture / Me

Choosing the new curtains / Alice McLane

Hanging the new curtains / Alice McLane

**Figure 7.5**

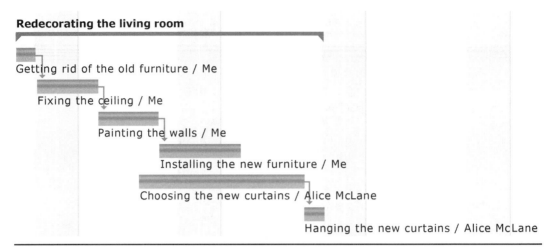

**Figure 7.6**

To keep an eye on your noncritical tasks, you should always keep your schedule up-to-date. That's the only way you'll know exactly where your project is at any given moment in time and whether it will be delivered as it was initially planned.

Keeping your schedule realistic can be tough without the proper technology at hand.

### 5(e) Useful tools for building a critical path

If your projects have parallel activities, doing the scheduling calculations for the critical path method is quite laborious and feels like using pen and paper, instead of calculators, to do math. This becomes even work if you consider the fact that frequent updates to the schedule will force you to recalculate things. For large and complex projects, there will be thousands of activities and dependency relationships that need to be up to date. Fortunately, there is relatively inexpensive, Web-based project management software that can handle this with ease on a *pay as you go* basis.

Project management applications, like desktop-based Microsoft Project or Web-based Wrike.com, will help you visualize your project schedule in the form of a Gantt chart and draw dependencies between your tasks. Such a tool will automatically calculate your project's end date, as well as the length of your project. The tools also will help you identify the tasks that will not be on the critical path. Additionally, some software applications allow you to easily reschedule your tasks as your project develops. You'll be able to easily put the tasks on the path and take them off. You'll also be able to move whole task chains on the chart, according to your real project conditions. The Gantt chart you've seen above is an approximate schedule for our sample project created in an online tool, on Wrike.com.

Web-based tools that focus on collaboration can be useful when you work on a team. They allow your team members to update the schedule, making it realistic. This way, you immediately see the progress and changes on your project, without having to pull the information from your team members and put it into the project plan manually by yourself.

### 5(f) Tips and tricks when creating your critical path

*Pay close attention to the human factor.*

Critical path analysis and project management tools can be really helpful in administering and managing projects. The dependencies that you put on your project are usually fairly easy to grasp. Thus, the formal critical path for small projects is often obvious enough for project managers and for project management software. Project management tools are helpful in the visualization of the schedule, and in quick calculation of an approximate end date when there are estimates in place. However, they are not a substitute for the *human factor*. Experienced project managers know that tools are important, but they must always remember that they are dealing with human beings when planning project tasks, deadlines, milestones, and implementation dates. The human factor should also be taken into consideration when creating your project schedule.

We mentioned the *resource critical path* method earlier in the chapter. Another method that can complement your use of critical path and help you deal with resource constraints is called the *critical chain*. The critical chain method (CCM) is a way of planning and managing projects that puts the main emphasis on the resources required to execute project tasks. A critical chain tends to keep the resources levelly loaded, but it requires them to be flexible in their start times and to quickly switch between tasks and task chains to keep the whole project on schedule. Dependencies used to determine the critical chain include both logical hand-off dependencies (where the output of the predecessor task is required to start the successor), and resource dependencies (where a task has to wait for a resource to finish work on another task). The identification of the critical chain uses a network of tasks with *aggressive but achievable* estimates that is first *resource leveled* against a finite set of resources. More information about resource constraints is found in Chapter 5: Dealing with Constraints, Assumptions, and Scope, especially 5.3—*We don't have the resources we need*; and Chapter 9: Managing Risks, especially 9.4—*My project is too dependent on a few key people*.

*Involve your team in the planning process.*

The people doing the work should be actively involved in scheduling. They're motivated to get it right, have the skills to understand the dependencies, and need to accept the schedule. It is also helpful to involve your stakeholders and clients. They can provide you with valuable insights on when they need the project to be completed, and other important information.

When choosing project management software to build your project plan and your critical path, keep in mind that the application should give your team members and clients an opportunity to contribute to the plan.

*Move tasks that involve risks closer to the start of your project.*

All projects have activities with potential risks that can lead to problems or delays. Some of these can be averted or reduced through advance planning. This is always a good approach and carries a great chance of project success. Identify the most risky tasks on your project because these will require special attention. If you manage to complete them earlier, you will be able to reduce the project's overall risk profile sooner. Therefore, putting these tasks closer to the beginning of your critical path, if possible, is highly recommended.

*Check the plan and see whether there are any tasks that can be completed a little earlier when your critical path is delayed.*

It is often a good idea to communicate clearly to stakeholders if your project may be delayed, along with reasons for the original deferral and the actions you'll take to compensate for the delay. If the delay is unavoidable, you have to make a decision and consult with stakeholders about whether to deliver later than the due date or to reduce the scope of the work to be on time. This will change your initial critical path. For more information, see Chapter 5: Dealing with Constraints, Assumptions, and Scope.

# 7.9 I made some wrong assumptions.

By Stephen Maye

## 1. Problem

You have been charging ahead confidently—until now. Based on your experience and the guidance of trusted contributors, you factored reasonable assumptions into your plans, decisions, and actions. Now, new information has revealed that some of those assumptions were wrong. It feels like everything has changed. What will you do next?

## 2. Warning Signs

Sometimes this problem shows itself simply because you learn something that proves one of your assumptions is wrong. Often though there are other, less obvious signs:

- Key actions are not yielding the expected result.
- Progress has stalled because decisions are being revisited or deferred.
- Good work is not received as well as it should be.
- You feel like you're losing your ability to predict the future.

### You Made a Bad Assumption; Now Deal With It

Dave knew the scope for the large initiative he would manage would include subprojects in the product development and professional services organizations. The initiative's goal was to develop and implement new processes and technology (and required organizational changes) to support better collaboration and consistency in the way these groups service customer needs. Three months into the project, as success measures became clearer and the subprojects became more tightly integrated, it was obvious that a critical assumption was wrong.

Dave and the team had assumed there would be little to no involvement with the Sales and Marketing organization. No one had mentioned them (except in passing), and they did not play prominently in the project charter.

Although there were related activities underway in Sales and Marketing, it was not integrated with the larger initiative. The sequencing of activities was not consistent with the initiative's key milestones, and the lack of shared management and oversight created a blind spot for both progress and the details of scope and integration.

Dave needed to develop a solution that brought all of these activities into his project. He needed to revisit his assumptions and understand the impact that this wrong assumption would have on his project, and he needed to manage the overall impact. Where should he start?

## 3. What will happen if I do nothing?

The short answer is that you can end up failing entirely after having worked harder than anyone could have expected.

What you know about a project can be separated into facts and assumptions. Facts like the budget, schedule, and team makeup are typically held together by assumptions that can introduce risks if not managed well.

Project assumptions are often in one or more key areas:

- The definition and priority of project success measures
- Sponsor availability and support
- Team effectiveness
- Solution fit and effectiveness (including scope)
- Pace or degree of change adoption
- Market or environmental variables

When (not if) some of these assumptions begin to give way and unravel, the entire machine can go with them. The result can be a project that breaks down along the road or motors into a place no one actually wanted to go. After a very rough ride, you slip out of the driver's seat looking like someone who either can't drive (manage) or navigate (stay in synch with the business).

## 4. Solution

We've all encountered the bumper sticker advice *assume nothing.* This pithy, and misguided, sentiment may have contributed to your sense that you've been negligent. Let's be clear that the solution is *not* to stop making assumptions. Assumptions are necessary and unavoidable, and increase in number and potential impact with the size, duration, and complexity of a project. Don't punish yourself because you made assumptions or because some were wrong—this is the case in every project. (Ninety-five percent of project managers make inaccurate assumptions; the other 5 percent have been known to lie.) Your approach should be to avoid unnecessary assumptions, manage the necessary ones, and know the difference between them.

Although it is best to be mindful of your assumptions from as early as the creation of the business case, it is unlikely that you are too far along to benefit from taking steps now. (You were probably more aware of your assumptions at the start of the planning process when you were forced to make assumptions in order to get started. Unfortunately, in the midst of all the project activity, you may have lost sight of some of those assumptions.) You need to deal with the impact of the assumptions that have proven to be wrong, eliminate assumptions that have no business threatening your project, and implement an approach to manage the necessary assumptions that remain.

That approach is as follows:

1. Understand the role of assumptions in project execution
2. Explore wrong assumptions made to date
3. Eliminate unnecessary assumptions
4. Define an approach to manage necessary assumptions

5. Gain support for the role of assumptions in project execution
6. Integrate assumption management into existing project plans and processes

## 5. What should I do?

You are dealing with a problem that requires both a point-in-time solution and an ongoing process. At the end of the day, you need to have squeezed all of the ambiguity that you can out of your project. Then you need to help everyone around you understand how much ambiguity is left and how you are dealing with it.

First, you have to deal with the political and material impact of wrong assumptions to date. Equally important, but slightly less urgent, is the need to eliminate unnecessary assumptions. Once the current problem and blind spots are addressed, you will need to gain support for the role of assumptions in project execution, define, and implement an approach to managing necessary assumptions, and integrate it into everything you do.

### 5(a) Understand the role of assumptions in project execution

If you are making assumptions when reliable information is available that means assumptions are unnecessary, and you are setting yourself up for trouble, especially when those assumptions are pivotal to the success of the project. You need to ensure that all of your assumptions are needed—that facts aren't available when you need them.

Part of your job is to factor assumptions into the project, and a disproven assumption is simply a trigger in a planned process. For example, when you craft an implementation strategy that covers many months or multiple years, you are required to apply assumptions about the direction of the business or business unit, market trends and market position, shifts in the labor pool, the effectiveness of the solution, speed and quality of change adoption (new processes, new technology, new structure, new ways of thinking and working), and even the stability continuity of the sponsors driving the project.

When you acknowledge the assumption, you have the opportunity to relate it to risks and other project implications. You can track the assumption and replan based on the degree to which the assumption proves to be accurate or inaccurate.

### 5(b) Explore wrong assumptions to date

You might be reading this chapter because some of your assumptions have proven to be incorrect or inaccurate. You saw the signs, you analyzed for cause (the erroneous assumption), and now you know. The first thing to do is address both the original assumption and the implications of the new information.

Document a corrective recommendation for the project sponsor as follows:

- We made this assumption _____.
- New information now suggests _____.
- The potential impact to the project is _____.
- We explored these options _____.
- We recommend this course of action _____.

With a clear decision from the sponsor(s), document the change and integrate it into the project plans, work assignment, role and responsibilities, communication plan, etc. With the urgent problems solved, you can turn your attention to the systemic risk of weak assumption management.

### 5(c) Eliminate unnecessary assumptions

With trusted members of your team (representing key areas of the project: tech, people, process, strategy, business justification, and such) and the customer, brainstorm the assumptions that are still at play in the project. Looking at each major phase of the project, ask:

- Why are we taking this approach?
- Why do we believe that is important?
- Why are we moving at this pace rather than faster/slower?
- What do we believe is the most important outcome of the phase, the project, and the larger program (where relevant)?
- Other questions relevant to that project.

The idea here is to ask *why* until you reach the hidden assumptions on which the project rests. Why, why, why, why, why? Peter Senge described the *Five Whys* in *The Fifth Discipline Field Book*, a good resource for the thinking project manager. As you move through the discussion, capture assumptions on three lists that all can see and name the lists: Confirm, Track, and Verified.

- *Confirm* items are assumptions for which we have not done appropriate due diligence.
- *Track* items are assumptions for which no further due diligence is required (or possible) at this time, but for which we must create a link to the project plan, including a point at which the assumption should be proven, disproven, or adjusted.
- *Verified* items are assumptions for which appropriate due diligence has been done and for which no change is expected. (These are, in effect, not assumptions at all. They may not be empirically provable, but they have been verified from an authoritative source and appropriately documented and communicated. These might include resource availability, sponsor priorities, and the project's role in a larger strategy. *Verified* items are assumptions for which a known authoritative source is identified, for example, the executive sponsor provided a list of prioritized outcomes for the project).

### 5(d) Define an approach to manage necessary assumptions

The remaining verified and unverified assumptions should be integrated into the reporting and plan management processes. Each should be linked to a point in time where it can be confirmed, disproven, or adjusted. Each time an assumption is disproven and adjusted, it should be reported with the resulting implications and recommendations for changes to the plan. The implications of each assumption should be documented for future consideration when the assumption is proven, disproven, or adjusted. Document them as follows:

- Assumption name
- Description
- Verified—yes or no
- Will be resolved _____ (time when it will be confirmed or disproven)
- Status (open, proven, disproven, adjusted)
- Adjustment details

You may be deploying a technology solution to five user communities within a six month period with a critical assumption being the rate at which the users can adopt the new technology, related processes, and role changes necessary to achieve the anticipated business benefits. The assumption should be stated explicitly with a decision point identified where expectations will be adjusted if the assumed rate of adoption proves to be other than expected. The assumption is overt, the point at which it will be proven, disproven, or adjusted is known, and a process for managing it is in place.

### 5(e) Gain support for the role of assumptions in project execution

Clearly, sponsor commitment is needed for both the identified assumptions and the process of managing the assumptions as part of the project.

As a result of following the steps previously mentioned, you now have a body of documentation to present that essentially says, "This is all that we can know and what we feel it's logical to assume." You should now be prepared to:

- Present the list of assumptions to be tracked.
- Present the process by which they will be managed, reported, and updated or adjusted.
- Address questions and incorporate changes based on sponsor input.
- Gain explicit commitment to proceed with these assumptions in place and manage them as you have just discussed.
- Update plans accordingly. Assign new task and responsibilities to address the change in process.

### 5(f) Integrate assumption management into existing project plans and processes

Review the project roles and responsibilities to ensure identification and management of assumptions is addressed.

- The project plan and schedule should include a link to key assumptions with potential replanning points identified to address disproven or adjusted assumptions.
- Risk management should be linked to key assumptions to ensure the interdependency between assumptions and our assessment of project risks are understood and maintained.

- Assumptions about related projects can be just as significant as those made within your own project. Key assumptions about the relevant program (or portfolio) to which your project belongs must be identified and managed.
- Key assumptions can have a material impact on the business justification/ROI for a project. Each key assumption from the business case must be made explicit and incorporated into the ongoing management and re-planning of the project.

# 7.10 The company's project management process doesn't work for me.

## By Ian Stewart

## 1. Problem

With deep experience implementing financial reporting systems for consultancies, you were brought on to manage a significant overhaul of a major bank's core accounting system. Several weeks into the project it has become clear that many of the methods and vernacular that you've been accustomed to using as a consultant are not considered a standard practice for delivering projects at your new company.

The nature of the project management profession encourages mobility and a cross-pollination of ideas on project delivery. A common mistake, though, is to assume that all organizations either deliver projects the same or are necessarily open to or encourage innovations in their project delivery methods. These assumptions can actually be damaging to the project if the project begins to progress significantly with a delivery method that is not well-supported or considered non-compliant.

---

*Form* **Here to Eternity?**

During the weekly project team meeting, Louise looked up from her printed agenda and paused before asking her lead business analyst, "What is the STS again?"

Five weeks into her new job at Provincial Bank, Louise began to wonder if she had made the right choice by leaving the consulting firm where she had worked most of her professional life. She thought, "Sure, the travel was hard, but at least there I knew what was expected." All of her years of experience had not equipped her with what she needed to navigate Provincial Bank's endless matrix of required artifacts and forms.

Delivering new general ledger software systems was something Louise did know about though. Successful implementations of these software packages had been her calling card for years, and now she was saddled with an inefficient project delivery process that required a seemingly endless series of project lifecycle tollgates and peer reviews. As a consultant, this was rarely the case. Fixed-price contracts and a proprietary methodology offered Louise the mandate she needed to move quickly without impediment. Now, as a senior project manager at Provincial, impediments and obstacles were everywhere.

Louise was beginning to feel helpless. If she could just talk to somebody and explain what she was trying to do. "I don't need a deliverable approved three times. Why do I have to do this?"

For now, Louise decided to keep her resignation letter archived. After a few moments with her eyes closed, she looked out into the faces of her project team and asked for suggestions on what to do next.

## 2. Warning Signs

The project management process should support you as the project manager and should assist you in managing the project. Any of the following are indications that things might not be happening that way:

- Project team members question key tasks in the project schedule.
- Poor early performance against project quality performance indicators.
- Lack of existing support for a preferred project toolset.
- Lack of understanding of the organization's required project toolset.
- Confusion over some of the project management terminology.
- Confusion on roles and responsibilities within the project team.
- Confusion on areas of responsibility with central support area, like a PMO or test/product quality group.

## 3. What will happen if I do nothing?

When questioning a company's project management processes, a project manager could opt to follow the existing processes or move forward with a preferred set of project steps and processes that might be considered nonstandard. The first option, following the processes, could lead to a less efficient delivery of the project. The second option, ignoring the project processes, could lead to rework, political battles, or reprimands from senior management.

Your project team's success depends on your ability to understand the landscape and the roles of key stakeholders within an organization. While delivering on the expectations of the project's sponsor is always critical to success, the needs of other stakeholders, like those responsible for supporting the final delivered product, have an important stake in determining the project's success as well. Ignoring the process requirements of those stakeholders will lead to an inevitable showdown that could put your project's success in jeopardy.

## 4. Solution

At the risk of stating the obvious—there is more than one way to deliver a project. Project managers who have delivered projects for different organizations will already know this. What begins to get a bit more complicated, however, is when the *most efficient way* is considered. Project managers, especially those who have a proven record of success, will form opinions on how a process, standard, practice, or approach is best used. There can also be pressure on PMs in some industries (software development is a good example) to innovate to a most efficient approach.

To resolve a conflict with an organization's project processes, a PM will have to put aside predetermined approaches and reconcile differences directly and as soon as possible. The alternative to doing this can include rework for the project team and reprimands or even termination for the project manager.

To move forward and reconcile differences with a project process, methodology or standard, a PM should act quickly. To increase the chance of success, a PM should ADOPT a five step approach to working these differences out.

1. **A**cknowledge your own assumptions and bias
2. **D**on't be dogmatic
3. **O**utline the drivers behind the process
4. **P**oint to alternatives and middle ground
5. **T**alk it out

## 5. What should I do?

A project manager should move quickly to resolve any differences around project methodology or a supporting project process. Circumventing the issue will increase the risk of rework or reprisals for the project team. By taking the following steps a project manager can address the underlying issues and reach a negotiated agreement that is acceptable to all sides:

### 5(a) Acknowledge your own assumptions and bias

Maybe you have found yourself thinking, "I've worked as a project manager for years. I know this is a waste of time." Have you ever asked yourself *why* you think this is good therapy? Keep in mind that how we think is influenced heavily by our past experiences, and our past experiences are not the same as the past experiences of others. This is especially relevant for PMs who are working for a new organization. If you find yourself in this situation, it is reasonable to think that your past experience might provide you with some insight that your new organization might not have. The insight that you might *not* have, though, is what is unique about the new organization and why things are handled differently.

We all have assumptions about how things should be done and have some degree of bias based on past experience. Understanding that not everyone will share these is a critical first step toward the resolution of problems related to project process.

### 5(b) Don't be dogmatic

Delivering projects is about delivering value for the business or organization, period. Zeal and dogmatic belief is best reserved for personal faith or sports fans. Organizational or business circumstances will always dictate the best approach for doing something, and there really are no absolutes when it comes to managing projects.

### 5(c) Outline the drivers behind the process

In the history of all organizations, no one has ever come into work one day, sat down, and decided to develop and implement a process that they felt made no sense and added no value to an organization! There will always be cases where certain factors should have been given more careful consideration, or where specific aspects of a process need to be updated, but in the end no process is created in a vacuum. There are always drivers that contribute to why something is designed or used a certain way.

In a project management process, consider the following:

- *Industry:* The most comparatively uniform functions within an organization—Finance and Human Resources for example, can vary significantly from one industry to another. No two industries are entirely alike, and even industries that are commonly grouped together can be very different from one another. Manufacturing cars is different than manufacturing boats. A nuclear power plant is different than a hydro-electric plant. Banking is different from insurance.

- *Organizational history:* While theorists on organizational behavior will examine the elements of an organization's culture, it's the history—young or old—that will be the primary contributor to what makes an organization unique. Mergers, years of success, years of failure, positive press, negative press—all of these can contribute to how an organization sees itself and its appetite for risk (see Figure 7.7). Ultimately, the process is about controlling risk.
- *Regulatory environment:* Some industries will be completely free of regulation or at least close to it. Others will be profoundly influenced by it.

### 5(d) Point to alternatives and middle ground

If an organization lacks processes or roles, the PM will usually be empowered to add those for their project. Certified project management professionals (PMPs) may recall specific sections of the PMBOK that outline professional responsibility. A recurring scenario is one in which a PM is delivering a project for a less mature project organization. In this scenario, it is often mentioned that the PM's professional responsibility to the PM profession is to model the right approaches to project delivery and help the organization to mature its processes.

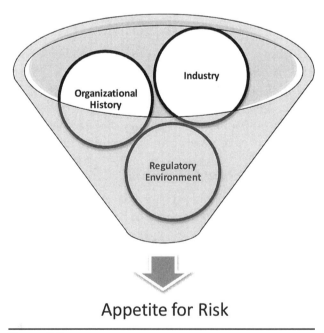

**Figure 7.7**

This scenario tends to be less frequent. What is more common are instances in which either (1) a PM who prefers an innovative, streamlined approach is delivering for an organization that has a rigid, methodical methodology, or (2) a PM who prefers a rigid, methodical approach is delivering for an organization that has an innovative, streamlined methodology.

Regardless of the scenario, most project organizations will have exception or variance processes. Through variance request processes, special consideration can be given to allow the project to take a different approach. In requesting the variance, it is critical to separate personal preference away from the unique nature of the project. Additionally, a compromised approach should be pursued, not an all-or-nothing proposal.

### 5(e) Talk it out

Organizations will typically have specific, designated roles that create methodology, processes, standards, and such. These often reside in a Project Management Office (PMO) or Center of Excellence (COE). Regardless, knowing the roles and the players will be essential for resolving any differences. In most cases, talking through the differences in a face-to-face setting can yield some remarkable results.

In talking through project process differences, emphasize what is unique about the needs of your project. Stay away from any discussion that encroaches into the area of opinion or personal preferences. Many organizations will have process improvement feedback loops in place to provide input on project process. While these can be typically helpful, resolution or updates implemented through them will likely take time to implement.

# 7.11 Everything is urgent, and I'm behind.

## By Mike Donoghue

## 1. Problem

The projects that you are working on are asking a lot of you. Forget about things like lunch or free evenings and weekends because, for whatever reason, more work has come your way and you are swamped. Sometimes you might be able to take a breather while you wait for updates, answers to questions, further instructions, and so forth, but even when you have downtime, you are still thinking of ways to juggle everything. It is when you reflect on all of your commitments and constraints that you come to the hard realization that some deliverables are at risk. Given the resources you have, is there anything you can do to turn this situation around?

## 2. Warning Signs

There comes a point when you know that you are in trouble because you are behind and don't believe that you can recover. The key is spotting the problem early. Look for the following signs:

- You are receiving an increasing number of telephone calls, emails, and such. from people who are checking on the status of your projects.
- Other project leaders, managers (including your own), and those in the higher ranks are being included in these communications.
- Communications are becoming more focused on *when*.
- More meetings are being called with the supposed intent to either check in or keep things on target. More people are being invited as well.
- Tasks are becoming increasingly hard to schedule, even those you used to perform regularly and without reminders.

### I Am Drowning in Work Here!

When Debra was asked to collaborate on a new product development effort, she was happy to accept the offer. Her quarterly project work was winding down and it seemed like a good time to tackle another project. She had heard great things about this latest endeavor and was enthusiastic. She knew there would be challenges working on a fresh product versus an update to an existing one, but with her schedule opening up and the fact that the request came from a well-respected colleague, it felt like a great opportunity.

Unfortunately, things heated up quickly for her when the quarterly project was recalled. Debra's current project had to be restarted with an aggressive timeframe and the new product development work ramped up simultaneously. Between the two projects, Debra found herself with too many demands of her time. The impact was not on her alone; many other people were struggling to meet the accelerated needs of the projects, too. That meant that the assistance Debra might normally be able to get was hard to come by. And now, here was Akshay, another manager, coming down the hall with a smile on his face and a pile of papers in his hands, heading in Debra's direction.

Debra found herself being short with people, both at work and after work, raising her voice, and getting angry at the slightest things. She had stopped going to the gym a while ago and cancelled getting together with friends on many occasions. She also found herself feeling weak at many meetings and was using energy drinks, junk food, and vitamins to help her out. Debra wanted to have a sit-down with her boss and the project leads to see how they could resolve these conflicts and issues.

Since associates are having similar problems with this burden of work, what kind of questions do you think she should ask to seek assistance and prioritize her tasks?

- Your sleep is becoming irregular. When you go to bed, you cannot stop thinking about the tangled mess of priorities you have to deal with. You also are probably losing sleep by working late and/or going early because of these issues.
- You are more irritable. You do not feel as if you can leave your job concerns behind when you are not working. It feels like you have no time for anything else, let alone fun.

## 3. What will happen if I do nothing?

Unless you get help soon, there may be repercussions on multiple levels. Project delays may impact others who are waiting for your project tasks to be completed and may even affect the project delivery date. Small breakdowns in meeting project needs are easily overlooked. Repeated failure will impact how others perceive you and your project teams. In the long run, this can erode the confidence others have in you, leading to a degradation of your role within the organization. Additionally, your physical and mental health, confidence, relationships, and other factors may be at risk, potentially impacting you further.

## 4. Solution

The first thing that you need to do is recognize that you have an issue that needs to be addressed. There are a number of options open to you to improve the situation, but until you recognize that things need to change you won't be in a position to take advantage of those options. When you recognize the need there are a number of things that you can do:

1. Maintain open and frequent communications with people who can assist
2. Identify the work that you should focus on and the best people to assist with the rest
3. Implement a time management discipline
4. Put yourself first
5. Monitor for improvements

## 5. What should I do?

Project manager is not another word for *hero*. No one is expecting you to go to extremes for the project, and you will be ultimately measured by the success of your projects, not by the amount of time that you spend working on them.

### 5(a) Good communications

Open and frequent communication keeps people informed of your workload and conflicts. It can help reinforce the need for assistance, generate an acknowledgement of what is possible, and build an understanding of your limitations. It also means that you can focus your efforts on your real priorities and ask people to seek assistance for noncritical issues elsewhere.

Having a dialogue provides you with a way to reach out and negotiate with colleagues and managers about how to share your overload with others and come up with better solutions. Setting up a plan with management helps provide the details you need to make a case for additional help.

### 5(b) Focus on priorities

If you have authority in your organization or can solicit it, try delegating some responsibilities to others. Even without imposing the will of a manager, asking for help among peers or within project groups may be enough to get the assistance you need. If those people or other resources are not easily available, can you hire someone or a service to provide you with assistance?

While saying, "no," would be something to do before you take on too many tasks and problems start appearing, its power can still be exercised after the fact. If others are observant of what has happened to your workload and you have communicated with leads and your superiors about your deadline issues, then it is possible to bring these parties together and negotiate a priority list to determine just what is possible and impossible.

### 5(c) Practice time management

Many people assume that busy people are better able to take on more work. While it is possible that talented people may be able to do more than others, their day is still only 24 hours long. Planning out the time you have and the tasks that need to be performed is important for yourself and those impacted by your work. It is also necessary to have management engaged in this process and on board with how and when deliverables are to be accomplished.

Use some form of time management system to come up with ways to segment your time during the day. Plan, as best you can, for interrupted time and noninterrupted time. You can consult with various experts to find the method that works for you, but utilizing a way to monitor and judge your responsibilities over projects is helpful for you, project leads, and your management.

### 5(d) Put yourself first

Healthy habits are always important, but seem to be forgotten when project work becomes harder to complete. Regular sleeping, nutritional eating, and basic tactics of simplifying your life as much as possible will make you a more focused and productive individual.

Try not to carry conflicts, worries, and concerns past your workday and think of tomorrow as a fresh start. Start work early the next day before meetings and other conflicts get the better of you, and make one hour in the morning equal three hours in the afternoon. Use time at the start or end of the day to plan out activities for the upcoming workday.

### 5(d) Monitor for improvement

After identifying the things that will work for you, and implementing the solutions, develop a way to check in on yourself over the following days and weeks to see whether things have improved. Engage colleagues and managers for their perceptions as well. Be prepared to revise and refine your actions if you still need to improve things.

# 7.12 Oops, I forgot a chunk of work that needs to be done.

## By Andy Jordan

## 1. Problem

You have worked with your team to build out the project plan, and you are really happy with what you have managed to put together. Everything seemed to be going pretty well, and the sponsor and customer have all signed off on the project plan. However, one of your team leads has come to you with a problem—it's impossible to complete the work as defined—there is another piece of work that's necessary. It was missed in the requirements and missed in the planning, but there's no getting around it, you can't complete the project without it. Now what?

## 2. Warning Signs

This problem can come about from a number of sources—stakeholders, the team, your own analysis of the project, and the like. However the warning signs are all fairly consistent:

> ### Beverly, We Have a Problem!
>
> Beverly was a relatively new project manager, but she had done things the right way. She had undertaken the various training courses, was studying for her certification, and made it a point to talk to more experienced project managers and learn as much as possible from them.
>
> All of that seemed like a complete waste now. Beverly couldn't believe that she had been so stupid. A few minutes ago, Jeff, her chief construction engineer, had stopped by and announced "Beverly, we have a problem!" Jeff was trying to build the solution that the design team had handed him, but he couldn't make it work. There was a whole chunk of the design missing. Beverly had just gone back through the requirements and design documents, and realized her mistake. She had only given the designers part of the requirements. Sure, other people were supposed to have reviewed it, and obviously the people signing off hadn't checked it very thoroughly, but it was her mistake. Now Beverly was faced with a project that couldn't be completed as planned, a group of stakeholders who were going to be livid, and a project team that couldn't proceed—and it was all her fault.
>
> Was Beverly's project management career over, or was there a way for her to recover this project?

- Someone starts talking about work that has to be done that hasn't been identified in the plan.
- You or your team realize that the project cannot be delivered as defined and requires some additional elements that have not been included in the requirements and/or design.
- There is a gap between the requirements and the plan.

## 3. What will happen if I do nothing?

This is not the kind of problem that will get better on its own. The problem comes down to the fact that the only way that the project can be successful is if you complete more work than you planned for. If you ignore the problem, the project will not be successful, with either incomplete requirements or functionality that does not perform properly. As the project manager, your only choice is to act swiftly and decisively.

## 4. Solution

There is a way out of this problem, and the key is to remain focused on the problem itself and not let yourself get caught up in the emotional rollercoaster that you are likely going through when you realize that a big chunk of work has been forgotten. You need to take a structured approach and complete the following steps:

1. Analyze the project to ensure that you have identified the full scope of the problem.
2. Work with the appropriate experts to identify the potential solutions and the impact that they will have on the project constraints.
3. Develop a recommended course of action and present it to your stakeholders.
4. Integrate the approved actions, replan your project and perform a *post mortem* to try to prevent the problem from recurring.

In addition, you need to maintain good communications with everyone involved in the project. They need to understand that you have things under control and are working to implement the solution.

## 5. What should I do?

With a problem like this, there is the potential for the entire project to be derailed. Emotions are likely to run high with both your team and other stakeholders, and people may start blaming one another for the mistake. While it's important to understand how the problem occurred so that it can be prevented from happening again, your initial focus has to be on ensuring that the full magnitude of the problem is understood and then developing solutions.

At the same time, you need to make sure that everyone knows that you are in control of the situation. You need to take charge, and that means proactive, action oriented communications. You need to let everyone know what the problem is, what you are doing about it, and when you will provide further details. Then, you can focus on getting the project back on track.

### 5(a) Analyze the problem

Before you can solve the problem, you need to be sure that you have fully understood the size and complexity. Identify the people involved on your project (team members and other stakeholders) who best understand the issues and bring them together to answer the following questions:

- Has the full magnitude of the problem been identified? Are you sure that there is nothing else that has been missed, no additional prerequisites or features that need to be addressed?
- Does the team understand, at a high level, what the options are to address the problem? Can you buy in the missing elements or do you have to build them, and does the missing functionality have to be incorporated into the first product release or can it be added later? If you don't know what the options are, do you know how to investigate and determine those options?

- Which areas of the project are impacted, and which aspects are free of impact?
- Do you know the people who need to assist you in developing alternative solutions, and do you have access to them?
- What is the priority of the project constraints—which is the most important of budget, schedule, and scope? Which is least important?

Once you have answered these questions, you will have a better handle on the magnitude of the issue and you can start looking at the possible solutions. Remember to communicate the progress that you have made to get to this point so that everyone remains up to date on the situation. As soon as practical, you should also look to reallocate resources so that areas of the project that are not impacted can continue to move forward. This may also mean temporarily releasing resources to assist on other projects or operational tasks if they cannot be utilized on your project for a while.

### 5(b) Identify your options

In some ways, this piece of work is the same one that you went through when exploring the different approaches that you could take to deliver the requested functionality at the start of the project. You will be faced with project constraints—is the schedule or the budget more important, for example. It may be that one of the constraints can't be missed. For instance, if the people responsible for hosting the Olympic Games are faced with this problem, they can't delay the start of the Olympics to give themselves more time to complete the tasks; they have to find a way to get it done on time. You need to find solutions that work within the constraints of your project, just as you did when developing your work breakdown structure initially.

However, you also have additional challenges that you didn't face when first working with your team to build out the work breakdown structure. The most obvious of these is the need to find a solution that works within the remainder of the project tasks that have already been defined. Wherever possible you want to avoid changing the work that has already been planned (and potentially completed), which will cause more upheaval and impact on the budget and/or the schedule.

You need to ensure that the right people are involved in the exercise of identifying solutions. That may require resources that are not currently assigned to your team. For example, if your project is for home renovations and you forgot the wiring portion, then you likely don't have any electricians on your team. You have to identify and secure the expertise that you need to build the possible solutions.

### 5(c) Develop a recommendation and present it.

At the end of this exercise, you should have a number of different approaches that have been developed by your experts and you need to develop a team recommendation for your preferred solution. You should consider:

- Which solution minimizes the negative impact on the project constraints of scope, budget and schedule, in particular the constraint that is most important? Remember that the most expensive option may be the best if it can be delivered in the shortest time (if schedule is the primary constraint).

- Which solution exposes the project to the least risk? Depending on how risk tolerant the stakeholders (particularly the sponsor and customer) are, it may be preferable to pursue a more expensive, more time consuming solution if it reduces the risks.
- Which solution is the easiest to implement? Consider the type of skill sets that you need, reliance on third parties, availability of resources, reliance on new or unfamiliar technology, and other factors.

The answers to these questions should help you identify the preferred solution, and then you need to present that preference to your stakeholders.

In order to approve the recommended course of action, stakeholders will need to be satisfied that:

- The solution will address all of the missing functionality.
- The solution is the best one to minimize the impact on the project considering the priority of the project constraints.
- The solution is feasible and can be achieved with the identified resources, within the timelines and for the identified budget.

As the project manager, you should be prepared to defend the team's recommendation and handle questions as to why alternative approaches were rejected. This isn't because the stakeholders mistrust you; rather, it is because they need to be sure that all variables have been considered and that the recommended solution is the best one.

### 5(d) Integrate the approved solution

Once the stakeholders have approved the solution, you need to communicate the changes to your team as quickly as possible. That means incorporating the additional work into the project plan and refocusing your team on the revised tasks. The schedule is a key element of this, but you also have to replan the budget and the risks.

At this point you may have to negotiate to secure additional resources or retain existing resources for a longer period of time. You may need to renegotiate contracts with suppliers, or enter into new contracts, and while all of this is happening, you need to ensure that your existing resources are moving forward as quickly as possible to implement the new changes as well as the original project.

You also need to conduct an analysis of how the missing piece of work came about in the first place. It may be that someone simply made a mistake, and that's okay, but if there is a more fundamental process problem, then it needs to be identified and communicated to your PMO so that the process can be improved before another project experiences difficulties. Even if it is simply a mistake by one or two people, there will be opportunities for coaching and perhaps additional training to ensure that the team members involved have the skills that they need for the next project.

# 7.13 We have no Plan B.

## By David Arias

## 1. Problem

You diligently planned your project and figured you would trudge through any issues as they arose. However, despite having committed valuable resources and great efforts, your project has not progressed much. To make matters worse, you just hit a dead end. A Plan B would have definitely come in handy.

## 2. Warning Signs

Signs that you are in trouble here include:

- Project components are taking a lot longer to deliver
- Excessive rework is necessary throughout project effort
- Continually missing deadlines or milestones
- Observation of low morale among project team members
- You are not looking forward to status meetings
- The project sponsor and/or customer are requesting detailed status reports more frequently
- Risks not considered are making their unscheduled appearance
- You feel that for every step forward you take two back

## 3. What will happen if I do nothing?

### Planning for the Best, Not Expecting the Worst

Avalanched by yet more problems, Phil needed to get away. It was 3:00 P.M., and all day long he had been putting out fires: a vendor threatening to pull out due to ambiguous specifications; the test system down for yet another day; changes approved months ago but yet to be implemented; another slipped deadline; and the customer uneasy and wanting confirmation of adherence to stipulated system deployment. With every problem encountered, he wondered *why*. So, running on empty, he had had enough; he silently crept out of his office for a well needed break and snack.

As Phil made his way to the local hotdog stand, he felt the chase and echo of his project team members' voices stir in his head. There was no getting away from his problems. As Phil chomped away on his juicy hotdog he couldn't help but wonder what went wrong; after all he is the most experienced project manager at the company given both his tenure and cross industry experience. This project was a no brainer, but it was giving him grief.

The project incorporated various technical aspects and cross functional team members. He had vast experience championing projects of the sort and driving them to successful completion. But none of that mattered now because as he bit down he could see that he had been found. Monica, the Corporate Project Director, was charging at him; before she could say a word, he blurted out "I've been busy managing the day to day activities of the project — I can have last week's daily status reports to you by tomorrow morning." She simply grunted and told him, "I'll see you in your office in 10 minutes to discuss your Plan B."

Then and there Phil finally realized the reason for his problems. He got hung up on his dominance of previous projects and during the project planning neglected to factor variables that could cause issues. So he never anticipated the need for a Plan B.

Having to attest, "We have no Plan B," carries with it a great responsibility to take action. To do nothing is akin to failure and as such, repercussions will vary per tolerances of the performing organization, which can include:

- Early project termination
- Project reassignment to another PM

- Demotion
- Losing your job

## 4. Solution

When you don't have a clear plan for mitigating current project obstacles, you need to fight the urge to follow through with your current mode of operation and simply stop. Yes, stop the project in its tracks, but only so that you may adequately *replan*. Not having an alternative, you need to regroup so that you have a fighting chance in completing your project objectives. As shown in Figure 7.8, you will need to:

1. Identify a sponsor for support
2. Perform a project audit
3. Identify project risks
4. Replan the project

## 5. What should I do?

Placing a pause on your project allows you to analyze it, so that you can gauge exactly how you came to be in such a predicament. That said, your focus should shift to strategizing, so that what seems as a doomed project can be transformed to one of opportunity where your commitments are met. Here are some steps to take:

### 5(a) Identify a sponsor for support

In order to stop and replan your project, you will need the help and support of a sponsor. This sponsor is key because it must be someone who has a stake in the outcome of the project and carries enough executive leverage to ensure naysayers are checked while your replanning efforts are developed and take effect. In addition, your sponsor will be essential in garnering resources not originally contemplated.

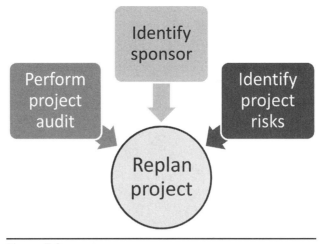

**Figure 7.8**

### 5(b) Perform a project audit

A project audit is essential to determine what was missed during the initial project plan. The following work will be involved in the audit:

- Review project objectives (scope) and see how they match up to what was being produced. Try to identify causes for rework and whether it was per changes during natural process of execution or changes due to incomplete scope definitions.
- Review time and cost estimates to make sure they are aligned to scope requirements.
- Do you have the right human resources? Determine if the skill set of your project team members are enough to meet the needs of your project requirements.
- Is communication structured to allow for proper communication among team members? Does everyone know their role within the project? Are there scheduled status meetings with stakeholders and the project team?

### 5(c) Identify project risks

Risks are inherent in all projects. Unfortunately, they are not always included during project planning. Some don't include them because they figure they will deal with them as they present themselves, while others omit them altogether because they are comfortable with their technical knowledge and figure it won't happen to them. However comfortable you are with the project, risks are an integral part and as such they must be identified and listed. If a risk is critical enough to sidetrack a project, a mitigation plan should be created. Risk identification is necessary because it will directly impact project timing and costs. In the end, you must account and plan for probable risks so that if they occur your project is not affected, or at least that the impact is managed.

### 5(d) Replan the project

Having obtained the support of a sponsor, identified issues that caused problems, and listed possible risks, you are ready to integrate these elements into a single action plan. Your action plan should consist of a formal document that clearly outlines a path forward to properly reinitiating your project. The action plan should indicate the impact on time, cost and scope of your project.
   Elements of an action plan:

1. Summarize need for the action plan
2. Outline changes required from the original project strategy
3. Establish need for each change
4. Highlight impact on project scope, time, and cost
5. Establish human resource skill sets
6. Incorporate communication methods to be deployed
7. Provide method(s) to be used for measuring project success

Once your action plan is complete, your sponsor can go ahead and sell it to other interested parties to get further support in driving the project to completion.

# 7.14 Whenever I propose a project schedule, I am asked to compress it.

By Imad Alsadeq

## 1. Problem

Every time you have a new project, your manager asks that you develop a project schedule. No matter how much time and effort you spend developing it, once the manager sees it, he says, "No—no—please go and compress it, do some fast tracking, and feel free to crash."

Then, after a lot of discussion and negotiation, the manager approves the schedule. But wait, this is not the end of the problem; it is just the beginning. The next day you go and discuss the project schedule with your client. Once he sees the total duration, he also says, "No—no—please go and compress it, do some fast tracking, and feel free to crash."

Guess what? From what I have seen over the years, you will then execute these compressed schedules over a time period that exceeds the original schedule by at least two or three times.

## 2. Warning Signs

This problem is essentially black and white—the plan provides an estimate based on realistic assessments of the work and then you are asked to compress it. Look for:

### FasTraCra Law

I was asked to propose a schedule for a crucial high security project. "This project should be finished quickly; the budget is open, requirements are very clear, and it is easy—like moving boxes. That is it." My manager kept repeating that whenever he saw me developing the schedule.

After studying the *clear* requirements, I proposed my schedule to be as short as possible. In that first schedule I moved some sequenced tasks to be parallel (known as *fast tracking*). I also allocated different resources on the same task (known as *crashing*). So the total project duration was six months.

Once my manager saw the schedule, he asked me to compress it. I answered, "I already did," and started to explain. But suddenly something glowed in his eyes when he said "Okay! Now do some fast track and crash." It did not matter how long I discussed the meaning and applicability of doing that. After a few days when the client saw the schedule, the same glow shined in his eyes and he said the same thing. "Do some fast track and crash."

At that moment, I remembered my son at home repeating the magic word, *abracadabra* while hoping to make himself fly or turn his brother into a frog. I gathered the two compression techniques and imitated my son's magic word to come up with, *FasTraCra*.

Over time, and after observation and discussion with schedulers and project managers, I have become 100 percent sure that, "Too much compression explodes the schedule." Most projects I have seen with a FasTraCra schedule (compressed too much using fast tracking and crashing), when implemented, finish three times over the first proposed schedule. My project was one of them.

- Dissatisfaction over the estimates that you provide
- Suggestions that you have padded the estimates to buy yourself more time
- Stakeholders wanting to know how much time can be saved with *working harder* or *a little overtime*

## 3. What will happen if I do nothing?

If you don't resist pressure to compress your project then you will be faced with a project plan that doesn't provide enough time to complete the work—the amount of work hasn't been reduced just because you have reduced the allotted time for it. You'll try and compensate by having your team work longer hours and look for ways to shortcut the process, or otherwise increase project risk in an attempt to save time. As you start to fall behind schedule, you will get ever more desperate and you'll create an environment where at least some, and possibly all, of the following will occur:

- You will lose confidence in your ability to develop the right project schedule
- Your team will lose faith in you as a leader, and as someone who cares about their welfare
- Your manager will lose all confidence in your ability to schedule and plan effectively
- Your client will lose confidence in you and your company
- Your deliverables will suffer
- You will limit your future in this company and others

## 4. Solution

Success depends on the ability to *consider* the positions of the stakeholders, *prepare* an appropriate response, and *communicate* effectively with all parties. To develop an effective solution, you need to understand why you are being pressured to compress your schedule, and what is it that is driving stakeholders to ask for the compression (the *consider* part).

Next, you need to be able to develop solutions that will assist the stakeholders in achieving their goals without compromising the integrity of the project schedule (the *prepare* part). Finally, you need to be able to *communicate* effectively with stakeholders about the importance of a realistic schedule, and of the flexibility that you do have to be able to help them meet their goals.

Remembering the concepts of consideration, preparation, and communication, you can build a structured process for dealing with this issue:

1. Build trust
2. Communicate understanding
3. Educate stakeholders
4. Implement peer reviews
5. Use the *FasTraCra* law
6. Say, "no," the right way

## 5. What should I do?

You cannot ignore stakeholder requests, but neither can you give in to the requests to compress the schedule. You need to find an alternative that is acceptable to all parties, and you need to understand the implications of that approach.

### 5(a) Build trust

Unless there is mutual trust, top managers will consistently think the project manager/scheduler is adding contingency reserve to the schedule. Clients think the same of any vendor or subcontractor. This problem can be solved through building trust between the different parties.

But how do you build trust effectively? Remember the two key requirements needed for there to be trust: character and competency. They need to see your character; that you are working hard to manage an effective project, bring quality deliverables, and balance the best interests of the company and the client. They want to see that when there is a problem, your first concern is the project objectives, not your own interests. When they can trust you to act in their best interests they will believe you. But in addition to character, a company and its clients need to see competency, that you can do the job.

You need to master the project, understand those compression scenarios, and demonstrate that you have the skills needed to find unique solutions to scheduling and resource problems. Be the one who is the most competent, explain your scenarios and reasoning and show that it is the best for reaching the project objectives. Remember to consider the needs of the stakeholders and explicitly address those. When you demonstrate character and competence, trust develops. With trust your communication is effective—then they will trust your judgment when you object to compressing a schedule.

### 5(b) Communicate understanding

First, internally communicate to your manager that what you are delivering is a reviewed and examined schedule, not a haphazard one. There is good reasoning and planning underlying all your scheduling decisions, so explain it. If there is new information or constraints, that is one thing, and a reason to change, or maybe compress, a schedule. But you cannot just compress the schedule for the sake of compression. You know your job and have the best interests of the company and client in mind, and that was one of the considerations used when you planned the project.

Second, communicate to the client when they want to *FasTraCra* (see Sidebar) that the schedule you set up is the best schedule for the project objectives. You are open to scheduling changes, but the client needs to understand the consequences of the various compression scenarios they want. Remember, consider their perspective, prepare for their needs and pressures, communicate with character and competence, and seek compromises all stakeholders can be satisfied with.

### 5(c) Educate stakeholders

Imagine presenting the schedule with a tip about scheduling, it is an indirect teaching way. Every time you present a schedule, mention the real aim behind the compression, and the consequences of each technique. Share your knowledge and demonstrate your competency. They will view you with more respect and you will have more influence in the scheduling process.

### 5(d) Implement peer review

Asking for more compression for a schedule developed by two is harder than by a schedule developed by one. Through the PMO or a senior project management colleague, ask for a review of your schedule. This will have the double benefit of identifying any areas of the project where there may be errors, and will also reassure your stakeholders that the schedule has been reviewed and confirmed as realistic.

### 5(e) Use the FasTraCra law

Explain to them that a *FasTraCra* schedule is against the project's goals at the end. Explain to them that you are trying to protect their best interests by resisting compression. It is not *your schedule* you are protecting; it is the project objectives and their deliverables. Protect your clients from themselves. The amount of time *needed* to do the work doesn't change because the time *allocated* has changed.

Wherever possible use historical information from previous projects, show the client statistics illustrating how projects were behind schedule because of over compression. Carefully explain how overcompression can explode a schedule.

### 5(f) Say, "no," the right way

Agreeing to ill-considered schedule compression is never the right step. You have to push back. However, after going through this series of steps you cannot simply say "no." There are other things that you can do that may be able to assist with delivering an earlier delivery date, such as increased funding or reduced scope.

## References

Senge, Peter M. *The Fifth Discipline Field Book: Strategies and Tools for Building a Learning Organization*. New York: Crown Business, 1994.

White, J. Chris. 2010. "The Dynamic Process Method." *Dynamic Process Method*. http://www.DynamicProgressMethod.com

# 8

# MANAGING PEOPLE DAY TO DAY

## 8.1 Meetings are a waste of time.

### By Dave Prior

*"A meeting is an event where minutes are taken and hours wasted."*

—*Captain James T. Kirk, Star Trek*

## 1. Problem

Meetings—can't live with them, can't live without them. In order for your project to run well, you need to make sure that the right people are getting together at the right time to have the right conversations. The reality of work today is that there are an infinite number of things competing for the attention of the people you need in the room, so you need to make sure that when you call people together, you are adding value for both the participants and the project. How do you make sure that your meetings are not a waste of everyone's precious time?

## 2. Warning Signs

You know when your meetings are not achieving what they need to, but look for some of these early indications that things may be going wrong:

- Invitees consistently arrive late, or not at all.

### Hijacked!

*"The one who figures on victory at headquarters before even doing battle is the one who has the most strategic factors on his side"*

—*Tzu, 2005*

Unbelievable! This is the third week in a row that Susan has hijacked Stan's meeting. This is not cool. What she's talking about isn't even on the agenda. To make matters worse, Stan and Susan work in the same PMO and are supposed to be on the same team, and she agreed not to do it again when he spoke to her about it last time.

Stan spends a lot of time preparing for his meetings. He creates a detailed agenda, has premeetings with specific attendees to make sure they will be there, and knows what to expect. He even asks the other people in his PMO if they have any agenda items to add that are relevant to the project. Each week Susan says, "no," but for the last three weeks she's interrupted him right after he reviewed the agenda and has taken the meeting on a 45 minute tangent about *her* project. Yes, her project is pretty high profile; and yes, Stan is able to get all the executives in the room (something she struggles with in her own meetings), but what about all the items people were expecting him to cover?

On top of this, Stan is concerned about the impression this is making on senior management. It

*Continues*

- Attendees often use the meeting to spend time catching up on email.
- Continual requests to reschedule meetings are received.
- Decisions made in the meeting frequently change outside of the meeting.
- Invitees are not empowered (or willing) to make decisions.
- Attendees are physically present, but disengaged.
- Attendees hijack the meeting.

probably looks like he can't control his own meetings. He could just call Susan out in the meeting and shut her down—maybe. But that wouldn't look good in front of the executives, either.

Looking around the room, Stan starts to pay attention to the faces and body language of the other attendees. A few of them look a little disturbed. Maybe they don't like being hijacked. After all, they also came prepared to discuss Stan's agenda items. Stan starts to wonder if maybe he can figure out a way to enlist their help to keep Susan from taking over again.

## 3. What will happen if I do nothing?

If you see any of these warning signs and do not make some changes, you will likely find that attendance continues to drop off. It is also likely that you will not obtain the results you are looking for from the meetings you schedule, and this could endanger your project, as well as your credibility.

## 4. Solution

If one or more of the warning signs listed above are present, your meeting may actually be a waste of time. If this is the case, you have two options:

1. Cancel the meeting(s) in question.
2. Change your approach in order to make sure your meetings are not wasting time.

Since you probably already know how to cancel a meeting, we will focus on a process to change your approach in order to make sure that your meetings are effective:

1. Establish the meeting purpose (why are you having the meeting?).
2. Establish whether the meeting is adding any value to the project.
3. Consider if the list of invitees is correct and complete.
4. Review if you are leading the meeting effectively.
5. Establish backup for your position.

## 5. What should I do?

If one or more of the warning signs listed is happening, it may be an indicator that your meetings are not perceived as providing the necessary value for people to consider them to be a good use of their time. Here are a few questions that you can ask yourself to get a better understanding of the value of your meetings:

### 5(a) Why are you having the meeting?

When leading a team, especially if you are a project manager, it can be easy to lose sight of the real point of holding a meeting. After all, our job is to manage the process and if the process dictates that we need to have a meeting, then we need to have it. However, if you look at it from another angle, the most basic and valid reason to have a meeting is that it is necessary to delivery. So, the question to ask yourself is, "how vital is this meeting? Will the project be delayed, at risk, or fail if we do not have it?" If you do not know the answer to this question, you probably need to spend more time working that out before you actually send out the invites. If skipping the meeting is not going to stop, impede, or endanger the project delivery, then do you really need to have it? Keep in mind that each minute someone from your team spends in the conference room is a minute they are not spending getting work done on the project. If anyone else wanted to pull your resources away, you'd probably demand proof that doing so was a business necessity. We need to ask the same of ourselves.

Conversely, if you are ready to cancel a meeting, make sure doing so isn't going to endanger the delivery. There are some meetings that are important to hold, such as ensuring that you are doing everything possible to inform the most critical stakeholders about what is going on. One of the hardest parts about being a PM is that we need to not only push for discipline on the rest of the project, but for ourselves as well.

### 5(b) Is the meeting adding value?

Are you able to quantify the value of the meeting you are holding and what it is providing to the project and the team? For example, is the meeting identifying critical risks and issues, which require input from all of the participants? It may be obvious, but there will be times when the answer to the question appears to be, "Yes," because the meeting was predefined as something that was needed. However, just because there was agreement on the importance of it earlier, does not necessarily mean that is still the case. As the person keeping watch over the project, it is your responsibility to reevaluate the validity of any decision previously made at any point in time.

Ask yourself what you are basing the answer about value on. Holding a meeting simply for the sake of holding it may not help you deliver the end product any faster. In fact, there are some schools of thought that place the responsibility for discovering and removing any unnecessary or wasteful activity directly on the shoulders of the person leading the project. Balancing this with the need to follow a predefined process can be confusing at times, which is why careful reevaluation of the reason for the meeting is so important.

### 5(c) Do you have the right people in the room?

Deciding who to invite, and getting them to show up, is often the most challenging part of holding a meeting. You will likely be competing with a number of other projects or events for people's time, so establishing how important the meeting is can be the very thing that gets them into the room.

First, make sure you are inviting the right people. In order to determine who the correct people are, you need to know why you are holding the meeting, what your objectives are, and what individuals are willing and able to make decisions. Once you have your list, identify which participants are critical (the decision makers) and which are being invited for other reasons (political reasons, out of courtesy, and such).

Once you've identified the critical participants, you may need to track them down and have a one-on-one conversation with them to make sure they understand how vital it is that they attend, why they are needed, and what is expected of them. Depending on your situation, the role of the nondecision making attendees and why you need them, you may want to have similar conversations with them as well.

If the critical (decision-making) attendees can't participate, they may be able to send a proxy. If this happens, make sure to confirm with both the proxy and the decision maker who was invited so that the proxy will be authorized and willing to make decisions on behalf of the original invitee.

When nothing you can do or say will get the critical people into the room, you may need to consider cancelling or postponing the meeting to make sure you do not waste the time of the people who can make it.

There is no shame in cancelling a meeting, but wasting people's time is something that will weaken your ability to get them to the table when you really need them.

Bottom line, remember, just because the meeting is important to you, does not make it important to anyone else. You have to give people a compelling reason to attend and make sure that you and they are clear about their role in the session. This will make it easier for you to lead the meeting when things get underway.

### 5(d) Are you leading the meeting effectively?

> *"You've got to be very careful if you don't know where you are going because you might not get there."*
>
> —*Yogi Berra*

Getting everyone into the room is only part of the battle. The next step is making sure you aren't wasting their time once they are there. Here are five simple steps to help get you ready to run a successful meeting:

1. **Know the room:** Make sure you are familiar with the space in which you'll be leading the meeting. Think about where you want to position yourself, and how you can use the environment to make the meeting more effective. For example, are there a lot of windows that will be open during the meeting, causing distractions? Will the sun be shining in and heating up the room, which will have a tendency to make people sleepy?

2. **Have an agenda and stick to it:** Whether you distribute it beforehand or not, have an agenda for the meeting. Taking the time to plan out what you want to happen and how you want to get there will help you keep the conversations on track and realize when you are getting derailed. If you are able to lock in on a single, specific desired outcome, then the whole meeting can be used to basically guide people toward the outcome you are seeking. When you are running the meeting, move through the agenda from point to

point, leading people toward the end goal. Doing this will show the participants that you've respected their time by having a carefully planned series of items to cover. As soon as you have covered the items on your agenda and reached a decision on the necessary points, end the meeting and dismiss the attendees. Keeping them only as long as you absolutely need them in the room will demonstrate your respect for their time.

3. **Study the politics:** Spend time considering the people who will be in the meeting and what they each have to lose and gain from their attendance and participation. Make sure you have enough material included to keep them interested and focused. Ideally, have something that offers potential gain for them. If there will be people in the room who are at odds politically (within your organization), consider how you will try to manage that in order to keep the attendees passionately engaged.

4. **Study the leadership:** Whenever possible, sit in on meetings run by others that include your participants. Study their behavior and learn how to read their reactions. If you can tell when they are getting angry, bored, or whatever, you can use that information in running your own meeting. Again, the idea is to be able to keep them focused and engaged while you guide the conversations towards your objective(s).

5. **Meeting Tao:** *Tao* is a term that translates to English as *the way*. How are meetings held at the organization? Is it one of those places where everyone shows up late, spends 15 minutes talking about personal stuff, and then gets to the topic? Is it an organization that places a high value on arriving on time and keeping on task throughout? Learn what you need to do in hosting the meeting in order to be taken seriously by the attendees and earn their respect every step of the way during the event itself. This will help you determine how the organization relates to, and ascribes value to, meetings.

### 5(e) Get some backup!

For the times when you will be leading meetings that include a lot of strong personalities or personalities who are hard to keep on track, it is not a bad idea to enlist the help of a backup person. This will typically involve meeting with a trusted individual before the meeting and talking about the possibility of something specific happening, and how they can help you move past it.

Suppose, for example, that Senior Executive Jim has a tendency to hijack everyone's meetings and has a history of specifically disregarding you in the role of meeting facilitator, but he has demonstrated a fair amount of respect for your close friend, Steve. You may want to talk to Steve before the meeting and ask him to speak up at the first signs that Jim is warming up. Steve can help you and Jim keep on track to make sure all of the critical items are covered.

This may not result in you looking like the master facilitator, but a little applied social pressure may be just what you need to keep the meeting on track and get results from it. At the end of the day, you are responsible for getting the deliverable done and there are times when you have to sacrifice a little ego to get there. It is all part of the job.

# 8.2 Vendors are not delivering.

## By Andy Jordan

## 1. Problem

Your project is dependent on external suppliers for part of the functionality. You've been through the process of reviewing vendors, selecting the right partner for your needs, and negotiating the contract and statement of work. The vendor understands what you need and when you need it, but it's not happening. Deadlines are being missed and deliverables are falling short of quality targets.

## 2. Warning Signs

When you have to deal with suppliers on your project, the need for clear and open communication is even higher.

> ### Why Did We Choose That Vendor?
>
> Nathan thought back to the meeting three months earlier with a vendor. It had been a great meeting (and the champagne that had been broken open to toast the future success of the partnership hadn't hurt). Everything had seemed so positive! After an exhaustive search, you and your stakeholders were confident that you had found the perfect vendor to help make this project a reality. They had a good track record, were a sound company, and seemed like a great bunch of people to work with. This was going to be a fun project.
>
> Now Nathan came back to the reality that he was facing today. The first major deliverable from the vendor was due a week ago, and it hadn't shown up. Nathan had left multiple voice mails and sent numerous emails, but no one was getting back to him. He had no idea what else to do—how could he get himself out of this mess?

You are completely reliant on a good relationship with your counterpart from the vendor to understand what is happening. Otherwise, you only find out that there is a problem when the vendor misses a deadline or provides incomplete or low quality deliverables. Early signs that you may have a problem are if:

- Your contact with the vendor is communicating less, is harder to reach, or avoids answering questions directly.
- The vendor wants to split deliverables into different phases or only provides some of the functionality initially.
- Early review of a vendor's deliverables shows a large number of problems.
- The vendor starts talking about how difficult or complex the work is, suggests that some of their suppliers are being difficult, or begins to complain that your requirements, design, or schedules are not clear enough.

## 3. What will happen if I do nothing?

Although the relationship between you and your vendors should be a partnership, vendors are still in it for themselves. They are going to put their interests first, and if you allow them to *get away* with things, they will take advantage. If you don't let them know that missed deadlines, incomplete deliverables, and quality problems are unacceptable, things will continue to get worse as the vendor will feel that you are passively agreeing to a shift in schedule or quality.

## 4. Solution

The solution to this problem is not to immediately refer to the contract between you and your vendor and insist on enforcing every clause; that option will always be there as a fallback position, but it should be your last resort. Success in managing suppliers depends on maintaining a positive relationship, treating your vendors as equal partners, and working together to come to a mutually satisfactory solution. In this scenario you need to:

1. Make sure that your vendor absolutely understands that their performance is not satisfactory.
2. Work with them to develop a plan to bring the project back on track, and ensure that no further problems occur.
3. Closely monitor the vendor's performance against the plan.
4. Implement any contractual/financial adjustment that is necessary as a result of the vendor's failure.

## 5. What should I do?

This problem is a tough one. On the one hand, you need to manage your project against its scope, schedule, and budget (as well as resources, risks, and quality), so you need to aggressively manage your vendors if they are starting to slip. On the other hand, you need to maintain a constructive relationship with your suppliers, so you can't be too aggressive.

In many ways, a vendor missing a deadline, or not providing a full set of deliverables, is no different from a team member in the same position. The hard part is that you have less day-to-day influence over your vendor, and potentially less control over their actions.

### 5(a) Advise that performance is unsatisfactory

One of the most important things to do with your vendor is to maintain good, open communications. This should happen right from the start of the project rather than only when problems occur, but it's never too late to start. You should identify one contact person from your vendor (likely their project manager or equivalent) and manage all aspects of the project through them. It is okay for you to have members of your team work with members of the vendor's team on day-to-day details, but you need to work directly with your counterpart to manage the project status and progress.

In an ideal world, ongoing communication will help to ensure that you aren't surprised by a missed deliverable, but as we all know, we don't manage projects in an ideal world. If you are faced with the situation where a vendor has not met their deadline, or where the deliverable that they provided is unsatisfactory, you need to immediately contact your counterpart and advise them that there is a problem with their performance. The vendor needs to understand that you are on top of the situation, so don't let time pass. Let them know as soon as the problem occurs or as soon as it is discovered.

Ensure that you remain professional, you still need to work with this vendor to achieve your project goals, but there is nothing wrong with saying something like, "I noticed that you failed to meet your deadline yesterday. I need to understand what the problem is, what you are doing to correct the problem, and why we weren't advised that there was an issue. We also need to discuss the steps that you are taking to ensure that the problem doesn't happen again."

You are remaining professional, but you are also making it clear to your vendor counterpart that there is a problem, they need to fix it, and you need some reassurances.

### 5(b) Work with them on a plan for this issue and to prevent further problems

If the vendor has a problem, it's their responsibility to put it right, not yours. However, you also need to be realistic and recognize that you will need to work with the vendor on the solution. They didn't miss their deadline to be difficult; they did it because something went wrong. A good, strong relationship with the vendor will allow you to have an open conversation about what they can deliver and when it can be delivered. You need to work with them to establish:

- When will they be able to deliver what they owe at the standard that is required?
- Are they able to provide a partial deliverable, and if they do, will that help you?
- What is the impact of this problem on any future deliverables, and what are they doing to ensure that other deliverables aren't missed?

If the deliverable is relatively straightforward, and the delay fairly small, this may be all that is needed, but in most cases you will also need to work with them to establish interim milestones to help ensure that they are on target to correct the problem. You do not have as much visibility into their work as you do with your own team, so these milestones are vitally important.

You also need to manage your project to minimize the impact of the delay on other aspects. This may mean rescheduling or moving resources around, and other actions.

Perhaps more important, is to establish why the problem occurred, and work with your vendor to try to ensure that it doesn't happen again. The problem may be something that you can't control, such as an internal issue at the vendor that they need to get control of. That can be frustrating, but there is little that you can directly do to influence it. However, if there is something that you can do to assist the vendor, you should look at those options—remember, this is a partnership. That assistance may be as simple as providing requirements further in advance, or a case of doing an in-person walkthrough of those requirements to assist in understanding.

Getting to the bottom of the problem may require you and the vendor to work together on the root cause analysis, especially if the problem was one of the quality of the deliverable, rather than the delivery date. In that situation, it is not uncommon for a vendor to provide their deliverable thinking that there is nothing at all wrong, only to find that you as the customer are dissatisfied because the deliverable was not what you expected. Clearly, communication has broken down and you need to work together to find the breakdown and correct it.

### 5(c) Manage performance against the recovery plan

When the vendor and you have agreed on the plan to bring the project back on track, you need to carefully manage that plan. Make sure that the communication is open and frequent, and act quickly if you sense that the vendor is experiencing additional problems or if the communication is becoming more difficult.

Make sure that the milestones are close enough together that you can quickly act if one is missed, and ask for evidence of progress. This isn't a case of not trusting the vendor; rather, it's about ensuring that the progress meets your expectations.

### 5(d) Implement adjustment or a penalty

If your contract has been well written, there will be an established penalty, generally financial, that applies in the event of a vendor's failure to meet a deadline or to deliver a subpar product. This makes things much simpler as you don't need to negotiate any correction that needs to be applied; however, it is often not included in the contract.

If you have a contract management or procurement function available to you, ask for assistance in this piece; they are the experts. However, if you need to work with the vendor directly to agree to the compensation that will be provided, then focus on something that will actually help the project. A financial penalty is always a possibility, but you may find it easier to obtain things like increased training, discounted support, additional features at no cost, and the like that are of lasting benefit. Don't accept something that the project doesn't need, but work with the project stakeholders to ensure that you get a form of compensation that is of the most benefit to your project and organization.

# 8.3 People are ignoring my emails.

## By Josh Nankivel

## 1. Problem

You have been sending your team emails for a long time. Some people on the team are good at responding and others—well, let's just say they don't seem to be as *on top of it* as they should be.

You were talking about a specific topic in a meeting, and half the room didn't know what you were talking about. "Didn't you get my email?" you chided in frustration. What was wrong here?

## 2. Warning Signs

You need to get on top of this problem early. Be ready to act if you see one or more of the following signs:

- People are missing important points in your email, or missing them altogether.
- It is as if some of your important messages were accidentally deleted or marked as spam.
- You are worried that your team members have misunderstood your email instructions.
- You pick up signs that your team members do not take your email communication seriously.
- Your team is overwhelmed by hundreds of email messages in their inbox and unable to keep up with them.
- Results reflect a lack of understanding over time.

> **Email: What's the Problem?**
>
> Mark was frustrated. Several people on the team were obviously not getting or reading his countless emails on the Alpha project. While most of the team seemed to *get it*, it was difficult to be sure.
>
> Mark decided to ask a few of them: "John, did you get my email?"
>
> "I'm really not sure, Mark. I've got a few hundred e-mail messages sitting in my inbox. There's just not enough time in the day to get to everything. What's the exact time and subject line so I can find this needle in my haystack?"
>
> "Sam, did you get my email?"
>
> "Yeah, but I didn't really understand it. What is the Obfuscator 3000, anyway? What does it have to do with this project? What did you mean when you wrote..."
>
> A flustered Mark asked, "Sam, why didn't you ask me these questions before? We should have been weeks along by now!"
>
> "I don't know," Sam replied. "I had so many questions I just figured I'd wait until I saw you again. Then I kept forgetting to bring it up. I mean, I have Project Ultima and the Zeta Release 4 on my plate too."
>
> Does this situation sound familiar? How could this miscommunication have been avoided?

## 3. What will happen if I do nothing?

If you continue communicating in the same way, similar results will continue. In fact, the communication gap may widen further as time goes on. Team members will feel less comfortable coming to you with questions about the nuances you did not cover in an email, and make assumptions instead. One day you may go into the office and find results that are completely unacceptable due to months of misinterpretations.

Deliverables will not meet requirements, resulting in cost and schedule overruns after rework. Your professional relationships, especially with your team members, will deteriorate as miscommunications and lack of face-to-face time mount. If you continue to use ineffective communication practices, you will continue to experience ineffective results. It really is that simple.

## 4. Solution

The problem is you, not them. The solution lies with you as well.

Email can be great for certain types of communication, but in general, it is an overused means of communicating, especially when so many of us have the option to walk over and visit, or get on the phone and talk to someone directly. It can be a great method of communicating when the needs are asynchronous and when people are disconnected geographically, but in general, it gets overused.

Think about your own preferences when it comes to communication. Do you prefer knowledge transfer via text on your computer? Perhaps, but not everyone feels the same way. In fact, the majority of people respond much better to face-to-face or phone communication.

Much of the context is lost via email. Body language is absent, and so is the tone of your voice. Emphasis can be misinterpreted via email communication. For all these reasons and more, email communication retains an important but limited scope of efficacy in the workplace.

You need to clarify:

- The scenarios when email is a valid form of communication
- Time when email should not be used
- The most effective forms of communication

## 5. What should I do?

Start with an analysis of your current methods of communication. Delve into your sent items and categorize them based on what are good uses of email and what could have been communicated more effectively in person or over the phone.

### 5(a) Valid uses of email

Email can be used with great effect for many things. They include some of the following:

- *Agendas:* Sending meeting agendas well in advance is always a good idea to ensure productive meetings.
- *Replies, forwards, and thanks:* When you are entering a communication stream that has already started, many times it makes sense to stick to the communication media that has already been invoked.
- *Sending documentation:* A document must be sent via email many times, and even though a common file share may be even better, this can be a valid use of email.

- *Remote communication:* Phone conversations are still preferred, but email may serve well for remote situations, especially when you are in different time zones.

## 5(b) Invalid uses of email

Email can be overused, especially when other more effective communication channels are available. The following may be considered inappropriate by many recipients:

- *Tasking:* Issuing tasks via email is usually not a good idea. So much can be lost to interpretation, and with an asynchronous channel like email, the natural series of questions and answers to clarify scope is stunted. Additionally, if your email is lost among hundreds of other unread messages, it may be weeks before someone sees it.
- *Questions or information sharing:* If these are in direct relation to another email from someone else (a forward), it may make sense to keep it in the same channel. Most of the time, however, these are best left for another time when you are speaking face-to-face or via phone. Again, a synchronous channel allows for clarifying questions and feedback.
- *Urgent matters:* If a matter is truly urgent and important, communicate using a synchronous channel (face-to-face, phone, real-time chat,and such). Otherwise, it may be hours, days, or weeks before your urgent situation comes to the attention of the recipient. In critical situations, the ability to ask clarifying questions and gather feedback in a real-time fashion becomes even more important.

## 5(c) Effective communication

Here are some examples of other communication methods in conjunction with or instead of email that can make a positive impact in your professional life:

- *Technical interface meting (TIM):* Get everyone in a room who should contribute and has a stake in the problem at hand. Frame the question(s) clearly in an agenda so you can come out with a solid decision. Follow up with an email documenting the decisions made and action items, if any. These are variable in length, and held as needed.
- *Team meeting:* Rather than sending out email messages to your team, if it can wait for the team meeting, you should only talk about it then. This allows for questions and real-time discussion, eliminating the need for assumptions. These are 30 to 60 minutes in length, weekly.
- *One-on-ones:* A short, face-to-face or phone conversation includes time for your team member to voice issues, risks, and anything they want to tell you. It also allows you to gather status and discuss their current and upcoming work. These are 10 to 30 minutes in length, weekly.
- *Timely feedback:* There are countless opportunities to encourage effective behavior and correct ineffective behavior. In the author's experience, most

of these opportunities come in the form of effective behavior that you should be encouraging. Most project managers miss these opportunities. Focus your feedback on behavior, impacts, and future expectations. Feedback takes about 15 to 30 seconds to give when it becomes habitual. Give feedback as soon as possible after observing behavior. Strive to give at least one piece of feedback to each of your team members weekly.

# 8.4 I may not have the right team.

## By Cicero Ferreira

## 1. Problem

It feels as though the project is not meeting the stakeholders' expectations. The quality of the products generated is lower than expected and the team cannot reverse the situation. You have analyzed the situation to try and come up with the source of the problem, and no matter which way you look at it, you keep coming back to the fact that it looks like you don't have the right team to deliver this project.

## 2. Warning Signs

You need to be careful with this problem. You are dealing with people, and you don't want to cause hurt or upset. You also don't want to mistake caution for a lack of ability. However, you need to address issues quickly if the project is to be saved. Look for:

- Team members who seek your opinion on each simple task and demonstrate a lack of confidence or shortness of thought or leadership on the subject.
- The activities are being performed with relative autonomy, but the amount of reworking needed to arrive at the final product is quite high.

### Do I Have the Right Skills in the Project?

Shannon's supervisor called her into his office and announced that she was to lead the next major project for the organization. It was a high-priority project involving the improvement of an end-to-end business process responsible for the bulk of company revenues.

He also said that participants in the multifunctional, full-time project team had been appointed from each department involved, and she would have all the necessary support to do a great job. The success of the proposed project could mean the fulfillment of a long-awaited promotion for Shannon.

Shannon met with the team and, within days, completed the planning work. She was well prepared for the new challenge.

She held the project kickoff meeting. Each member of the team, as well as other stakeholders, learned what the project should achieve, what products were to be generated by the deadline, and what the roles and responsibilities of the participants were. Moreover, she prepared the participants with an overview of the methods and techniques that would be useful in their daily work.

When the work started, though, things did not go according to plan. Dates were slipping, people looked confused, and deliverables were low quality or just missing. The stakeholders were starting to look a little nervous.

"Do I have the right team for the project?" Shannon wondered. Even the simplest tasks were subject to hours of discussion between Shannon and the team members, sometimes to respond to basic questions, other times to analyze errors that would generate more rework in the near future. Two weeks had passed, and Shannon was now very concerned with the team's performance. The nominees for each of their respective departments seemed to have neither the qualifications nor the experience necessary to perform the job. Are there problems with individuals, management or the group?

- Customers and other project stakeholders demonstrate discomfort regarding the performance of a significant part of the team, and even cast doubt on the possibility of job success.
- A significant number of team members do not feel real empathy toward one another, cannot work in an integrated way, and even avoid one another.

## 3. What will happen if I do nothing?

Possibly, the problems will get worse. Within one or two executive meetings, if you have not made a decision, someone else will make one for you. A project that involves many people, full-time, is very expensive. Low productivity is not acceptable, and it won't take much to get to the point where the project can never be successful. You don't want to be the project manager who lets that happen!

## 4. Solution

In one story, Shannon was not involved in the team selection process. She did not have the chance to review the resumes of candidates before their selection. It is highly recommended that the project manager participate in the selection of professionals that will make up his or her team.

Remember, a project is a temporary endeavor undertaken to achieve a specific goal. It is planned, executed, and monitored, usually by people with limited resources.

Among other important factors, successful projects demand the right people, with the right profiles, in appropriate roles in the project. Additionally, to work as a team, people need to be properly trained and prepared. This is one of the hardest parts of the PM's job. It is necessary to know precisely which competencies, skills, and experience are required to generate each product expected from the project. Only after that can we begin to think about candidates. Before you begin building (or rebuilding) the team, there are four significant considerations:

1. Consider the required competencies, skills and experience
2. Consider the existing competencies, skills and experience and analyze the gaps
3. Consider the need for a team (not just a group of experts)
4. Consider your role

## 5. What should I do?

As soon as you think that your project team may not have the right people, it is time to conduct a diagnosis to determine the extent of the problem. It could be a situation where the problem affects only a small part of the team, or it may be a more serious situation that could jeopardize the entire project. You should conduct this diagnosis through three different lenses: competencies, skills, and experience.

### 5(a) Consider the project needs

Let's start by identifying the products to be generated by the project at hand. Let's take, for example, a project such as led by Shannon in the same story, aimed at improving business processes. Perhaps the end-to-end process in the story was the order-to-cash or O2C process, the heart of the manufacturing company. The objectives for this project could be: (a) the reduction of working capital related to accounts receivable; (b) operational cost reductions; and (c) faster resolution of customer issues to improve customer satisfaction.

The project deliverables could be the main O2C subprocesses (e.g., customer presence, order entry—creation/booking of orders and order fulfillment—physical and digital fulfillment, distribution, invoicing, customer payments/collection, cash application, and receipts). In a complex effort like this, we need to put together at least three disciplines in addition to the industry content component: project management, process management, and change management. Based on this, we can identify the major competencies for this project:

- An industry content SME (subject-matter expert) for each business sub-process
- A process designer for each business subprocess
- BPM (business process management) specialists
- ERP (enterprise resource planning) specialists
- Change management specialists
- PMO (project management office) specialists
- Professionals to perform each part of the process
- Executives to sponsor and link the effort with strategic direction
- Others

Notice that for the correct application of these competencies to the project, it will be necessary to check the skills in addition to the duration and type of experience possessed by the professionals to be allocated to the project. Let's analyze, for instance, the change management specialist profile for this O2C project using The Management Consulting Competency Framework from the Institute of Management Consultancy (IMC). It defines the competencies and standards for management consultants in three developmental stages: early, advanced, and mastery (see Table 8.1). Now, it is possible to identify Shannon's needs in a more accurate way. Do we need a more junior or more senior professional?

### 5(b) Consider the available resources

With the appropriate knowledge, skills, and behaviors identified, the second step is to assess the existing competencies of the project team.

This process requires a certain amount of rigor that should help the organization answer the following questions during the expertise assessment phase (adapted from Bopp, 2010):

- Which employees possess the required skills?
- Which other employees demonstrate the aptitude and baseline knowledge to quickly master these required skills?
- Will the current skills be adequate to address the needs?
- If not, what measures must be taken to close skill gaps?

**Table 8.1** The Management Consulting Competency Framework (Institute of Management Consultancy)

| Developmental Stage | Early | Advanced | Mastery |
|---|---|---|---|
| Expertise | Provides technical skills/experience to a project. Developing skills defined by Common Body of Knowledge and Competency Framework. | Secures, designs and manages small consulting projects. Practices skills consistent with Common Body of Knowledge and Competency Framework. | Can secure, design and manage large, complex, team-based consulting projects. Meets highest international standards of competence, including IMC USA, CBK, and CF. |
| Scope | Narrow specialty in a technical discipline/industry. | Applies expertise across industries and disciplines. | Creates new approaches to applying expertise across industries and disciplines. |
| Organization Focus | Tactical support to middle managers. | General business advice to managers and executives. | Broad strategic advice to senior managers and executives/Board of Directors. |
| Value to Client | Solves technical/tactical problems. | Recommends and implements solutions to client needs. | Sought by and considered a partner by executives. Long term engagements and retainer relationships are the norm. |
| Commitment to Profession | May belong to technical and/or trade associations and to IMC USA. Does not subscribe to a formal code of ethics. | Member of IMC USA and bound to IMC USA Code of Ethics. Has obtained CMC® certification. | Member of IMC USA and bound to IMC USA Code of Ethics. Has obtained CMC® certification. Actively contributes to profession. |
| Experience | Up to 3-5 years as an external or internal consultant. | Up to 5-15 years as an external or internal consultant with experience managing increasingly large, complex projects. | Greater than 15 years as an external or internal consultant. |

- Will the company's actions include external recruiting for new talent to the business?
- Will the company's actions include a blended approach, such as formal training, the use of technology to deliver the training, experiential learning such as mentoring, job shadowing, mentoring, or other means to close skills gaps?
- What are the implications to the business if such gaps are not closed?

After that exercise, you should have a solid understanding of the competency gap for the project (the difference between what you have and what you need). In our example, Shannon now would have objective information necessary for informed decision making. She could possibly have several gaps to address. The solution could be training, the recruitment of other members for the team, the replacement of team members, or even the occasional participation of specialists. Thus, the project could be recovered and put back on track, and Shannon placed closer to that promotion.

Therefore, to prevent problems, we should include a thorough analysis of project risks when planning the project. Surely, not having the competencies, skills, and experience required is a risk for the project.

### 5(b) Consider the need for a team

As we learned previously, complementary skills are needed to conduct the project successfully. There are many variables involved, so it would be almost impossible to conduct the work as a production line or as an individual effort or even to carry it out within each department in isolation.

There is a common purpose established for the project, which in turn creates mutual accountability between the participants—the first step towards building a team. However, you can't create a team just by bringing them together around a common purpose. Teams need to develop and learn to work together, which is covered in depth in Chapter 4: Navigating People Challenges. When you build your team, you need to consider a number of factors about the potential members:

- *Different personality types and how well they will work together:* Will the detail-focused team member and go-with-your-gut team member be able to work well together?
- *Different knowledge and experience levels:* Will senior members get frustrated with their more junior colleagues, or will they see an opportunity to create a protégé?
- *Different working styles:* Can the early-in, early-home type of person work successfully with the in-by-lunchtime, stay till midnight person?

Effective teamwork is not easy to obtain, but it is a powerful tool. Team-based organizations are more likely to be successful in adapting to market demands. People are not only a cost, but also an intellectual content and asset of the firm. What can make people with different personal backgrounds, experience, and professional goals work well in teams? Individuals must meet at least some key requirements in order for them to work as high-performance teams (adapted from Rees, 2001). There must be:

- Common goals
- Leadership
- Members' integration and involvement
- Individual commitment and the maintenance of self-esteem
- Easy and continuous communication
- Empowerment to make decisions both individually and as a team
- Mutual trust
- Respect for differences
- Constructive conflict resolution

### 5(d) Consider your role

The project manager has a key role in establishing the *modus operandi* of the team. He or she can assume a leadership style that drives people to do what was planned and how he or she wants it to be done. In this style, the project manager predominantly assumes a controlling role. In another style, one better suited to high performance teams, he or she acts as a facilitator, taking a more neutral stance and helping the team find methods and solutions based on the experience of team members. Of course, this means that sometimes the project manager will have to abandon the facilitator role and will need to give direction, make decisions, and provide guidance.

You need to review the competency, skills, and experience profile that you have created for your team, overlay the interpersonal elements, and determine the management style that you need to assume. You also need to recognize that you won't be able to use the same style all of the time, and that you will have to change your style for different individuals.

# 8.5 I am not sure how much process is enough.

## By Michael Wood

## 1. Problem

Faced with an ever growing portfolio of projects, you feel the pressure to get them done as quickly as possible. The challenge is in knowing how much process (what and how many steps) is needed to successfully take projects from beginning to end. Too much process will most likely meet with push back from the project team, needless forms, and bureaucratic costs that could slow the project down. Too little process could lead to unpredictable results, false starts, unwarranted risk, and even project failure. So how much process is enough to consistently get projects done quickly, accurately, and efficiently?

## 2. Warning Signs

How do you know when the process you are using to manage and oversee projects is not producing the outcomes needed? How do you know if your project processes are too light or too tedious in nature? Consider the following warning signs.

### 2(a) *Project processes are too light:*

- Results are inconsistent.
- Failures are increasing.
- Progress tracking reporting is chaotic.
- Scope creep is severe.
- Stakeholders are critical and unhappy.

### 2(b) *Project processes are too tedious:*

- Resistance to process protocols is high.
- Team morale is low.
- Progress tracking and reporting takes too long.
- Stakeholders resent the volume of sign-offs and approvals.

---

**Process Adaptability Is the Key to Ending Project Governance Woes**

After six months as the head of the company's project management office (PMO), Samantha was at her wit's end. She took the governance of the organization's project portfolio very seriously, and thus implemented a strict discipline over how projects were evaluated, tracked, managed, and executed and evaluated.

However, smaller projects seemed to get bogged down in paperwork, yielding a constant barrage of complaints from project staff and stakeholders alike. Even medium sized projects seem to languish under the comprehensive *best practices* framework. When upper management had taken notice of the lack of satisfaction being expressed by stakeholders, Samantha knew something had to change.

Samantha's first step toward finding a remedy to the problem was to listen to what project teams, managers, and stakeholders were saying and to gather their ideas about alternative approaches. She quickly realized that no one had an issue using the prescribed processes on large, complex, and costly projects. It was the smaller projects where phrases like *overkill* and *paperwork intensive* prevailed.

Samantha quickly learned that a common sense approach needed to be implemented—one that scaled down the process to the project. The result was the implementation of multiple process packages, each designed to be used in conjunction with specific project profiles. This streamlined project paperwork, lowered oversight costs, and allowed teams to stay focused on project related tasks.

- Oversight costs are growing.
- Feedback from team and stakeholders indicates the process is too complex and bureaucratic.

## 3. What will happen if I do nothing?

When you encounter the above warning signs, corrective action is needed. Doing nothing will lead to a slow erosion of the project management function as projects continually fail to meet requirements and stakeholder expectations. Eventually, upper management may intervene to:

- Make sweeping changes to project management leadership
- Impose strict and overbearing controls over projects
- Cut project funding
- Outsource the governance and management of projects to third parties

When the project process is chaotic, out of control, or too bureaucratic, doing nothing is not the answer.

## 4. Solution

The solution to right-sizing your project processes is to realize that one process does not fit all projects. Therefore, a more adaptable approach where the steps used to evaluate, approve, conduct, and manage a project are aligned with the project would involve:

- Complexity and intricacy
- Failure risk
- Duration
- Cost
- Geographic diversity
- Resource requirements

Using these elements to right-size the project can yield attractive results.

A scalable project process can help to streamline the evaluation and execution of projects without compromising governance maturity. It can also improve team compliance to established standards and protocols, while enhancing stakeholder satisfaction. All-in-all, a scalable approach to aligning project processes to project attributes is a good thing.

## 5. What should I do?

When developing an adaptable, scalable project management process framework, you need to understand how the project attributes (complexity, risk, duration, cost, geographic diversity, resource requirements) affect the amount of project process discipline needed to ensure timely success. Each project should be scored in terms of these attributes. In general, the higher the project's score, the more formal the processes need to be. For example, consider a project where:

- Complexity = 10 (thousands of tasks)
- Failure risk = 7 (failure has significant bottom line impact)
- Duration = 8 (2 years)
- Cost = 5 (over $2 million)
- Geographic diversity = 7 (5 or more geographic locations)
- Resource requirements = 5 (multiple teams, large capital outlays, etc.)

These scores would warrant a significant level of process discipline and structure in order to ensure the project was executed in a prudent and effective manner. Thus, the steps required to collect project status data, measure milestone achievement, manage change requests, manage vendor contracts, approve payments, and other tasks would need to be well controlled as the stakes are high and failure enterprise threatening.

Conversely, a project scoring low across these dimensions may warrant a set of minimal steps to ensure successful completion. Contrast the following projects using the attributes found in Table 8.2.

Common sense dictates that the oversight, diligence, and process discipline needed to build a backyard shed is far less than needed to build a skyscraper. A *statement of work* might suffice for the shed, but a *detailed project charter* would be needed for the skyscraper. Likewise, the project plan for the shed might consist of basic assembly instructions while the project plan package for the skyscraper would include many types of blueprints, detailed work plans, detailed communication plans, human resource utilization plans, calendars, and more planning tools.

By developing standard process scenarios built around the various project attribute scores, you can maintain high process maturity and ensure that you deploy just enough process to achieve consistent project success. You can also use those standards as references to demonstrate to your stakeholders that the level of process that you are applying to their project is appropriate for that type of project.

**Table 8.2** Project attributes

| Project attribute | Build backyard shed | Build skyscraper |
|---|---|---|
| Complexity | Low | High |
| Failure risk | Low | High |
| Duration | A few days | A few years |
| Cost | Under $3,000 | Hundreds of millions of dollars |
| Geographic diversity | One location | One location |
| Resource requirements | 2 to 3 people | Hundreds, maybe thousands of people |

# 8.6 I do not know enough technical stuff to manage.

## By J. Chris White

## 1. Problem

You have been brought in to manage a project in a completely new and different group, and you are unfamiliar with the details of the kind of work they normally do. There are a lot of specialty requirements and terms that you don't understand, and you have no context to know if the estimates and explanations that the team are providing are accurate or not.

## 2. Warning Signs

Like some of the other problems in this book, this problem is a lot about gut feeling—you know when you are uncomfortable. However, you can also look for the following signs:

- People use terms and acronyms that are *Greek* to you.
- When you hear a status report or are shown the work completed to date, you have no way to judge how close the task is to being complete.
- You blindly accept progress status reports.
- After hearing the details of activities performed on the project, which you thought would help you, you are more lost than you were before.

### What Did the PM Say?

"Talk about being in over your head. Why did I take this project?" Ken found himself having this conversation in his head a lot more than usual. "I've managed several projects for the financial products our company offers, but I don't know anything about manufacturing. CNC? PCB? Pre-fab? SMED? Black belt? Goodness gracious! What planet did I land on?"

Ken had a lot of confidence in his ability to manage projects. Some people would probably even describe him as arrogant. Ken was always quick to point out, "Like Dizzy Dean always said, it ain't bragging if you can do it." Of course, that didn't help with his image either. But, many in the company would readily admit that when it came to managing projects, Ken was definitely one of the best. People did not mind being on his projects because they were always successful.

Well, perhaps Ken had finally bitten off more than he could chew. He had never met a project he could not manage, but now he was staring one face-to-face. Ken liked high-priority projects. He thrived on pressure. In the manufacturing group, there was an opportunity to take the helm for a project for a new product being developed by the company. Ken's current project was in the closure stage, so Ken was looking for his next assignment anyway. How hard could it be? Just like paper flows through a financial process, widgets flow through a manufacturing process. No problem.

This quickly changed at the project kick off meeting. Not only did he not know a lot of the people working on this project, he had a list of acronyms longer than the Constitution. Not good. Ken was beginning to doubt himself, which was also not good. How could Ken get to know the technology and its new terms that were associated with this project?

## 3. What will happen if I do nothing?

Without a vision, your team will perish. You are typically the one they look to for that vision. If your lack of technical knowledge prevents you from understanding what needs to happen from a project perspective, the project will suffer. In the end, this can impact your credibility as a project manager, and perhaps, even your career path and the likelihood that you'll be assigned another project like this. If you cannot prove that you can handle a wide variety of projects, you may be limited to projects that only fall within your domain of known expertise with very little room for growth.

## 4. Solution

There are two options. First, you can back out of the project. If you are truly over your head, it may be best to step down and avoid failure. There are plenty of sophisticated and graceful ways of saying, "I'm not the right person" without damaging your reputation and career. Second, you need to buck up and learn some of the technical stuff. You don't need to know it all, but you need to at least know enough to understand conversations. Either learn the rest of the technology related to the project, or find someone who knows it and become good friends with them.

## 5. What should I do?

Assuming that you are not opting out of the project, there are two opposing schools of thought on the subject of technical expertise. One school of thought is that the project manager needs to be an expert in the technical aspect of the project, too. This school of thought contends that the best project managers are technical people who have *risen through the ranks* and been promoted to project manager.

The other school of thought is that project management is a separate discipline in and of itself, and that a project manager does not need to know the technical content to successfully manage the project. This school of thought contends that the project manager can move around to any project and be just as successful. As with many spectrums of thought, the real world often lies somewhere between these two extreme viewpoints. In some situations, the extreme viewpoints may work, but for most situations, there is a blend of both.

So, for the sake of discussion in this chapter, let us assume that you need to know at least some of the technical content. Where to draw the line is hard to say, and depends on the situation. You can do some learning on your own via company material, searches for key terms on the Internet, and related white papers. Most likely, though, that will not be enough. The best thing to do at this point is to sit with some of the experts on the team and ask them to explain the processes, procedures, and technical aspects of the project work.

The motivation for learning technical aspects is that you have to know enough to be able to judge whether work tasks are accomplishing their objectives, are behind schedule, are efficient, and such. Of course, the more you know, the better. This is critical to you being able to do the job you were brought in to do—manage the project. Don't feel like you have to know everything; knowing everything is not a requirement. Knowing enough of the information is the only requirement. If you are too proud to ask people for information, just think of the alternative if you don't—chances for project success decrease significantly.

You need to retain a balance. Your ultimate priority is to manage the project successfully, so you need to regularly check that the technical knowledge that you are gaining is supporting that goal. Ask yourself, will I:

- Better understand the work that my team is doing?
- Be better able to judge the accuracy and reliability of estimates and updates?

- Understand the potential risks more thoroughly?
- Be able to spot potential trouble areas sooner?
- Be able to have more meaningful conversations with stakeholders?

As long as you are able to answer, "yes," to at least one of the questions above, the knowledge that you are gaining will assist you in managing the project.

Your team won't see asking for help as a sign of weakness. They will have increased respect for your willingness to recognize and admit when you don't yet have the knowledge that you need. You will be better able to support them if you have a better understanding of the issues that they are dealing with.

Another strategy to help with the lack of technical knowledge is to befriend one of the experts in the field at your company. This person may or may not be on your project team. The key is that you establish a relationship with this person to whom you can ask technical questions and receive straightforward feedback on whether or not the technical elements of the project are being met. If this expert is not on the project team, try to get him or her to attend a few status meetings, so that he or she can get a feel for the work being done and have a proper context for assisting you. If this person is on the project team, that is fantastic. It's a natural fit.

# 8.7 There are too many issues to handle in a timely fashion.

### By Andrew Filev

## 1. Problem

Today, in order to successfully operate in the modern business environment, we need to process a huge flow of information and to handle a lot of responsibilities. Every team member gets his or her own share of this pressure. When your to-do list gets longer and longer, do you ever think it would be good if the day lasted not just 24 hours, but, say, 30? It's likely that such a situation is familiar to many of us.

When you combine this with a project that has a number of issues to resolve, you can have some big problems. You are faced with not knowing which issue to focus on first, which can wait, or which should be delegated to other team members.

## 2. Warning Signs

Every project has issues, and every project generates lots of work for team members, including the project manager. Recognize that you may have a bigger problem when:

> **The Death Spiral**
>
> Janice had that awe-struck, *deer in the headlights* look on her face. She had been managing her first project for several months, and at first everything was going well. Lately, though, she seemed to be in a death spiral headed for an inevitable crash of project failure. It seemed as though things had gone like this:
>
> 1. She was working very hard to complete her work and had no capacity for extra work.
> 2. The project team raised a couple of issues that she needed to deal with and that took her away from her other work, which fell behind.
> 3. Because she couldn't resolve all of the issues as quickly as the team needed, there were new issues that arose.
> 4. Trying to deal with them put her further behind on her *real* tasks.
> 5. Her failure to complete her work on time caused more issues.
> 6. She was unable to deal with those issues in time, which caused yet more issues.
>
> Janice could see where this was headed—project failure and loss of her job. There was just no way out of it for her, or was there?

- You are finding new issues faster than you can solve existing ones.
- You aren't sure which issue you need to focus on first.
- You don't feel that you understand some or all of the issues that are being raised.
- Your team feels overwhelmed by the number of issues that they are dealing with.
- You are spending huge amounts of time working, but not achieving much.

## 3. What will happen if I do nothing?

This is not a situation where you can even think about doing nothing. There is way too much going on. If you do nothing, issues and outstanding work will escalate and you will lose all control. However, you also can't continue doing the same thing that you are doing now—that's not working either, as the number of outstanding issues is continuing to grow, and that, too, will lead to a loss of control and ultimately project failure. You need to change your approach.

## 4. Solution

The solution to this problem has two distinct elements to it. First, you need to understand the problem around your issues and get a handle on what is causing so many problems to surface. Second, you need to ensure that you are working as effectively as possible so that you can handle the high workload that the issues are contributing to. You need a structured approach to:

- Focus on, and do, one thing at a time
- Follow the two minute rule
- Learn to delegate
- Prioritize
- Set deadlines
- Get a system to help you

## 5. What should I do?

It's easy to become overwhelmed by the volume of work when issues start arising. Each issue needs to be dealt with and needs handling in addition to all of the other work that is ongoing. You need to remain calm and in control; don't let the project control you.

### 5(a) Focus and do one thing at a time

There are physiological reasons that explain why working on several tasks at the same time is impossible. In *The Myth of Multitasking: How 'Doing It All' Gets Nothing Done*, Dave Crenshaw (2008), a business coach specializing in time management, says that what most of us call *multitasking* should actually be referred to as *switchtasking*. He explains that the human brain cannot physically do several things at the same time. We don't type a document and check email *simultaneously*. We switch back and forth from one task to another very rapidly. If we keep this up for a long time, stress accumulates, and we start experiencing focus problems. According to Crenshaw, no matter how quickly we switch, this has a high cost.

In 1927, Bluma Zeigarnik (1967), a Russian psychologist, described her experiment where 164 people were given a list of simple tasks that they needed to complete as soon as possible. After the participants started, they were interrupted a few times so that they couldn't finish some of the tasks. The main revelation was that, at the end of the experiment, the interrupted tasks were remembered much more so than the completed ones. This is how Zeigarnik explained why unfinished tasks stuck in participants' minds: "If a task is not completed, a state of tension remains, and the quasi-need [for completion of a task] is instilled" (p. 7). In other words, when you start working on a task, you experience some kind of tension that remains until you're done with the task. When you finish it, your mind is released of the anxiety. But if you're distracted or interrupted, your thoughts will return to the uncompleted task again and again. In an interview with Michelle Kowalski, Joe Hartnett, associate professor of business at St. Charles Community College, says that you can only intertwine things, such as doing one thing while waiting on another. Hartnett explains that trying to give adequate time and energy to more than one objective at a time is simply counter-productive.

It's important to focus and give your full attention to the task in front of you. If you put aside what you're doing, and if you have to go back to it three or four times, it will take you longer to allow yourself to get back on track and tap back into your creativity. Your brain takes time to adjust to the next thing. If you give something less attention, your work will suffer. You will find that if you multitask, you don't spend as much time on each item. When multitasking, you sometimes think you're working harder than you really are.

If we apply this to our project problem here, with an increasing number of issues, it is easy to allow issues to become the interruptions that Zeigarnik referred to. We have our regular project responsibilities, but then we are distracted by issues that are coming to the surface. This can happen not just when the issue first arises, but all the time that it is unresolved; it can invade our thoughts and start causing us to lose focus on other tasks.

### 5(b) Follow the two-minute rule

The Zeigarnik effect shows that *switchtasking*, and thus overloading your brain with a lot of uncompleted tasks, is stressful. It looks like a reasonable deduction of this phenomenon to refer to the two-minute rule. It is one of the key elements of David Allen's (2002) *Getting Things Done (GTD)* organizational method. In a nutshell, the idea is that if you have a task requiring less than two minutes for completion, don't procrastinate and do it right away. This simple rule helps you to keep focused and save time. Here's how Allen explains why the rule is efficient: "The rationale for the two-minute rule is that that's more or less the point where it starts taking longer to store and track an item than to deal with it the first time it's in your hands—in other words, it's the efficiency cutoff" (p. 131).

### 5(c) Learn to delegate

According to Andrew Carnegie, one of the most successful industrialists of the nineteenth century, no person will make a great business who wants to do it all himself. The ability to delegate is very important for a project manager so as to handle multitasking successfully. Think of such a situation: you've assigned an important task to a talented employee and given him or her a deadline. Now, do you let the employee do the work and simply touch base with you at predefined points along the way, or do you keep dropping by the desk and sending emails to check on progress?

If it is the latter, you might be a micromanager. The *micromanager* is the manager who must personally make every decision, take a lead role in the performance of every task, and, in extreme cases, dictate every small step the workers take. Micromanagement is mismanagement, and under it, the manager, employees, and business can suffer.

Do not do everything yourself. You will never have time to do the entire job for all of your projects. Even *Super-You* needs help and support. Remember that your most powerful leverage is your team. Your team members are experts in their own areas. Together, they can act like a powerful collective brain. The only thing you need to do is guide them, showing the right direction of project development. It helps to remember at all times that a manager is there to ensure that the work gets done as efficiently as possible. If the manager is attempting to dictate all actions and otherwise trying to control the employees' every move, the group will not be as efficient and effective as it could be under rational, enlightened management. Recommended books about management are *The Seven Habits of Highly Effective People* by Stephen Covey (1989) and *Good to Great: Why Some Companies Make the Leap... and Others Don't* by Jim Collins (2001). These books have some great thoughts on delegation, management, and leadership, which will not only help you to become more productive, but might inspire you to change your whole management style.

For instance, one of Covey's (1989) *habits* is synergy. To put it simply, two heads are better than one. Covey explains that several people working as a team can achieve better results than if they work separately. Everyone contributes their personal experience and expertise to the collaboration, so the team as a whole gets a new insight. Together, you can notice something you never noticed before. It can help you to come up with a new solution to an old problem. Thus, it means that trying to do everything on your own is not only stressful, but also less efficient than if you share the tasks with the team.

Delegation is a win/win strategy in managing multiple projects. On one hand, you empower your teams to do well by giving them opportunities to excel. On the other hand, you get rid of a part of your job. Giving your team more freedom in collaboration and contributing to project plans will save you time and give you a chance to think over strategies, set priorities, and sequence tasks across your numerous projects. Delegate to cut your routine work. But don't forget to coordinate your team's actions.

When it comes to issues, these will always be escalated to you by your team, but that doesn't mean that you have to deal with them yourself. You need to be aware, and you are ultimately accountable, but you can still hand the issue back to team members to investigate the cause and develop possible solutions. Indeed, in many circumstances, that is the best approach as your team members are likely in a position to better understand the details of the issue.

### 5(d) Prioritize

You need to master the skill of prioritizing to make the best of your own and your team's resources. It is extremely hard to be effective in time-bound endeavors (like projects) if you can't prioritize appropriately.

The famous Time Management Matrix divides the items we have to deal with into four categories according to their urgency and importance. Its principles were first stipulated by President Dwight Eisenhower, who said that the more important an item, the less likely it is urgent, and the more urgent an item, the less likely it is important.

As shown in Table 8.3, Quadrant I contains items that need to be managed without delay. In Quadrant III, there are items that should be minimized. The items of Quadrant IV should be minimized or eliminated completely. Quadrant II is what should be further prioritized and have our focus for the long-term perspective. These are the strategically important items we need to thoroughly plan for to maintain control over the work.

David Allen (2002) explains that *stuff* we have on our mind (coming from emails, memos, self-generated ideas, and such) isn't a task list yet. When a new item appears in your *stuff*, the main question that you need to answer about it is whether it is actionable or not. If the answer is, "no," there are three things that can be done with the item. First, it may be deleted if it has no relevance. Second, it may be labeled *to do someday*. The third option is that you might keep this information for reference.

Actions that you identified as "actionable" are to be further organized. When you've decided what projects the items belong to and how they range in priority, you get a clear picture of "the next-action" category. Having completed a task, you move to the actionable item that is the next one on your list. So the target is set, and you focus on moving toward it.

This principle goes back to the same idea that incomplete tasks cause cognitive dissonance, or simply speaking, remain *stuck in our head* and overload our brains. By selecting the next action item and either completing it or storing it in some external system that will reliably remind you about it later, you complete the task for now, getting rid of the dissonance and offloading the task, leaving your brain with enough capacity to productively focus on the next thing.

Apply these principles to the issues that are raised to you:

- How many issues are not really issues at all, and can be ignored?
- How many issues are technically issues, but not really something to worry about?
- How many are true issues that need dealing with, and then:
  - Which need handling now?
  - Which can wait?

**Table 8.3** Time management matrix

|  | URGENT | NOT URGENT |
|---|---|---|
| IMPORTANT | I<br><br>Items that require immediate action | II<br><br>Items that need focus for long-term perspective |
| NOT IMPORTANT | III<br><br>Items that interrupt and distract us from main activities | IV<br><br>Items with little value and time-wasting items |

### 5(e) Set deadlines

After you have prioritized the items on the to-do list, you can set deadlines for tasks that you think require them. This way, you'll know exactly when action is required.

You've probably heard that a lot of people find themselves working better when they have a deadline. If you're that kind of person, you should be careful with this method because if you use it as the *only* gear to accelerate your performance, it may soon become very stressful. However, if you apply it reasonably, it may be helpful for ensuring timely task completion.

Deadlines can be a good tool for mobilizing your resources and kicking yourself into action. If your motivation is running low, you can set a timeframe to beat procrastination. For example, a productivity system can be geared toward to-do lists that have either daily or weekly deadlines. With these deadlines, it is easier to get started.

Whether your deadlines should be rigid or flexible depends on your reaction to tight time limits, the project you're working on, and your business environment. The main thing to remember is that deadlines should always be realistic. Just because you set a deadline for next week to bring $100K in new revenue for your company out of the blue doesn't necessarily make it possible. Setting extremely challenging deadlines usually has the opposite effect from what was intended. As soon as you start to doubt your ability to finish on time, you'll lose motivation to try.

How should you organize the items that have no deadlines, so that the Zeigarnik effect is avoided and no tasks get lost along the way? In Scrum methodology (part of Agile project management) such tasks are called *backlog*. You need to keep them recorded in order of priority in some external system. Thus, you'll free your brain from the pressure of uncompleted tasks. This system should support you in the following ways:

- You meet hard and important deadlines, if it's physically possible.
- You do the important work before you do the unimportant work.
- You are very productive and constantly move forward to your goals.

With the help of this system, you'll be able to review the priorities from time to time. If a minor item gets pushed down the list by more important (sometimes new) ones, you'll still have a clear overview of all the tasks.

### 5(f) Get a system to help you

Let's elaborate on the recommendation given above. In order to follow the tips that were mentioned—not only regarding deadlines—you need a system that will help you facilitate task management, so that the tips don't turn into extra tasks and increase the pressure, instead of eliminating it.

When you have such a system at hand, you don't need to keep all the information in your head. You can focus on the current task, and all the upcoming ones are safe in external storage. Some people still prefer paper and pen for this purpose, but if you truly have a lot of tasks and multiple projects running, you will outgrow this solution very quickly. Thus, a *system* usually means software that would be effective for handling the organizational part of your teamwork, one that will let you focus on the main goals of your project while it does the *secretary job* for you, like integrating the plans of the team members, requesting status updates, or shooting off reminders about the upcoming deadlines.

Don't choose project management software that will make you create a separate *workspace* for each project. Separating project data and schedules is a common mistake. Many of the traditional project management tools make it difficult for you to make changes to your initial project plan.

Choose a flexible application that will let you easily keep your plans up-to-date. Some Web-based applications allow your team members to update tasks assigned to them directly in the plan. This saves you lots of time, as you don't need to collect all the updates and integrate them manually into your schedule. Such a tool will also help you accelerate your delegation skills.

Let's summarize what you need a system for; a system helps to:

- Have all the tasks listed in one place—urgent and non-urgent ones—so that none of them get lost or forgotten
- Keep track of the tasks' delegation among your team members
- Enable team members' contributions to the project plan
- Set priorities for your team and yourself
- Set deadlines for the tasks
- Remind you about those deadlines

When you start a project and then take on several more, you'll need a reliable tool that will help you to integrate your data. You need a tool that will let you have all the data neatly organized in one place, so that you have a good overview of what is going on in the team. Tools should make your life easier, not create even more duties for you. While choosing a project management tool for a multitasking environment, make sure it will integrate the project schedules for multiple projects and that the schedules will be easy to update. Also, seek the tools that don't force you to duplicate your work. For example, if you're heavily using email for team coordination, get a tool that can integrate with email nicely.

### 5(g) A note on out of control issues

This chapter assumes that you can get issues under control with a more effective way of working, and by not allowing new issues to distract you from the work that you are trying to complete. However, you have to recognize that, at times, a project is in such serious trouble that there is an explosion of issues, and you may need to stop progress and examine the cause of all of the issues.

In this case, you need to get to the root of the problems and solve that before proceeding. This will obviously have short term impact on the project, but it's the only way that you can be sure that the cause of the issues has truly been dealt with. Potentially, if the problems are serious enough, the project may end up being cancelled.

# 8.8 How much status is enough?

## By Dave Prior

## 1. Problem

Suppose that you are managing two separate projects. On one project, things are going very well. You have clear lines of communication with the team; progress is being made toward the deliverable on a consistent basis that is in line with the project schedule. Best of all, management seems happy. Since things are going so well, you backed off on status reporting. After all, status reporting is really only a big deal when things are off track, right? Besides, if management isn't asking, why spend time on it?

Your other project is a different story. Its current state is somewhere between screaming disaster and chaos theory, and the constant demands for updates from panicked senior executives have resulted in you spending almost all your time on the project doing nothing but creating and sending out

> **The Status Trap**
>
> Jim looked at the clock and noticed that he had lost another day in preparing status reports. The project was not supposed to go like this. He knew how critical status reports were necessary, since they were one of the primary tools he used to communicate with the organization about the project. But he was pretty sure the report should not be getting in the way of him doing any actual work on the project or removing obstacles for the team.
>
> Unfortunately, Jim has five senior stakeholders watching his project and each of them has a separate demand for what they want to see in the report and how it must be formatted. Oddly enough, no matter how much time he spent on this report, they would still stop him in the hallway for a verbal update. It is almost as though they had not even read what he had sent them.
>
> Jim needed to make a change with how he was handling status if he was ever going to take on the role of actively managing this project. Based on what he had been putting in the reports, he needed to make the change quickly to help get his work as PM back on track. How could he balance the work required to manage the status reports with the efforts required to lead the project?

special status reports. The good thing is that because you are so focused on status, you are gathering a lot of important information with great frequency. Sure, it is completely disruptive to the team when you make them stop working every other day to individually give you a full run down on their work, but how else will you please the sponsors? The biggest problem you can see here is that while you are finding lots of things that could be tweaked or optimized, you are so busy working on collecting and reporting on the status that you never have time to do anything about the issues you are seeing.

So, which of these projects is set up to fail? The answer is, both of them. They may or may not deliver the desired end product, but they are both set up to fail from a communication standpoint.

## 2. Warning Signs

If there are problems with the status reports you are sending out, one or more of the following warning signs may indicate you are reporting either too much, or too little for them to effectively communicate in the way they are intended.

- You spend more time collecting and reporting on status than you do working to solve problems that will enable the delivery to happen faster or more efficiently.

- The collection of status is disrupting the team's ability to get their work done.
- You've skipped on sending in status reports for a week or two, and no one noticed.
- You began to use status reports as a way of flooding management with so much information they are afraid to ask questions.
- You are not sure what the organization's regulatory compliance policies are regarding status reporting.
- You do not know who will be using the status report, how they will use it, or what end goal it serves.

## 3. What will happen if I do nothing?

Regardless of whether you are working on a project where you've decided to blow off status reporting because no one notices, or you are spending all your waking hours collecting and reporting on status, you are likely to be headed towards the Land of the Unhappy Client. Once you get to that place, you are no longer able to truly serve the project because you will spend all your time trying to win back a client you never had to lose in the first place. This will likely happen regardless of whether or not you deliver what the client has asked for because their perception of how things went will be filtered through the status report issue.

## 4. Solution

On any project there are a few things you can do to make sure that your status reports are providing as much value for the client as possible without having a negative impact on the team due to demands on your time. The first is to ask yourself a few questions:

- Are there any organizational or regulatory compliance requirements that must be adhered to with respect to status reporting?
- Does the client have any established formats, frequencies or other practices around status reporting? If so, will they fit with your project or do you need to seek an alternative?
- What is the most convenient, easily digestible way for the client to receive the status updates?
- What is the best way to capture status from the team without having a negative impact on their productivity?
- Who are the recipients of the status report, what will they use it for and what information will make it valuable to them?
- When you look at the status report, do you know why the information requested for each field will be valuable and why?
- Have you established guidelines for the stakeholders to get updates between status reports?

This chapter will show you how to find the answers to each of these questions. This will give you all you need in order to be able to determine just how much status is necessary, how often and why.

## 5. What should I do?

When you are managing a project one of the most important things to keep in mind is that, as PMs, we are supposed to be spending the majority of our time communicating. Unfortunately, one thing a lot of people in project leadership roles forget is that we also need to always remain focused on selling the value of our work, the project, and the team to the client. Status reporting is one of the most important tools we have available to us that helps us communicate with the team and stakeholders while also selling the value of our work (regardless of the news) to the client.

And now that we've listed some key questions to ask when trying to determine *how much status is enough*, let's take a closer look at each question to see why we are asking it, and how it could help.

### 5(a) Are there any organizational or regulatory compliance requirements that must be adhered to with respect to status reporting?

*Why are we asking?*

Many organizations will have requirements to adhere to specific standards that may filter down into how you manage projects. This could come through the presence of legislative requirements like Sarbanes-Oxley, specific requirements for keeping the organization compliant with best practices defined by industry organizations like the International Organization for Standardization (ISO), or the Software Engineering Institute's Capability Maturity Model Integration (CMMI). These kinds of predetermined standards may dictate how much leverage you have in terms of making adjustments to how you handle status reporting.

*How will this help?*

If you are managing a project in any environment, you need to ensure that you are doing so in a way that is compliant with the practices and norms that are part of the environment. If the organization has a requirement for your project to adhere to a specific way of reporting status, you need to tailor your approach to those requirements and manage the project in a way that does no harm to the organization's established best practices.

### 5(b) Does the client have any established formats, frequencies or other practices around status reporting?

*Why are we asking?*

The reason we provide status is to communicate to an organization how things are going. We do this primarily because we want them to understand what they are facing in terms of completion, risk, decisions that need to be made, and such. If there are established ways in which we can prepare to deliver this information, those established ways make it more digestible for the recipient.

*How will this help?*

In our role as project manager, we are responsible for making sure our communications are received and understood in the way in which they are intended. Providing information to the client in a familiar way reduces the number of barriers they may face when trying to access the value in the information. Keep it simple, speak their language, and it will be easier for them to understand.

### 5(c) What is the most convenient, easily digestible way for the client to receive the status updates?

*Why are we asking?*

Even when there are established patterns of delivering status, it is important to ask questions about whether or not the methods are effective for the recipient. Just because there is an established method does not mean that it cannot be improved upon. If our goal is to get the message into a state that is consumed by the client as simply as possible, we need to know what the client's preferences are.

*How will this help?*

This is also about removing barriers to the message. If we can update the client with information they need in a time, place, and method that makes it easier for them to understand, there is a better chance our client will have the information necessary to make the right decisions about the project at the right time.

This is a common problem for many PMs who are trying to manage Agile projects in traditional organizations. Often times, traditional senior management and PMOs are not accustomed to receiving and interpreting things like backlogs and burn down charts, and they don't know what to make of them. It may be in the best interest of the project to come up with a status report mash-up that uses the most critical elements from the traditional report and the essential elements from the Agile process.

### 5(d) The team is responsible for providing status, but what is the best way to capture their updates without having a negative impact on their productivity?

*Why are we asking?*

So far, most of these questions have been about the recipient of the information, but we haven't discussed the source yet. The thing is, every time we interrupt the team to collect status, we are pulling them away from their work on the deliverable, so even though they are responsible for providing it, there is a cost to the project for gathering status. We want to collect the information we need in a way that has as little negative impact on the team's productivity as possible.

*How will this help?*

Since collecting information is going to disrupt the team's capacity to deliver the work they've been charged with, it makes sense that we'd want to collect the information in a way that is as easy for them as possible. Asking the team to contribute ideas about how and when they'd like to be interrupted will allow them to make the best use of their available working time and also go a long way towards establishing the perception among the team members that the PM respects them and their work.

The important thing to keep in mind—which many project leaders lose sight of—is that the team and their work need to take priority over the work of the PM. Status reporting is vital to a successful project, but at the end of the day, if the reports are all done, but the team did not complete the work because they were too busy providing status, the work is still not done and a perfect status report record will not save the day.

### 5(e) Who are the recipients of the status report, what will they use it for, and what information will make it valuable to them?

*Why are we asking?*

When we communicate status, we can be more effective in how we deliver our message if we know who we are trying to communicate to, what information is most valuable to them, and why they need it.

*How will this help?*

Knowing what the recipient of the status report considers to be valuable, what they need the information for, and how they like to be *spoken* to will allow us to be more efficient in how we craft the status report by tailoring it to the specific needs of the recipient and their end goals. The easier we can make it for the recipient to understand, the better off we are.

### 5(f) Have you established guidelines for the stakeholders to get updates between status reports?

*Why are we asking?*

No matter how much time you are spending putting status reports together, there will always be one or two people who have special needs for updates about their own specific concerns at times when you were not planning on working on status. This can be very time-consuming and frustrating for both parties. Establishing guidelines about when status will be delivered, and in what format, will go a long way toward keeping the client feeling like they are having their informational needs addressed with a degree of frequency they are comfortable with, and in a manner they can digest.

*How will this help?*

Setting norms for behavior is an important part of any project. When there is uncertainty around the work being done, having a process that is reliable can be a very important part of a successful project. The clients need to know when they can expect to get updates and (hopefully) will then allow the PM time to focus on more than just status.

# 8.9 I don't know how to test to ensure things will work.

### By J. Chris White

## 1. Problem

The project is a development project that is designed to build something and you don't want to get stuck at the end with a failed inspection or quality assurance test that could have been prevented. However, you are not sure how to build testing into your project. You are sure that you can't just wait until the end and then test everything, but what should you do?

## 2. Warning Signs

Some signs that you may have this problem on your project include:

- There are not many quality tests shown in the project plan.
- The product commonly fails the quality tests that you do have.
- Other team members are getting an uneasy feeling about whether or not the technical requirements of the product will be met.
- Team members are testing for *success*, but not for *failure*.
- There is not a good, solid testing plan in place.

## 3. What will happen if I do nothing?

If you don't plan comprehensive testing throughout your project, you are completely reliant on one final test at the end, and inevitably there will be problems. When the final test fails, it will be extremely difficult to find out where the problem is. Sure, it can be done, but it will be time consuming and resource-intensive. You'll blow through any profits made on the project (and possibly lose money). Moreover, the client or end customer may be frustrated and relationships may be damaged (perhaps beyond repair).

### Climbing the Stairs One Step at a Time

Kayla had always enjoyed making things. That's why she was thrilled to be the project manager assigned to the development of a new product for her company. It was a great opportunity for her, and best of all, it would actually be fun.

However, Kayla had never managed a product "development" effort before. She had managed several maintenance projects out in the field, but that was after a product had been developed. Even though she looked forward to the development project, she had heard many horror stories from project managers of other development projects where finding and fixing issues and problems was required. In some cases, it was actually the customer that found the problem. Yikes! That couldn't happen to Kayla on this project. She could not afford to mess it up. Her career would come to a grinding halt.

So, how could she make sure that this project would be a success? "Well," she thought to herself, "I feel comfortable with the resources that I have available and I feel comfortable with the time we've been allotted." But, she couldn't help feeling a bit uneasy about ensuring that the final product would work as proposed. She knew she could do a lot of testing at the end of the project before the product went out the door to the customer. Yet, that is what her predecessor did and the project was still a failure. Kayla remembered the previous project manager saying, "No matter how much testing we did at the end, it wasn't enough. It felt like there was no way we could test our way out of that problem."

Kayla knew product testing and quality assurance was vital. So, was it the way in which the previous project manager scheduled the quality assurance tasks near the end? Or, was it that they were not testing for the right things? Or both?

## 4. Solution

The solution to this problem is not inherently difficult: you need to test from the *bottom up* (i.e., test parts, then components, subsystems, and the total system in that order). However, that does not happen by itself. As the project manager, you need to ensure that your project plan includes all of these tests, and that there is consideration of the work necessary to address any testing failures:

- Plan for testing of parts, components, subsystems, and full system.
- Build contingency into the project for rework or corrections.
- Build gateways that control progress to the next phase.

## 5. What should I do?

The more parts, components, and subsystems that get assembled or combined to form a total system or product, the more interconnections there are. And, the more interconnections there are, the more opportunity for the system or product to fail. For the purpose of this chapter, assume that the *hierarchy* for a system or product starts with individual parts (e.g., screws, sheets of metal) at the lowest level. Multiple parts are combined to make components, which are the smallest *unit* of assembly. Multiple components are combined to make subsystems, which are larger units of assembly. Finally, multiple subsystems are combined to make the end system or product. There may be even more *levels* to the system hierarchy in your situation, but for the purpose of discussion, let's keep it simple.

Given this system hierarchy, you want to test from the bottom up. So, start with testing the individual parts before they are assembled into components. In the project plan, include tests, quality assurance (QA) activities, and/or inspections that make sure the parts meet their various specifications (e.g., length, width, weight, color, form).

It is not realistic to assume that every part will pass the test, so make sure that your plan includes time and money to address the issues that are found by:

- Fixing and correcting the parts that failed
- Replacing the failed parts with others

When all the necessary parts have passed their tests and/or inspections, they can be assembled into components. At this point, since you know all the parts are correct, the only issues that arise will be from integrating and combining the parts. This limits the scope of your investigation when you are trying to figure out why a component failed a test. You already know all the parts are good, so the problem cannot be an individual part. The problem must have something to do with the interconnection of the parts. Perhaps the original specifications or requirements for the parts were incorrect. For example, the tolerances on width for several individual parts begin to *stack up* as these parts are assembled side-by-side.

Similarly, once the components have passed all of their respective tests with regard to specifications and requirements, you can move up testing to the subsystem level. If all the components passed their respective tests, all problems and failures that arise at the subsystem level are the result of combining or integrating components. As mentioned, perhaps the failure is due to poor or incorrect requirements at the subsystem level. These will need to be reviewed.

Next, once all the subsystems pass their respective tests, the final step is to combine subsystems into the final system or product. As you move further through the project, the solution to problems is going to shift from replacement (the norm at the parts level) to fixing or correcting.

Remember, tests that occur at each level must be explicitly written into the project plan or resources and time will not be allocated to them; the plan also needs to include time and resources for implementing fixes. It is much easier to find errors and problems working through the levels of the system hierarchy than to find errors and problems on a completed system or product.

The worst case is if the end customer finds the error or problem. Yes, adding these tests at each level adds cost and time to the overall project, but they are absolutely necessary in the development process. The key is that you *do not* move to the next level of testing without successfully passing all the tests at the previous level. This is when things get confusing and a great deal of time is required to figure out what went wrong.

To get started with establishng a testing plan, here are some key things to think through, particularly for a specific *level* of the product hierarchy, like the project described previously:

*What should be tested?*

- Any technical aspect relevant to the usability of the product as defined by the client or end customer, including physical attributes (e.g., size, dimensions, weight, speed of movement, color), electrical attributes (e.g., conductance, voltage), or other features (e.g., getting an *acceptable* rating from seven out of ten people in a focus group).

*Who should participate?*

- Team members or other personnel outside the project team who are held accountable for the specific component, subsystem, or system. For instance, there may be someone who is manager over all printed circuit boards (PCB's), regardless of the electronic product the PCBs go in.
- Subject matter experts within the company, who have expertise in the technical aspect or function being tested (e.g., electrical, mechanical) and who may or may not be on the project team.
- Quality control or quality assurance personnel (who can testify on behalf of the company, perhaps not on the project team, that the tests were conducted correctly and that the component, subsystem, or system has adequately passed the test(s).

*Deliverables from each test:*

- Description of test(s) conducted
- Test(s) results
- Discussion of test successes as well as failures

- Corrections needed for product, based on test failures
- Action items and assignments for corrections to be made to product, as well as a schedule of due dates, which is essentially a mini-plan for getting the product back on track
- A Final Report of findings that should include all the things listed earlier and is to be passed to the group of people conducting the next test.

Note: This may be an iterative process for which the tests at the same *level* of the product hierarchy must be conducted, fixed, and reconducted to reach a successful conclusion before moving on.

# 8.10 I can't work well with people at a distance.

## By Jennifer Whitt

## 1. Problem

My customer and project teams work remotely, with core staff located in a main office; however, the other project team members are scattered throughout the country and abroad in different time zones. It is difficult to get everyone together, and when we finally do, it doesn't feel as if anyone is paying attention or contributing to the virtual meeting, let alone accomplishing the tasks at hand.

## 2. Warning Signs

Just because you have a remote team (or some remote team members), it doesn't mean that you will have this problem. It will arise only if the team isn't working effectively with the physical and time differences. Look for:

- Tasks take longer than expected to complete, or are completed with higher cost and questionable quality. Note: This could be a symptom of other problems as well. Issues involving working with people at a distance could be just one of those problems.

### Out of Sight, Out of Mind?

Julie had finished another conference call with her team and the client. She let out a sigh of despair as this was the third meeting in a row where nothing had seemed to change and the project schedule continued to slip. Her problem seemed to stem from the fact that the project team members and the client were in different, remote locations. She was finding it increasingly difficult to keep everyone focused and engaged.

She reflected on the call she just concluded. It was one symptom of a problem that continued to get worse. Everyone showed up to the call, eventually. Unfortunately, some members from her team were five minutes late and needed to be caught up by Instant Messenger behind the scenes. Worse yet, key stakeholders from the client showed up even later, and the meeting regressed in order to bring everyone up to speed.

There were moments of silence where she felt as if she was the only person on the call. She needed to repeat the same question a number of times. One time the question remained unanswered, and she had to move on to the next point on the agenda. To make matters worse, there was a misunderstanding about a deliverable that needed to be finished. One of Julie's team members blamed it on the sloppy requirements and a lazy client project manager—who just happened to be on the same call!

Julie knows that something has got to change or this project, and possibly her PM position, would be on shaky ground. She knows that just because she can't see everyone face-to-face, there has to be a better way.

- Long periods of awkward silence experienced on conference calls.
- Frequent requests to repeat yourself during conference calls.
- Team members show up late to the virtual meetings.
- Misunderstandings due to the fact that people are not working together as a team.

## 3. What will happen if I do nothing?

The energy and excitement that are necessary to move a project forward will quickly deteriorate. Key decision makers will disengage from the project and fewer people will attend standard or virtual meetings. Meetings will become nothing more than going through the motions with disengaged team members and the project will quickly derail.

## 4. Solution

To overcome the challenges of working with remote teams, you need to address the situation with project leadership—that ranges from picking people who can effectively work in a remote team environment (even the ones who will be in the central office) to effectively conducting virtual meetings. There are a number of items that you should be sure to address:

1. Know your team
2. Set clear expectations
3. Keep in touch
4. Start small (and short)
5. Conduct effective meetings
6. Consider the remote team members
7. Recognize the challenge of remote management

## 5. What should I do?

It goes without saying that there are things that some team members do when other people can't see them that they would never do when people are around. This certainly applies to working remotely. Multitasking, partial listening, and becoming distracted by nonwork-related issues create a challenge when working with people who are not in the same office.

### 5(a) Know your team

It takes a self-disciplined, self-motivated, and self-energized person to be able to work remotely. Not everyone is able to handle the responsibility that comes when they are put in that environment, and many do not enjoy being away from the core team.

Some people need the schedule, discipline, camaraderie, and structure that accompany the workplace. As a project manager, it is easy to make this determination on a person-by-person basis based upon their previous work history, how much ongoing direction someone needs, and the person's motivation.

If it is within your authority as that person's project manager, you can prevent setting them up for failure (and yourself up for frustration) if you only allow those who can handle the responsibility to work remotely. In some cases, that may mean taking a less skilled or experienced local team member over a more experienced individual who can only work remotely from the core team for this initiative, who is not effective in that capacity.

### 5(b) Set clear expectations

Once you have chosen team members who are able to handle the responsibility of the project and the additional challenges presented with a remote team, you need to set clear expectations with them. One principle that seems to work well has to do with the military phrase of *Going Dark* which means that someone has gone incognito, has gone into hiding, or has become noncommunicative. As a project manager, you should be clear with your people that, while they are on company time, they should *never Go Dark*.

What does this mean in practice? If there is a question that needs to be answered, a change in direction, or another important reason for you to get in touch with your team member, you need to be able to reach them immediately and receive a response or confirmation that they have received your message. This is as simple as the team member answering the phone when you call, sending a quick note back to confirm an email has been received, or jumping on a conference call immediately for an ad hoc meeting.

Remote workers should expect to overcompensate by doing everything within their power to become even *more* responsive than when they are in the office in person.

### 5(c) Keep in touch

Disconnects will arise if you only meet with your remote team members during scheduled virtual meetings. Team members may be reluctant to bring up topics that need to be addressed in a group setting. Make sure to set up individual conversations, incorporate these into your communication plan, and use collaborative technologies that are available such as webinars and video conferencing.

### 5(d) Start small (and short)

It is easier to give than to take away. If someone is asking to work remotely for convenience and not geographic necessity, rather than agreeing to them working remotely a couple of days a week or the entire week, start with one day here and there to finish a particular part of a project. Evaluate how someone does, and expand from there. Another approach to transitioning would be the ability for someone to work remotely on a trial basis for a short period of time. Either way, a gradual change will afford you the opportunity to see how someone does in a remote setting and make adjustments to communications as necessary.

While working remotely is becoming more common, it needs to be stated, up front, that this would be considered more of a benefit or perk to reward outstanding performance, not a standard part of being on the project team.

### 5(e) Conduct effective meetings

Working successfully with remote workers has to do with how effectively conference calls and virtual meetings are conducted. People need to view meetings they attend remotely as being just as important, or more important, than the ones they attend in person. It is hard to sneak into a face-to-face meeting without everyone knowing you are late, disrupting the meeting while you are finding a seat, and getting caught up with what everyone has already discussed. This frustration is compounded when you add the element of distance, not being in the same building, or not being able to get in touch with someone who is critical to the call.

Here are some suggestions on how you can make virtual meetings as effective as possible when you are conducting them:

- *Make the purpose of the meeting engaging:* Routine status meetings and reports consume a lot valuable time. Status updates can be sent out in advance and read by the stakeholders. The meeting itself should be about issue identification, risk mitigation, and problem solving.
- *Make sure everyone is on time:* A cardinal rule for conference calls is to make sure that everyone shows up on time and the meeting starts promptly as scheduled. It is extremely awkward to have dead air over the phone while the minutes tick by because a key member is late. Make a *big deal* to your team that this is one *rule* that you have—that everyone be on time for conference calls. If someone is running late, they need to let you know so you can move the agenda around or reschedule. This *rule* applies to internal meetings and especially applies to meetings where a client will be attending.
- *Turn control over to other team members:* Just because you called the meeting doesn't mean that you have to run the meeting. Turning control over to other team members will keep them engaged. This works especially well if there is a presentation, demonstration, or other event that is being done through a webinar, where the team member can run it from their desktop.
- *Say their name up front:* Those on the phone should be paying 100 percent attention to the call—see stop multitasking. However, the reality is that sometimes this does not happen and people are distracted or multi-tasking. Rather than take the risk of catching someone off guard and having them ask you to repeat the question, you can start with something like "Cheryl, you know that is a good question..." and then repeat the question that was asked. This will allow your team member the ability to tune back in and provide a focused answer.
- *Work out the technical issues up front:* Never assume that everything is going to work okay when it comes to a virtual meeting if there is technology involved, especially if a lot of people are attending. Always do a dry run to make sure everything is going to work as expected.
- *Turn off email notifications and instant messaging:* There is nothing more horrifying than sharing your desktop and everyone seeing the subject line

of a confidential email you received or someone sending you an instant message about someone who is on the call and can see your computer screen. Do not risk the embarrassment or misunderstandings that could arise from an inappropriate email or instant message. Turn them off!

### 5(f) What if you are a remote attendee?

Below are some recommendations on how you can make the most out of attending a meeting:

- *Stop multi-tasking:* It is hard not to multitask when there is a subject or topic on the call that is not of interest to you. The first thing you do is start checking your email, finish up on a task you have been assigned, or even take another call! Get into the habit of treating a remote meeting the same way that you would treat a meeting in person. If you would not do those things when you are in front of a group of people, do not do them remotely. This will allow you to get more out of the meeting and stay engaged.
- *Know who is attending:* Always make sure you know who is on the call. We've all heard stories about someone who was discussing how unreasonable, or clueless, or impatient the client was—only to find out later that the client was on the call! Don't let that happen to you by not going down that path in the first place, and by always knowing who is on the other end of the line.
- *Ask questions:* A good remote attendee is always audible or visible. When the meeting is wrapping up and someone asks if there are any questions— have some questions. Everyone will appreciate well-thought-out questions and the fact that you listened enough through the meeting to come up with them.

A couple of other things to keep in mind whether you are conducting or attending a remote meeting is to not type furiously on your keyboard while someone else is talking (due to distracting noise and motion), and make sure you have good phone equipment. Trying to make out garbled sentences that come from a cheap microphone or speakerphone is frustrating to anyone who is trying to listen to what you have to say.

### 5(g) Recognize the challenge of remote management

Pay personal attention to those who are on your team. You may notice a trend where performance or quality deteriorates. Establishing a candid and trusted relationship with all team members up front will allow you to have a candid conversation with them. Is there something going on in their personal life? Are they hesitant to escalate when they have problems? Knowing their history and challenges will enable you to help them work through any issues that may be impacting your project.

# 8.11 I don't know how to balance my project and team needs!

By Jennifer Russell

## 1. Problem

Your project has a really aggressive schedule. You are going to need to pull out all the stops to get this project done in time. But some of your team members are slowing down. They are not as motivated and committed as they were when the project started. Now, you're worried about team morale *and* the project schedule!

## 2. Warning Signs

You need to quickly recognize when your team and project's needs are out of balance, otherwise the situation may not be recoverable. Look out for:

- Team members who are starting to appear less engaged, and declining morale.
- There is an increase in conflict and arguments among people in the team.
- Everyone seems sensitive, including you.
- Some of your team members are showing signs of burnout, such as downing coffee like water, not getting enough sleep, working long hours, and breaking down crying.
- You have really smart people on your team, but they are not bringing their best, A-game ideas.
- The project progress is slowing down.

> **Know Your Team Members!**
>
> I once was working on launching a Web site for a huge corporation. Today that sounds ordinary, but in the late 1990s, not a lot of people had the knowledge needed to get a great site up and running.
>
> I asked a placement agency to find an intern, someone who could spell-check content as we aggressively designed and threw up hundreds of pages for our new site. Alex, who the agency sent, was fine at spell-checking, but every so often I'd walk by his desk and he'd excitedly show me the new thing he'd figured out—how to fix problems with images and text that our technical people were struggling with.
>
> It was clear that Alex was not born to spell-check.
>
> I talked to one of the engineering managers, showed him the work Alex had done, and quickly transferred him to their department so he could work on the kinds of challenges that engaged him, where his particular skills were desperately needed. The other department had no funding for an intern, but I was doing what was best for the overall project, not just my part of the project.

## 3. What will happen if I do nothing?

You may get through this project, but it will get more painful as it goes along, and you will end up dragging each team member across the finish line.

You will waste the excellent talent you have on this project by not using the people to the best of their ability. A good project, no matter how important, is not more important than each individual project team member. The unhappy reality is that most projects are full-time jobs for team members. If you only think of your team members in terms of what they can provide for the existing project schedule, you won't be using your team to its full capacity.

All your excellent plans will be for nothing if your team ends up unmotivated, uninspired, and uncommitted, because people with no passion have a *really* hard time meeting project objectives.

## 4. Solution

You know you need to balance cost, schedule, and scope for your project. Letting any one of those factors get out of control guarantees failure. In the same way, you can't manage the execution of your project plan and expect all to go well all the time (see Figure 8.1). Success of your project depends on you to:

1. Execute your project plan
2. Develop and guide your project team to maximum effectiveness
3. Help individual team members develop their full potential
4. Engage all team members and provide them appropriate levels of autonomy

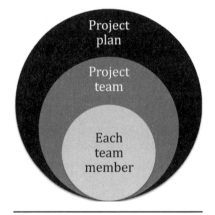

**Figure 8.1**

## 5. What should I do?

As the project manager, it is tempting to focus entirely on the project plan. Successful execution of your project plan is entirely dependent on your project team—and, your project team is dependent on each team member! If you focus only on execution of your plan, and neglect the project team and each individual member, your project will experience problems. For example, if your team is working well together except for one person, who might be lacking motivation and missing deadlines, then the whole team will start having trouble, and your project success may be in jeopardy. Here are your responsibilities in balancing individual and team needs with overall project plan execution:

### 5(a) Execute the project plan

All members of the project team must thoroughly understand the reason the project is being undertaken, to make the best decisions for the project. Communicating this information to your team is your responsibility.

- All of your team members thoroughly understand the objectives of the project, and what success looks like.
- You've clearly communicated project schedules, resource constraints, quality standards, risks and issues, and your team understands them.
- You manage, update, communicate, and make available a detailed project plan with all critical milestones.

### 5(b) Develop and guide the project team

It doesn't matter if your project team members don't report to you. It's your responsibility to ensure that they have all the tools they need to be successful on your project.

How are they going to work together? This can be as formal as establishing policies and procedures, or as informal as agreeing to daily stand-up meetings to cover status and issues. However you do it, you need to come to an agreement with your team.

What will be the methodology you use on the project? Setting expectations about what will happen when, and talking through any concerns about those choices, will help minimize unpleasant surprises. It is absolutely critical to truly lead the team, versus simply *managing the schedule*. You need to truly *own* the following issues and challenges, along with the overall results that the team produces.

- Do project team members clearly understand their responsibilities?
- You are responsible for ensuring that project resources are available, including team member skills and training, to help the team accomplish project objectives.
- You owe it to your team to make sure that you are competent as a project manager and available to them.
- Encourage dialogue and debate. If everyone immediately agrees on a course of action, that's a strong sign that there is not complete understanding.
- Do not forget to provide regular, constructive feedback on your team's performance. Do not get hung up by the fact that they may each have their own managers; they need to hear from you how they're doing, and where they can improve.

You want team members to share ideas with each other and establish high levels of innovation and creativity. You also want your team to be committed to the work they do and the promises they make. A highly functional team shares information freely, and team members are consistently open and honest with each other.

Part of your job as the project manager is to position yourself as the intermediary between your project team and the rest of the organization. You report on your team's successes and failures—you represent your team to management. At the same time, you also filter the requests of management down to your project team. You are a like a car's *shock absorber*. You absorb shocks and bumps so your team doesn't have to.

You communicate clearly with your team about management expectations, without adding to their stress. Your job is to help teams stay focused, accomplish goals, and help your people feel rewarded for their hard work.

The best teams invest a tremendous amount of time and effort exploring, shaping, and agreeing on a purpose that belongs to them both collectively and individually. They translate their purpose into specific performance goals, such as getting a product launched in a shorter time. If a team fails to establish specific performance goals or if those goals do not relate directly to the team's overall purpose, team members become confused, pull apart, and revert to mediocre performance. But when purposes and goals build on one another and are combined with team commitment, they become a powerful engine of performance.

### 5(c) Help each team member reach his or her potential

- Taking care of the group as a whole isn't enough. You need to get to know each team member, find out what drives them, and figure out how to best utilize them for the greater good of the project.
- Make sure that you spend some one-on-one time with each member of your group: identify their strengths and weaknesses, their needs, and special skills they can bring to the group.
- Work out plans with each team member on how they can accomplish their individual goals while delivering on the project objectives. Find out what is important to them—what gets them excited about their work.
- For each person, find out how independent and experienced they are. Make sure that they have the right level of competence for how you plan to manage the project. If you will give each team member lots of latitude in how they solve problems in their area, do they have the experience and emotional intelligence to handle that responsibility well?
- Make sure each person has the skills to perform his or her role successfully.
- Don't forget to praise and reward each individual for his or her contribution to the overall team and the success of the project.
- Help define each person's role within the group, and agree on the tasks they are responsible for.
- If any project team members seem to lag behind, coach them until they are back on track.
- Is each project team member committed to the delivery dates?

It is easy to forget that project managers are more managers of people than they are managers of technology. If you manage the people correctly, the people will manage the technology.

You need to manage your individual team members effectively in order to prevent burnout. In some environments, the customer will always be there with new demands and priorities that require you to drop everything else and fix immediately.

It's your job to manage these demands, not to just acquiesce and keep pushing your team members, but to present trade-offs to the customer. Showing the value of the current path, demonstrating the impact the change will have, and helping the client make a more informed decision. The result is a more engaged client or customer, who gains more satisfaction from feeling more in control of the output. At the same time, your team members are also more engaged.

### 5(d) Engage your team members and provide autonomy

The best way to motivate team members is to respect them, give them autonomy, and tie them to a strong purpose. It used to be that project managers believed that you needed to crack the whip over team members, that if you gave them any leeway they would slack off and surf their favorite sports websites.

Now, we know better. Being focused and excited by your work comes naturally to most people. Creativity is widely distributed on your project team. People want to be proud of their work. People will seek responsibility, if you let them.

If you think your team is mediocre, and needs your leadership to be successful, trust me, they will rise to the occasion and give you mediocre work. If you want your folks to surprise you with amazing work, you need to engage them.

When you let your team members figure out how to solve a problem, and how to work together, it can have a powerful effect on individual performance and attitude. Autonomy leads to higher productivity, less burnout, and more enjoyment of work.

Make an effort to see issues from your team member's point of view. You provide the problem, and listen to find the answer. Let your team figure out the best solution.

Involve people in goal setting. Employees have greater commitment to goals that *they* helped create, making individuals feel more engaged. If you create a goal for someone, it will be less aggressive than the goal he or she chooses, as people like to stretch their skills and do work they can be proud of. They will do everything they can to meet this goal.

Autonomy creates motivated, happy employees. If you need your team to be creative and do problem solving, why not get into the habit of engaging them on that level?

*Autonomy on steroids*

So you know you need to deliver on your project. How can you integrate team member's own ideas and desires into that reality?

People work better when they're working on something they are passionate about. Take for example, Atlassian, a company that makes tools for software developers. Once each quarter, the company sets aside an entire day when its engineers can work on any software problem they want, as long as it's something outside of their regular job. It works like this: on Thursday afternoon, they begin working on building code or designing a new idea. In 24 hours, on Friday afternoon, they present the results to the rest of the organization. They began calling these *FedEx Days*— as something that absolutely, positively had to be delivered overnight. In fact, many workers got so caught up in their projects that they worked through the night to get them done!

These 24 hour bursts of freedom and creativity resulted in fixes for some long-standing problems, and some new products which ultimately generated more revenue for the company. Lots of other companies have taken on a similar *hackathon* concept. Team members look forward to the day for months, thinking about what projects they can do on their own, and the result is high energy, high productivity, and a lot of joy.

How can you make this work on your project? Set aside an entire day where employees can work on anything they choose, however they want, with whomever they'd like. Make sure they have the tools and resources they need. However, impose just one rule: people must deliver something, whether a prototype, new idea, or better process design on the following day.

### Autonomy on crack

Some companies, after experimenting with the once-per-quarter freedom day, decide that they want to get more traction in team-member-led initiatives, so they have extended the idea to *20 percent time*. They offer one day per week to employees to allow them to work on whatever is important to them. Sometimes that is fixing bugs in existing products; sometimes it is creating something new. Devoting this much time to autonomous development means that each hackathon isn't a one-off event, but a weekly commitment. It means that a new idea can be developed over time and brought to fruition.

People are more efficient with their 20 percent time than they are with their *normal* time. Given a gift of autonomy, you don't want to waste it and risk it being taken away!

Organizations like the Mayo Clinic, Google, and 3M offer 20 percent time to their employees, and they have found less turnover, more meaningful work, and lower burnout.

### What's the right autonomy level for your team?

You can grant your team members a lot of autonomy, but this doesn't mean abdicating project leadership. Your project and your team need your strong leadership to be effective.

It is up to you how far you want to go with giving your project team members autonomy. Just remember that if your team is only operating under your direction, they can only be as smart as you are.

As wonderful as you are, you can't think of everything. Your company hired smart people for a reason! Here are some things to think about in figuring out how much freedom your team members should have and how much you may want to grant going forward:

- Are people on your team able to make decisions by themselves and adapt to changing situations, or do they need to come to you for everything?
- Do team members figure out how to solve their own problems?
- Can your team pick the standards and practices for themselves that better allow them to produce the right solution?
- Can your team split up and share the work as it chooses?
- Do training, holiday, and vacation time get cancelled when the project falls behind schedule?
- Can team members *bump* someone, choosing who is on or off the team?
- Does your team maintain a high rate of productivity without being overworked?

Like anything else with project management, different levels of autonomy work for different projects and different teams in different companies. You can experiment and find out what works well for your team. You may be surprised at what great results your team can deliver!

## References

Allen, D. *Getting Things Done: The Art of Stress-Free Productivity*. New York, NY: Penguin Books, 2002.

Berra, Y. November 17, 2010. "Quote by Yogi Berra." http://thinkexist.com/quotations/meetings

Bopp, M. A., Bing, D. A., and Trammell, S. F. *Agile Career Development: Lessons and Approaches from IBM*. Crawfordsville, IN: IBM Press, 2010.

Collins, J. *Good to Great: Why Some Companies Make the Leap... and Others Don't*, New York, NY: Harper Business, 2001.

Covey, S. *The Seven Habits of Highly Effective People*. New York, NY: Free Press, 1989.

Crenshaw, D. *The Myth of Multitasking: How "Doing It All" Gets Nothing Done*. San Francisco, CA: Jossey-Bass, 2008.

Golembiewski, R.T. *Handbook of Organizational Consultation*. 2nd ed., revised and expanded. Public Administration and Public Policy. Boca Raton, FL: CRC Press, 2000.

Katsenbach, J. R., and Smith, D. K. (March 1993), "The Discipline of Teams." *Harvard Business Review*.

Kerzner, H. *Project Management Best Practices: Achieving Global Excellence*. Hoboken, NJ: John Wiley & Sons, 2006.

Kirk, J. T. November 17, 2010. "Quote by Captain James T. Kirk." http://www.quotesdaddy.com/quote/694399/james-t-kirk/a-meeting-is-an-event-where-minutes-are-taken-and

Kowalski, M. September 27, 2010. "Multitasking: An Effective Habit Or a Productivity Killer?" *bnet - The CBS Interactive Business Network. CBS, Daily Record and the Kansas City Daily News-Press*. http://findarticles.com/p/articles/mi_qn4181/is_20051129/ai_n15871071

Medina, J. *Brain Rules: 12 Principles for surviving and thriving at work, home, and school*. Seattle, WA: Pear Press, 2008.

Mediratta, B. October 21, 2007. "The Google Way: Give Engineers Room." *The New York Times*. http://www.nytimes.com/2007/10/21/jobs/21pre.html?ex=1350619200&en=f4b2cd9d18f162bb&ei=5124&partner=permalink&exprod=permalink

Odell, J. September 27, 2010. "Distributed Computing Architecture/e-Business Advisory Service Executive Report." *The Cutter Consortium*. http://www.bioteams.com/Cutter00-04%20ExecRpt.pdf

Pink, D. *Drive: The Surprising Truth About What Motivates Us*. New York: Riverhead, 2009.

Rees, F. *How to Lead Work Teams: Facilitation Skills*. San Francisco, CA: John Wiley & Sons, 2001.

Taylor, L. November 17, 2010. "Make Meetings Matter." *Fast Company*. http://www.fastcompany.com/partners/gotomeeting/articles/20060901/lead.html

Tzu, Sun. *The Art of War, Shambala Classics*. Cleary, T. (Trans.). Boston, MA: Shambala, 2005. 20.

Zeigarnik, B.V. (1967). On finished and unfinished tasks. *A Sourcebook of Gestalt Psychology*. New York, NY: Humanities Press, 1967.

# 9

# MANAGING RISKS

## 9.1 I didn't realize what could happen if this project fails.

By Andy Jordan

## 1. Problem

You happily took control of the project at the beginning and your confidence built steadily as the plan was developed, the team started to come together as a single unit, and the work started. That seems like a long time ago. You just had a meeting with the project sponsor, who spelled out how critical the project is to the company's success. If this project fails, the company could be in *serious* trouble. Suddenly, you don't feel so confident that your risk management has considered the severity of that impact.

## 2. Warning Signs

This problem can be easy to miss. You need to look past any preconceived ideas that you may have about the importance of the project, and pay attention to the information that you are getting from any of the following situations:

- Stakeholders seem more interested in the progress of your project than you would expect.
- When you communicate what you believe to be a slight delay, the response is as if the world is ending.
- Stakeholders keep checking up on you.

### What Do You Mean, "We're All Doomed"?

Fred's jaw almost hit the floor. He had walked into the sponsor's office with his status update on the project he was managing and reported that things were going fairly well. There was a minor technical issue that had caused some problems, but the team was sure that they could figure it out.

The sponsor had turned as white as a sheet. He put his head in his hands and said, "We're doomed, we're all doomed!" Fred almost laughed, but the sponsor didn't look like he was joking. Fred tried to reassure the sponsor that it was just a minor issue and that he knew that the team would get through it.

The sponsor's response was almost shouted: "Don't you get it? If this project fails, the whole company will go under. We'll all be unemployed."

Fred was shocked; he didn't know what to say. This was just a minor product improvement project, wasn't it?

- Everyone in the organization seems to know that you are running the project.

## 3. What will happen if I do nothing?

Well, quite possibly nothing will happen if you do nothing. The project may continue on and be successful, and you end up wondering what the fuss was about. On the other hand, the company could be in serious trouble; the fact that you have a failed project could be the least of your problems. If you don't take any action once having learned the implications of project failure, then you are rolling the dice that nothing will go wrong.

You won't have as good a handle on the risks, and the impact that they might have, as you should, and that's not a good position to be in. Do you want to wager your career, and possibly your employer's survival, on things not going wrong?

## 4. Solution

When you are made aware of the fact that the implications of a failed project are much more severe than you thought, the first natural thing to do is to revisit your schedule, budget, scope, etc., and make sure that the plan is realistic and achievable. There's nothing wrong with that; it's a sensible precaution, but the area that requires your biggest focus is the project *risks*. You determined your risk response strategy (accept, mitigate, transfer, eliminate for negative risks) based on your understanding of the project. That understanding has now changed, and there needs to be a review of the risk management strategy to determine:

1. Does the management plan for existing risks have to change?
2. Are there additional risks that need to be considered and managed?
3. Is the overall project approach still appropriate?

## 5. What should I do?

Once you are sure that you fully understand the implications of a failed project, you need to engage your core team to review the project. Replanning is covered in depth in Chapter 7: Planning. In this chapter, the focus is on risk elements. Before we start, let's look at some risk basics.

When you plan a project, you need to identify as many risks as possible. You don't want to have any surprises. However, if you aren't able to actively manage all of those risks, you will never get anything else done. Therefore, you need to review the risks in order to determine which ones are the most significant.

Risk assessment is usually done by considering the likelihood of the risk occurring and the impact to the project if it does occur. This gives us a score from which to determine the biggest risks—the ones that require management. We then apply a risk management strategy to those risks. While there are positive and negative risks, we usually focus on negative risks, where the strategies are:

- **Accept**: Recognize that this is a risk, but don't do anything (either because nothing can be done, or because the cost in time or money would be prohibitively expensive).

- **Mitigate**: Work to reduce the likelihood of the risk occurring, the impact on the project if the risk does occur, or both.
- **Transfer**: Move the risk on to someone else; usually this only works for financial elements of risk. Insurance is an example of this strategy.
- **Eliminate**: Completely remove the risk from the project. Usually this requires a change to the way that the project will be undertaken.

We then monitor these risks, and the others that we determined to passively manage and adjust our strategies where necessary. Wherever possible we also build in a *contingency plan*, which is a course of action to take in the event that the risk becomes real.

So, now back to assessing the risk of the situation at hand.

### 5(a) Review the risk management plan

When you learn that the implications of a failed project are much more severe than you first thought, that can cause a change in each of your risks. When we scored risks, we considered the likelihood of the risk occurring and the impact. The likelihood of the risk occurring probably hasn't changed (although recognize that team members, including you, are under more pressure now so may be more prone to make mistakes), but the impact definitely has the potential to have changed. Furthermore, the steps that you are taking to manage the risk may need to change.

You need to consider every single risk in your plan (not just the ones that you are actively managing) and ask the following questions:

- If this risk occurs, is the impact still the same, or has it changed?
- Is the mitigation strategy that we are executing still appropriate?
- Is our contingency now sufficient to address the situation that we will face if the risk becomes reality?

Inevitably, you will identify a number of changes that need to be made to respond to this new awareness of what will happen in the worst case scenario:

- Risks that you were previously monitoring will now need to be actively managed with a strategy and contingency.
- Risk management approaches for some risks will need to be stepped up and the strategy may need to change. Risks that previously could be accepted may now need mitigation or elimination.

An example from our personal lives may serve as an illustration. Car insurance is an example of risk transfer; we transfer the financial risk of owning and driving a car to someone else, and the insurance company puts a price on the risk. If an 18-year-old driver changes their car from a 4-cylinder, front wheel drive, four-door sedan to a 12-cylinder supercar, they can expect the insurance company to charge more because the risk has increased. That is essentially the analysis that we are doing here: pricing and managing the risk.

### 5(b) Consider additional risks

It is almost certain that the implications of project failure are causing you additional risks that you did not previously consider. You need to make sure that all risks are identified and analyzed using the same process as at the start of the project. These new risks then need to be considered alongside the existing risks that you analyzed at first, until you have a comprehensive list of:

- The risks that now exist on your project
- The severity of the risk (likelihood and impact)
- The management and contingency that can be applied to each risk
- The owner and review schedule for each risk

Just like at the start of the project you need to decide which risks are going to be actively managed, but the likelihood is that you now have additional, and more significant risks that need to be actively managed than previously. At a minimum, that will require additional resource effort dedicated to risk management and an increase in overall project contingency (money and time), at worst, you may need to change the project, and that's covered next.

### 5(c) Review project approach

All projects have a number of different ways that they can be executed. The plan you built was based on the overall project budget, schedule, scope, and such. But now that has changed. The risks are more severe than you thought, which can have a tremendous impact on you. We have already seen that the budget and scope are likely to change (and if one can't move, other constraints have to allow for that). As we need to spend more time and effort managing risks, we also need to add contingency plans. However, it is also possible that we have to fundamentally alter what we are doing.

Suppose, for example, that we had two alternative approaches to completing the project:

1. An approach that would deliver the project on time and budget, but where there was a 10 percent chance that the deliverables would not work properly.
2. An approach that would result in a 15 percent cost overrun, and 10 percent delay in the schedule, but only a 2 percent chance that the deliverables wouldn't work properly.

It would be perfectly logical to choose Option (1) on most projects, but now that we know that the implications of failure are great, Option (2) is looking like a better bet!

Once you have completed all of your risk analysis, you will need to present the updated plan to your stakeholders for review and approval. You should also have discussions with your sponsor and customer, in particular, to understand how the implications of failure were not understood at the outset. Did you make a mistake or did they try to *protect* you from the potential implications if things went wrong. In that case, the sponsor may have been trying to help you, but the impact has been significant.

# 9.2 Problems keep popping up that I did not expect.

## By Peter D. Carothers

## 1. Problem

Unforeseen events are part of project management. But constant buffeting of your project by unanticipated events suggests that you have a problem. Unless you are stepping back to look at the big picture, and considering all that *could* impact your project, you may get trapped into constantly reacting to the unexpected events, rather than leading your project.

## 2. Warning Signs

This is a fairly easy problem to recognize and be aware of:

- Issues you did not anticipate keep popping up on your project.
- You spend most of your time in crisis management mode, reacting to *fires* rather than proactively managing your project.

## 3. What will happen if I do nothing?

If you don't address this problem, unexpected problems will continue to arise, taking more and more time away from managing the project. This is likely to result in delays and cost overruns, and may put the entire project at risk of failure. Additionally, if the team sees problems arising all of the time, they will become dispirited and their effectiveness will be reduced.

## 4. Solution

As a project manager, your fundamental responsibility is to lead your project to a successful conclusion. To accomplish this, you will find the demands on your time fall into a few, basic categories of responsibility:

### No Time for Planning, We Need to Start Now!

Does your workplace value working hard over working smart? Have they lost the difference between working on what's important rather than what's urgent? As a project manager, it will be your responsibility to resist that culture and establish professional practices on your projects.

*We were working so hard we never saw that coming.*

Does this work culture sound familiar? Head down on the task at hand, not looking ahead. No time for planning, too much work to do? As a leader of your project, your team looks to you to set the agenda, map the road ahead, and scan for trouble.

*I'll plan once these fires are out.*

Are you an adrenalin junky who gets satisfaction from the chaos of the battlefield? Are you most comfortable *being busy* rather than proactive? Is everything you do treated as though it is already late or on your critical path? Do you contribute to a culture that favors action over forethought? Even if you excel under this pressure, this is likely holding you back as a PM.

*Take a timeout.*

Look back at your most recent project. How many adverse events occurred that caught you off guard? What was their impact on your final deliverable? How many could have been avoided, or their impact minimized with greater attention to *what if* forethought and planning? What can you change in your behavior to lead your projects more proactively?

*Fight back!*

Short-term thinking rarely delivers a project on time and within budget. It is your job to prepare your project for success, and that requires dedication to *planning time*. Regardless of your company culture or your own comfort zone, you need to build that time into your day to succeed as a project manager.

- Defining the objective and the path to achieve it
- Leading your team along that path, and proactively avoiding pitfalls and events which may jeopardize that objective (and a successful project outcome)
- Reactively applying the skills of your discipline to put out the fires that inevitably arise, which place your objectives in peril

You need to ensure that you have as much control as possible over the project, and particularly around unexpected events. To be successful, project managers need to master three distinct areas of action:

1. **Analysis:** objective knowledge of yourself, your project, and the environment in which you work will allow you to assess your project's overall risk profile.
2. **Preparation:** proactive attention to communication, project planning, and building strategic relationships.
3. **Decisiveness:** responding to risk and change events with confidence.

## 5. What should I do?

No one expects you to control the future, but how you prepare for and manage the unexpected will likely determine your success as a project manager. Nothing will prepare you better than understanding the bigger picture surrounding your project. Armed with analysis, we can move to the proactive steps to prepare for the unexpected, so we are poised to decisively lead during change events.

### 5(a) Analysis of three critical elements

Before we can fix anything, we need to understand the cards we have been dealt. First, we must determine what our baseline or starting point is in three areas.

*Know thyself.*

Having a realistic view of your own strengths and weaknesses is invaluable as a project manager. Where have you had the most practical experience, and where do you lack experience? Look back over your recent performance reviews or peer evaluations. Step back and give yourself an objective appraisal of your strengths and weaknesses as a project manager. Review any assessment tests you have taken, or consider taking assessments online to help in your self-evaluation. Once you have an objective picture, consider asking a trusted mentor or peer to corroborate your assessment. An objective self-evaluation is an essential first step to developing a plan to address gaps or weaknesses in your skill sets, and will inform your approach to handling risk for your projects.

Areas of inquiry:

- Am I an effective communicator?
- Am I an effective problem solver?
- Am I an effective planner?
- How is my decision making and judgment accomplished?

- How do I rate my ability to lead in each of the project phases of initiation, planning, execution, monitoring and control, and closure?
- How are my skills as a leader?
- How am I perceived by others?

### *Know your client, stakeholders, and environment*

Now let's take a look at factors influencing your project. It is essential to assess your client's expectations and tolerance for risk. This will allow you to determine if your project can achieve that standard within constraints. What environmental factors, such as maturity of company processes, or organizational structures, might influence your project? Is your client relationship a true partnership? Who has *approval* authority? How vulnerable is your project to outside influences?

Areas of inquiry:

- What is your client's tolerance for risk (at what threshold are they uncomfortable with more risk)?
- What are your client's hot buttons and their *real* success criteria?
- What outside forces might impact your project?
- What is the culture of your company and that of your client?
- What support structures can you rely on—for example, the project management office (PMO), project management information system (PMIS), or mentors?
- What is the strength of your client relationships and how good are they?
- Who owns sign-off on deliverables?

### *Know your project*

Now let's take a look at your project to assess the general complexity, risk factors, and your confidence in your ability to meet project objectives within current constraints. Has this project been done before? Do you have the right people? Are the success criteria defined and objectively measurable? What are the results of failure? (A human heart transplant carries far more risk than replacing a server.) What is the contract type, and how does it limit your options? Does the overall risk quotient for your project warrant an increase to your management reserve (a manager's contingency fund to address unknowns)?

Areas of inquiry:

- How well defined are your objectives?
- What is the degree of complexity for the endeavor?
- Has the objective been done before?
- What are the impacts of failure?
- Considering the triple constraint of cost, schedule and scope, do you realistically have sufficient resources to meet objectives?
- How suited is your team to the tasks?
- Based on your contract type, what happens in event of budget or schedule overruns?

- Is scope of work negotiable?
- How much funding is allocated for a *management reserve* (a cash reserve to apply towards unexpected costs)?

### 5(b) Be prepared

Armed with a thorough understanding of these factors, we can now invest proactive efforts to be ready for contingencies. We can't eliminate the unexpected, but we can be ready for it.

#### *Communication to control risk*

Too often the role of an effective communication plan for your project is ignored as an essential component of minimizing risk on projects. The concise and predictable sharing of project information among project team members and stakeholders will build common purpose, set common expectations, facilitate collaboration, and share project risk across all parties. An effective communication plan will:

- Define your team's *culture* of shared responsibility in managing project risk
- Establish communication channels and protocols for reporting potential risk events
- Establish expectations for participation, interaction, and collective responsibility concerning risk
- Share risk decision making with sponsor with sign-offs on risk planning and event responses

#### *Preparing for unknowns: Fundamentals of risk management*

A comprehensive project management plan includes a strategy and tactics to manage project risk. Preparation is your best defense in managing unanticipated events. You need a basic plan to:

- Guide your actions on how you will handle risk throughout the project—this is your plan that defines the how and when of steps below.
- Identify potential risks—this is the process of listing potential risks. A risk breakdown structure (see Figure 9.1) can serve as a framework and checklist when considering risks to your project. Tailor your own RBS to the unique demands of your project, then walk through each category and itemize potential risks to your project.
- Prioritize risks for further planning—each risk can be plotted in context to its probability of occurrence and its potential impact on your project. Since there are diminishing returns to trying to address absolutely every potential risk, use a probability-impact grid (see Figure 9.2) to help identify priority risk events. Be sure to consider your client's *risk tolerance* when determining what risk events are *actionable*. Items to the right and upper right deserve priority consideration in prioritizing risk.
- Prepare responses to risks you identified above your risk tolerance threshold—typically those found to be *high* and *moderate* in your probability-

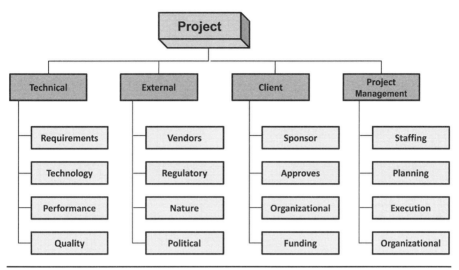

**Figure 9.1**

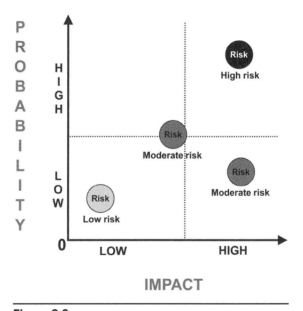

**Figure 9.2**

impact assessment (see Figure 9.3). Prepare a risk response defining your action plan to remediate each risk.

- Devise the methods you will use to monitor your project for risks and changes throughout your project's life cycle—set calendar dates and project milestone triggers for risk reviews. Have a protocol for evaluating new risk events as they are identified. Remember, managing risk is an ongoing project management activity throughout your project.

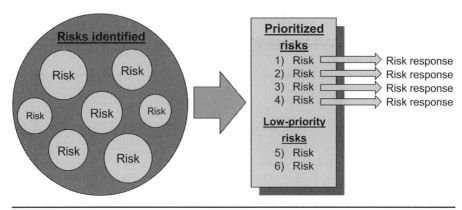

**Figure 9.3**

*Leveraging relationships*

Carefully cultivate relationships with your stakeholders before you find yourself in a sticky situation. Treat your relationships like bank accounts; you need to make deposits to be able to make withdrawals at a later date. Invest in them deliberately before you need them; this includes your team, your sponsor, your boss, and your mentors.

With your clients, attempt to cultivate a climate of partnership to achieve a common goal. Build trust with honest and frequent communication. Set expectations, and understand theirs. Engage sponsors in sign offs of critical planning milestones and consensus in response to change events.

Leverage existing tools or develop your own support processes and solutions. If your organization is unwilling or unable to do so, build your own PMIS, which is an archive of past project artifacts such as performance data and documents, from your own projects and experiences. Create your own templates like risk registries to use on future projects. Create your own lessons-learned process to drive your own continuous improvement. Empower yourself to control your own success.

Create your own support network. Invite peers whom you respect to share their experiences. Seek out mentors and solicit their advice. That established network will be invaluable if you need counsel during a crisis.

The more work that you can do up front to strengthen the relationships on your project, the less likely you are to be exposed to nasty surprises, and the better able you will be to call on your team and stakeholders to address the issue.

### 5(c) Decisive reactions to change

When an event crops up that has the potential to impact your project, take immediate action. Consult your action plan. Check if this event is in your list of anticipated risks (your risk registry). If so, review your response plans, adjust them as appropriate, and implement your corrective actions.

Is this a new risk event you did not anticipate? Analyze its potential impact to schedule, cost, project scope, and quality? What options exist, and what is your best course of action? Other questions to ask are:

- Can we ignore it? Depending on the nature of the risk, it might reasonably be ignored if it does not meet risk tolerance thresholds.
- Can we negotiate with sponsors to recast it as a non-risk or change order? Treating it outside of existing scope can save your schedule and budget.
- Can we make risk someone else's responsibility? Don't forget this does not make the risk go away, just who has to deal with it.
- Finally, do we need to take corrective action to address the risk? Bring in your team and support network to devise the best solution and then implement it.

Communicate! Enlist your team in planning actions and responding to risk events, and keep stakeholders informed.

# 9.3 The importance of my project changed.

## By Aaron Porter

## 1. Problem

You just found out that the importance of your project has changed. You don't have a lot of detail about what has changed or what the impact of the change is. All you know is that there has been a shift in the priority of your project in relation to other projects, and you need to determine the most appropriate way to respond.

## 2. Warning Signs

Interest in your project increasing or decreasing over time is not a guarantee that the importance of your project is changing. It is likely that interest in your project will fluctuate over time. This could be due to factors such as hitting a busy season, or due to having demonstrated your competence and built trust. You don't want to be paranoid, but you don't want to be caught off guard, either. Below are a few signs that your project may be becoming more important:

- You are asked for more frequent status updates.
- You are asked to provide more detailed reports.

### I'm Sorry, Did You Say Project B?

You take a deep breath and release it slowly, quietly, hoping nobody will notice. You spent the better part of the past week preparing your presentation for Project A, with your sponsor calling you every other day to make sure you would have it done on time and reminding you how important it is to make a good impression in the meeting. And then—they skipped Project A.

They didn't ignore it at least. They did acknowledge you and your scheduled time on the agenda, and then told you that they would not need your updates for Project A this month. You know, the one everyone has been talking about for the past six months. Instead, they want you to talk about Project B, your backburner project that you haven't touched in two weeks, which nobody has asked about in three months, and that you are not prepared to discuss in depth.

"Where is Project B?"

"How long until Project B is done?"

"Why haven't you been making progress?"

Your sponsor for Project A looks as frustrated as you feel. Amidst the many thoughts and expletives rushing through your mind, one question rises to the surface, "What changed?"

- You are asked for more meetings.
- You are asked to invite more people to meetings who are not part of the project team.
- Managers and executives previously uninvolved in your project begin showing increased interest.

These could be few signs that your project may be becoming less important:

- The project schedule is slipping due to resources splitting time with other work.
- Your resources are pulled for other projects (personnel, financial, or material).
- You are asked to place work on hold.
- You are rushed through your status updates, or passed over during group meetings.

## 3. What will happen if I do nothing?

Doing nothing is an option. It is not always the best option, and you should not choose to ignore change without understanding what will happen if you do. But it is still an option. Change, in some form, is regularly ignored by just about everyone, everywhere; ignoring change does not mean that your project is destined to fail. But, do yourself a favor—before you choose to ignore change, take a little time to understand the impact. This way you can explain your decision, when asked, and others won't think that you are just not paying attention.

At the same time, not responding to change can be one of the worst choices you can make. You may only need to do something minor, but, you may need to make significant changes to your project. Whether or not the change can make or break your project, you need to understand the impact the change will have on your project to determine whether or not doing nothing is a viable option.

## 4. Solution

While there are many reasons that a project can change in importance, there are really only two ways that the importance of your project can change. Your project can become more or less important; it is the degree of importance that should have the greatest impact on your response(s). Regardless of which direction your project takes, there is some basic discovery you need to perform before you can determine the best course of action.

1. Discover the degree of change in importance
2. Discover what has changed and why
3. Discover how your stakeholders are affected
4. Discover how project scope is affected
5. Determine how to respond

## 5. What should I do?

You need to start with the understanding that the purpose of your project is to support the business. If the outcome of your project is either no longer desired by the business, or suddenly becomes critical, there is a reason for the importance of your project to change. In any case, it is your responsibility to determine the best way to respond to the change in support of business objectives and not a personal agenda.

### 5(a) Discover the degree of change in importance

Warning signs can be misleading. This is due, in part, to the emotional nature of people. Some people panic at the smallest change, and others sit calmly while things crash down around them. Once it is clear that the importance of your project is changing, or has changed, figure out the degree of change.

You should work with your sponsor to determine how much the importance of your project has changed. They should be able to provide you with the details about external factors affecting the importance of your project. If the change is minor, there may be little to do. If the change is major, there may be nothing you can do, or you may spend several long days locked away with your team coming up with an appropriate response. Understanding the degree of change is a necessary part of determining how to respond.

### 5(b) Discover what has changed and why

If the importance of your project has changed, chances are the importance of at least one other project has changed; changes rarely occur in a vacuum. As you continue to work with your sponsor, find out what other projects have changed in importance and how they changed in relation to yours. You should also find out if it is your whole project that has become more or less important, or if it is the priority of specific deliverables that changed.

Understanding why the importance of your project has changed is equally important. Does your project need to be completed before a new law goes into effect, or the scope of the project will change? Did your biggest competitor just announce a new release that threatens your company's market share? Did someone uncover a critical requirement that was initially overlooked, which will delay the project? Is there an internal power struggle over resources resulting in false inflation or deflation of your project's importance in order to shift resources? Understanding what changed, and why, is the next step in determining the best strategy for responding to the change.

### 5(c) Discover how your stakeholders are affected

You might ask yourself what stakeholders have to do with the importance of project changes, and why you need to understand how they are impacted. Stakeholders can be a double-edged sword. They both drive, and are impacted by, changes to the importance of your project. If one has not already been completed, you need to conduct a *stakeholder analysis*. There are two key pieces of information you need to know that the stakeholder analysis should tell you about your stakeholders: (1) their interest in your project, and (2) their interest in other projects. If your project became less important as a result of conflicting stakeholder interests, you hopefully discovered that when working with your sponsor. Your sponsor should be your champion in that battle.

On the same project, you may also have a stakeholder that needs the project to complete successfully, and on time, in order to meet his or her objectives. In this case, you have a stakeholder who may be upset by your project becoming less important, and that stakeholder may be willing to work to protect the interests of the project, assuming those interests are also in line with the interests of the business. A thorough understanding of your project champions and detractors can also guide you in preparing your response to the change.

### 5(d) Discover how project scope is affected

Changes in project importance don't always involve changes in project scope. You may or may not need to change your work plan or schedule. Take what you have discovered, working with your sponsor, and go through a change management review. You may find that nothing needs to change, from a project perspective, but there may be plenty of work at the sponsor level to protect the project and allow it to keep running smoothly. You may also find that you need to crash the schedule, eliminate project work, or increase the scope of the project, among other things.

One consideration that you may not agree with is that even if there is the potential for scope change from a change in project importance, you may not want to act on it immediately. There may be other factors external to the project that your sponsor may want to address in order to protect the integrity of the project. Let your sponsor make the decision about whether to make changes external or internal to the project, or both. Regardless, make sure you have effective change management in place, so that you can quickly and appropriately respond to scope changes should the need arise.

### 5(e) Determine how to respond

Everything you have been doing up to this point has been part of determining how to respond to your project's change in importance. Now that you understand the degree of change, what changed and why, who was affected, and the level to which project scope was affected, you are in a better position to answer the question, "Is doing nothing in response to the change a viable option?" and to develop alternative responses. A few responses that you might consider are:

- *Terminate the project:* Is the impact significant enough that the project cannot recover, or does the project no longer support business objectives?
- *Enhanced Marketing efforts:* Do you need to do more to make the benefits of the project known and understood?
- *Reality check:* Is the change in importance artificial and making other projects either more or less important than they should be? You should work with the sponsor to determine this and let the sponsor determine how to continue.

Just as you wouldn't want someone else to artificially deflate the importance of your project, don't create circumstances to artificially inflate the importance of your project. Aside from possible ethical and legal issues, the truth will eventually come out and could damage your credibility. If there is a good reason for your project to become less important, fighting against the change reflects poorly on you and can negatively impact the company.

In the end, you are not alone. You have the project sponsor, stakeholders, and your team to support you as you work together to determine the best response to the change in your project's importance.

# 9.4 My project is too dependent on a few key people.

### By J. Chris White

## 1. Problem

You have a team of people assigned to the project, but you are finding that the tasks are not balanced between them. Instead, you have a few experts whom you are reliant on for the vast majority of your tasks, and they always seem to be assigned to the critical tasks that can't slip. You are really worried that if you lose one of those resources for any length of time, your project will be in serious trouble.

## 2. Warning Signs

There are a number of things you can look for that may indicate that you have this problem on your project:

- Progress slows down dramatically when certain resources are not available.
- Many milestone approvals involve the same resources.
- People are constantly asking, "Where's so-and-so? I have a question."
- The same names keep appearing on the project plan resource assignments.
- You strongly believe the project will fall short of its objectives if certain resources are pulled away to work on other projects.

### Not Enough Cooks in the Kitchen

"Where's Jennifer? Where is Steve?" Tim had been asked this question many times this week. He was starting to think that Jennifer and Steve were the project managers. Jennifer and Steve were critical to this project. Without them, the project would not meet its goals. This would hurt both the company and Tim's reputation.

Tim tried talking with Jennifer and Steve to let them know how critical they were. This seemed to help for a while. Tim could see that they were both sincerely trying to make themselves available to work on the project. But, they kept getting pulled in other directions because they were valuable to several groups in the company, not just Tim's project.

Tim then talked with his project executive to make it *formal* that Jennifer and Steve were assigned to Tim's project. This definitely helped. Jennifer and Steve were now dedicated to his one project. "Fantastic," thought Tim. Problem solved.

Not exactly. At times, the workload was just too much. Jennifer and Steve became the bottlenecks that everyone was waiting on. Sure, it was better to have these two people dedicated than to not have them, but too much work was funneled through them. Tim felt like Chief Brody in the movie *Jaws* when he said, "You're gonna need a bigger boat." Having the two of them was not enough. The schedule was starting to slip.

How was Tim going to deal with these critical resources and his project's reliance on them?

## 3. What will happen if I do nothing?

If things go as they should, there may not be any impact. You may find that you *get away with it* and the project is successful. However, it's more likely that, at some point, you will experience a problem that will cause a significant dilemma. If you are totally reliant on just a few individuals, then the fate of the project is not in your hands, it is in theirs. If they become unavailable, or are unable to get through the work in the times assigned, you will likely experience project delays and not have any way to address them. This will cause stakeholders to question your ability to manage risk and potentially damage your career.

## 4. Solution

This problem is essentially one of risk, so the solution requires a risk management approach. Consideration and analysis of the risk should lead you to four distinct actions, the first three of which are aimed at managing the risk, and the fourth is a contingency if the risk becomes real:

1. Secure the key resources' involvement on the project for the duration of the initiative.
2. Look for additional experts to help reduce the reliance on individuals.
3. Provide training and skills development.
4. Look at ways to remove the reliance on the individuals.

## 5. What should I do?

Remember that you are essentially dealing with managing risk here, and before you take any steps to correct the problem, you need to make sure that it has been fully identified and analyzed. Make sure that you know who all of your critical resources are—the people who are your *single points of failure* where the loss of the individual to your team will leave you without a backup plan. Ensure that you are also aware of how long the problem will persist—is it for the whole project, or just one phase? Only when you fully understand the problem, can you act.

### 5(a) Secure the key resources

The first thing you need to do in this type of situation is to try and get key resources officially committed to your project, preferably dedicated to only your project. This will involve several actions on your part.

Start working with your project sponsor or project executive immediately. Make the sponsor/executive aware of your situation so that he or she can work with you organizationally and politically to get these resources dedicated to your project. Let him or her know that the progress and success of your project is highly dependent on these people. The necessary discussion may be a level above you in which your sponsor must talk with other project sponsors or functional directors to secure these resources. This may involve talking with the key resources' bosses (e.g., in a matrix organization) to alter their schedules and workload to accommodate your project.

Hopefully, these key resources will not be key resources on other projects that have a higher priority.

You may need to *trade* resources to secure what you need: provide a non-key resource from your project who may have the right skills to assist on another initiative in exchange for increased commitment for your key resource. Also, recognize that you may not need the key individual for the entire duration of the project and you need to be prepared to release them when their key functions have been performed.

### 5(b) Find additional experts

Next, see if there are other resources than can be added to the project team. Even if you secure the key people, the project is still dependent on them. An unexpected absence or reallocation could cause one of them to miss a segment of work time on your project. Consequently, you need a Plan B, which is getting a few more resources to help with workload.

Just because you have a dependency on one or two people, that doesn't mean that their skills don't exist elsewhere in the organization. You may be able to identify other people with the skills that you need and arrange for them to be allocated to the project to help to reduce the reliance on these key people.

To get additional resources, you will likely need the help of your project executive again. Also, make sure to ask your key people who else in the organization could possibly help on the project. Usually, people within certain areas of expertise know where other people with similar expertise are within the organization. If the key people know they are bringing in resources that will help take some work off their plates, they may be happy to find other resources for you.

If you cannot find additional resources within your organization, you may be forced to seek outside expertise and bring them on as subcontractors. Depending on the type of work (e.g., proprietary), this may, or may not, be allowed for your project. It is definitely a last option, compared to finding these types of resources within your own organization.

### 5(c) Develop skills

One of the most successful strategies in the long term is to address dependence on one or two people by developing those same key skills in others. By building knowledge capacity in other team members, you are building more productive and effective resources for the project. In essence, you are growing your pool of key resources. In this regard, part of the role of the key people will be to train other resources.

In the short term, this may slow down progress on your initiative. You are creating additional tasks (training, coaching, and such) for resources that you have already identified as crucial for a number of project tasks. However, in the longer term, you are reducing the reliance on these resources and therefore reducing overall risk. From an organizational perspective, you are also helping to remove this risk from future initiatives.

### 5(c) Remove the reliance

This approach is more of a contingency solution than a risk management solution; removing reliance is an option that you likely won't want to implement unless you are faced with losing a critical resource for an extended period of time. However, you should be discussing this option before you are faced with the situation so that the solution can be implemented quickly, if necessary.

Make sure that your stakeholders understand that if these key people are not fully available (or are not available to the extent that your project needs them), key milestones and deliverables may slip. If they don't slip, the quality or scope may suffer. The point is that you need to make the end customer aware of these possible impacts.

You need to understand what the options are for dealing with that situation. Is the preference to reduce scope in the areas where reliance on the unavailable expert exists? Is an extension of the schedule preferred? Can the budget be increased to recruit a replacement (although the search process may impact the schedule)? Is a lower quality deliverable acceptable?

By understanding the options and discussing the preferred choices as part of risk management, you can save yourself a lot of time and effort if the risk becomes real—you can confirm with your stakeholders that the agreed upon contingency plan can be implemented and the disruption can be minimized.

# 9.5 Some of this project is beyond my control.

By Luis Crespo

## 1. Problem

This is a problem that every project manager will face at some point in their career. You are accountable for the project's success, but not all of the success factors are within your reach. You feel as though you cannot control your own project, and you feel exposed—that you are reliant on things that you cannot impact.

## 2. Warning Signs

This is a problem that relies a lot on the project manager's gut feelings to know when there is a real problem—it just feels wrong. However, look out for the following warning signs:

- Problems are happening on your project that are unperceived by you, but are perceived by your team or stakeholders.
- Decisions are being made that affect your project, and you are either not reacting or simply do not know how to react.
- Situations are often arising within your project team, but you are not reacting.
- Your project scope or expected benefit is unrealistic, and you have not even mentioned it.
- Your project is in trouble, and you think you can fix it by yourself.

### A PM with an Uninterested Sponsor

Mary has just inherited a project with an uninterested business sponsor. Her business sponsor feels the project has been forced on the team by executive management, and therefore the sponsor will now do anything possible to make the project fail.

The project sponsor does not bother to show up at the kick off meeting and does not send a delegate. During the planning phase, she constantly changes her mind on the requirements and purposefully delays sign off meetings with Mary, the project manager.

Mary performs her due diligence and lets her business sponsor know that the sign off delays will cause further delays at the back end of the project and possibly budget overruns. Additional change requests are also likely. It doesn't seem to matter to the sponsor; the harder Mary works to keep the project in line, the harder the business sponsor works to derail it.

Finally Mary decides to have a face to face with the business sponsor and express her concerns over the constant delays that this project is having due mainly to delays from the sponsor side. The sponsor candidly lets Mary know that she is not interested in the success of the project.

What should Mary do? Is this within the realm of Mary's control to reinterest the sponsor in the project? Should Mary *grin and bear it*, rationalizing that it's her sponsor's money so let her spend it as she wishes?

## 3. What will happen if I do nothing?

If you do nothing, the problem will continue to get worse. Stakeholders and team members will perceive that you have no control and will bypass you, going instead to the people that they feel can control what is happening. Over time your role on the project will become more and more marginalized, and people will question why you are involved in the first place—and that's not good!

## 4. Solution

To solve this problem, you need to understand whether the situation is truly beyond your control, and if it is, how you can put yourself in a position to gain control or influence to the project's benefit. Consider the following structured approach:

1. Consider whether your problem is truly one of control, or whether there are other underlying issues.
2. Establish whether the issue cannot be controlled or whether you can control it with an appropriate level of authority.
3. Identify your ability to influence.
4. Incorporate the lack of control within your project risk.
5. Identify and execute your next steps.

## 5. What should I do?

Control is an illusion. As a project manager you already know that. You know that as a project manager you are usually accountable for much, but in control of very little. That being said, you need to determine those things that are truly outside of your realm of control. Many times, what we feel is out of our control is just a symptom for something else that may be going wrong in our project.

### 5(a) Is this truly a control problem?

Before you can solve the problem, you need to understand the underlying issue. The sense of having no control is one of the symptoms, but it may not be the real problem. Consider a situation where you are managing a project within a matrix organization. Your resources are assigned to the project, but their line managers are within operational units.

Now suppose that you are having difficulty getting your team members to work on their assigned project tasks; they always seem to be working on operational items assigned by their line managers. Is this a problem where your lack of control is affecting the situation? Possibly it is, but perhaps the project's communication plan is flawed and your team members aren't aware that they have assigned tasks. They are working on operational items, not because their manager told them to, but because they don't think that they have any project tasks assigned to them.

Before you can solve the problem, make sure that it truly is control-related and not another, completely unrelated issue. Each chapter in this book has a series of warning signs, and if you can match what you are observing with those warning signs you will have a good sense of what might be happening.

### 5(b) Control or authority

Once you have established that at least some of the issues that you are facing are related to control, then you need to establish whether you can regain control with the appropriate level of authority.

Have you ever been stuck on the tarmac waiting for your plane to take off only to find out that your flight has been delayed or, even worse, cancelled due to weather conditions? There was not one person you could have called, emailed, or texted who could have changed the conditions. The reason is simple. None of us has control over the weather nor can we get that authority from anyone on Earth.

The same is *not true* for all aspects of your project. For instance, if you are going to be a on a long term project, you may not have the control over certain matrixed resources and their day-to-day assignments or allocations. You may be concerned that these resources may end up not being available for your project. For that reason, you may request for the authority to have these resources functionally report to you for the duration of the project.

The same would hold true for other aspects of your project. Perhaps you are concerned that you are not seeing all timesheets that are being charged against your project. You may request that any of the timesheets that have time charged against your project be routed to you for approval first.

Before you can proceed in determining whether it is a matter of control or authority you can ask yourself the following questions:

- Is this something that someone else is responsible for?
- Should this be part of my responsibilities as part of this project?
- If this becomes part of my responsibilities will I be able to execute on this?
- If this becomes part of my responsibilities am I capable to execute on this?
- Is this something which has not been defined as being owned by someone?

Why are these questions important?

Let's take a couple of questions and answer them. Say that you do request that the resources functionally report to you for the duration of the project. Is this something that someone else is responsible for? Sure. It was the functional manager. Then there needs to be communication with this functional manager as to when the transition begins and when it ends, among other things. Will you be able to execute as a functional manager along with all your other project management responsibilities?

The old adage, "Be careful what you wish for," holds true. Once you request something such as the management of resources you will need to make time for tasks such as reviews and ad hoc meetings with your resources. Do you have this time available to you and how will it impact your ability to manage the project? Another aspect to ponder is: are you capable to execute as a resource manager? Just because you want the resources reporting to you doesn't mean that you actually should. Being a good project manager doesn't make you a good resource manager just like the inverse also holds true. Do you have any experience as a functional manager? It's more than just having people report to you in an org chart, therefore you need to make sure you are qualified to execute before you ask for the authority. These are just some questions that could, and should, be asked as part of this process.

Even with these questions, it is important to keep in mind that just because the authority could be given to you, it doesn't mean that it will or it should.

One final thing to consider here is that the authority doesn't have to be yours. You can have control through other people involved in the project. Go back to the example of resources working on operational issues instead of project tasks. The solution of having them report to you for the project's duration would work, but so would a request from a senior stakeholder (ideally the sponsor) to the line manager to ensure that the resources are dedicated to the project work assigned to them. That also has the added advantage that it doesn't position you as the *bad guy* in the eyes of the resource's supervisor.

### 5(c) Circles of influence

Realizing that certain things are beyond your control is very healthy. For one, this realization helps you understand your limitations and what aspects of your project you can personally control. That does not mean that if you cannot control something you cannot affect it.

For example, most project managers do not have control over what budget gets assigned to their project. Sure, they may have contributed planning estimates during earlier phases of the project, but usually they get assigned a budget along with a hard end date. Given this lack of control over the budgetary process, does this mean all is lost? Definitely not. This is where the circles of influence come into play.

When project budgets are put together they are, for the most part, an exercise in creative estimating. A budget is usually (all high level) resource estimation plus hardware and software estimation multiplied by a time factor, sprinkled with a great level of guess work. But how can your circle of influence factor in? If you have built up a reliable reputation in your company, you will inevitably be called to assist directly or indirectly in this process. Considering that one or several of these efforts may end up being your projects to manage, you can apply influence to help to ensure that the budgets are closer to the reality you will be dealing with. Granted, once you provide your input, they will go through some corporate cleansing, but at least they will be a lot closer to reality.

What about project scope? Unless a project will be benefitting your department directly you will not have a say in project scope. Does that mean you really don't have a say? Not exactly. Many times your business sponsor is looking for someone to bounce ideas around with, or perhaps looking for new ideas. Don't be afraid to be this person. There also may be a perfect opportunity to automate a business process or introduce a cost savings. Regardless of the situation, you need to be careful not to inadvertently introduce scope creep or begin to gold plate deliverables in the interest of your sponsor.

Alternatively, if your sponsor is staunchly holding onto a specific scope that you know will introduce risk to the project you can influence the process by providing subject matter experts who will speak to your sponsors regarding the matter and try to change, or should I say influence, their view point.

### 5(d) Managing your project risk

Once you understand the issues that are truly beyond your control, and you understand the ability that you (or your team) have to influence the problem, you need to make sure that the risks are captured and analyzed as part of the risk management plan.

The inability to control these problems will inevitably add risk to the project, so you need to ensure that you are monitoring for signs that the lack of control is causing you tangible problems (such as resources not working on tasks in the earlier example), and then implement appropriate contingency plans. You can also look at ways to manage the risk before it becomes a real problem by building a good relationship with relationship owners to try and ensure that you can work through any conflicting priorities.

### 5(e) Your next steps

The steps listed above can lead you to different actions. Regardless of what actions you take, you will need an action plan. Here are some questions that can help you formulate an action plan:

- What can I do to prevent communication issues from seeming like my project is out of control?
- What steps have I put in place to ensure that project issues are not repeated through the life of the project?
- What steps have I taken to identify what additional authority I may need during my project in order to make it a success?
- Have I adequately identified the key project stakeholders in case I need their support in matters that are beyond my reach or control?

These questions highlight some of the preparation needed to move forward when you address items that are beyond your control.

# 9.6 Costs are much higher than we thought.

## By Andy Jordan

## 1. Problem

The project has been moving forward for some time, and you have noticed that the costs seem to be out of control. It's not that your estimates were a long way off. You read Chapter 5.4 of this book and applied the lessons there, so that's pretty much where you thought it would be. The issue seems to be that you are spending a lot of time and money on items that are not in the project plan, and that is sending the costs skyrocketing.

## 2. Warning Signs

The warning signs here are fairly obvious; you need to be on the lookout for:

- Status reports start to show cost overruns, even though individual project tasks and deliverables are coming in on schedule and budget.
- The amount of time that team members are spending has increased for tasks that are not part of the project plan.
- You have a lot of issues in each week's status meeting.
- You are trying to manage many potential risks, as well as risks that have been realized, requiring a contingency to be implemented.

> **Hey, Where Did the Budget Go?**
>
> Natalie didn't get it. She had worked really hard with her team to ensure that the estimates for her project were as good as they could be, and now, a couple of months into the project, the work was paying off. Tasks were coming in more or less on estimate. Good planning does pay off!
>
> Yet, when Natalie looked at the project budget, the project had spent way more than they were supposed to at this point. The way things were going, the project was going to be about 20 percent over budget, and that was unacceptable. But where was the money being spent?
>
> Natalie had checked the math and that was accurate, so that was not the problem. As she thought about what else had been happening on her project, she thought about some of the risks. For example, the team had an amazing risk management plan, but there were still some risks that were becoming real. Could that be the cause of the budget overrun?
>
> Natalie wasn't sure, but she knew that she had to solve the problem quickly before the sponsor decided that she wasn't capable of managing this project.

## 3. What will happen if I do nothing?

I think you know the answer to that question! Costs will not magically come back in line. They will continue to make a mockery of the project budget, and people will notice the problem further up the organization's hierarchy. If you are lucky, your project will simply be cancelled for being too expensive, and if you are unlucky, you will be out of work.

## 4. Solution

Let's provide some good news: your project probably isn't actually over budget. More likely, you had not planned for all of the costs that are involved. The cost of a project is not simply the sum total of the tasks that have been identified; there is a lot more to it than that. You need to understand:

1. What are the costs of managing the project, particularly the risks?
2. What are the costs of dealing with things that we know might be problems?
3. What are the costs of dealing with problems that we don't know about?

## 5. What should I do?

It's a lot easier to deal with this issue at the beginning of the project, but it's never too late. Before you start, recognize that you will be wrong! There are too many assumptions throughout this process to come up with an exact figure, but that's okay. If you have done the work properly, the errors will offset and you will have an approximately accurate estimate. Remember, it's an estimate—it's supposed to be wrong!

### 5(a) Project management costs

Projects cost money. I don't just mean the deliverables; I mean the whole project. Think about it from your own perspective. You have a million things to do to keep control of the project, and yet there is a lot of your time that is spent on tasks that are not on the project plan. However, you still get paid for them, and they still cost money.

There are a lot of tasks like this—costs incurred to prevent other things from going wrong elsewhere on the project. Consider risk management as an example. Risk management (at least for negative risks) is about doing things now with the intention of preventing something else from happening later, or to reduce the severity of that event if it does occur.

Those tasks take effort and time from people—time that those people won't be spending on the tasks that have been assigned to them, which costs money.

When you plan your project, you need to make allowances for these costs (time and money) either by including *management* tasks with costs incurred against them, or by reducing the effectiveness of the resource on their assigned tasks (i.e., increase the effort and duration of each task to reflect that they can't be focused on the tasks exclusively).

This discussion considers only minor costs relative to the next two, though—and they are doozies!

### 5(b) The costs of dealing with what we know might go wrong

Of course, things go wrong on projects. Risk management is all about identifying those risks and trying to put some degree of control in place. However, we can't eliminate risks entirely, and some risks are going to become real. That costs money, and you can estimate how much money it will cost.

Consider this example: You are buying a piece of software that costs $100,000 that will take 3 months to implement, but the vendor is concerned that it might not work for what you need. They estimate that there is a 20 percent chance that it will need customizing at a cost of $50,000 and a delay of two months. Alternatively, you can buy an additional piece of software now for $20,000 that will eliminate the need to customize, but will extend implementation to four months.

So, we know:

- The task (software purchase and integration) will cost $100,000 and take three months.
- There is a risk that the software won't work. That risk has a 20 percent chance of becoming real and will cost us $50,000 and two months.
- You can eliminate the risk now by buying an additional piece of software for $20,000 and one extra month to implement.

Based on this information, we can determine some of the costs that we are facing. If we decide to *take the risk* and not buy the software, we need to put a cost on the risk of failure. We do that by considering the impact and multiplying it by the likelihood of it happening. In our example that's $50,000 and two months multiplied by 20 percent = $10,000 and 0.4 months.

On the other hand, if we decide that we want to eliminate the risk and incur the additional cost, things are a little simpler. We spend $20,000 and incur a one month delay.

If we make a decision about which approach is better based solely on dollars and time, then we take the risk, although remember that, in reality, the impact will be $0 and 0 days four times out of five, and $50,000 and 2 months on the other occasion.

That's not what this is about though. The decision needs to consider a lot of other factors beyond the pure numbers. The point is that we need to allow for those costs regardless of which option we pursue.

As project managers, we may adjust the budget and schedule to allow for the additional software, but how many of us will increase the schedule and budget if we decide to take the risk?

This is one of the biggest areas where costs can get out of control. As project managers, we like to think that we can manage risks to the point that things won't go wrong, and our sponsor and customer certainly don't want to put money and time aside for things that might go wrong. They expect us to manage the project so that things won't go wrong.

Well, I've never found that perfect world. If risks are real, then they will become real, which will delay the project and cause us to incur additional costs. If we plan for it, we can incorporate it into the budget and schedule, if we don't then our costs will get out of control.

Project risks like this are often referred to as *known unknowns*, and the money and time that we put aside to deal with them is called *contingency reserves*.

### 5(c) The costs of dealing with things going wrong that we don't know about

We all like to think that when we plan our projects, we are able to identify all of the risks that are likely to impact the project, but that's not true. There will always be unforeseen events that cause delays, and we need to be prepared to deal with them as they arise. If your project experiences these events, it is not a reflection on you or your team for not managing risks properly; it's just *one of those things*. Consider the next (extreme) example.

You have built your project plan with your team and completed a comprehensive risk management exercise. You know that things will be tough, but you feel confident that you can deliver on time and budget. Then you get a call one Sunday night—your team has just won the jackpot in their office pool for the lottery. They are all now millionaires and won't be going in to work.

Of course you didn't plan for that on your project, but somewhere in the world, that phone call is being made. When these unplanned events occur to your project, they will have real cost and time implications, and you can't make your project immune from them.

This event is called an *unknown unknown*, and the money and time set aside to deal with such events is called a *management reserve*.

### 5(d) Contingency and management reserves

Best practices say that between the contingency reserve (for known unknowns) and the management reserve (for unknown unknowns), 10 to 25 percent of the project budget should be put aside. Think about that for a minute: on a $1 million project you should add between $100,000 and $250,000 for reserves. The exact amount will depend on how much risk is being accepted on the project.

The theory says that contingency reserve should be managed by the PM and used as needed as some of the risks become real. It is not *spare* money; it can only be used to offset the impact of reserves. Management reserve is usually managed by the sponsor and made available as needed to deal with unforeseen events.

Of course, reality is somewhat different. Very few sponsors will agree to putting aside formal reserves at all. Certainly if you tell them that you need to add 25 percent to the budget to deal with reserves, the response will not be pleasant.

However, the bottom line is that these numbers were developed for a reason. You can't make the need for reserves go away just by not providing them. If you do that, you'll be faced with the problem that this chapter is all about—a project that appears to be significantly over budget despite the fact that each task is being completed in line with the plan's estimates. The reality is that the project is not really over budget; the budget is insufficient because reserves were ignored.

# 9.7 I don't know if a real risk is an *issue*.

## By Andy Jordan

## 1. Problem

Project managers are always talking about risks and issues, but isn't a risk also an issue? If you aren't sure what is a risk and what is an issue, or how to manage them properly, you may make mistakes about how big the problem is that you are dealing with, which can have a significant negative impact on your project. Additionally, your team is going to get confused about what is a risk and what is an issue, and what they need to do.

> **That's a Big Risk, Oh, I Mean an Issue!**
>
> Gary was confused. Two members of his project team had just sent him emails. The first email subject was "We've just found a huge risk!" The second email subject was "Big issue to deal with!" The emails described the same situation. After reading the emails, Gary agreed that this was something that had to be dealt with straight away.
>
> Gary's confusion came from not being sure what he was dealing with, a risk or an issue. Therefore, he did not really know what to do. Was this really a risk, or was it even an issue? In fact, what's the difference between a risk and an issue—are they the same, do they need the same solution? Or, is it a bit more complicated than that?

## 2. Warning Signs

This problem can really sneak up on you . You may be well into the risk planning and management tasks before you realize that you are in fact dealing with an issue and not a risk. Similarly, you can be dealing with an issue for quite some time without realizing that it is in fact a risk, and needs to be handled differently. You may have a problem if some of these things are happening:

- You are having problems identifying an appropriate risk management strategy for dealing with a risk.
- You can't actually identify the trigger event that will signal when a risk has become reality.
- The actions taken to deal with a risk or an issue are not working.
- When an issue or a risk is identified, it takes too long to deal with.
- Your team is unsure whether something needs to be brought to your attention to deal with now, or whether it needs to be assessed for possible future impact.

## 3. What will happen if I do nothing?

If you aren't able to successfully identify the difference between a risk and an issue, you won't be able to manage either of them properly. If you aren't taking the right steps to manage aspects of your project, you will not get the best outcomes and potentially could make things worse.

Your team will also follow your lead, so if you aren't sure about the difference between a risk and an issue, or how to identify them, the team will likely also be confused. That may mean that problems aren't identified as early as they could have been, and it may mean that risks result in problems that could have been prevented.

## 4. Solution

There are a number of ways to identify whether you are dealing with a risk or an issue. You must be able to analyze the problem you are dealing with and identify the characteristics of the problem that *make* it a risk or an issue. Then, you can implement the appropriate management strategy.

## 5. What should I do?

When you are managing a project, you don't want to have to spend a lot of time analyzing risks and issues. If you have a good understanding of the difference between the two, you will be able to quickly determine which you are facing and can spend your time developing appropriate solutions. Here are a few approaches that will help you get there.

### 5(a) Definitions

Every risk and every issue is unique, but there are some ways to identify whether you are dealing with a risk or an issue that can apply in all situations. Let's start by defining a risk, or at least borrowing the definition from the Project Management Institute (PMI®) *Project Management Body of Knowledge, 4th Edition*. It says that:

A *risk* is an uncertain event that, if it occurs, may have a positive or negative impact on the project and its ability to deliver its objectives.

In some cases, there may be a larger impact that goes beyond the project and affects the organization as a whole, but generally speaking we are talking about the project and its objectives. It's also important to note that risks are not always bad. They can have positive outcomes. We refer to negative risks as *threats* and positive risks as *opportunities*.

Examples of negative risks are: staff may leave, suppliers may be late delivering, or costs of a component may increase. Examples of positive risks are: the possibility that in completing the project you are also able to address performance problems that aren't included in the project, or advantages that happen to be delivered by the changes that the project will implement.

When considering whether you have a risk or an issue, the key phrase is *uncertain event*. Only risks are uncertain. You don't know whether it will happen or not. With an issue, the problem has already occurred, there is *no uncertainty* involved. We can define an *issue* as: *a situation that may prevent the project from achieving its objectives*.

There is some similarity in the wording between a risk and an issue. In both cases, we are talking about the project objectives being impacted, but there are more differences than similarities. In addition to the lack of uncertainty, with an issue we don't have the concept of positive or negative. Issues only have the potential to create negative outcomes.

When the uncertainty of a risk goes away (i.e., the risk becomes reality), the risk ceases to exist. With negative risks we are left with a situation that may prevent the project from achieving its objectives, in other words, an issue.

### 5(b) Identifying the problem that you are dealing with

If a problem is discovered during a project, you need to quickly identify what it is. Ask yourself:

- Has this already happened?
- Could it negatively affect the project?

If you answered yes to both questions, you have an issue. The first question rules out the possibility that it is a risk, and the second question establishes whether you need to act on it. Lots of little things happen on projects, and you can't manage all of them, so focus on the ones that can impact your project objectives.

Consider some real examples to illustrate the point:

1. A team member may resign and leave part way through your project.
2. A team member is called to jury duty and will be absent for the next four weeks.
3. A team member won't be in today because they aren't feeling very well.

All of these situations deal with staff being unavailable, but they are very different. Situation (1) is a risk, which may happen, but hasn't occurred yet. You may be able to take steps to reduce the chance of someone leaving (offer them a bonus at the end of the project, for example), or reduce the impact if it does occur (make sure that you don't have any areas of the project where only one person can do the work), but you don't yet have to deal with someone who has actually resigned.

Situation (2) is an issue. You are going to lose a team member for four weeks and you can't do anything about it. It is happening now and you need to take steps to address the situation by perhaps finding a replacement resource, hiring a contractor, extending the project timeline, and so on.

Situation (3) is also a problem, but is it an issue? During the course of a project, there will be occasions when someone isn't available, either their car breaks down, they have a sick day, or something else happens. As a project manager, you should expect these and be able to work around them; they don't need to be considered or dealt with as project issues. Instead, the team member can catch up over the next few days, someone else can help for a day or so, and so on.

### 5(c) Dealing with issues

When we build risk management plans, we are concerned with two different types of actions:

1. **Actions to take before the risk becomes real:** For negative risks, these are focused on reducing the impact of the risk should it occur, reducing the likelihood of it occurring, or both.
2. **Actions to take after the risk occurs:** These are generally known as *contingencies* designed to reduce the impact to the project after the risk has been realized. Contingencies are identified during risk planning and implemented if the risk becomes an issue. However, it doesn't mean that the only way to deal with an issue is to implement a contingency plan.

Issues from risks that have occurred are only one type of issue, but there are many more types of issues. Examples include:

- *A problem that impacts scope, budget, or schedule:* This could be a delay in the project, a cost overrun, a change in available resources, a problem in delivering what has been asked—in short, just about anything that threatens the project is an issue.
- *A communication problem between two or more project stakeholders:* (team members, project manager, sponsor, customer, and the like).
- *A process problem:* Either processes aren't being followed or the processes aren't meeting the needs of the project.
- *An expectation problem:* The expectations of one or more stakeholders differs from the agreed upon scope, budget and schedule.

These are all very general because an issue can arise from almost any situation. No matter how the issue occurred, it needs to be dealt with immediately. The specific actions will depend on the individual situation, but the process is similar for all of them:

- *Make sure that you understand the issue:* If necessary, engage team members and stakeholders to assist you in understanding the specifics and the extent of the problem.
- *Understand the impact that the issue may cause and what the implications are:* It may be that the issue is relatively minor and you don't need to do anything. On the other hand, the issue could threaten the success of the entire project.
- *Take action to prevent, minimize, or correct the impact:* Not all issues can be solved completely. You may need to take actions to both solve the problem and deal with the affect that the issue has caused.
- *Validate that the steps have worked:* You need to ensure that the actions that you have taken solved the issue. This may be a case of reassessing the project, or it may be a conversation with stakeholders in the event of a communication or expectation issue.
- *Take steps to prevent the issue from occurring again:* Some issues are one-off events that you can forget about once they have been resolved. However, in some cases, there may be an underlying problem that needs to be addressed in order to prevent more issues from surfacing later in the project. The project manager needs to be using team members and stakeholders to assist in assessing, resolving, and preventing issues.

# 9.8 How do I know what might be a problem in the future?

By Aaron Porter

## 1. Problem

Scenario 1: One minute everything is fine, and the next you feel like your hair is on fire. It doesn't matter how detailed the project plan is, how much time has been spent planning, or the size of the project—something unexpected seems to raise its ugly head on almost every project at your company. Scenario 2: You've heard about risk management, but you're not sure when is the best time to identify risks, or how to identify risks effectively.

## 2. Warning Signs

Taken by themselves, some of the following warning signs may not mean that there is a problem with identifying risks at appropriate points during the project. They could point to different problems, or may not indicate problems at all.

> **There Is Never a Hole in the Ground to Swallow You Up When You Need It!**
>
> Bob knew he had a big problem. He sat quietly, staring down at the pen he was about to snap in half. He placed the pen, carefully, on the table, not wanting to draw unnecessary attention to himself or shower the people on the other side of the conference room table with plastic shrapnel. Bob sank a little deeper into his chair, wishing he could hide under the table, as if that would really help. He flinched when he heard his name called. "Bob." The voice echoed in his head and Bob looked up, slowly. "Tell us about your project."
>
> Bob vaguely remembered stumbling back to his cubicle. How had things gotten so bad, so quickly? Everything had been going so well. How had all of these problems crept up on him without his knowing? Could he have done anything to help prevent them, or at least see them coming?
>
> In spite of the problems, he felt lucky that he was being allowed to fix them. Bob knew he had to learn from this experience or things like this could keep happening until his luck ran out, but where to begin?

Other warning signs should not be ignored. Like risks, you should not ignore any warning signs until after you have determined that they are harmless. Possible warning signs are:

- Risks are not being identified.
- Only simple risks are identified, such as not enough personnel, money, or time.
- Project team members and stakeholders regularly bring previously unknown problems to your attention during meetings or while you are at your desk, after project work has started. While this could indicate a problem, it could also be a sign that your team is learning more about the project over time as opposed to having missed important steps earlier. This can be a good sign, all by itself.
- Project tasks are regularly late or over budget due to time and resources spent fixing unexpected problems.
- The general opinion of you as a project manager is low, and others make jokes about fixing the problems you cause.

## 3. What will happen if I do nothing?

If your actions don't change, your circumstances won't either. If your projects are currently experiencing avoidable delays and costs because of unexpected problems, they will continue to do so until you start doing something different. This is not to say that you are the root cause of the problem or that you have control over what needs to be done. But, at a minimum, you are the one that should identify that something needs to be done and bring it to the attention of someone who can do something about it.

Companies don't like to bleed money due to delays or lose out on market share because they can't make it to the market. As a project manager, you face the standard risks of poor risk identification and this can include losing your job, trust, and credibility. But it doesn't stop there; getting fired is not the worst thing that can happen. Rarely, a project manager in charge of business applications misses something that results in someone else's death, but what if you are in construction, automotive engineering, civil engineering, or the military, where the missed management of risk can have dire consequences. Never mind that you may have ruined your project management career; think of how harm to others would affect you emotionally and the impact on the lives of those left behind. Don't get stuck in the *it's just project management* mindset; risk management is critical.

## 4. Solution

Risk identification is not a one-time task. It needs to take place at critical points throughout a project: initiation, requirements and design, schedule development, and so on. In this chapter, there are steps that can be followed as a whole, or you can use the steps that make sense for you and your organization, to help you increase your chances of identifying and dealing with problems before they occur.

## 5. What should I do?

There are companies that have defined risk management processes and will provide you with the training you need to implement their processes. I hope you work for one of these companies. If you don't, you may have your work cut out for you. Organizational change can be difficult, to say the least. When project managers try to change the organization, it is not always well received, but you are in good company—when CEOs try to change organizations, it is not always well received either. There are two basic approaches you can take to implement risk management, neither of which is as easy as it sounds or as quick to complete as you might like.

The first approach is to treat implementing risk management like a project, which can be a long process. If the process is successful, you will have templates, guidelines, and leadership support to make it happen. The second approach is to slip risk management processes into existing processes. Hopefully, others will notice your improved successes and it will catch on. But if your efforts fail or encounter resistance, you won't have anyone to support you or the new processes.

You shouldn't be scared away from risk management because you can't implement everything described in this chapter, or you can't do it in the manner described. Some of the steps outlined here can be omitted or combined; figure out what you and your company can do and make it work. Remember, this is just one person's perspective on a very broad topic.

There are three main points during a project that provide logical points for risk assessment that will be discussed in more detail later in this chapter. These are:

- Prior to project approval, such as during creation of the business case
- During requirements development
- During creation of the work breakdown structure (WBS) and project schedule

### 5(a) Risk assessment prior to project approval

A good starting point for your first risk assessment is after the sponsor and high level deliverables have been identified. It could be as simple as asking, "What are the risks to deliverable 1?" But is this enough? You will come up with a list of risks, but you will come up with a better list of risks if you give the question context. What does that mean? In this case, context refers to types and categories of risk which can be applied by borrowing a couple of tools from strategic planning.

The first tool is the SWOT Analysis. SWOT stands for strengths, weaknesses, opportunities, and threats. Taking these types of risk in reverse order, *threats* are risks; *opportunities* are positive risks; *weaknesses* are vulnerabilities that increase the likelihood of a risk occurring and negatively impact the ability to seize an opportunity; and *strengths* are attributes of a company that make it possible to take advantage of opportunities and overcome threats. Looking at each of these factors at the beginning of a project will help you to build a team and assign activities that will increase the likelihood of project success.

The second tool is the political, environmental, socio-cultural, and technological (PEST) analysis. Categories and types of risks are shown in Table 9.1.

You begin by identifying risks and placing them in the cell at the cross-section of the SWOT columns and PEST rows. As you input data into the cells, ask these questions: Are there political threats to your project? Does your company have environmental strengths or weaknesses? Are there technological opportunities you can take advantage of that will benefit the project or the company?

### 5(b) Risk assessment during requirements development

Before you can complete a detailed risk analysis of a system, you (or others involved in the process) need to understand the system, making requirements development the next logical point for risk assessment. This section makes the following assumptions about your organization:

- You have access to a documented enterprise architecture
- Your company performs enterprise analysis

**Table 9.1** SWOT/PEST Matrix

|                | Strengths | Weaknesses | Opportunities | Threats |
|----------------|-----------|------------|---------------|---------|
| Political      |           |            |               |         |
| Environmental  |           |            |               |         |
| Socio-cultural |           |            |               |         |
| Technological  |           |            |               |         |

In the book *IT Architecture Toolkit* by Jane A. Carbone (2004), *enterprise architecture* is described as all the components of an organization that are needed to run the organization, including data, people, processes, and tools, and how they work together.

*Enterprise analysis* is actually a process that begins before the project is approved, benefits from an existing enterprise architecture, and involves:

- Identifying why a change to the organization is needed
- Identify new capabilities required to meet the project objectives
- Determining the best approach to meet the project objectives
- Defining project deliverables
- Creating a business case for the project (International Institute of Business Analysis, 2009, p. 81)

Armed with this information, you are on your way to documenting project requirements. The enterprise architecture provides input into *current-state documentation*, which is completed for the purpose of creating a snapshot of today's reality. Enterprise analysis provides input into *desired-state documentation*, which can include diagrams, processes, and rules for what you want the organization to look like when the project is complete. Keep in mind that you can get to this point without enterprise analysis and enterprise architecture; you will just have to do a little more work, first. You can then conduct a *gap analysis* between the current-state and desired-state for the purpose of determining where you are, where you want to be, and how you are going to get there. It is during the gap analysis that you will find the next opportunity for risk assessment.

You could use the SWOT/PEST matrix to identify risks during the gap analysis. However, you may find that the gap analysis starts you off in a different direction. Ask yourself, what does a gap potentially represent? A risk, of course, but not all gaps are risks.

There are several ways that gaps can be represented, and you may find it useful to borrow a tool from *root cause analysis* known as the Ishikawa or Fishbone diagram (shown in Figure 9.4). This diagram will list the gaps, instead of using the SWOT/PEST matrix. If you want to, go ahead and use both!

You can use the categories of People, Processes, Tools, and Technology, or define your own that fit your organization. The benefit of this approach is that it provides you with a visual tool that allows you to see all of the gaps at a glance, and makes it easier to differentiate between gaps that you are going to fill as part of the project and risks that need to be addressed.

## 5(c) Risk assessment during WBS and schedule development

Let's recap. So far you have project approval, completed a couple of rounds of risk analysis, completed the requirements and design, and have a solid understanding of the project deliverables. Now, it is time to work with your project team to develop the project tasks and schedule.

During the first round of risk analysis, you looked at both positive and negative risk. While it is always a good time to look for opportunities, now is the time to focus

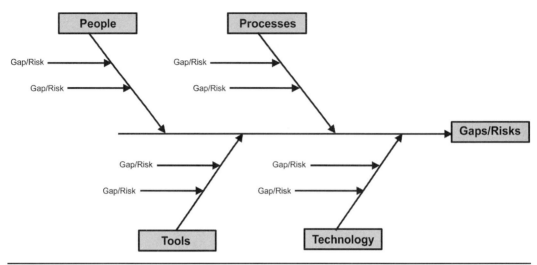

**Figure 9.4**

on threats. You are committed to the project and project scope has been established; it's time to get up close and personal with those pesky potential problems.

The starting point for developing your task list is the WBS, which is basically a graphical view of project deliverables and tasks that resembles an organization chart. As you create this, you want to keep an eye out for risk, and then go back over it in detail once it is finished. This can be done by listing work packages and tasks on a spreadsheet or in a table, and then listing potential risks next to them. A few things to consider are whether or not you have the right tools or people to accomplish the tasks. Are you using new technology that your team knows little about? How reliable are your tools and technology? What are the financial circumstances of the vendor(s) you are working with to accomplish specific tasks?

There can be a lot of tasks on a project, so use your time wisely. You may not need to spend nearly as much time assessing risks for a task to create a report that will take less than two hours to create and publish as you would for a set of tasks that result in setting up a secure network for protected health information.

An important aspect of tasks, and the risks they are affected by, is schedule. You need to understand the relationship between work that needs to be done, how long the work will take to accomplish, and how delays to one task will affect another. Some tasks can slip a little without seriously impacting the project, but if a task on the critical path, its slipping could jeopardize the entire project. Creating a project network diagram, a visual representation of project activities, can help you understand this relationship. If you find it difficult to create project network diagrams by hand, you can easily find software at varying prices that will create them for you, once you enter some basic task information.

### 5(d) What's next?

Time to take a breath. You've spent more hours than you care to count identifying risks, although you probably have been counting and have the timesheets to prove it. You know several ways, at specific points in a project, to identify risks so you can avoid unexpected problems. But what are you supposed to do with this information?

The whole point of identifying risks is so that you can do something about them. By the time you are done evaluating risk to the project tasks and schedule, you should already have dealt with a number of risks that were identified earlier in the project, but you could still have a big list. Without spinning off a whole new chapter on managing risk, below is some basic information you should capture about each risk, beginning with your first risk analysis, so that you can determine which risks are worth the effort to address:

- *Event:* A risk is easily characterized by an event taking place.
- *Impact of event (qualitative):* What will happen as a result of the event? Keep the description of the impact of the risk separate from the event; there can be multiple impacts to the same event.
- *Likelihood of event (H|M|L):* How likely is it that the event will occur?
- *Cost of event (quantitative impact):* A financial measure or H|M|L, depending upon available information.
- *Time to impact:* Timeframes can be used, although some risks can be constant if they are not addressed; when the risk could make itself known is an important factor in determining how soon you need to dedicate resources to addressing the risk.

Impact, cost, likelihood, and time to impact are all factors that need to be considered when reviewing risks—which should be done regularly. Weekly might be too often, and monthly might not be frequent enough. Let's assume that you have a weekly status meeting. Instead of reviewing every risk that has been identified every week, review only the risks that affect the immediate tasks and those that are actively being worked on in the weekly meetings; once a month, go back through your identified risks and reevaluate the impact, cost, likelihood, and time to impact. You may find that some previously identified risks are no longer a concern, and others have become more critical.

Understanding what might happen, when it might happen, how likely it is to happen, and how much it could cost if it happens will help you to determine the appropriate response to the risk. Some risks can be ignored, and some have to be dealt with. Sometimes you can find another person or entity to take responsibility for the risk, and sometimes you just need to change your plans so that the risk no longer has an impact on the project. However you choose to respond to a risk, document the reason for your response. For the risks that you choose to deal with, incorporate your responses into your project plan and track them to completion.

# 9.9 Should we end this project early?

## By Alex Brown

## 1. Problem

All projects need to come to an end. To a project manager, the ideal project ends on time, within budget, and delivering 100 percent of promised scope. Some projects need to end early, though. Sometimes the best decision a project manager can make is the decision to stop. How do you end a project early without being seen as a failure?

## 2. Warning Signs

It's important to see the warning signs for this issue as soon as possible. If you don't, you could have a big hole to crawl out of. Look for:

- At the start of the project, there were a dozen good reasons to get this done. Last week, we were down to only six. Now there are only two. Next week, how many will be left?
- Something big has changed. It was not on your risk list.
- Your team knows *what* they need to do, but people are having trouble remembering *why* they are doing it.

> **Failure or Success?**
>
> Dan dreaded the next status meeting with the team. How could he tell them that the project was over? All that hard work, and the company was now walking away from it.
>
> Dan looked up from his desk as Sam, the project sponsor, walked into the room.
>
> "Dan, I want to thank you for what you've done," Sam said.
>
> Dan was not sure what to say. Was she kidding? Their project had just been killed. "Um, okay," he said, and waited to see where this conversation was going.
>
> "I know that I have been tough on you and the team. Six months ago we really thought that this project was going to help the company. But the market has changed," she continued. "I just ran some numbers. We will be saving over five hundred thousand a month by stopping this project now. Instead of wasting time and money on this project, we can get your team to work on a new product line."
>
> "Invite me to your next team meeting. I want to thank everyone personally for their hard work, and talk about the next project we are launching," Sam finished, and walked out the door.
>
> Dan realized that Sam was not kidding. Suddenly he realized that the next team meeting would not be so bad.

## 3. What will happen if I do nothing?

When things change, sometimes the *worst* thing you can do is nothing. However, if you let a project continue you may waste time, money, and resources. To a project manager, doing nothing usually means following the plan. If your project has a good reason to end early, though, you really should do nothing. In other words, *stop*!

## 4. Solution

A good project charter and a good business case will tell you not only what to do, but *why* to do it. As a project leader, you should keep that question, "Why?" in your mind at all times. Watch what is happening to your project, to your team, and to the world.

Often people know that things have changed, and they avoid thinking about it. After all, their job is to complete the project, right? It seems like failure to stop. A courageous leader knows when to tell people that it is okay to stop.

You need to make sure that you have the right information about the project and the circumstances surrounding the project to know when to put a halt to the project (or at least recommend to your sponsor that they stop it).

## 5. What should I do?

Make your project charter and business cases into living documents. Understand why you are doing the project, and talk to your sponsor about business justification for the project on a regular basis. Remind your team about the purpose of the project, and they will understand when it is time to finish the project early. The best way to recover from a canceled project is to start a new one. Figure out what your team will do next, and everyone will find it easier to move on.

### 5(a) Project charter and business case

According to project management textbooks, the project charter and business case are important at the start of a project. You need them to prove that the project has value and to get authority to do the work.

In real life, the project charter and business case are important from the beginning to the end of the project. The reason to complete a project might change partway through the effort. Experienced project managers and sponsors do not look at change as wrong or evil. Instead, they see that change is part of normal life and normal business.

If you review the project charter and business case regularly, you get a chance to ask yourself and the sponsor, "Does this still make sense?" Every project has a set of deliverables. We launch projects because we *want* those deliverables. Make sure that you still want those same deliverables when you are partially done with the project.

Sometimes minor changes will require small changes to the charter, business case, and plan. If there are major changes, though, it might be better to stop the project.

### 5(b) Remind your team why

An enthusiastic, motivated project team is made up of people who want to accomplish a goal. They spend their working time imagining what the world will be like when the project is complete. They work to try to make that vision into reality.

It is hard to let go of a vision, even if it has become dated or irrelevant. It is sometimes easier to keep working, pretending that there will be something useful at the end. Abandoning a project can be difficult and emotional.

As project manager, part of your role is to look outside of the project team, and to understand the reasons for doing the project. If you remind the team of the value of the project at each team meeting, then the team will see (maybe even before you do) that something has changed, and that the value is gone. Reminding team members of the value of a project can be a great way to sustain their interest in a valuable project, and it is also the best way to break the news that their project needs to end early.

Even if you disagree with the business decisions that led to the cancellation of your project, find a way to explain the reasons to your team. Get an old copy of the charter and business case. Remind everyone about what the world looked like when you started the project. Explain what has changed. If you do not understand or agree with the project cancellation, you must keep that to yourself. You need to communicate an objective business decision and avoid editorial comments about whether you agree or not. Try to include your sponsor in the delivery of the message; the team needs to still feel that they are valued, even if the project is no longer considered necessary.

### 5(c) Proper closure

Just because a project is ending early, doesn't mean that the closure can be fast tracked. You need to follow all of the normal project closure processes, and ensure that:

- A lessons-learned or post mortem session is completed and the information captured as part of the project record
- All project related contracts are appropriately dealt with and deliverables from both sides are complete
- The project documentation is archived in your organization's project repository
- All resources are released (human and other)

Too often when a project ends early, everyone involved wants to run far away from it as quickly as possible. These projects may well be the ones where you have the best opportunity to capture improvements in the way that projects are executed.

### 5(d) Next!

Most organizations have more ideas than they have time and people. Often projects are canceled because there is something better that the company needs to do. Figure out what your team will be doing next.

Perhaps the team will remain together and take on a new assignment. Perhaps the team will break up and work on separate projects. No matter what, let people know that there is a next project. Celebrate the good work you did together, and look forward to the work of tomorrow.

You need to recognize that people need time to accept bad news, and that some people will take longer to process the news than others. If there is another initiative that team members can focus on, it will make the process of letting go much easier.

### 5(e) Failing projects do not get better with age

If your project needs to end early, then stop work on it as quickly as possible. Sometimes it is possible to salvage something useful from the project. The sooner you end work on a failing project, the less time and money you waste on it.

Team members sometimes find it hard to stop working on their projects. They had plans, and they want to see their work completed properly. The sooner you give them new, useful, and valuable work, the better.

There is sometimes a belief that you have invested too much into a project to stop, but that's a false premise. You can't get the money back that has already been committed, but you can avoid *throwing good money after bad.* If the project is no longer capable of meeting the goals that were set for it, then investing further in it will be futile and wasteful.

# 9.10 There's been a serious crisis, beyond the scope of my project!

## By Paul Lukas

Project managers function as bandleaders who pull together their players, each a specialist with individual score, and internal rhythm. Under the leader's direction, the players respond to the same beat.

The foresight and the dynamic interpersonal skills of many individuals is the reason why an organization, and more crucially, an individual person lives to work another day. In the days following a real crisis, superb leadership is a necessary skill.

The crisis in this case resulted from a real, intense, and enormous disaster: the September 11, 2001 destruction of the World Trade Center towers in New York City, which were the headquarters of my firm and the workplace of my project team members. This chapter examines lessons that can be learned from an extreme crisis for application in more routine project crisis contexts.

## 1. Problem

A project manager's mindset primarily focuses on the scope and schedule of the project plan. Project plans usually assume that working conditions will remain unchanged for the duration of the project. The unforeseen crisis can

### What To Do With the Pile of Shoes?

Designer high-heel shoes were scattered all over the upper lobby of the World Trade Center on a beautiful, late-summer day on September 11, 2001. Yet, nobody seems to pay it much attention.

These shoes, impractical in the circumstances, were abandoned by many women during a frightful exodus. The shoes escaped the notice of many colleagues, now exhausted after a 45 minute descent of 60 or more flights of cramped concrete fire escape stairs. The pile of shoes was possibly the least bizarre scene of the past hour. The image of an airliner piercing the North Tower and exploding into a ball of black smoke and fiery debris kept replaying in our minds.

Many, who remembered the bombing of 1993 with gut-wrenching disbelief, followed the painstakingly prepared and meticulously rehearsed New York City Fire Marshal's instructions for yet another descent of the fire escape stairs, but this time was not a drill.

During the descent, half-way down, I and many others were thrown against the walls as our own building lurched and whip-sawed upon impact of the second plane. Few could conceive of what was happening. Calm prevailed; after a moment the descent continued. Upon reaching the twentieth floor, smoke began drifting up from the lobby. Oh no, fire on top of everything else?

Once out on the streets, we watched with disbelief the implosion of three skyscrapers. The sky filled with plumes of dust and thousands of documents floated quietly to the ground. The feelings of disbelief were counterbalanced by the elation of safe escape from both explosion and implosion.

At the recovery centers over the next few days, some team members confronted the crisis, others

*Continues*

leave project team members disoriented and possibly paralyzed with fear or indecision.

Anything can happen under the best of circumstances. There are always the unknown unknowns. Even mundane, routine crises can stress the project team, resulting in resource shortages or disappearance, new requirements, changed deadlines, or start dates.

denied it. Some were afraid to come out of their homes. Others had eye, throat, and lung irritation from the smoke and dust still blowing across the moonscape of lower Manhattan. Many felt disoriented by the disturbing sounds and images, unfamiliar surroundings, new equipment, and disruption of daily routines.

Despite the crisis, as a group, we managed to overcome many difficulties, rallying to ensure that the firm was ready for business the following Monday. Keeping the team focused on doing the job became the primary leadership challenge in the face of crisis.

## 2. Warning Signs

The warning signs for an extraordinary disaster such as acts of terrorism are outside the scope of this book. Such circumstances are difficult to foresee. However, there are signs that a project manager might more routinely encounter, even on small projects:

- Changes in leadership or organization structure
- Austerity measures in your company or division

Team members are feeling:

- Emotional or physical symptoms that they acknowledge or deny
- As if they are in uncharted territory, unable to anticipate next steps
- That the crisis has created an excuse to unilaterally change scope, deliverables, or schedule.

## 3. What will happen if I do nothing?

If your project has just been hit by a serious crisis and you do nothing, you will have big problems. When something major happens to your initiative, everything (or at least most things) needs to change. If you don't recognize that and act on it, the project won't be able to get out from under the problem and the project will be doomed to failure.

## 4. Solution

When you are dealing with a crisis, you need to focus on establishing an environment of trust and safety. Safety and trust will allow team members to speak freely, knowing their concerns will not be used against them. It is important to reestablish the relative priority of the project given the changed circumstances, but don't force people to accept things until they are ready. Different people will need different amounts of time. Immediate and frequent communication with the project team will be necessary to help the team understand whether routine ground rules and processes still govern.

## 5. What should I do?

When you are dealing with a crisis situation, you need to be a people leader before you are a task manager. Of course, a crisis will have a significant impact on the tasks, but it will also have a very significant impact on the people, and those are the people who you will need to help you get the project back on track.

### 5(a) People leadership

Make sure that you give consideration to all of the following:

- *Communications:* Communicate what is needed in a way that each of your team members can relate to. Recognize that you will likely have to communicate the same message on multiple occasions until people are ready to process it. Make sure that you remain calm too; otherwise, the team will respond to your anxiety with increased nervousness.

- *Validate strong emotions:* During any crisis, don't ignore the strong emotions and feelings your team members may blurt out or even try to hide. Observe and let your team members know the feelings are not unique. Heavy feelings in crisis circumstances are a normal response and may be shared across the team. Feeling these emotions is not a sign of weakness, but a normal human response. If possible, redirect the emotional energy to serve as strong motivation to move ahead and overcome the crisis.

- *Connect to similar past activity:* While the situation might seem foreign or strange because of the circumstances causing or resulting from the crisis, it is not difficult to connect the task at hand to prior, more routine, yet stressful, circumstances, such as a job interview, external audit, or a pending performance evaluation. Connecting to these more *routine* contexts will reduce the stress brought about by the unusual or extra-stressful circumstances.

- *Connect to a shared goal:* Find a way to connect otherwise routine accomplishments to an awareness of the *extraordinary* or *heroic response* in the face of duress. At the beginning of a project, project managers orient team members regarding project purpose and benefits as well as external factors driving project timing and priority. Reintroduce this orientation, perhaps saying, "Remember when we started…?" Most people cannot envision themselves as heroic, so remind them that almost every hero, when asked about his or her experience, will claim they were, "just doing their job." Reiterate the project team's shared goal and how the team member's contribution aids the team in achieving the mission.

- *Demonstrate vision:* Think beyond the immediate scope or context of the project. In the case of the architecture company's security director at the World Trade Center, vision allowed them to prepare for scenarios most stakeholders would dismiss as too improbable and costly. They boldly stuck to their vision to ensure that proper precautions were part of the plan. Project managers with vision know that the unexpected may occur on their projects, and they have a tool kit of back-up plans to keep their project from sinking.

### 5(b) Moving past the crisis

Whatever crisis the project manager faces, there are ways to adapt or continue with success, and eventually your project team will be ready to move forward. In fact, the project will give them something to help focus their minds. While the crisis may be unforeseeable, the organization's reactions can be a bit easier to forecast.

As a project manager, be the bandleader. It's important for the bandleader to know the score, the venue, and the strengths and weaknesses of the players. In project management terms, monitor your team for safety, and scan the environment for changes in process or priority. Connect and close ranks with stakeholders to communicate consistently with the team.

The specific steps that you take to move forward with the project will depend on the phase of the project that you had reached when the crisis hit. Using PMBOK phases, you may want to consider the following approaches:

- *Initiating:* If you were only in project initiation when the crisis happened, it likely makes sense to reinitiate the project. You may need to revalidate the business case, but otherwise, there is probably more effort in adjusting the work that you have already completed than in simply starting again.
- *Planning:* If you were in planning when the crisis occurred, you could be facing some very significant rework to scope, schedule, budget, resources, quality, risks, and so on. Each of these could all have changed dramatically. You need to compare the original situation with the current state, and determine whether you can move forward or whether you need to restart the initiative. Planning is the *tipping point* where you can move forward or backward, and it is important to understand the change so that you can make the right decision.

Remember to consider whether the changes are temporary or permanent. You may lose resources to crisis management activities, but they may be returned to the project after a period of time.

- *Executing, monitoring and controlling:* By this point in the project, it is probably too late to turn back, but you need to recognize that you can't just go forward as if nothing had changed. Some elements of the project may no longer be necessary, while there may be whole new sections that need to be addressed (and those do need planning from the beginning). The temptation here is to get back to normal as quickly as possible, but first you need to confirm what *normal* is. Normal is not the same as it used to be.

Identify the elements of the project that are relatively unaffected by the crisis and use those as your starting point for moving the project forward. Progress in these areas will buy you time to deal with the areas that are significantly impacted by the crisis.

- *Closure:* The temptation, if you had reached the closure phase before the problems hit, is to ignore the project and treat it as if it had finished. However, that is not something that you can do. You need to ensure that the project is closed properly and that the documentation and lessons learned are captured. You also need to recognize that a project that was being closed may now need to be reactivated to deal with expanded scope.

## References

Carbone, J.A. *IT Architecture Toolkit*. Upper Saddle River, NJ: Pearson/Prentice Hall, 2004.
International Institute of Business Analysis (IIBA). *Business Analysis Body of Knowledge*. Toronto, ON: International Institute of Business Analysis, 2009. 81.

# Index